Estrangement, Alienation and Exploitation

Part I Economic Theories and Legislation

Estrangement, Alienation and Exploitation

A Sociological Approach to Historical Materialism

JOHN TORRANCE

First published 1977 by
THE MACMILLAN PRESS LTD
London and Basingstoke
Associated companies in New York
Dublin Melbourne Johannesburg and Madras

ISBN 0 333 19850 6

Printed in Great Britain by
REDWOOD BURN LTD
Trowbridge and Esher

Contents

Acknowledgments

I should like to thank the Principal and Fellows of Hertford College for the two spells of leave in which this book was conceived and then written. During the first of these the Warden and Fellows of Nuffield College kindly gave me the benefits of Associate Membership. During the second I was Visiting Lecturer at the University of Auckland, New Zealand, and I am especially grateful to Professor David Pitt and his colleagues in the Sociology Department for providing the most favourable conditions for academic production.

I and the publishers also wish to thank the following who have kindly given permission for the use of copyright material: George Allen & Unwin (Publishers) Ltd, for the excerpts from *Capital*, Vol. 1, by Karl Marx, translated by E. & C. Paul and George Allen & Unwin (Publishers) Ltd (Humanities Press Ltd), for the excerpts from *The Phenomenology of Mind* by G. W. F. Hegel, translated by J. Baillie; Basil Blackwell & Mott Ltd, for the excerpts from *Early Texts* by Karl Marx, translated and edited by D. McLellan; Lawrence & Wishart Ltd, for the excerpts from *The German Ideology* by Karl Marx and F. Engels, translated by R. Pascal *et al.*; for the excerpts from *Economic and Philosophical Manuscripts* by Karl Marx, translated by M. Milligan and D. J. Struik, and for the excerpts from *Theories of Surplus Value*, Part III, by Karl Marx, translated by E. Burns; and Penguin Books Ltd and Random House Inc., for the excerpts from *Grundrisse: Foundations of the Critique of Political Economy* by Karl Marx, translated by Martin Nicolaus (1973), translation copyright © Martin Nicolaus, 1973.

Hertford College, Oxford   J. T.
August 1976

Introduction

Commentators on Marx have always noted that his concept of alienation contains two semantic elements, alienation in the sense of renunciation or relinquishment, and alienation in the sense of estrangement. Few, however, have pressed this distinction very far, being content with remarking that in both Hegel and Marx – the watershed from which alienation theory descends into modern thought – the two senses are closely linked, if not conflated. Since this may be a reason why the idea of alienation, despite all that has been written about it, remains unclear and far from univocal, the present study will attempt the opposite approach. It will maintain a sharp distinction between the two senses of alienation, and seek the theoretical significances of each, and of their conjunction, primarily in their divergence and heterogeneity. The aim will be to clarify the theoretical basis of Marxism, while emphasising its sociological character, and to supply sociological theory in general with some missing conceptual elements.[1]

Writers in English and French have perhaps been more apt than Germans to use 'alienation' as an unanalysed compound. If so, this is no doubt because, in these languages, the word carries both of the two meanings which, in German, correspond to *Entäusserung* and *Entfremdung*, the terms actually used by Hegel and Marx. Since the ease with which these two quite different meanings can be conveyed in translation by a single homonym has encouraged the mistaken idea that their close conjunction in Hegel and Marx is in fact an inextricable fusion, let us begin by sorting out the two notions involved, irrespective of language. For this purpose, the term 'alienation' itself will henceforward be restricted to one of these, and the other will be denoted by 'estrangement'.

'Alienation' in this restricted sense (*Entäusserung, entäussern, veräussern*) refers to the renunciation or relinquishment of possession, or of a claim to something, or of a liberty or power to do some action – usually, but not necessarily, in favour of some other person or persons specified or unspecified. It is not surprising that this sounds like a lawyer's definition, for legal contexts are where the word is most often found. Nevertheless, it is not, or need not be, a 'legal concept'. It denotes simply a type of social action, or social practice: an action which has the effect of altering a social relationship previously existing between a person and any others affected by the claims or powers relinquished. So, although the word may come to have special application in law or commerce or politics, the primary location of the idea is in general reference to social life. If it is to be a scholarly or scientific concept at all, therefore, it is, at least potentially, a sociological concept. A possible usefulness, in this connection, is its high level of abstraction. For it includes all voluntary acts of disposal of claims – whether by sacrifice, gift, exchange, bequest, abandonment or any other action – and, arguably, compulsory acts of surrender and abdication as well. At this level, 'alienation' functions as a correlative of 'appropriation', which includes any taking possession or assumption of powers not previously held – whether with consent or, if we are prepared to define 'expropriation' as 'forcible appropriation', by compulsion. Together, alienation and appropriation, without any undue stretching of their everyday meanings, can therefore be used to describe a complete transfer of claims from one party to another, representing the beginning and end of a social process and the two poles of a social relationship. The parties concerned may themselves be individuals or collectivities. Further consideration of the sociological bearings of these terms will be left for later; there are, however, some extensions of the social usage of alienation which deserve mention here.

Obviously, persons may alienate their own autonomy, partially or wholly, so that we may have to speak of 'self-alienation' in this sense. Furthermore, like most other ideas having a primarily social reference, alienation may be transposed into various contexts where the relationship is internalised to the psyche, or exists only in an imaginary or figurative way. Thus, to take a trivial example, an individual may renounce the liberty to smoke and simultaneously assume, as his own moral censor, power to prevent himself from smoking. Such a case is only directly social if he makes known his resolution and thereby inevitably delegates some of his powers of self-discipline to his acquaintances – in so far as he values their opinion of his strength of character, and hence avoids their censure as well as his own. Less trivially, a person may dedicate himself or his possessions to his god. Even when privately performed, such a vow will generally have social consequences; but again, it is only directly social to the extent that priests or others, acting as representatives of the abstract entity to which the devotee has relinquished his autonomy, actually assume and exercise the powers that have been surrendered. In so far as these cases are less than directly social, I shall treat them as secondary applications of the idea, derivative from the social usage. The justification for doing so cannot be presented at length here. But the argument, in brief, would be that, on the one hand, both the internalised conception of the individual's moral personality (his 'self') and the idealised conception of the cultural group's religious personality (its 'god') are abstractions which arise out of, and are sustained by, processes of social interaction; while on the other, the basic mechanism by which individuals 'represent' cultural abstractions – whether of individual or collective personality – to both themselves and others is universally implicated in all social processes, including those of alienation and appropriation. These examples, which resemble the social paradigm, yet where it would be eccentric to use the words 'alienation' and 'appropriation' in ordinary discourse, incidentally serve as a reminder that, linguistic though the discussion must be, it concerns concepts, not words.

'Estrangement' (*Entfremdung, entfremden*) – which I am substituting for the other English sense of 'alienation' – also seems to have a primary reference to social relationships. It denotes a process, or condition, by which people become or are strangers or enemies to one another. Usually, but perhaps not necessarily, its use implies a contrast with a previous state of solidarity. Certainly, for this sense of mutual estrangement, 'solidarity' denotes the opposite condition. Unlike the sense of 'alienation', just considered, which refers only to actions, not emotions, estrangement refers in the first place to how people feel about one another and describes the affective tone or texture of a relationship, or the direction in which its emotional content is changing. It is an incidental disadvantage of restricting the use of 'alienation' as I have, that 'estrangement' is rather milder in its emotional connotation than the sense of 'alienation' for which I am making it do duty. For 'estrangement' has as its core the idea of people treating each other as strangers, whereas 'alienation' includes this but also extends to the extremes of enmity. The sense of 'estrangement' being proposed here, therefore, will be extended to cover the normal range of 'alienation', part of the justification for this being that *Entfremdung*, in Hegel and Marx, has a similar extension. In taking the interpersonal process or state of estrangement as the primary reference, rather than actions, I am treating as secondary certain related transitive verb-forms. For instance, we might speak of a person's action estranging another from him, or of one person estranging two others who had been friends or married (or of one country's diplomacy 'alienating' another country from a third). All these refer to actions from the standpoint of their effects in 'cooling' or 'distancing' partners in a relationship, and can perhaps be regarded as secondary in the same sort of way as 'to cool' or 'to distance' – or for that matter, 'to heat' as in 'heating a room' – seem secondary to the concepts expressed in 'cool', 'distance' and 'hot'.

The basic sense of mutual estrangement refers to situations where there is matching of reciprocal orientations. People regard *one another* as strangers or enemies. These orientations are types of 'self-other' orientation, and as such have two aspects, affective and cognitive. The affective range, from indifference to hostility, has already been commented on. Although one cannot be too positive in an empirical matter, it may be suggested that the cognitive aspect has six linked elements. These are (i) whether the salient features of the other's identity are familiar or unfamiliar; (ii) if familiar, whether or not they are an object of hostility for self; (iii) depending on (i), whether his attitudes are known or unknown, and (iv) his behaviour predictable or unpredictable; (v) whether his attitudes are likely to be hostile, and (vi) whether his behaviour is likely to be dangerous. With the aid of these variables one could construct pure types of stranger-orientation and enemy-orientation. Others are treated as strangers to the extent that the salient features of their identity are unfamiliar, and hence their attitudes unknown, possibly hostile, and their behaviour unpredictable, possibly dangerous, and in any case dangerous merely by being unpredictable. Others are treated as enemies to the extent that salient traits of their identity are familiar and objects of hostility for self, and their attitudes also thereby known or presumed to be hostile; their behaviour is predictable only as being dangerous for being guided by malice. An intermediate type of orientation is that of persons who become estranged having been solidary. Here, newly salient and unfamiliar features of the other identities make them strangers to each other, but in addition, by disturbing the predictable basis of the old relationship, these features are dangerous in themselves, and all the more so if the other's new features are themselves objects of hostility for self, or his new attitudes known or thought to be hostile, or his new behaviour dangerous. Although the presentation of these types assumes interpersonal contexts, either or both of the parties may just as well be collectivities.

Obviously, orientations having cognitive aspects similar to these may exist which are not of the self-other type at all. Stranger and enemy orientations specify at the self-other level a general mode of defensive and offensive orientation which may relate to animals or inanimate things in so far as they are objects of hostility for self, or are seen as unfamiliar or dangerous. Such instances would fall outside the concept of 'estrangement', however. On the other hand, relationships of estrangement may be introjected, or projected upon ideational objects, so there are corresponding secondary uses to consider, whose relationship to the primary sense of mutual estrangement parallels the relationship to real alienation of alienative 'transactions' with internal or imaginary others. We might speak of 'self-estrangement', therefore, where one becomes a stranger to oneself, which resembles the case where unfamiliar features of identity emerge between intimates and estrange them from each other; or where one is one's own enemy.[2] (For example, one's self may be partially in the power of a hostile other, so that one is self-active in self-destructive ways.) Secondly, there may be estrangement between a person (or people) and a god, whether their own or another's.[3] As with alienation, so here this estrangement would only be directly social to the extent that it appeared as relationships of estrangement between persons whose salient identities were religious roles. A roughly similar point can be made about cases of estrangement between persons (or groups) and secular cultural entities, such as the state: the 'outlaw' is in a state of war with all or any who represent 'law'. To be distinguished from all these cases of mutual 'estrangement between' are cases of one-sided 'estrangement *from*' — whether from persons, gods, authorities, the dominant culture, or 'reality itself', etc. These are *attitudes* of individuals or groups which, in so far as they influence orientations in interaction, do have social consequences but cannot by themselves comprise the emotional texture of relationships. For the latter is always the resultant of two or more inputs. One-sided estrangement, therefore, in so far as it does not *produce* mutual estrangement, may contribute to relationships of misunderstanding, frustration, etc.

Hitherto the fact that English and French have one word for both the concepts which have been separated as alienation and estrangement has been treated as if it were no more than a coincidence. However, this etymological datum indicates an important semantic linkage between them. This is the association of ideas between what is strange or foreign, and what is 'other than' something else. This association turns into an equivalence of meaning where we are dealing with what is 'other than' the familiar, or 'other than' what is identified with the self and its extensions – which is the 'otherness' to which objects are consigned when they are alienated. Thus 'alien' in English can mean either 'foreign in *nature*' (i.e. strange) or 'belonging to *another* person, place or family'. The Latin root, *alienus* ('belonging to another') derives simply from *alius* ('other', 'another'). The same connection reappears in German, but in the reverse etymological direction: instead of the apparent association running from otherness to strangeness, it runs from strangeness to otherness. Thus the root of *Entfremdung* – i.e. *fremd* ('strange', 'foreign') – has the second meaning 'belonging to another or to others'. In this sense it is the antonym of *eigen* ('one's own', 'belonging to oneself'). In Marx, the relationship between *Entfremdung* and the *eigen-fremd* polarity (within which occur the processes of alienation and appropriation) is an important part of the theoretical problem.[4]

Obviously, strangeness is a much narrower and more concrete attribute than otherness, and they only tend to equate when we use 'alien' or 'foreign' to mean 'radically other' or 'other in essence' than something else. But what the two ideas have in common is that they qualify their object only by defining it negatively. What is other than X is simply not-X, and what is strange is merely not anything familiar, where the familiar is necessarily finite and known. The tendency to equate the terms, attested by etymology, is presumably due to the assumption, warranted in most practical contexts or where X is an existential predicate, that what is defined negatively by a property that it lacks is necessarily less familiar, finite or knowable than what is defined by possession of the property itself. It may not be so clear that cases where 'alien' and 'other' are commonly equated could also involve any notion of hostility or antagonism. However, just as the use of 'property' in the sentence before last indicates how the language of traditional logic contains metaphors drawn from the language of appropriation and alienation, so dialectical logic – from which our pregnant senses of 'alienation' arose – drew metaphors from the social processes of estrangement. The merely indifferent opposition of X and not-X thus contained the possibility, which the dialectical process could convert into necessity, of developing into a contradiction and clash of irreconcilable opposites.

In this context a further semantic linkage comes to light. For what is defined as other than X, and thereby alien or foreign to X, is thus *excluded* from X and put outside its sphere. But this is almost exactly the root meaning of *Veräusserung* and *Entäusserung*, which unlike the Anglo-French 'alienation' comes from the root 'outside' (*ausser*). Thus to alienate something is also to exteriorise or externalise it, in a moral sense: to place it beyond one's control and exclude it from one's circle, or private area, by renouncing one's claims upon it. But equally, persons or groups that are estranged are, at the least, mutually excluding entities who, if they enter one another's spheres, can only trespass and encroach, as outsiders whose different interests become antagonistic by the mere fact of intrusion.

These semantic and etymological linkages, which help to make the concept of alienation such a resonant instrument in the hands of a dialectician, clearly derive much of their force from the usages of a society dominated by private ownership. For the concept to be useful in the scientific analysis of such a society, these connotative ambiguities would have to be purged, and the extent to which Marx achieved this is a measure of the sociological importance of his theory.

In this introduction, the two unit ideas of alienation and estrangement have been distinguished and delineated as sharply as is possible at this stage. Then some of their semantic interconnections, which inevitably blur the distinction, have been reintroduced. The further refinement and elaboration of these ideas as sociological concepts is taken up at the beginning of Part II. Part I, meanwhile, contains a historical discussion of the interplay of these two unit ideas in traditions of social theorising, up to and including the works of the young Marx. Readers who are already surfeited with such historical surveys, therefore, are advised to turn straight to Chapter 4.

Part I

Estrangement and Alienation in Pre-sociological Thought

1 Estrangement and Alienation in Ideology

Hegel, whose philosophy has bequeathed us the 'problem of alienation', was himself the heir to numerous ideological traditions. This chapter attempts a brief résumé of three of the most important of them – Judaeo-Christian religious ideology, the political ideology of seventeenth-century contract theorists, and the enlightenment's ideology of education and culture, together with the counter-ideology of its critic Rousseau – from the standpoint of estrangement and alienation. The aim is to show how these two unit ideas were already interrelated in each, and how both common and divergent patterns of interrelationship emerge. Only the main outlines will be sketched in each case, no doubt superficially enough, and there is no claim that this represents a detailed or researched history of ideas or of intellectual influences, for which the reader must go elsewhere. At the same time, in order for the patterns which interest me here to stand out clearly, these traditions will have to be subjected to a certain amount of sociological and historical interpretation.

1 RELIGION

A basic theme of Hebrew and Christian mythology is the estrangement between man and God. Conceived as man's breach of a pre-existing harmony – whether by Adam's disobedience or 'the dark idolatries of alienated Judah' or the Christian sinner's fall from grace – it is amply reciprocated by the wrath and vengeance of Yahweh and by Christ's final damnation of the unrepentant. Common to both mythologies, too, is the Messianic mission of redemption by which part of mankind will ultimately be reconciled with God. What these myths try to justify in eschatological terms, by depicting a reunion of God and man in the imaginary past and future, is simply the inevitable present state of estrangement between the two. Thus Old Testament writers often expressed man's sense of God's indifference to human problems with the phrase 'we are but strangers and sojourners before thee.' And complementing this was the realisation, experienced with religious awe, of the alien character of the divine powers themselves: 'My ways are not your ways', etc. Christian versions of the same idea are the dark 'cloud of unknowing' that awaits those who attempt the *via mystica,* or Calvin's doctrine of God's inscrutable providence and the related Jansenist idea of a *deus absconditus.*

This notion of religious estrangement, with its mythological and theological rationalisations, cannot adequately be interpreted as just an illusory reflection of tribal and class divisions and their imaginary transcendence, even though it may have subserved these ideological needs. For it derived from specialists in religious ideology, whose role was to expound and justify the ways of God to men. I would suggest that what it expressed, and sought to justify, was the basic datum of religious experience itself: the radical separation of the sacred from the profane. But it expressed this, of course, in contexts where religious experience provided a conceptual and evaluative framework for experiencing the whole of social life. For whether or not we accept all of Durkheim's explanation of this social phenomenon, we can scarcely deny the prevalence of the dichotomy in precapitalist societies, or its importance as a framework of social consciousness. Prior to their adaptation to situations of tribal or class conflict, therefore, these myths and metaphysics of religious estrangement functioned as legitimating charters for the institutional separation of sacred times and places, persons and properties, powers and symbols, from encroachment by the demands of profane life and secular interests. They thereby *indirectly* legitimated the social orders to which these partitionings belonged.

Not only this, but they also supported the primacy of the sacred sphere by asserting that mutual estrangement among men is itself the result of man's estrangement from God; and that only by seeking to overcome the latter can the former be assuaged. Thus the expulsion from Eden was followed by the quarrel of Cain and Abel, and universal strife is to precede the Second Coming. In the Old Testament, men's mutual estrangement appears as ritual discord, competition and confusion of cults, where all 'go whoring after strange gods.' In the New Testament, it appears in ethical terms, as the social and political anarchy of those who are 'strangers from the covenant of promise': as 'enmity, strife, jealousy, anger, selfishness, dissension, party spirit, envy.' According to the Hebrew priests and prophets, only by forsaking their idolatries for the common cult of Yahweh could the Israelites heal the divisions which weakened their nation and enslaved it to its enemies. For Paul, only belonging to Christ and living in the spirit could call forth the virtues of solidarity – love, peace, patience, kindness and self-control – that would dispel the conflicts of the flesh.

But if religious ideology bade men transcend their mutual estrangement from God, it had also to furnish the means of doing so. It was not enough to proclaim that at the end of the world all things would be made one: some present method of privileged access was needed, within the estranged relationship itself, to the divine side of the persisting dualism. It is here that the notion of alienation enters religious ideology.

Just as religious estrangement makes its appearance as soon as there is differentiation between sacred and profane, so religious alienation in the form of sacrifice appears universally as its remedy. Though it has the form of an exaction, sacrifice is none the less the primary means provided by religion of enabling the believer to feel at home in a divided cosmos – for the gods from whom he is estranged are not only powerful, but also personify some of his deepest needs. Originally, no doubt, sacrifice was simply an application, within the context of religious estrangement, of the general practice of ceremonial giving in social life, and it has the same function. Exchange of gifts tends to become institutionalised between units which are to some degree divided and estranged from one another, but which share some kind of underlying or superimposed solidarity – between families of kinsmen, lineages in a tribe, tribal rulers in a culture-area, etc. The gifts express this solidarity, but also, since they pass from the exclusive ownership of one to that of the other, the separation and independence of the partners too. Thus, by extension, giving can also be a means of trying to create solidarity between strangers by asserting the existence of a bond of which the gifts are the practical expression. Sacrificial giving expresses or seeks to elicit an underlying solidarity between gods and men, without denying or annulling their estrangement. It is the human side of an exchange of gifts, in which the gods contribute the beneficence of nature, social successes, and any kind of good fortune or misfortune avoided. Just as secular solidarity is momentarily actualised in giving, and in the festive community thereby called into being, and may remain memorialised in the gift as its 'sentimental value', etc., so sacrificial rites briefly actualise solidarity with the divine as a cult community. The devotee, suitably purified, enters the sacred sphere and relinquishes his offering, which henceforth remains as sacred property, set apart, a memorial of his ritual presence with the god, but also a reminder of the gulf which reopens when he returns to his profane existence.

Sacrifice, or ritual alienation, is therefore the most elementary form of religious alienation. It expresses and maintains a cult community between believers and their god, which bridges, but thereby also recognises their irremovable estrangement. Whether such cults are based on a pre-existent, e.g. tribal, solidarity, or emerge as the clientèle of an oracle or *genius loci*, etc., is immaterial. In either case they originate in a setting where the idea of a multiplicity of spiritual beings, each with its particular places and powers, is as natural as the idea of a multiplicity of men and of social groups. Like all institutions of gift exchange, also, sacrifice implies a kind of equality between the partners. Each must have something to offer, and either party may accuse the other of failing in his obligations. Thus the devotee, when he leaves his gift in the sacred precinct and withdraws into profane life, is also returning to his own secular sphere of autonomy with his ritual personality intact. He, or his group, can in principle carry their religious custom elsewhere. In this way, proliferation of cults may lead to anarchy and competition of divinities; the solidarity of each cult community, furthermore, is likely to be reflected in their mutual estrangement and antagonism, which is abetted by all kinds of mundane interests. It was in this type of situation that Judaism, seeking a monotheistic national monopoly for Yahweh, introduced the idea of religious alienation which we find in the doctrine of the Covenant.

Whereas ritual alienation is an ideological practice, the alienation of the Covenant is part of an ideological historical theory. The Hebrews were said to have renounced, and alienated to Yahweh, not just the regular offerings which expressed their national solidarity with him, but, once and for all, their national, tribal, and individual ritual personalities. They could no longer choose how to exercise their power of ritual disposal of their goods by following tribal or household deities or the gods of neighbouring peoples and localities, for Yahweh had chosen them already as his holy people, and ancestral patriarchs had alienated their loyalties in advance. By this doctrine, the cult community was no longer to be actualised merely intermittently, in ritual gatherings and ceremonies, but was incarnate in the life of the nation as a whole. It was itself a sacrificial gift, to be kept pure and intact. Ritual, the norm governing the conduct of the cult community, was generalised as the Law; just as scrupulous observance of ritual had been necessary to ensure the efficacy of sacrifice, so strict obedience to the law became the condition of divine favour continuing towards national and individual enterprises. Thus Judaism placed the entire political community permanently within the sacred sphere: the profane world began at the external boundary of national life. As a 'holy people unto the Lord', the Jews' social and political estrangement from their tribal neighbours and rival kingdoms, and later from their host societies throughout the world, was legitimated as religious estrangement. Foreign peoples were aliens beyond the law, and could therefore be conquered or exploited for the glory of Yahweh. At the same time, the collective appropriation by the religious community of the ritual powers alienated by its members, and thenceforth exercised on their behalf by a centralised priesthood, could communicate a vastly enhanced supernatural force to their pursuit of economic and political prosperity. Internally, this concentration of ritual power entailed a steeper stratification of religio-social status, as between 'the sojourner within the gates', the chosen people themselves, and the professional servants of the holy of holies, and hence, an intensification of religious estrangement.

Christianity likewise developed in contexts of religious anarchy, within Judaism and Hellenistic paganism, both riddled with competing sects. Stemming from the prophetic tradition which challenged ritualistic observance of the Law in the name of ethical conduct, it recast the major themes of Judaism as a 'new covenant' around the messianic claims of Jesus. Evolving the doctrine of original sin out of the Hebrew myth of the fall of man, Christianity postulated an extreme condition of religious estrangement as the inheritance of every individual. Simultaneously, it provided a 'means of grace', accessible to all and any through voluntary participation in an act of collective self-alienation made by Christ on behalf of all believers. The Messiah therefore has become himself the perfect sacrifice, and also the pattern of self-sacrifice to be followed ethically and ritually, by all who would avail themselves of his salvation. The believer renounces his worldly personality – his freedom to pursue profane ends, including the preservation of life itself – and alienates himself wholly to the service of the sacred. By this 'death' – in the limiting case, by martyrdom – he becomes by his symbolic participation in Christ's death and resurrection a member of an idealised cult community, conceived as existing eternally in transmundane spirituality and actualised in the Church. Thus the dichotomy of sacred and profane was individualised and subjectivised. The Christian, by his self-alienation to God, is estranged from himself and from all others as natural selves, yet solidary with others as risen souls. At the same time, the frontier of Christendom divides the community of risen souls from the heathen, 'strangers to Christ', who, together with apostates and heretics, may be more or less forcibly brought into the fold of the saved. Satan, conceived as Christ's adversary, symbolises both the internal and external estrangements of the elect. The stratification of religious roles is incorporated into a hierarchy of grace, which extends upwards into the ranks of heavenly beings. For the first time in history, the sacred-profane dichotomy could emerge as a specific and universal duality at the level of ideology and institutions. (However, as long as the prepotence of the sacred was embodied in the political claims of the Church against secular rulers, or of established national churches against Rome, it remained enmeshed in political particularism.) Although it would be tedious, one could in principle follow through the analysis in terms of estrangement and alienation to show how the different strands in Christianity – monastic, mystical, predestinarian, salvationist, etc. – represent different modes of estrangement from the world and varying conceptions of self-alienation to God.

Judaism and Christianity, therefore, contained a common ideological theme. Beginning from a conception of undesirable estrangement amongst men, due to their common estrangement from God, they claimed to create harmony and order by asking men to renounce certain powers and alienate them to God, through his earthly representatives. In return, men would receive new powers and a new life, as a result of the new condition into which they had entered, and which they constituted, by their renunciation: a sacred community set apart and estranged from others and from the profane world. Within the framework of the new community, what had originally appeared as the oppressive division between sacred and profane received its justification as a functional stratification in terms of religious values.

2 POLITICS

The Hebrew doctrine of the covenant appears in various forms in the Bible. Most important for the Jews were the covenants between God and the patriarchs, which provided foundation myths for their sacred national community. When Hebrew theocracy took the form of a kingdom, however, special covenants were sometimes said to have been made between God, the people and the ruler, establishing the latter's political authority. In the Middle Ages, especially amongst apologists for papal supremacy, and again in the early and theocratic phases of Protestantism (in the American colonies, for instance) these special covenants were made a precedent for doctrines seeking to give governments a legitimacy at once popular and sacred.[1] The social contract theorists proper, however, from Grotius to Rousseau, made a different use of the biblical model. Their 'original contract' was conceived by analogy with the patriarchal covenants, not the special covenants, yet depicted a purely secular act of association between men, whose aim and result was the foundation of a political, not a religious community. Even theorists like Hobbes and Rousseau, who emphasised the authority of the sovereign in matters of civil religion, construed this only as a power of interpretation, within the secular sphere, of sacred and spiritual beliefs which pertained to another world.

If we examine the structure of social contract theory at the same level of abstraction as we have taken the theological doctrines of covenant – a level which obliterates most of the distinctions that have divided political philosophers, just as it also ignored theological differences for which men once fought and died – it can be seen to transpose the biblical model into the profane sphere quite faithfully. It should be emphasised that this was a reproduction within the profane, rather than a new application beyond the sacred-profane opposition. For social contract theory ran its course in the shadow of religious beliefs whose imagery was, at first, no less compelling for having become more abstract and remote. In this, social contract theory was heir to the Christian separation between the world and the spirit, with its depreciation of earthly life, and also to a specifically Protestant transcendentalism. On the other hand, Protestant influence also appears in the fact that the theory sought the basis of a new political morality in the very conditions of mundane existence themselves, in the laws of human nature, just as Protestant businessmen imbued with ascetic activism found a new social morality and meaning for life in the pursuit of economic achievement. Both cases exhibit the same paradox, though one is theoretical and the other practical: men sought in worldly existence itself 'signs' of the intentions of a God whose purposes were no longer directly revealed, and with such success that the divine will itself at last became an unnecessary hypothesis. Profit-making and the science of man both became self-justifying human pursuits in a godless world.

Social contract theory was thus a secularising ideology, and its content also reflected the secularisation proceeding in the world around it. For while it began with an image of human nature borrowed from Christian doctrine, assuming an initial condition in which men's estrangement from God was manifest in their estrangement from one another – the Hobbesian view – it culminated, with Rousseau and others, in a denial of original sin and in explanations of men's primitive isolation in terms of environment, history or chance. As soon as men began to be seen once more as naturally sociable, rather than natural strangers and enemies, the idea of social contract became superfluous. Kant, with his notion of man's 'unsocial sociability' and his qualified acceptance of contract theory as an 'idea of reason', stood on the very brink of this transition.[2] The ideological career of social contract thus reflected the entire movement by which the medieval subordination of the profane to the sacred was reversed, and their opposition finally superseded – a movement initiated, paradoxically, by the Reformers' determination to exalt the sacred even higher, beyond the institutions by which Rome had made it accessible to a fallen world, and the world thereby amenable to Rome.

The religious myths explaining man's estrangement from the gods, and the doctrines of religious alienation with their institutional remedies, have been interpreted here as responses to the basic religious datum, the social division of sacred and profane. Similarly, the seventeenth-century emergence of the ideological problem of political obligation, of the need to justify the ways of the state to men, can be seen as a response to the basic datum of political experience as it became differentiated from religion: the opposition of the public and private spheres. The causes of this are no doubt to be sought in the supersession of the feudal political economy by capitalism. As private commodity production and the sale and hire of labour became general, 'feudal' rights either dissolved into the private proprietorship and contractual freedoms of families (or of their individual heads) or accrued to the crown (or to its individual wearer). Public powers thus became concentrated at the level of the nation, in the hands of the ruler and at the opposite pole to the subjects, but could only be maintained as a state through continuous exactions from the people's private revenues. Thus the basic datum of political experience came to be the opposition and estrangement between rulers and people, sovereign and subjects, public authority and private interests.

Just as social awareness had previously been structured by the religious cleavage, so now the political opposition of public and private, state and society, provided a new framework for cognition and evaluation of all social experience – at first, especially, in the form of law. Social structure was codified and discussed in terms of positive law, public and private, and the ethics of social behaviour in terms of natural law; Montesquieu could take the first step towards sociology by analysing the 'spirit of the laws'.[3] Social contract theory was the political ideology *par excellence*, for its predecessors had enveloped politics and laws in religion, while its successors tended to subordinate them to broader secular, cultural and economic ends. Thus although the owners of the means of production were the private beneficiaries of public order, at the expense of the masses, this underlying class-struggle was as yet by no means a direct object of social awareness, precisely because it was underlying and apolitical, enclosed within the unitary category of the private in a society whose oppositions were structured around the polarity of private and public.

Hence the period spanned by social contract theory was dominated by two problems: to resolve the relationship between the sacred-profane and public-private divisions, and to find institutional means of bridging the latter. Social contractarians addressed themselves to both, by trying to establish the autonomy of the public realm on a profane basis, freed from the trammels of divine delegation and divine right; but also on a basis of private rights, so that the subject, as possessor of his life, liberty and estate, should have access to political authority and recourse against tyranny.

Whereas religious ideology had described the mutual estrangement of men apart from God in ritual or ethical terms, social contract theorists described their mutual estrangement apart from the state in legal terms. Individuals in the state of nature were conceived as 'sovereigns' over themselves (Grotius), as mutually excluding possessors of their persons, deeds, and such things as they needed and could obtain by 'natural right'. They had as it were, a natural legal personality, consisting in their authority to interpret the law of nature each for himself, to be judge in their own cause, and to acknowledge no human superior. Lacking any restraint but one another's and without redress before an impartial judge, these individuals are 'not only perfectly able to injure each other, but for various reasons very often willing to do so.' Hence any man 'with whom we live in the natural state, is to be regarded, not indeed as an enemy, but still as an inconstant friend.' Thus Pufendorf;[4] many theorists, of course, simply followed Hobbes and treated the state of nature as a state of war.

The way out of this general mistrust was by an act of 'political alienation': each was to renounce part or all of his natural legal personality in favour of the collectivity of those so doing. Whether rights and powers were conceived as alienated directly to a particular individual, who thereby became the bearer of the corporate legal personality, or whether it was a matter of 'the total alienation of each associate, together with all his rights, to the whole community'[5] — which were then redistributed as public and private powers to government and citizens — makes little difference. In all cases, this act of political alienation — which stood in somewhat the same relation to ordinary contractual undertakings as the religious alienation discussed above stood to ordinary propitiatory offerings in a world of many gods — created a political community, solidary within and estranged externally from all others, with whom it remained in the natural state. With a new, positive legal personality stemming from their membership, the subjects now enjoyed security of property and contract. Though the sovereign had a claim on their private revenues, it was only for public purposes. The concentration of force and legitimacy in the hands of the ruler provided defence against enemies external and internal, and allowed impartial justice to be administered amongst the citizenry. In place of an irrational estrangement between rulers and people, the theory justified the existence of a functional graduated hierarchy of magistracy and citizenship. Thus both in structure and function, there was a close parallel between the doctrines of covenant and contract, as ideological applications of the ideas of estrangement and alienation to religion and politics respectively.

3 CULTURE AND SOCIETY

Rousseau's contribution to the doctrine of political alienation in *The Social Contract* contained little that was original. The idea of a direct transfer of powers to the collectivity, creating a democratic body, was already present in Spinoza. What made Rousseau's social contract explosive was the critical import of his political philosophy as a whole. And this can only be understood in the light of the social and cultural criticism contained in his other books. For a gulf divided Rousseau from other contractarians which is scarcely visible from the vantage-point of social contract: they were, in Mannheim's special sense, ideologists, theorisers of social order on the basis of the *status quo*, whereas Rousseau was a utopian who condemned present conditions by contrast with an abstract ideal. And it is in this connection, rather than as a social contract theorist, that Rousseau has usually been thought to have partly anticipated the ideas of self-estrangement elaborated by Hegel and Marx. Unlike his contract theory, however, Rousseau's cultural criticism does not employ the language of alienation. Is there nevertheless a kinship of ideas between his cultural criticism and the estrangement – alienation model that we have discerned in religious and political ideology? I want to approach this question in a roundabout way, through the sociology of ideological production.

It is remarkable that social contract theory could dominate political thought for some two hundred years, despite being always regarded as something of a makeshift. Its historicity was always dubious, and seldom insisted on. But its analytical value was not great either, for only those who already approved of existing political arrangements would be likely to agree that they were parties to a tacit compact, so that the legitimacy of governments rested in the end simply on the balance of approval and disapproval amongst their subjects. This was already clear from the internal contradiction of Hobbes' theory, and one suspects Hobbes himself was not unaware of the difficulty. In view of its evident internal weaknesses, the long-lived appeal of the theory requires some external explanation. The considerations which follow approach this question from the supply side, by examining the social position of its producers.

The demand for a theory of political obligation, I have argued, arose when the public-private opposition emerged in the glaring form of estrangement between more or less absolute monarchs, surrounded by their courts, armies, bureaucracies and trading monopolies, and more or less disaffected or rebellious subjects. Although social contract theory was stretched in various ways to suit the interests of élite factions, it was mostly a justification of order, seeking rational grounds for maintaining or stabilising the existing political dualism. But what sort of person would be most likely, and best qualified, to invent a theoretical justification of this order as resulting from a beneficial exchange, in which individuals could attain security and the advantages of civilisation by renouncing a life of independence that was 'poor, nasty and short' and binding themselves to obey a superior? Surely the answer must be: an intellectual who has been upwardly mobile on account of his talents, and who has himself benefited by renouncing his humble origins and serving a powerful patron or the public power itself. Estrangement from his kin and alienation of personal independence to his protector, or through employment by the state, has been the condition, for him, of realising the benefits of membership in the political community. It will have been a good bargain, because by exchanging the obscurity of private life for the prominence and comfort of the public sphere he has in fact joined the few who benefit most from the cleavage between them. On the other hand, since he has had to rise by his abilities, his experience inclines him to see this as an option open to any man of reason, making it easy for him to project his own social biography into a fictitious, 'rational' history of the community as a whole. Thus the form taken by social contract theory, its pseudo-historical and pseudo-rational character, as well as the interrelationships of the ideas of estrangement and alienation within it – are all consistent with its being a theoretical abstraction, made for a specific political purpose, from the upwardly mobile intellectual's experience of the balance of advantage won through his personal ascent in a system of patronage. And in fact, most social contractarians fit this specification fairly well, being lawyer-bureaucrats and academics, or protégés of political aristocrats. The few who do not, like Spinoza and Rousseau, produced democratic or otherwise deviant theories, while other theorists of the period with quite different social biographies, like Harrington or Montesquieu, avoided social contract altogether.

If this hypothesis helps to explain the appeal of the contract model to political ideologists, it could possibly be applied also, *mutatis mutandis*, to religious ideologists. For them service of the temple or the church was likewise an avenue of upward mobility; they too saw the entire community as 'called' to serve, as they had been. Thus the general structure of the estrangement – alienation theme in ideologies of covenant and contract is perhaps explicable by the conditions of intellectual production by institutionally dependent ideologists.

If so, this also accounts for the decreasing appeal of the contract model in the eighteenth century, after it had dominated Jewish and European religious and political ideology for so many centuries, and at a period when contract was becoming more rather than less widespread and familiar as the legal form of everyday social relations. The conditions of intellectual production were altering: princely patronage of ideologists became less dictatorial and more discreet, reflecting more honour on the patron than on the protégé, as the status of intellectuals rose with that of the bourgeoisie in general. To be an independent man of letters, living by the pen, depending only on publishers who were his equals or even inferiors, was becoming a possible if precarious role as reading publics and book production expanded. The general function of patronage – the recruitment of talent into the élite – was exercised less by the organs of state and church or by powerful noblemen, and more through the impersonal system of *salons* and the general admission of intellectuals into a 'polite society' which prided itself on its culture but needed much leavening of its intellectual lump by gifted outsiders. Institutions in the public domain became less demanding of the private loyalties of their servants, so that academic freedom increased and offices of church and state could furnish intellectuals with incomes while leaving them much of the freedom of an independent *rentier*.

Under these conditions, we should expect the upwardly mobile intellectual's sense of having crossed a social gulf to take a different shape It was no longer just a matter of having ascended out of the stratum where all life is private life into the light of the public arena; it was more a matter of quitting the rough, superstitious and uncivilised masses to enter the charmed circle of the cultured, the educated, and the enlightened. It was thus more of an ascent from one type of private life to another. The basic division within the experience of intellectuals would therefore shift away from the stark political duality of the seventeenth century towards the vaguer and more complex opposition between cultivation and crude simplicity, as society itself grew softer and more complex with economic growth. Consistent with this change, we find that the central theoretical opposition in ideology was less that of private and public, and more that defined by such pairs as savage-civilised, rude-polite, superstition-enlightenment, prejudice-reason: a much more complex set but one which seems to have corresponded to the self-image of the new and largely apolitical aristocratic-cum-bourgeois-literary élites.

The various terms of the old contractarian ideology began to shift their meaning and relationships accordingly, around the new theoretical poles. The 'state of nature' ceased to be an abstract image of an unregulated world of private law, tinged with original sin, and began to be taken more concretely – anthropologically, psychologically, and pedagogically. The 'natural' condition was, in this sense, a state of primitive savagery and simplicity which European man had happily transcended through the 'education of the race', just as it was also the instinctual state of the individual psyche, to be transcended by cultivating sympathy and by disciplining and sublimating self-love. Human history was written as a *Bildungsroman*, and educational novels symbolised the saga of human progress in the struggles of their heroes. But, for these denizens of a social stratum which had so highly developed the art of sociability, man was no less naturally sociable than he was competitive. Cultivation, therefore, merely developed a natural inclination into a 'second nature' of artifice, convention, self-control, good manners, and wit. In this theoretical outlook, in fact, the notion of a *conventional* order, with its overtones of etiquette, is the formal equivalent of the idea of legal order for seventeenth-century theorists, and it was in terms of the discovery, testing and transmission of useful conventions, and the moral sentiments they attract, that Hume recast social contract as a theory of political allegiance. In place of the fierce Hobbesian ruler whose tyranny is the price of legal security, the benevolent despot came to be seen as guardian and arbiter of the conventional order. Educator of his people, he was promoted to the status of honorary intellectual and man of taste. Since the division between the cultured and uncultured condition was not a sharp or sudden one, its surmounting was not conceived as a deliberate decision of mankind, as an act of 'cultural alienation', but rather as a natural progress by which individuals and peoples came to join the ranks of civilisation.

Inasmuch as the ideology of enlightenment turned upon differences of degree within the private realm rather than the opposition of public and private life itself, it might seem to reflect a more trivial preoccupation with society than that of the seventeenth-century contractarians. But in another way it was much more ambitious. For social contract theory had only prescribed for the profane sphere, whereas the ideology of enlightenment inevitably clashed directly with the Christian view that man's estrangement from God, through original sin, was the source of social conflict and all the miseries of this life. For if man was perfectible through the cultivation of his faculties, his own reason sufficed to build a harmonious world, and moral freedom and virtue were to be attained by overcoming the ignorance and cowardice on which religion throve. From this standpoint, religious alienation was not man's part in a good bargain, but man's loss, his self-betrayal and self-enslavement to priestcraft. Hence, already implicit in the Enlightenment's view that man's natural progress and happiness had been thwarted, in history, by the impostures of religious superstitions – keeping him in an artificial state of barbarism, and preventing the peaceful unification of the species through worldwide trade and communication – was the critical, negative idea of religious alienation only expressed in those terms later, by Feuerbach.

From this standpoint, religious alienation was not a means of palliating an estrangement of man from God proclaimed and accepted as inevitable, and thus of justifying and bridging the felt opposition of sacred and profane. On the contrary, it was a process by which men created a god in opposition to themselves, thus artificially cleaving reality into sacred and profane, necessitating thereafter a continuous stunting of their powers through repeated acts of renunciation and self-denial, palliatives for an illusorily divided cosmos. Instead of seeing the remedy for men's mutual estrangement in the reduction of their estrangement from God by religious alienation, therefore, eighteenth-century rationalists saw religious alienation itself as the cause of men's mutual estrangements, both directly, by fostering the antagonism of different faiths and sects, and indirectly, by keeping men in ignorance and political impotence, a prey to false ideas and sinister interests. In this way, as it moved away from the abstract individualism of the seventeenth-century view of man, Enlightenment ideology moved to the opposite extreme of an almost equally abstract universalism. 'Man', the species, had alienated its natural essence – that of a free, rational, happy and sociable being – to impostors and vested interests, who oppressed it and divided it against itself in the name of absurd or false beliefs. But nature, aided by reason, could not be gainsaid for ever, and the natural progress of the human mind had now set man on the road towards moral and material perfection.

It should now become clear where Rousseau stands in relation to this development. First, he shared the rationalistic deism of his age, and carried to an extreme the denial that man was by nature estranged from his maker. As a champion of 'natural religion', he took the enlightened view of traditional religions as superstitions to which man had alienated his autonomy, to his detriment. He went beyond this, however, by extending a similar analysis to the traditional state and attributing a larger share of human misery to political than to religious oppression. It is well known that Rousseau advanced two accounts of the social compact. That in *The Social Contract* is prescriptive, and a deliberate idealisation, while that in the *Discourse* is a conjectural history of how 'All ran headlong to their chains, in hopes of securing their liberty; for they had just enough wit to perceive the advantages of political institutions, without experience enough to enable them to foresee the dangers.'[6] In all this, Rousseau was no more than an advanced exponent of contemporary arguments against feudalism and absolutism, and at this level *The Social Contract* merely sets forth an improved version of the received theory, which could not be abused to justify monarchical or aristocratic oppression, and which favoured republican and democratic institutions.

But beyond this point Rousseau was wholly at variance with his age, whose estimate of enlightenment he reversed. For where his contemporaries criticised religious alienation as unnatural for a rational man, Rousseau thought it superfluous for a man of unsophisticated virtue. Where they dismissed social contract theory as superfluous, given the progress of civilisation and the spread of enlightened conventions, condemned civilisation and the conventional order itself as a corruption of man's innocence, and returned to social contract as the means of creating an autarchic refuge for simplicity. Thus in one way he was far ahead of his time, for he extended the Enlightenment's critique of religious and political ideology to its own ideologies of culture and progress, correctly diagnosing them as manifestations and masks of social inequality. But in another way he was a reactionary, for instead of going beyond the abstract universalism he criticised to a concrete analysis of society's contradictions, he retreated towards an extreme individualism. This was perhaps really a borrowing of seventeenth-century clothes to dignify and conceal his wounded petty-bourgeois pride. For in Rousseau we see an intellectual who was sufficiently upwardly mobile to have internalised the entire ideology of enlightenment, but socially thwarted and hurt to a degree where he revolted and turned its own weapons against it (and against himself, as an example of its corrupting influence). His critique was certainly radical, but its roots were no deeper than Rousseau's own, in the ethical solipsism of the Swiss middle class.

Thus, repelled by the degrading effect on men's minds and bodies of the extreme social inequality in France, he believed that he had found its origins in basic processes of human interaction. In speculative terms, he described the sources of social prestige in primitive life: 'Each one began to consider the rest, and to wish to be considered in turn; and thus a value came to be attached to public esteem.'[7] This secondary value reinforced the primary cultural values of the community, causing emulation in achievement and a ranked distribution of honorific rewards. With economic development and heritable property, ascriptive inequalities came to be accorded status in the same way. Political authority, as it appeared, favoured the rich and prestigious, and made social inequality permanent and profound. In all this, Rousseau showed a sociological imagination unique in its period. Yet he failed to make the crucial distinction between levels of development of material and intellectual culture, on the one hand, which determine the general type and character of social stratification, and on the other, those universal social processes which promote conformity and distribute status in any social group whatever. Thus, rebelling against the particular cultural ideology and social inequalities of his age, which he saw as the end-product of an evolution that had begun with the most primitive social distinctions, he mistakenly identified the latter with man's universal social interdependence in group life. Only outside society, he concluded, in the 'natural' isolation of his imaginary primordial man, or through the artificial insulation of persons from each other's influence, in the ideal state or the ideal pedagogical environment, was inequality avoidable.

'Social man', he wrote, 'lives constantly outside himself, and only knows how to live in the opinion of others, so that he seems to receive the consciousness of his own existence merely from the judgment of others concerning him.'[8] This remarkable statement might have recorded a *discovery* that could have led him on to inquire into the conditions under which man's other-directedness was most conducive to equality. In fact it is part of the final and damning peroration on the plight of 'civilised man', who is here the 'social man', as compared with the integrity of 'the savage' who 'lives within himself'. In turning away from his insight into the nature of social man – an insight into himself, of which his morality made him falsely ashamed – and back to his hypothetical savage, Rousseau closed a door to the sociological study of inequality. Instead of going on to examine the ways in which the alienation of goods and services *within* social life both depends upon, and maintains, relationships of estrangement between 'social men', he retained a purely ideological conception of social life as itself the product of pre-social man's self-alienation.

This ideology can now be rapidly summarised. Men, in their prehistoric state, were mutually estranged – not in the sense of being hostile or mistrustful, for Rousseau did not deny a natural sympathy – but in the minimal sense of being isolated by choice, indifferent towards one another, and having no innate need for company beyond sexual gratification. As population increase brought about a more gregarious life, men inevitably alienated their natural independence and autonomy to their associates. Thus societies, and ultimately political and religious communities, came into existence. But they were all premised on the self-alienation of individuals, who become slaves to the conventions and values of their milieus, exchanging their natural virtue for the opinions of others, so that estrangement and hostility between men and groups grew as society developed. Not only war, conflicting interests and the mutual hatred of social unequals; but also secret malevolence and manipulative enmity, which exploit the superficial solidarity of social conventions. The only remedy, short of becoming a hermit, is the political enclave of the ideal democracy described in *The Social Contract*, where each alienates himself, not to any other, but to all, thereby remaining as free as before. But such a remedy, Rousseau admits, is really only for the gods. 'So perfect a government is not for men.'[9]

It is, I think, clear that as between the 'bad' and the 'good' self-alienation there is only a verbal play on the inevitably duplex nature of man's social identity: as 'member' and part of a social whole, he, together with all other members, confronts himself as an individual; but simultaneously, as an individual, he confronts all the other individuals. It resolves nothing, because in the end there is no real problem to resolve. Rousseau succeeds in stating some of the basic conditions of all social existence, in terms which his predecessors had used to state the conditions for associating as a religious or political community. Along with these ideas went the model of estrangement and alienation, whose origins I have tried to locate in the social experience of intellectuals. In applying this model to social existence in general, Rousseau had to assume a non-existent position outside society. The alienation he condemned has no human or social remedy, because it is purely a construct of ideology and lacks any concrete reference. On the other hand, it eloquently expresses the social outsider's *feeling* of estrangement from his society and his culture. For the *révolté* intellectual, who has become estranged from his stratum of origin without winning solidarity with his stratum of aspiration, and therefore has publicly taken up a stance of individualistic self-sufficiency, to seek re-entry into society would indeed mean a painful 'alienation' of his social self. For this reason Rousseau's idea of social life as alienation, or of other people as hell, has had many echoes amongst marginalised intellectuals in bourgeois society, from Stirner to Sartre.

It could be argued that Rousseau's most enduring influence has been in educational rather than political theory. Traditionally, education had been conceived in terms of religious alienation, as it was also, for instance, by Rousseau's contemporary Wesley. A Christian education fulfilled the baptismal promise to renounce the Old Adam, as the pupil advanced in piety and learning to become a full member of the Body of Christ. Enlightened educators in the eighteenth century replaced this notion of an alienation with that of a natural progression under rational guidance, through which the pupil came to see for himself that sociable and conventional behaviour was in accordance with enlightened self-interest. Rousseau's individualism restored the emphasis on alienation, but as a negative critique of the enlightened practice. Education for social conformity was an alienation of the natural independence with which every child was born, and stifled his capacity for spontaneous feeling and genuine virtue. The educational programme of *Emile* aimed to insulate the pupil from social pressures, while exposing his faculties directly to nature. And it could perhaps be thought that here, in the region of primary socialisation, Rousseau's idea of a self-alienative confrontation between individual and society does have a factual reference. Especially in a Freudian perspective, it might seem that the human instinctual endowment gives men needs which only society can satisfy, yet allows this only at the cost of severe repressions and the sacrifice of psychical potential in childhood. This might seem to justify a psychological interpretation of Rousseau's 'natural man' and thus give empirical grounding to the idea that all social life involves a psychological alienation, a renunciation of possible selves and self-fulfilments for the individual.

Such a view, however, still involves making an abstraction of 'the individual' on one side, and 'society' and 'culture' on the other. We have no way of isolating either side, in such general terms, from all the various instances in which societies and cultures have moulded their psychological raw material into the 'individuals' they required, and in which individuals so moulded have produced the society and culture that suited them. The supposed subject of this psychological self-alienation cannot therefore be identified, in reality, nor can we say with any precision what 'he' would be giving up, nor to whom. On the other hand, we might perhaps say, within a sociological frame of reference, that socialisation processes contain a slightly different sort of alienation. For if we suppose that they typically involve social distance between 'teacher' and 'pupil' (a generation gap, relations of peer-group exclusion, or hierarchical distancing of institutional roles, for instance) we can also construe this as a combination of solidarity and estrangement. The teacher manipulates this balance in such a way that the pupil alienates parts of his autonomy in order to win the praise or avoid the blame of the teacher, i.e. to reduce their estrangement or avoid its punitive intensification. This 'autonomy' is not a vague or metaphysical potential, for it always has a concrete content, namely the object of the 'lesson', in so far as it involves a latent battle of wills. Successful socialisation requires the teacher to retain enough power to manipulate the balance of solidarity and estrangement so that the pupil ends up by internalising the norms and values which the teacher represents. Thus, in the only factual sense in which we can speak of alienation occurring in primary socialisation, it involves 'social man' on both sides, although at different levels of personal and social development: it gives us no warrant for returning to Rousseau, nor with him to nature.

That social mobility involves processes of socialisation, often 'anticipatory' on the part of the upward recruit, is a commonplace of reference-group studies. It is sometimes noted, also, that there is a partial formal identity between the actual processes usually classified separately under the headings 'socialisation' and 'social mobility'. In both cases, there is social distance, or estrangement, between a powerful established group on one side and less powerful individual aspirants on the other, so that the latter achieve solidarity with the former by internalising their values and norms, and renouncing those of their groups of origin under threat of continued or increased estrangement by the powerful. Thus, if the model of estrangement and alienation which has been so prominent in religious and political ideology reflected the experience of upwardly mobile intellectuals, they may have also interpreted this experience in the light of latent models of estrangement and alienation built up in consciousness during primary socialisation. Similarly, if models of covenant and contract made a wide appeal to their consumers, this may have been partly due to their reactivating such residual experiences of early life, which are in any case reactivated whenever individuals undergo the discipline of social learning. The dualities of sacred-profane and public-private would thereby have been 'domesticated' by subconscious assimilation to the familiar and long-transcended dualities of parent-child, sib-sibling, and teacher-pupil. In myths of religious alienation, which combine the idea of a covenant with those of the Fatherhood of God, the Brotherhood of Christ, etc., this is already an explicit connection. In political ideology however, the analysis has a certain irony in so far as social contract theorists prided themselves on finally routing the argument of their rivals, the patriarchal school, that political authority was an extension of paternal authority, and the state an enlarged family.

To the extent that these analyses are convincing, they help dispose of a number of ideological uses of 'alienation' and 'self-alienation' that still haunt the literature, and also suggest the sociological utility of concepts of estrangement and alienation defined concretely, with reference to elementary social processes.

2 Estrangement and Alienation in *The Phenomenology of Mind*

The ideas of estrangement and alienation received their first full-dress philosophical presentation in Hegel's *The Phenomenology of Mind*.[1] The climax of this presentation is in the second section (the 'antithesis') of the historical development of *Geist* (spirit, mind) in Chapter VI, entitled 'Spirit in Self-estrangement'. To discuss only that section, however, would not do justice to Hegel's arguments, which depend on preceding preparatory stages. Thus 'Spirit in Self-estrangement', which refers to the development of European Christendom, demands to be discussed against the background of its 'thesis', 'Objective Spirit', which refers to Graeco-Roman civilisation. Furthermore, as Hegel himself insisted, these analyses of historical socio-cultural systems can scarcely be understood in abstraction from the presentation of corresponding modes of self-consciousness in Chapter IV. These are the well-known sections that culminate, respectively, in the dialectic of master and slave and that of the 'unhappy consciousness'. Not only is the discussion of these earlier sections necessary to situate Hegel's treatment of self-estranged spirit in context, but in addition, each of these sections contains its own partial development of ideas of estrangement and alienation.

Hegelians may very well object that to isolate even these sections from the book as a whole is to risk distorting Hegel's ideas. There is force in this objection, especially as I shall largely ignore the later sections on morality, religion and absolute knowledge, which for Hegel contained the point and conclusion of the entire work. Up to a point, my selection can be defended on the grounds that faithful exegesis of Hegel is not the primary aim, nor one for which I would be qualified. I shall be content if, without gross misrepresentation, I can trace the double thread of estrangement and alienation through the relevant chapters. Even so, however, an important distinction and limitation is involved in the choice of only these chapters as relevant. For Hegel uses the term 'self-estrangement of spirit' in two quite different contexts, and indeed in two apparently different senses. One is the historical context already mentioned, where it unquestionably refers to relationships involving human beings. In Chapter VIII of the *Phenomenology*, however, and again in *The Philosophy of Nature*, Hegel uses 'self-estrangement' to describe the latency of spirit within nature, apart from man, as a dumb and still unrevealed essence awaiting appropriation by man as knowledge.

This appears to be a wholly metaphysical, or at best epistemological usage, and I propose to ignore it and confine myself to the historical sense. There is, however, a connection between the two senses which ought to be noted. It is (or seems to me) somewhat as follows. Man figures in the metaphysical self-estrangement of spirit in nature only as spirit's redeemer: human knowledge is the means and vehicle by which spirit returns to itself out of its alien material condition. But the process through which this actually occurs is that of history. And it can occur there because spirit undergoes a *second* self-estrangement in human history, within the sphere of human consciousness and by human agency. At a certain stage of his development, man comes to think of his true self as having its home in another world, estranged from natural existence. The return of spirit from *this* estrangement, through the historical awakening of reason and man's reappropriation of his earthly nature with the growth of secular culture, is also the condition for the return of spirit from its self-estrangement in external nature, outside of man, in the form of the natural sciences which form part of that culture. The metaphysical and historical self-estrangements of spirit are thus formally similar conditions. They are also separate conditions, although a single process overcomes both together. Since this inquiry is only concerned with estrangement and alienation as relationships between men, or between men and their objects, and not with their metaphorical extension to relationships amongst conceptual entities, detailed discussion of Hegel's metaphysical usage can, I hope, be omitted without loss.

The sections dealing with estrangement and alienation in history will be discussed in the following order:

Ch. IVA Independence and Dependence of Self-consciousness: Lordship and Bondage.

Ch. VIA Objective Spirit: the Ethical Order.

Ch. IVB Freedom of Self-consciousness: Stoicism, Scepticism and the Unhappy Consciousness.

Ch. VIB Spirit in Self-estrangement: the Discipline of Culture.

The main reason for interweaving parts of chapters like this is convenience of exposition, but there is ample justification also in Hegel's assertion that the forms of self-consciousness developed in Chapter IV are only abstractions from the real development of spirit in the world, as set forth in Chapter VI,[2] which they presuppose as the scene of their existence. It should also be remembered that the different 'moments' of the *Phenomenology* have a synchronic as well as a diachronic reference. The dialectic of master and slave, for example, or the relationships between family roles, both of which Hegel develops in connection with the ancient world, retain their significance throughout the later epochs, where social inequality and the family remain as subordinate moments. For the different moments are introduced and analysed at the point in history at which Hegel thought they first appeared as dominant structural principles; conversely, each historical stage is unique in that it brings forth new principles, new implications of the preceding dialectic, around which the accumulation of past moments is rearranged as a subordinate system. I shall give an account of what Hegel himself says on the subject of estrangement and alienation, in these four sections, and then conclude with a brief comparison of Hegel's categories with the ideas of estrangement and alienation, as I have used them up to now.

I MASTER AND SLAVE

The basis for Hegel's ideas about estrangement was established in the course of a line of reasoning designed to supersede both Kant's theory of the thing-in-itself and Fichte's theory of legal personality. Before dealing with *self*-consciousness, he had expounded the elements of consciousness, including our perception of things, in Chapter II. He claimed that in perception we establish a world in which thinghood consists of 'an *excluding* repelling unity' of a thing's properties[3] – its unity as *this* determinate object, defined by its not being any other. This notion of a thing as defined by negation, through the exclusion and repulsion of otherness, is the necessary foundation of the ideas of estrangement introduced later, although there is no suggestion that any such relationship as estrangement could occur in a mere world of things. The next stage of the discussion of consciousness, in Chapter III, which deals with the understanding, carries the analysis of thinghood further. If we are to understand how the thing subsists as a self-determining unity, in the process of becoming itself in opposition to other things, then we have to conceive the substance of the thing as *force*. Thus the world of finite realities appears to the understanding as a 'play of forces'. Things establish and maintain themselves in existence, amongst their manifold interrelationships, through the equilibration of antagonistic forces.

So far, Hegel has treated the conscious subject, who is constituting this world in its various modes, as a perceiving and understanding mind that does not interact practically with its objects. Now he passes on, in Chapter IV, to the active relations of the subject to his world, as a living being, which give rise to consciousness of self. Through needs and desires, the subject grasps objects not just as an external world of mutually excluding entities, a play of forces outside himself, but as objects of desire which, as such, exclude *him*. He has to set his own forces to work to overcome the otherness of things, by labour, appropriation, and use, if he is to attain satisfaction and to survive. In the process he acquires the sense and certainty of selfhood, and on the other hand, experiences in practice the independence of objects, outside and resistant to the self. Yet this is not the end of the matter. For among external objects are other self-conscious beings, and towards these the subject directs a special sort of need: the need to receive from another consciousness confirmation of the self-certainty which he acquires through his action on the world of inanimate things. This is what Hegel calls the desire for 'recognition'; its pursuit takes the form of the dialectic of master and slave, or lordship and bondage.

In this elementary contact of one self-consciousness with another, 'we see the process repeated which came before us in the play of forces; in the present case, however, it is found in consciousness.'[4] The self, at this stage of the argument, can only have a thing-like unity. 'Self-consciousness is primarily simple existence for self, self-identity by exclusion of every other from itself . . . But the other is also a self-consciousness; an individual makes its appearance in antithesis to an individual. Appearing thus in their immediacy, they are for each other in the manner of ordinary objects.'[5] Hegel's starting-point thus echoes that of Fichte, who deduced the 'science of rights' from the mutual recognition that he regarded as implicit in the situation of a community of egos, each defining itself as a free being by the exclusion of all others from its sphere of private potency. Beyond this starting-point the resemblance ceases, however. For Hegel, Fichte's merely abstract deduction was inadequate in that it could not explain why, if mutual recognition as free and equal moral agents was implicit in all interaction between self-conscious beings, mankind had had to pass through a long historical travail of enslavement, domination and struggle before men's equal rights were recognised by law. But he thought this concrete process could also be deduced from the implications of the initial situation, and if Fichte's treatment shows the influence of Rousseau's *Social Contract*, Hegel's dialectic is a subtilised elaboration of the argument of the *Discourse*, that 'Free and independent as men were before, they were now . . . brought into subjection, as it were, to all nature, and particularly to one another; and became in some degree a slave even in becoming the master of other men.'[6]

The dialectic of master and slave is well enough known to need no detailed rehearsal here. The force of their own self-existence which maintains the mutually excluding individuals over against each other also requires completion through each other. Self-certainty can only rise to the level of truth if others confirm it. 'Self-consciousness attains its satisfaction only in another self-consciousness.'[7] Yet others are neither able nor willing to grant recognition, simply by the fact that they are others. But yet again, all are equally desirous of recognition. Since each can treat the other only as a conscious object of his need – as a mirror for his ego – and not as a self-conscious being in his own right, a subject, the general desire for recognition turns into an all-round *struggle* for recognition. Logically, there is nothing in the assumptions of the model to prevent this becoming a life-and-death struggle, and only to the extent that it does can either party obtain their desire by, so to speak, imprinting their selfhood in the person of the other, so that the other reflects it back as a form of their own self-consciousness. Its only necessary limit is reached when one has another at his mercy, where it becomes apparent that to destroy him would defeat the purpose of the struggle, by breaking the mirror. *Life* is thereby recognised as a prerequisite of self-consciousness – the life of others as well as one's own. The vanquished is spared to become the living confirmation of the victor's self-certainty, and the completion of his self-consciousness. As a living conscious being, held under fear of death as means to this end, he becomes the slave or bondsman of the other; while the latter is confirmed in his self-certainty indeed, but only as lord and master of the slave, and on condition of remaining so. Thus in place of the former plurality of unconnected egos, a stratified community of living persons emerges in which self-consciousness is socially established, but in a one-sided way. The two main relationships of living beings to the world, desire and labour, can now be distributed between the two poles of the social relationship of master and slave, and shape the consciousness of each accordingly. Masters view the world, slaves included, as means to the satisfaction of their desires: theirs becomes the self-consciousness of the pure consumer. The world of slaves is a scene of labour on behalf of their lords: their selfhood is limited to fear and service, but they have also the self-assurance which labourers gain through their practical and direct experience with the world of things.

It is because these two aspects of the slave's consciousness come into conflict that the situation changes and can ultimately be transcended; for there is no motive for change on the part of the masters, dependent as they are on maintaining their supremacy. In tracing this dialectic Hegel makes the first explicit reference to estrangement in the *Phenomenology*. The slave's whole reality, defined and dominated as it is by the power and will of the master, is a coercive exteriority which he internalises as fear – or, in Hegel's words, an 'alien, external reality before which [his consciousness] trembled.'[8] By working in this very medium, however, the slave imposes upon it forms that spring from his own mind and will. His labour realises, through objectification, his *own* conscious designs within this alien sphere, whose extraneous and alien character is to that extent cancelled. 'Thus precisely in labour where there seemed to be some outsider's mind and ideas involved, the bondsman becomes aware, through this rediscovery of himself by himself, of having and being a "mind of his own".'[9]

It is significant that Hegel's first mention of estrangement should come at the point where the slave's self-consciousness, waking to its independence, challenges the master's consciousness of reality as dependent on his will. By implication, estrangement can only arise between independent self-conscious beings who are recognised as such. So long as the struggle for recognition was in progress, the antagonists were no more estranged than any other mutually excluding and repelling forces of nature. The master's victory produced a one-sided unity between his own power and the slave's fear, the latter being merely an external correlate of the former within the being of the slave. But as soon as the slave himself contrasts the reality created through his work with that defined by his fear, he knows both the master and himself as independent self-conscious beings, and as estranged by their inevitable hostility. Hegel's use of the idea of estrangement here therefore accords with its definition as a type of self-other orientation, for this also presupposes that the other is treated as another self.

2 THE ETHICAL ORDER AND THE SOULLESS COMMUNITY

Hegel did not explain how the dialectic of master and slave was supposed to relate to the presentation of the Greek *polis* in Chapter VI, as spirit objectified in an ethical order, but we can link them up from his hints. The first point to note is that there is no account, in Chapter IV, of the relationship between the individual masters. This would depend on the kind of society in which the system of personal bondage exists. But in the classic instance of ancient Greece, the union of slaveowners is presumed to take the form of the 'ethical order' of the city-state. On the other hand, the account of the city-state in Chapter VI does not mention slavery. This is doubtless because material production, comprising the moments of labour and bondage, is presumed to occur within the private household. The ethical order of the *polis*, we can infer, is that of the public arena in which only free citizens participate. The household appears here only in the form of the family, for the city is composed of families of freemen. If we look at the discussions of slavery and the *polis* together, however, as Hegel certainly intended, then their conjunction in the same historical instance would represent an extreme separation of two aspects of social order: of 'Ego that is "we", a plurality of Egos, and "we" that is a single Ego.'[10] Collective self-consciousness as a plurality of egos appears only in the antagonistic relationship of masters and slaves within the private household, while in public life the self-identification of all citizens with the universal will embodied in law and custom constitutes the *polis* as a single ego, a collective self. Hegel's aim, in the *Phenomenology*, was to show how the historical process, from antiquity to modernity, would eventually unite these extremes in a rational social substance, an ethical order which reconciled universality with individuality, where self-conscious individuals would fully recognise 'the perfect freedom and independence of their opposition as component elements' of the whole.[11] The separated yet historically compresent extremes of individual and collective self-identity were necessary starting-points for this theoretical journey. Hegel did not, however, conceive of this particular separation in terms of estrangement—for, as we have seen, he did not clearly situate it within reality at all. It can be registered only as an implication of the structure of his theory, or even of the presentation of his theory, as entailed by the deduction of the categories of self-consciousness in 'abstraction' from the dialectic of spirit. It was left to Marx to theorise the concrete relation of the worker's individuality to the universality embodied in the collective world of the masters, in terms of estrangement, by employing a notion of alienation that has not so far appeared in Hegel's theory, and by taking the standpoint not of spirit but of labour.

Hegel is anxious to present the ethical order of the city-state as containing no internal estrangement, despite being a complex unity of opposing principles. For example, there is tension between the political community as concentrated in government, and as diffused in the systems of personal and real rights, guilds and associations, which always tend towards fragmentation of the whole. The state reunites its parts and revives the national spirit in wars, and in peacetime preserves its unity by justice. Yet although coercive, justice here is 'neither an alien principle holding somewhere remote from the present, nor the realization . . . of mutual malice, treachery, ingratitude, etc.' On the contrary, 'justice is the government of the nation, and is its all-pervading essential life in a consciously present individual form, and is the personal self-conscious will of all.'[12] And again, Hegel sees the universality of ethical life as present on two levels, in the human law of the state and the divine law of the ancestral deities of the family. This leads to conflicting obligations and ultimately to the subversion of the unity of the *polis*. For the centrifugal tendency of the family, represented by its womenfolk's concern with the family's status and the wealth of its private life, can only be counteracted by increasing militarism on the part of the state, which therefore becomes more and more a specialised machine of male warriors. None of this struggle is described in terms of estrangement, however, for its various elements interpenetrate at every level. Family and state do not become estranged, because the warriors are still brothers and sons of matriarchs. The entire dialectic proceeds within a kind of intimacy and within the shared culture of the city. Its upshot, however, is that the family in its original form vanishes behind the uniform status of private legal personality, vested in the *paterfamilias*, while the collective spirit of each separate *polis* is dissolved through war and conquest into the worldwide despotism of military empires. The solidarity between individuals in the ethical order is thereby 'burst into a plurality of separate points' and there emerges what Hegel calls the 'soulless community', epitomised in imperial Rome.

Here, once again, Hegel employed the idea of estrangement. Political authority becomes naked and arbitrary domination, supported by no traditional bonds of common culture or national spirit: it is in this sense that the political community is 'soulless' (*geistlos*). The ruler, since he represents no collective self-consciousness, and none stands opposed to him either, takes himself to be the 'living god' of the world he rules; yet by the same token he can rule it only in accordance with personal caprice and his individual talents, for common customs and values do not exist. Yet this does nevertheless constitute a political *community*, in terms of the common legal system which defines all its subjects as persons and private proprietors, on a footing of formal equality, and gives the ruler his legitimate authority as the personal sovereign of each. The actual meaning or content of this empty legal status, however, depends on the chances of life, and hence mainly on the will of the despot. Thus on the one hand, all the separate individuals see control of their destinies 'gathered at the same time into a single centre, alien to them and just as devoid of the life of the spirit *(geistlos)*'.[13] But, on the other, 'The lord of the world becomes really conscious of what he is – viz. the universal might of actuality – by that power of destruction which he exercises against the contrasted selfhood of his subjects.' For (Hegel's words cannot be improved on here) –

> his power is not the spiritual union and concord in which the various persons might get to know their *own* self-consciousness. Rather they exist as persons separately for themselves, and all continuity with others is excluded from the absolute punctual atomicity of their nature. They are, therefore, in a merely negative relation, a relation of exclusion both to one another and to him, who *is* their principle of connexion or continuity. *Qua* this continuity, he is the essential being and content of their formal nature – a content, however, foreign to them, and a being hostile in character. . . . Juridical personality thus finds itself, rather, without any substance of its own, since content alien to it is imposed on it and holds good within it.[14]

The original cause for the estrangement characterising the soulless community is that individuals confront each other as foreigners, through the dissolution of tribal and national identities. No doubt this occurs mainly between different parts of the empire, or in cities where immigrants of many nationalities mingle, but in any case the universal legal categorisation of families and individuals as mutually exclusive proprietary units generalises relationships of estrangement. (In this connection, Hegel's treatment in the *Phenomenology* was usefully supplemented in *The Philosophy of History*.) Above all, however, it is the fact that the actual intercourse of individuals is mediated through common subjection to alien rule, and to the ruler's arbitrary and destructive violence, which completes the estrangement implied by their initial situation. For life in the soulless community is the antithesis of ethical order: it is what we should now call anomie. In an unpredictable, chaotic and violent world, individuals revert to Hobbesian attitudes of mutual mistrust and exploitation. Like Hobbesian men too, their social bond is anxiety for the security of their property, compelling them to obey a ruler who is nevertheless their enemy. The interest of Hegel's treatment of the theme of *Leviathan*, however, is that he does not depict it as a likely or inevitable general solution to man's natural predicament, but as the historical outcome of social and political dissolution. The situation where private property and private law is the sole bond of the political community corresponds to a specific mode of estrangement between ruler and ruled, and through this, of the ruled from one another.

This relation of the 'lord of the world' to his subjects echoes that of the master to his slaves. Like the master, the ruler only finds the truth of his self-certainty by denying the autonomy of his subjects in acts of oppression. In *The Philosophy of History* Hegel argued that slavery died out in the Roman empire as political bondage obliterated the distinction between freemen and slaves, while legal personality was available to all, whether born free or freed. Thus the soulless community is the first, negative, form in which Hegel united his separate starting-points of the state as universality of the collective ego, and society as plurality of individual egos. The state, now personified in the despot, 'is truly what it is only *qua* universal plurality of single units: cut off from this plurality, the solitary and single self of the ruler is, in fact, a powerless and unreal self.'[15] The soulless community, in fact, universalises the economic relationship between the many masters and their slaves, as a political relationship between the single, divinised ruler of the world and his subjects.

This is the main reason why, in Chapter IV, the independent self-consciousness attained by the slave through labour was made the point of transition to a discussion of Stoicism as the first form in which 'free self-consciousness' emerges. For this 'is a freedom which can come on the scene as a general form of the world's spirit only in a time of *universal fear and bondage*, a time, too, when mental cultivation is universal, and has elevated culture to the level of thought.'[16] Philosophical Stoicism is thus seen as a reaction to the world of the soulless community, for the latter actualises for a whole epoch of society (*politically*, therefore) the condition of estrangement from which the self-consciousness of the slave makes its flight into freedom.

3 THE UNHAPPY CONSCIOUSNESS

The triad of Stoicism, Scepticism and the unhappy consciousness, developed in Chapter IV, are the three stages of this flight. This 'freedom of self-consciousness' differs from the objective, positive liberty realised in the ethical order of the *polis* through public embodiment of law in the actions of individuals. The slave seeks a subjective, negative liberty, a private space in which he can escape the overwhelming power of the master. Since the master controls the whole of the slave's outer world, this desire turns inward and leads towards a diremption of consciousness. On the one hand, the outer world of desire, labour and social recognition develops as an objective sphere of bondage and necessity; on the other, an inner world of thought, doubt, and faith is elaborated as a realm of individual freedom. In this way, subjective personality develops for the first time. But Stoicism, the contemplative withdrawal towards pure thought, culminates in vacuous generalities. It is the first stage in that it merely makes consciousness double by seeking an inner calm of philosophical certainty, set apart from the restless mutability of the world of action. Scepticism, as second stage, expresses this doubleness of divided consciousness within the realm of pure thought itself through the attitude of doubt. As a critical dialectical spirit, forever moving from one position to another, it finds its justification in resigning itself to this restless contrariety. Hegel interprets Stoicism and Scepticism as 'moods of consciousness' that 'reduce to their abstract form' the two aspects of self-consciousness in the soulless community: the empty formalism of legal status on the one hand, and on the other the confusion and instability of real life. They give way to the third stage, the unhappy consciousness, epitomised in Christianity, which combines both sides of the opposition in a 'consciousness of self as a divided nature, a doubled and merely contradictory being.'[17] This dualism is expressed through an attitude of faith, by which the unhappy consciousness sets over against its own existence in the manifold and changeable life of here and now, a simple and unchangeable 'beyond' which is its own unattainable essence.

The consciousness of master and slave is the first, and the unhappy consciousness is the second type of mentality which Hegel characterised by estrangement. (In discussing estrangement in the soulless community we moved ahead of the order of presentation in the *Phenomenology*.) This is a somewhat different notion of estrangement from that encountered hitherto. In the case of slavery, as also in its political counterpart in the soulless community, 'estrangement' denoted an actual social relationship of external separation and hostility between self-conscious individuals. Here, however, we are dealing with a relationship between conceptual entities within a single (individual or collective) self-consciousness. It is only, as Hegel says, 'For *it*' that 'both are realities foreign to each other.'[18] But Hegel does not call this a kind of estrangement for nothing. His justification is that, for the unhappy consciousness, or the Christian believer himself, the relationship by no means holds merely between conceptual entities, but between 'himself' and a personal God. For in identifying itself with life in this world, unhappy consciousness exists as 'self', even though it treats this self as something negative, mere selfishness, to be annihilated. (In this sense, Hegel refers to the worldly self of the unhappy consciousness as 'the enemy', reminding us, no doubt, of the symbolic function of Satan as prince of this world, and lord of the flesh.) But by the same token, life eternal also appears to the unhappy consciousness as a self, and even as a particular existent self, for the divine self-consciousness is believed to have been revealed in Jesus Christ. Thus whether personified in God as 'the alien, external Being' or in Christ as the seemingly more accessible 'formed and embodied unchangeable' – which nevertheless remains still 'an alien extraneous reality' and 'absolutely remote'[19] – the sundered part of the unhappy consciousness seems to confront it as an actual and personalised self-consciousness. Thus it is precisely by internalising the interpersonal, *social* relationship of estrangement that the unhappy consciousness constitutes and maintains itself as a double self-consciousness. For although it also internalises merely conceptual dichotomies, conceiving its inner division as a severance between essence and existence, etc., these only receive and retain their distinctness and opposition as attributes of the personalities of God and man. Yet these in turn only preserve their separation and integrity as opposed 'realities' by virtue of the posited distance – and hence the felt estrangement – which keeps them apart.

The conscious aim of the unhappy consciousness, as man, is nothing less than 'complete and thoroughgoing fusion and identification'[20] with the divine. Yet this very aim, implying as it does a total shedding or purging of the 'merely' human self, logically requires that the divine should have first been posited as something alien, beyond man, and by definition unattainable by him. It is for this reason that Hegel saw the Christian project as inherently self-contradictory. 'Here, then, is a struggle against an enemy, victory over whom really means being worsted, where to have attained one result is really to lose it in the opposite.'[21] The unhappy consciousness is like a solitary chess-player who cannot win because he cannot outwit himself. All that keeps the tensions of the unhappy consciousness from collapsing through their own contradictoriness is the force of the *felt* estrangement between man and God, as an internalised social relationship structuring the individual and collective psyche of the devout.

In discussing the unhappy consciousness, Hegal introduces the idea of self-alienation, in the sense of renunciation and sacrifice. The quest for reunion on the part of the unhappy consciousness is developed through a triad whose first two moments end up in versions of the dilemma of self-estrangement. The first, passive contemplative devotion, exhausts itself in a yearning for a beyond which remains beyond reach. The second, the life of active piety and 'stewardship' in the world, contains a 'deception'[22] inasmuch as the believer gives the glory of his deeds to God, but keeps their worldly fruit for himself, together with the personal will expressed in the very act of giving praise and thanks. The notion of self-alienation enters at this point, for the flaw in the second stage was its incomplete self-renunciation. The third stage resolves this through submission to an institutionalised church. Henceforth, overtures to the divine are made only under the auspices of a mediating priesthood; the rewards of labour are tithed and enjoyments mitigated by fasting; private judgement is renounced in favour of rituals and the use of a sacred language. 'Through these moments – the negative abandonment first of its own right and power of decision, then of its property and enjoyment, and finally the positive moment of carrying on what it does not understand – the unhappy consciousness deprives itself, completely and in truth, of the consciousness of inner and outer freedom . . . It has the certainty of having in truth stripped itself of its Ego, and of having turned its immediate selfconsciousness into a "thing", into an objective external existence.'[23] Thus the slave's flight into freedom culminated in a new, spiritualised bondage.

This drastic solution is, according to Hegel, the only adequate escape from the *impasse* of the unhappy consciousness, and explains the institutionalisation of early Christianity in the form of the Church. It explains it not only as psychologically necessary, but sociologically, as the consequence of this religious self-alienation. The believer's self-alienation creates and sustains the mediating role of the priesthood as God's representative. 'For giving up one's own will is only in one aspect negative; in principle, or in itself, it is at the same time positive, positing and affirming the will as an *other*.' Thus the laity, by viewing the words and deeds of the church as those of God himself, brings into being the institutional consciousness of the priesthood as the 'middle term' consciously seeking to bridge the gulf between man and God, 'proclaiming to the unchangeable consciousness that the isolated individual has renounced itself, and to the individual consciousness that the unchangeable consciousness is . . . one with it, and reconciled to it.'[24] But in the intellectual life of the Church, professionally engaged in interpreting men and God to each other, a new element can now arise – 'the idea of Reason.' From the standpoint of a rational mind in the position of a mediating unity between extremes, the otherness of the divine ceases to be a source of estrangement. Instead, the solidarity with God that the laity attributes to the priest, and the solidarity with the laity that the priest assumes before God, now combine to prompt the conception that Creator and Creation form a single rational system, a great chain of being from the highest to the lowest. This theological idealism was, for Hegel, the supersession of the estrangement of the unhappy consciousness, but still on the basis of religious self-alienation. The further stages of the development of reason completed the return of man to himself.

4 SPIRIT IN SELF-ESTRANGEMENT

Stoicism and scepticism were the reactions of cultivated men to the soulless community, 'the counsel of despair to a world which no longer possessed anything stable.'[25] The unhappy consciousness, however, was the response, at first, of an oppressed foreign people under the yoke of Rome, then of persecuted minorities throughout the empire, finally it became the general mentality of the Roman world and of the European civilisation which followed it. To the extent that Christianity became general, the entire epoch came to have the character called by Hegel that of 'spirit in self-estrangement'. The contradiction which appeared within the un-happy consciousness between this life and the beyond is now seen to be merely the subjective manifestation of a similar opposition afflicting not just 'pure self-consciousness', but the whole sphere of spirit – culture, social institutions and action. 'Spirit in this case, therefore, constructs not merely one world, but a twofold world, divided and self-opposed.'[26] The outer, present world has the character of a mere objective actuality: its meaning and value lie in the world beyond. 'Nothing has a spirit self-established and indwelling within it; rather, each is outside itself in what is alien to it. The equilibrium of the whole . . . rests on the estrangement of its opposite. The whole is, therefore, like each single moment, a self-estranged reality.'[27] As such, it breaks up into two 'kingdoms' – the empire and kingdoms of the secular sphere, wielding temporal power, and the sacred kingdom of Christ, represented in the world, through processes that have been described, by the spiritual power of the Church.

Just as within the sphere of belief there is estrangement between man and God, so in the world of action there is estrangement between the individual and the socio-cultural reality that confronts him. This is simply an outgrowth of the estrangement that has already been traced in the soulless community, where it was associated with alien rule and political despotism. The development of this into what Hegel called 'the world of spirit in self-estrangement' is primarily just an intensification of these conditions. As in the soulless community, here too the 'absolutely insular, absolutely discrete' self 'finds its content over against itself in the form of a reality that is just as impenetrable as itself, and the world here gets the characteristic of being something external, negative to self-consciousness.' Here, too, 'this reality is the external element and free content of the sphere of legal right' over which the politically powerless individual has no control. 'Its existence is the work of self-consciousness, but likewise an actuality immediately present and alien to it, which has a peculiar being of its own, and in which it does not know itself.' The historical conditions for this intensified estrangement are indicated in *The Philosophy of History*. They would seem to be, first, the imposition of Roman rule on a people like the Jews, with a strong ideological revulsion against outsiders; secondly, the increasing chaos and misery of life in the Roman empire generally, where 'the supposed condition of Right turns out to be an absolute destitution of it'; but third, and most important, the situation of the invading barbarian peoples when they found themselves the occupants and cultural inheritors of the Roman world.

Only then did their *development* begin, kindled by a foreign culture, a foreign religion, policy and legislation. The process of culture they underwent consisted in taking up foreign elements and reductively amalgamating them with their own national life. Thus their history represents an introversion – the attraction of alien forms of life and the bringing these to bear upon their own . . . the German world appears, superficially, to be only a continuation of the Roman. But there lived in it an entirely *new spirit*, through which the world was to be regenerated – the free spirit, viz. which reposes on itself – the absolute self-determination of subjectivity. To this self-involved subjectivity, the corresponding objectivity stands opposed as absolutely alien.[28]

These sentences provide, I believe, the best clue to Hegel's intention in subtitling the section of Chapter VI which deals with spirit in self-estrangement 'Culture' (*Bildung*). For in this section he deals with the whole of European secular civilisation, from the Roman empire to the French revolution, making the Enlightenment the pivot of his argument. The subtitle thus echoes the Enlightenment's own idea of history as the education or training of the human race (which is also the meaning of *Bildung*). At the same time it covers a whole epoch in which the evolution of the 'Germanic' peoples was dominated by the prestige of the past, by the vanished greatness of Greece and Rome. At first positively, in the mediaeval Church, Roman law, the Renaissance, and the Reformation; later negatively, in the Enlightenment's struggle against Christianity. But even here, Rousseau modelled his utopia upon Sparta, and the French revolutionaries, heirs of the Enlightenment, borrowed their rhetoric from the history of the Roman republic. Thus, if 'spirit in self-estrangement' refers generally to European Christendom, the specific way in which Hegel develops the secular, active side of the opposition makes best sense if we think of it as treating European society as the *successor* to Rome, internalising its alien culture. At the same time, each exhibit in the historical picture-gallery of the *Phenomenology* was also intended to have a universal application. Viewed from this angle, European history provides a parable for processes of acculturation in human life generally, where every generation has to confront a cultural heritage which is to some degree alien because it comes from a distance, out of the past.

It is in connection with this acculturation that Hegel introduces the secular sense of self-alienation which gives the discussion of spirit in self-estrangement much of its originality and importance in the history of ideas. It makes its appearance in the introductory paragraphs which link the analysis of the soulless community to that of 'culture and its realm of reality'. There Hegel argues that the external reality controlled by 'the lord of the world of legal right', which confronts the atomised individuals as alien, is not just adventitiously present to them. It is, in fact, their own product, 'but not in a positive sense, rather negatively so. It acquires its existence by self-consciousness of its own accord relinquishing itself and giving up its essentiality.'[29] The substance of the self 'is thus just its relinquishment, and the relinquishment is the [social] substance, i.e. the powers of the mind forming themselves into a coherent world and thereby securing their subsistence.' This is a secular counterpart to the religious self-alienation, or renunciation of self, which constituted priesthood and church as the mediating agency between man and God. Here it is the chaotic secular history of the Roman world, corresponding to unlimited political despotism, which is constituted as the unintended result of individuals' relinquishing control of all autonomy save the nugatory personal rights contained in their legal status. Since Hegel explained Stoicism and Scepticism as speculative abstractions modelled on the experience of the soulless community, he would no doubt also allow us to construe the religious self-alienation of the unhappy consciousness as a reflection of this real self-alienation proceeding in the daily life of the self-estranged world, although he does not do so himself. Similarly, although Hegel does not mention self-alienation as a feature of the soulless community until this point in the book, it might be taken as implicit earlier, even in the dialectic of master and slave. For in that the slave labours in the lord's service, he continually relinquishes his autonomy, constituting the other as a material being and, socially, as his master. This absence of a concept of alienation which could allow the world of the masters to be deduced as an estranged product of the slaves has been noted before, in commenting on the lacuna which separates Hegel's treatment of slavery and of the Greek *polis*, and we shall return to it later. Here, Marx's analysis of estranged and alienated labour completed what Hegel left unfinished.

Hegel's concern, in adding self-alienation to the picture of the soulless community, was with its prospective rather than its retrospective implications. For when he moves on to 'culture and its realm of reality', the secular sphere of European Christendom, this self-alienation takes on a more positive meaning. This is still a world of solitary individuals confronting an alien outer reality. As before, 'the existence of this world, as also the actuality of self-consciousness, depends on the process that self-consciousness divests itself of its personality, by so doing creates its world, and treats it as something alien and external'. But whereas before this was the end of the matter, so far as individual self-consciousness was concerned, here this alien world has become something 'of which it must now take possession'. This is most easily interpreted as a reference to the position of the Germanic peoples *vis-à-vis* Roman civilisation and its cultural heritage. Especially as Hegel continues: 'But the renunciation of its self-existence is itself the production of the actuality, and in doing so, therefore, self-consciousness *ipso facto* makes itself master of this world'. This is a different process from that of the soulless community, where self-relinquishment by individuals merely delivered the world over to political despotism. Hegel emphasises this difference, although somewhat obscurely: it turns on the fact that the individual's status is no longer simply ascribed in terms of formal legal personality, regardless of content, but has to be achieved through conformity to an external model.[30] So now self-alienation involved proving oneself by alien standards. And in contrast to religious self-alienation which instituted a form of mediation between man and God but left the individual in 'thing-like' obedience to its own product, this secular self-alienation is *itself* a 'mediating process' by which individual life can acquire a kind of universal meaning.

'The means, then, whereby an individual gets objective validity and concrete actuality here is the formative process of culture [*Bildung*]'. Estrangement, which previously held between individuals as legal persons and their politically dominated reality, is now located between the individual's 'natural existence' and the external culture he must assimilate. By 'relinquishment of this natural state,' 'individuality moulds itself by culture . . . and only by so doing is it then something *per se* and possessed of concrete existence.' This process, which from the standpoint of the individual 'appears as self-consciousness making itself conform to reality, and doing so to the extent permitted by the energy of its original character and talents' is also, looked at from the social standpoint, 'the development of individuality *qua* universal objective being' – that is to say, as a cultural value in terms of which 'the extent of [the individual's] culture is the measure of [his social] reality and power.'[31] The passage from which these quotations are taken is full of allusions. No doubt the idea of a 'natural existence' to be relinquished contains an echo of the original situation of the barbarian peoples as *Naturvölker*. Similarly, the reader is inevitably reminded of the use which the Italian Renaissance made of classical models as means to the full development of individuality, and of an individualistic culture. Baillie detects a reference to Bacon's phrase 'Knowledge is power'. But Hegel's clearest debt here is surely to Rousseau's account of history as a process of acculturation accomplished through progressive alienation of man's natural existence. Of course, his presentation lacks Rousseau's characteristic pathos. 'Nature' was not a critical and utopian concept for Hegel, who esteemed complexity as highly as Rousseau valued simplicity. Nor was Hegel a historical pessimist, so that while he incorporated Rousseau's critique of European civilisation down to the eighteenth century, his standpoint was that of its later transcendence.

I shall not discuss 'Culture and its Realm of Reality' in detail, but merely sketch in the outline in so far as it develops the ideas of estrangement and alienation, up to the point where Hegel announces his rupture with Rousseau. The underlying idea is that the *world* of self-estranged spirit (as opposed to its heaven) is for the first time in history a world devoid of objective values. In the 'ethical world' of the city-state everything had its place and value in a consensually validated cosmos. Even the degenerate form of the soulless community rested on common faith in the reality and value of legal status, and in the absence of other values the 'lord of the world of legal right' could claim to be the only god. But existence in the soulless community was chaotic because consensus was so narrow. The potentiality, implicit in this confusion, for a stable order of values could only be developed in *thought*, as the ideal of a City of God; and could only be lived through faith in its existence in *another* world, as a flight from this one. This radical cleavage of sacred from profane stripped the secular world of Christendom of all value; even legal status lost its validity. Where nothing was ascribed, all had to be achieved. Beginning with purely subjective evaluations by individuals, on the one hand, and the given and inherited environment of an alien culture on the other, a new consensual order had to be forged. But it would be a purely secular order, which man could know to be his own construction, for the very reason that there were no longer any superhuman moral powers at work upon the earth. As such an order developed and became stabilised, so it would seem to have realised, in the living world, more and more of that estranged potentiality for order and value contained in the image of the world beyond. From the secular standpoint, this eventually enabled traditional religion to be challenged as a superfluous embellishment of the practical ideas of human progress: the 'world to come' would be simply the world of posterity. From the side of religion also, the growth of the secular order would meanwhile prompt its rational interpretation as a providential plan enacted through human agency, whether in Thomist, Lutheran or even Calvinist terms. By this means secular human action and social values could recover objectivity and sanctity, yet the religious view of the world would seem to owe more and more to man and less to God. These two trends converged towards the deism and rationalism of the Enlightenment, the point from which Hegel saw the human spirit as moving from the stage of self-estrangement to the beginning of self-certainty. But their convergence was fraught with self-contradiction, so that the movement led through the 'absolute freedom and terror' of the French revolution.

The social dialectic through which this transcendence of self-estrangement occurs depends on both estrangement and alienation. The initial presumption is of a world of mutually estranged individuals (or families, tribes, nations, etc.) confronting an alien cultural heritage. Individuals attain self-consciousness and social identity only to the extent that they alienate or relinquish their 'original' or 'natural' self and assume some given cultural role. By doing this, they bring their cultural heritage to life, and indeed breathe a new kind of life into it through the contingencies of interaction. At the same time, the life that these separate roles receive is the life of mutually estranged individuals. Thus the various aspects of the old culture develop in opposition to each other, infected with the estrangement that is the general result of the universal self-estrangement of spirit. Furthermore, since subjectivity is the only moral law, each cultural identity, as it achieves social recognition, claims ultimate moral value for itself. But precisely because it *does* claim legitimacy, the actual power and success with which the various aspects of culture are vindicated against each other creates, however conflictually, a secular moral order which, as such, is quite different from the ethical order of antiquity, where the human and divine law interpenetrated and were only latently opposed, and also from the mere anomie into which it collapsed.

> By means of the self *qua* inner soul of the process, the substance is so moulded and worked up in its various moments, that one opposite puts life into the other, each opposite, by its estrangement from the other, gives the other stability and similarly gets stability from the other. At the same time, each moment has its own definite nature, in the sense of having an insuperable worth and significance; and has a fixed reality as against the other.[32]

The actual pattern through which the new order grows is in fact determined by the salience of different aspects in the old culture. State power, wealth and language are its most prominent elements, and Hegel's treatment of the growth of European civilisation is a skilful, if sometimes fanciful, elaboration of these themes and the permutations made upon them by varying subjective evaluations. Through state power and wealth the dialectic of master and slave, with its double emphasis on the pursuit of enjoyment and the discipline of service and labour, is threaded unobtrusively into the argument. Key points are the discussion of patrimonial kingship and feudalism in terms of the 'noble consciousness', involving different types of self-alienation in the form of state power, and hence conflict between them; absolute monarchy as constituted by the language of courtiers, a type of self-alienation where 'The heroism of dumb service passes into the heroism of flattery';[33] finally, the pursuit of wealth as the characteristic activity of the modern age, with employees dependent on their masters and clients abasing themselves before rich patrons.

Wealth brings its specific forms of insincerity – 'the language of flattery, but of ignoble flattery' – a theme which Marx was to develop much further. But Hegel too attributed great importance to the type of cynical hypocrisy characteristic of the seventeenth and eighteenth centuries, whether in courtiers, economic dependants, or men of letters. For the constituent elements of flattery, he argued, were 'on the one hand, a self moulded by service into a shape where it is reduced to a bare existence, and on the other, the inherent reality of the power dominating the self.' This was the basic relationship of self-alienation, and since it occurred within the world of self-estranged spirit, the dominating reality, whether monarch or money, was a moral power, part of the universality of the secular order. Thus the flatterer was, in a sense, like a propagandist or devotee of the new values. But he was not sincere, for his self-alienation cannot be complete, he is not wholly identified with state power or wealth. For if he were, he would be their master instead of what he is, their slave. Hence, 'The object is consciously still the inherent reality in opposition to the self.'[34] Thus his language makes him *appear* as the personified self-consciousness of the moral order, but secretly he knows this as something to which he is wholly indifferent. His service is purely self-seeking, literally lip-service, with no inner bond of obligation. But, claimed Hegel, this is 'the perfect form of utterance for this entire realm of spiritual culture and development [*Bildung*]' in which it becomes 'conscious of its own nature as it truly is, and conscious of its ultimate and essential principle.'[35] For what is implied in the self-consciousness of the flatterer is the recognition that none of the moral claims of the cultural world 'possess real truth', but exist only in so far as individuals relinquish their autonomy to serve them. But this awareness, which only occurs here because men are in a state of estrangement from 'ultimate' reality and value, which they acknowledge as 'beyond' their sphere, is in fact true awareness of what is the ultimate reality about values and human life: that men make their own spiritual world.

This truth, hidden in the self-awareness of the flatterer, remains also unseen by 'the honest soul' engaged in the business of everyday life. He takes all the pretensions of the cultural universe at their face value: his 'is the uncultivated thoughtless condition that does not think and does not know that it is likewise doing the very inverse' of what appears. By contrast, 'The distraught and disintegrated soul is, however, aware of inversion . . . the conceptual principle predominates there, brings together into a single unity the thoughts that lie far apart in the case of the honest soul, and the language conveying its meaning is, therefore, full of *esprit* and wit.' Diderot's Rameau's nephew provided Hegel's model here, and he further contrasted this type of self-consciousness of estrangement with that of Rousseau, which is presented as the dilemma of the 'naïve mind':

Finally, should the *naïve* mind require this entire sphere of perversion to be dissolved and broken up, it cannot ask the individual to withdraw out of it, for even Diogenes in his tub is under the sway of that perversion; and to ask this of the particular individual is to ask him to do precisely what is taken to be bad, viz. to care for himself as individual. But if the demand to withdraw is directed at the universal individual it cannot mean that reason must again give up the culture and development of spiritual conscious life which it has reached, that reason should let the extensive riches of its moments sink back into the *naïveté* of natural emotion, and revert and approximate to the wild condition of the animal consciousness, which is also called the natural state of innocence. On the contrary, the demand for this dissolution can only be addressed to the spirit of culture itself, and can only mean that it must *qua* spirit return out of its confusion into itself, and win for itself a still higher level of conscious life. In point of fact, however, spirit has already accomplished this result.[36]

We need not pursue further Hegel's argument that the vanity excoriated by Rousseau contained a mocking consciousness of its *own* vanity, and was therefore a necessary critical ferment preparing for the recovery of man's estranged reality.

There does remain, however, a question which should be answered at this point. If Hegel rejected Rousseau's conception of natural innocence, what sort of 'natural existence' is it that he thought was renounced in cultural self-alienation? A possible solution is that it was, primarily, the 'natural man' in a sense borrowed from Christian theology. Christianity split the individual into a fallen being, conceived and born in sin, and an immortal soul destined for eternal salvation or damnation. By religious self-alienation, as we have seen, the individual puts off his sinful being by renouncing the world, the flesh and the devil, in exchange for the immortality already won for him by Christ's death and resurrection, placing the care of his soul in the hands of the Church. But inasmuch as he 'dies to sin' in *this* life, his earthly self remains as a spiritually inert residue – as Hegel says, a mere 'thing' from the standpoint of faith. It is an avenue of temptation to the soul, a mortal vessel of grace to be endured during God's pleasure, but of no value on its own account. This is the 'natural man'. Yet from the standpoint of secular life, this is the sole basis on which life in the world can be lived. And if this is what Hegel intended us to understand by the alienation of man's natural existence, then he claimed that in secular life, too, the natural man has to 'die' in the service of culture, to undergo a profane discipline of mortification and sacrifice on the altar of society and history before men can come to recognise social and cultural life as their own proper product and milieu.

If this was his meaning, then Hegel relativised Rousseau's concept of human nature, as he had relativised Hobbesian man in his discussion of the soulless community. The sentimental idealisation of the simple, amoral, quasi-animal natural man was a specific, historically conditioned 'perversion' (he implied) of the original theological idea – the twist given to it by a naïve moralist facing a world governed by vanity. The original idea was itself also a historically conditioned theological abstraction, but it corresponded to a real aspect of the self-consciousness of European civilisation, as the abstraction of the 'legal person' had also done in Rome. If it provided the necessary starting-point for the dialectical transcendence of the self-estrangement of spirit through self-alienation, then it was also itself a historically given starting-point, the result of the previous development of the soulless community and the unhappy consciousness, and of the conditions of collapse, under which the former was converted into the 'world' of the latter. And as it was a historically given starting-point, so its historical process changed its meaning: by the time of Rousseau the growth of secular culture had so emptied it of meaning (for even children had come to be seen as objects of culture through pedagogy) that it was available as an unattached ideological label for critical theory to use as it wished. (Some of the stages of this evacuation of the theological concept of natural man have already been reviewed in the discussion of social contract theories in Chapter I.) Rousseau's concept was its last fling at the level of philosophy, for as man reconquered all the developed moments of his historic self-estrangement the opposition of human nature and human culture would vanish along with that between fallen man and his immortal soul.

5 CONCLUSION

If we leave aside the metaphysical sense in which spirit is said to be self-estranged in nature, there appear to be four different uses of 'estrangement' in the *Phenomenology*.

First of all, there is estrangement between persons, a straightforward social relationship which is by now thoroughly familiar. Examples are the estrangement between master and slave, subjects and despot, or amongst individuals as exclusive private proprietors. By an enlargement of the same idea, an individual may treat any external reality, or even himself, as alien in so far as it, or he, is in the power of a stranger or appears as an extension of another, hostile personality. Thus the slave or the subject are estranged from their conditions of existence, and even from their own existence, in so far as they are self-conscious beings who see their lives surrounded and permeated by the will of the master or despot. This 'estrangement from' may either be one side of a social relationship of mutual estrangement ('estrangement between') or else an unreciprocated attitude. The latter is exemplified by the 'natural man' confronting an alien culture that he must assimilate. He regards it as embodying the purposes of others who were ignorant of his existence and indifferent towards him. As he begins to assimilate, of course, he inevitably interacts with representatives of the alien culture who will in turn see him as an outsider in so far as he has not yet learned to conform to their values. Thus the one-sided attitude of estrangement here develops into a social relationship, although it is an evanescent one in so far as the recruit actually does become acculturated and conforms. If, as in the case of the flatterer, conformity takes the shape of service to a despotic power which is indifferent to its servants, the superficial solidarity may conceal an attitude of estrangement like that of the slave. In all these cases where an individual knows his own actions to be determined by an alien will we can follow Hegel and speak of 'self-estrangement' as a division within the self, the internal and subjective counterpart of a situation of unequal power between persons in a social relationship of estrangement.

The second use is also a type of 'self-estrangement', but referring to an action or process rather than a condition. This use is dependent on the idea of self-alienation, as the renunciation or sacrifice of autonomy to another. Where self-alienation occurs between strangers, it is simultaneously an act or process of self-estrangement. In alienating part of himself to an alien or hostile person, the individual makes that part alien to himself, estranging himself from it and it from himself. Hegel only uses this idea in relation to acculturation. Here, however, total self-alienation is envisaged, for the self's 'concrete realisation consists solely in cancelling and transcending the natural self.'[37] To the extent that this occurs, the process of self-estrangement is self-liquidating, ceasing with the extinction of the natural self. In this case, says Hegel, 'The original determination of its nature is, therefore, reduced to a matter of quantity, to a greater or less energy of will, a non-essential principle of distinction.' Self-alienation may remain incomplete, however, as with the flatterer, whose natural self is still present in the calculating and self-interested manipulation of the language of self-alienation. In this case, the process of self-estrangement is arrested, and becomes the state of self-estrangement that has already been noted.

Before leaving this sense of 'self-estrangement' it is worth digressing briefly to see why Hegel only speaks of 'self-alienation' in connection with acculturation, in 'the world of spirit in self-estrangement.' After all, if the slave can be described as in a state of self-estrangement, he might be thought to have reached it by an *act* of self-estrangement, and hence of self-alienation. Likewise, if the citizens of the *polis* can be described as governed by duty and public virtue, sacrificing themselves for the common good, is not this a social system maintained by the self-alienation of each to all, as Rousseau had asserted? The answer seems to lie in Hegel's overall purpose. He wanted to show that the historical evolution of self-conscious reason would eventually lead modern man to know himself as the author of his social world and the source of the morality that sustains it. Men would *then* become 'conscious within themselves of being these individual independent beings through the fact that they surrender and sacrifice their particular individuality, and that this universal substance is their soul and essence — as this universal again is the action of themselves as individuals, and is the work and product of their own activity.'[38] But this is by no means the situation at the dawn of history. Hegel expressed this by positing initial situations in which social order was given 'in its immediacy': the individual would lack the standpoint or the language for separating himself from it enough to see himself as its author. Thus the social system of master and slave is said to originate in a collision like that of impersonal forces. Because the protagonists do not recognise each other as independent persons, the one cannot receive the voluntary submission of the other. The victor creates the social system by sparing the victim for his own ends and keeping him under threat of destruction, like any useful possession. Thus the bond established is based on self-interest, force and fear. Since there has been no self-alienation by the slave, there is no moral bond either. As the slave's self-consciousness awakens through labour, therefore, he wakes to a relationship of estrangement already present and given. The situation of the masters, united in the ethical community, is in some ways the exact opposite. Here also there is no recognition of the independent individual self, hence no question of self-alienation, but this is because each is an equal part of a single collective self, so that the social bond can *only* be a moral one. The collective self (or, strictly speaking, the two interrelated collectivities of family and state) is simply given, as the form of self-consciousness into which individuals are born and educated. Thus the element of self-sacrifice in public duty remains a secondary, subordinate and undeveloped moment. It is concealed within the particular self-consciousness of each citizen, for the public language has no resources to express and validate their private experience of corporate moral life.

Thus Hegel starts from two types of social order, coercive and consensual, assumed as historically given, with the individual conscious of himself only as their product, in order to trace the slow emergence of the individual's consciousness of himself as author and creator of his world. For this, the notion of self-alienation – the making of a collective order by the renunciation of individual autonomy – has to become the primary and dominant moment. Contract theorists had depicted this in a fanciful way, and Rousseau had developed their ideas into a utopian critique of the self-alienation of the 'natural man' through acculturation. Hegel historicised Rousseau's insight by deducing it as the form taken by human self-consciousness in its second, antithetical stage. This required that individuals should be both freed from slavish, thing-like passivity in order to be *capable* of self-alienation; and also severed from any moral order taken as objectively given, in order to be obliged to alienate themselves, as the condition of surviving in society at all. Thus the power of the masters had to be broken and their solidarity pulverised: the historical task of Rome. But also the acquired gains of human civilisation had to be transmitted – yet in a form where they would not appear as a given realm of objective values. This was the historical task of Christianity, itself a product of Rome, which it accomplished by disvaluing the secular sphere and attributing objectivity only to the City of God. Individuals, the 'natural men' cast off by religion, devoid of solidarity, had to build a social order in secular life, simply to survive. Since it could only originate through the actions of individuals, and could only use the cultural materials to hand, this had to emerge through coercion, creating a new order of lords and bondsmen; and through self-alienation, by which free men bound themselves to each other in the service of cultural powers – creating new political, legal and economic institutions. In a world cut off from ultimate values, institutional solidarities were stabilised more by common antagonisms than by shared ideals. As the new order of secular morality evolved, the moment of self-sacrifice and individual renunciation was inevitably accentuated, and the relationships it sanctioned were founded on estrangement – militarism, inequality, economic competition, etc. The consciousness of the lord, the conqueror, as a creator of social order could develop unconstrained by a received ethical order, but also lacking the unconditional mandate of heaven; for in the Christian heaven kings and commoners were equal. Thus, self-alienation was seen as the necessary price of avoiding the worst, but what it bought was no more than second-best. Between the vision of a lost Eden and the threat of anarchy, men resigned themselves to maintaining coercive and oppressive systems. In so doing, they learned to think of themselves as makers of social order, but within the narrow bounds allowed by man's sinfulness and God's providence. Only when separation between the here and the beyond was finally overcome, could the lesson of self-alienation be applied to building and inhabiting a social order for free and rational self-conscious individuals aware of their interdependence and collective power.

This leads us to the third use of 'self-estrangement' in the *Phenomenology*: the sense in which the unhappy consciousness was estranged within itself. Here the subject adopts an attitude of estrangement towards an imaginary being, and also imagines himself adopting a reciprocal attitude of estrangement on behalf of that being, towards himself. Thus a social relationship of estrangement has been internalised, and the subject's behaviour proceeds exactly as though a real social relationship of estrangement existed between himself and another. If we may call this mentality 'self-estranged', this would seem to be a perfectly good empirical usage. The subject may be either individual or collective, and in addition to Hegel's case, where collective consciousness internalises an imaginary social relationship posited by ideology, it is no doubt applicable to numerous other phenomena of both normal and abnormal psychology.

The fourth use of 'self-estrangement' is where Hegel calls 'spirit' self-estranged. This refers to the state of 'spirit' – i.e. human, or more precisely European, culture, society and consciousness as a whole – when not only consciousness, but likewise culture and society also are divided into two contraposed spheres whose representatives are mutually estranged. This is a less defensible usage than the last. For even if we allow that the mode of collective self-consciousness of a society or an epoch can sensibly be called 'self-estranged' in our third sense, it by no means follows that the society or epoch is itself something like an individual human being 'who' *is* thereby self-estranged. For however psychologically split, a human being retains, as a single bodily person, a potential personal identity – he remains a 'who' capable of being *re*-united, healed, as we should say. By contrast – as Hegel knew perfectly well – the identity of a social or historical whole consists, on the one hand, of what its collective self-consciousness proclaims it to be, and on the other, of real processes carried on by conscious and self-conscious individuals, but whose unity and systematic character can only be observed after the event by the historian. To conflate these two as aspects of 'spirit', so that the condition of the whole is diagnosed as self-estrangement because this is the state of the collective self-consciousness, is to impose a spurious personality on society and a teleological pattern on history. By means of this, to be sure, Hegel advanced an interesting and influential hypothesis: that the self-estrangement visible in ideology and collective psychology corresponded to a certain type of social structure and historical process, namely, one dominated by relationships of estrangement. But by personifying the whole, he merely obscured the causal problem of this 'correspondence'.

Furthermore, the implication of this hypothesis was precisely that since social groups came into being divided by mutual estrangement and lacking in common purpose, the social order resulting from their interaction would be one whose unity lay outside the collective self-consciousness of any of them. To call spirit self-estranged was therefore to call attention to the extent to which society was *not* a self-conscious unit, so that people failed to recognise themselves and their intentions in the collective consequences of their deeds. As such an unconscious, or extra-conscious, process society resembles nature. In referring to this as spirit's self-estrangement in history, therefore, Hegel was assimilating his philosophy of history to his philosophy of nature in the interests of the metaphysical unity of his thought.

Analysis of the *Phenomenology* is beset by the tedious necessity of continuous exegesis of its gnomic language. By following the threads of estrangement and alienation through the labyrinth I hope to have demonstrated that the book does contain a good deal of implicit sociology, and also what kind of sociology it is. The threads would have been impossible to follow if the trail had not been marked out before, and first of all by Marx. In the next chapter we shall see how Marx was led to the point of extracting and detaching this sociological content. He did so by taking the standpoint of the worker, and of the worker's estrangement from his society, and he attributed the mystification and distortion in Hegel to his taking the standpoint of the philosopher, and of the intellectual's social estrangement. Marx could not have read the 'system-programme' that Hegel had sketched out in 1796. But if we are justified in regarding the *Phenomenology* as the fullest realisation of this early project, then it amply justifies Marx's interpretation. For the young Hegel had expressed his aim as follows:

Until we express the Ideas aesthetically, i.e. mythologically, they have no interest for the *people*, and conversely until mythology is rational the philosopher must be ashamed of it. Thus in the end enlightened and unenlightened must clasp hands, mythology must become philosophical in order to make the philosophers sensible. Then reigns eternal unity among us. No more the look of scorn [of the enlightened philosopher looking down on the mob], no more the blind trembling of the people before its wise men and priests. Then first awaits us *equal* development of *all* powers, of what is peculiar to each and what is common to all. No power shall any longer be suppressed for universal freedom and equality of spirits will reign! – A higher spirit sent from heaven must found this new religion among us, it will be the last [and] greatest work of mankind.[39]

When Hegel wrote these words, the man in whom he later recognised this 'higher spirit' had just suppressed Babouvist communism in Paris and was carrying the banner of the bourgeois republic into the provinces of northern Italy.

3 Marx's Feuerbachian Metaphysics: The Self-estrangement of Man

Although ideas of estrangement and alienation had figured so largely in the *Phenomenology* (published in 1807) they attracted no special attention until the early 1840s, when Hegel himself had been dead for a decade. The reason for their neglect is well known. The ideas belonged to the critical part of Hegel's philosophy and echoed the progressive idealism of his youth. As the constellations of power and opinion that shaped the Restoration period grew up during the European struggle against Napoleon, the audience for such ideas vanished. Hegel himself covered his tracks. His later works blurred the sharp distinction made in the *Phenomenology* between religion as a merely human and historical phenomenon, and religion seen from the standpoint of theological metaphysics. The distinction was not revived in Germany until after the French revolution of 1830, when radical intellectuals began to challenge the reactionary prolongation of the *ancien régime* in Prussia, their first target being the established religion. As the hegemony of Hegelianism over Prussian academic philosophy started to totter, Hegel's heirs divided up his intellectual estate. To the Young Hegelians loosely grouped around Feuerbach's atheistic humanism fell the task of refurbishing the weapons of philosophical criticism lying embalmed in the master's works, and turning them against their maker. Amongst these ideas were those of man's self-alienation and self-estrangement in history, which thus began to acquire new content and new currency amongst these dissident few.

This new elaboration climaxed, of course, in Marx's economic and philosophical manuscripts of 1844. These provide the focus of this chapter and the starting-point for the next. But if the focus is to be accurate, we cannot avoid broaching and considering in some detail the question of how to situate the *Manuscripts* in Marx's thought, both in relation to his earlier development and his debt to Feuerbach, and in relation to his rejection of the Feuerbachian approach in 1845 and his development thereafter. As the amount of ink spilt over them testifies, these are extremely complex questions, despite the aphoristic simplicity with which Marx commemorated the rupture in his *Theses on Feuerbach*. So far as the debate over the 'two Marxes' is concerned, the argument of this book is in agreement with those who see 'alienation' as an important element of continuity, but will claim that the continuity should be sought at the sociological, not the philosophical level. Therefore an attempt has to be made to sort out sociological from philosophical uses of estrangement and alienation in the early works. Although both derived ultimately from Hegel, it will be argued that Marx's *direct* debt to Hegel was mostly sociological and terminological, while the substance of his metaphysics derived almost entirely from Feuerbach.

Marx acquired a critical method as well as a metaphysic from Feuerbach. Yet by 1844 he was far from being a mere epigone of Feuerbach, for his philosophical anthropology had already superseded and improved on Feuerbach's, both in substance and in method. Nor were these advances merely, or wholly, philosophical: some of them were consolidated on a scientific basis after 1845. The *Manuscripts* themselves are the record of a development, an unstable and transitional compound of the ideas to which Marx was so richly receptive during his months in Paris. Hence the complexity of situating the *Manuscripts* in relation to Marx's Feuerbachianism.

This chapter divides the task into four main sections. The first seeks to establish the nature and extent of the metaphysical debt to Feuerbach that Marx acknowledged in 1844 but repudiated in 1845, and also to trace some permanent effects of this influence in his later thought. The second examines the directions in which Marx had already advanced beyond Feuerbach's conception of man and society before 1844, and how far these were non-metaphysical gains that were retained after 1845. The third and fourth sections deal with two aspects of Marx's methodological indebtedness to Feuerbach in his early work: how he developed Feuerbach's reductionism into a critical phenomenology of social meanings and social cognition, and how he tried to improve on Feuerbach's failure to provide causal explanations. A fifth section combines these two themes in an attempt to extract a coherent theory of superstructures from Marx's early work.

I THE HUMAN ESSENCE

The prominence of the language of estrangement and alienation in the *Manuscripts* may have given the impression that these were central concepts for the Young Hegelians generally, and that Marx was simply applying to economics a pre-formed Feuerbachian doctrine defined in these terms. If so, it is a somewhat misleading impression. Of the Young Hegelians, Bruno Bauer was the first to revive the concepts,[1] but they were less conspicuous in his writings than other Hegelianisms. Only occasional phrasings of this kind occurred in Feuerbach's *The Essence of Christianity* (1841), a few more being interpolated into the second edition of 1843. His *Theses for the Reform of Philosophy* (1842) contained the important statement that 'theology divides man in two and alienates him (*entäussert* – perhaps 'externalises' is better here) in order to reidentify him with his alienated essence.'[2] But there was little else of this nature. By 1843 Moses Hess and Marx were also using the terms in the same occasional way, as part of the linguistic heritage of Hegelianism. Not until Marx wrote the introduction to his *Critique of Hegel's Philosophy of Right*, completed early in 1844, did he speak of man's self-estrangement in a way that indicated a greater centrality in his thought. For though even here the term was used once only, it was used to define the object of Marx's intellectual programme in its relation to Feuerbach's: 'The first task of philosophy, which is in the service of history, once the holy form of self-estrangement has been discovered, is to discover self-estrangement in its unholy forms. The criticism of heaven is thus transformed into the criticism of earth. . . .' (etc.)[3] By this time Marx was already deserting the study of law and politics for economics, and it was only in this new context that estrangement and alienation suddenly took the centre of the theoretical stage, in the *Manuscripts*. The main reason for this change seems to have been that his new subject-matter led Marx back to Hegel's analysis of needs, labour, ownership and slavery in the *Phenomenology*. Here, as we have seen, estrangement and alienation played a major role. Marx's preface to the *Manuscripts* paid a double tribute. To Feuerbach, as the founder of 'positive criticism', but also to Hegel; for Feuerbach's works are 'the only ones since Hegel's *Phenomenology* and *Logic* to contain a real theoretical revolution.'[4] Thus it is clear that in investigating Marx's uses of estrangement and alienation in his economic writings of 1844, we have before us a synthesis of Feuerbach and Hegel which was new and uniquely Marx's own. Far from being merely a new application of an established doctrine, it was a specific product of the first and last systematic Young Hegelian foray into the territory of economics.[5]

But although Feuerbach used the language of estrangement and alienation only sparingly, it is true that his main ideas were readily expressible in these terms. He had himself defined God as 'man's relinquished [*entäussertes*] self.' Thus 'The more subjective God is, the more completely does man divest himself [*sich entäussern*] of his subjectivity.' Christianity, the most subjective religion and the religion of universal love, therefore carries to an extreme the contradiction of love and faith: it qualifies love as 'Christian' and restricts it to those who share faith in the 'objective' incarnation of God as Christ. In this way faith 'estranges God from man, it makes him an external object.' Man's estranged essence usurps the place of the *human* essence which should unite man with man. Thereby, too, 'man estranges himself from nature' in placing his own nature outside himself as an alien personification.[6]

From this it should already be clear that in so far as Feuerbach's interpretation of religion involved estrangement and alienation, their meanings depended on a metaphysical conception of 'Man' and the human species. The individual's human essence consists in his membership in the species as a whole, for the human species represents man's 'essential nature' which 'has its adequate existence only in the sum total of mankind, and is therefore only an object of reason.'[7] To the extent that men are related to themselves, each other and their environment in the manner appropriate to the species, their essence is realised in their existence. But man, unlike other species, has no specific adaptation to his surroundings. Hence, though the species as a whole is man perfected, it is a perfection that is unlimited, infinite, for no term can be set in advance to human evolution. On the other hand, nothing can count as an ideal of human perfection which does not sooner or later appear in the actual life of the species. True species-life for man, therefore, consists in full and conscious participation in collective fulfilment of the possibilities of the species, and full and conscious acceptance of the limitations of the individual as part of the whole, a moment in the process.

But unlike other animals, 'the human individual is conscious of the distinction between the species and the individual; in the sense of this distinction lies the root of religion.'[8] Men cannot avoid perceiving it, since they are self-conscious beings and therefore aware of others both like and unlike themselves. They are inevitably conscious of individual differences – especially the distinction of sex, in which man's character as a natural species is directly manifest – and their individual limitations – especially mortality, which makes the life of the species a succession of generations. But because men are self-conscious *individuals*, they may also lose sight of the species as the only standard of human perfection. Their conception of the human essence may become an abstract idealisation of all that they lack individually, which they then personify as an imaginary being. 'Where instead of the consciousness of the species has been substituted the exclusive self-consciousness of the individual . . . Where therefore the species is not an object to him as a species, it will become an object to him as God.'[9] Thus the human essence becomes externalised, alienated, and set over against men as an extraneous personification of the essential powers that belong to the species, and which could belong to the individual too in so far as he is capable of living as a true 'species-being'. Religion only allows him to reappropriate these powers in a distorted way, mediated through faith in the alien will of a divine creator and judge. Sexuality and mortality, man's natural limitations, are denied by religion. But cut off from nature, man can only fulfil his potential for love and community in an exclusive, divisive fashion amongst his fellow-believers in a world artificially sundered into sacred and profane, the saved and the damned. Religion thus redefines as a religious need, as need for God's love, the isolated individual's need for completion by the variety and fullness of the species; and in satisfying this it provides compensation for his stunted life – which thereby becomes, however, even more stunted than before.

Though Marx modified this doctrine in various ways, the philosophical anthropology of the *Manuscripts* is substantially Feuerbach's. And in so far as estrangement and alienation have metaphysical connotations in the *Manuscripts*, they refer to the alienation by 'man' of his human essence and his estrangement from his species-being, though not necessarily, of course, in a religious form. Here, the 'self-alienation' and 'self-estrangement' of man are logically interdependent. In this chapter, therefore, no attempt is made to keep the two concepts separate.

If it seems paradoxical that Marx's metaphysics should owe more to Hegel's materialist critic than to Hegel's own idealism, it is also true, of course, that Feuerbach's metaphysics betrayed his own residual idealism. In the first place, he was no empiricist. He tried to replace Hegel's idealism with materialism, but within a Hegelian conception of what philosophy was entitled to say about the real world. Thus he extracted Hegel's critical account of the self-estrangement of spirit from its idealist wrappings, substituting 'man' and 'nature' for 'self-consciousness' and 'spirit', but he never seriously doubted that mere thinking could yield truths about 'human nature'. Though he shared the positivist conception of an alliance between philosophy and natural science, to replace the old alliance of philosophy with theology, he remained vague about the terms of their partnership. His notion of anthropology and psychology as bases for a new science of man stayed at the level of a proto-existentialist metaphysic.

The source of this unpurged idealism was, of course, the notion of 'essence'. Essences were accessible to philosophical reason, perhaps, but not to historical research or scientific observation. For Hegel, as an idealist, this was no reproach and no obstacle to speculating about them. For philosophy penetrated to a deeper level of reality and truth than empirical studies, precisely by discovering the spiritual grounds and ends of phenomena. Sense-perception and the 'understanding', though necessary, could by themselves yield only superficial knowledge, confined to the world of appearances. Feuerbach's attempt to preserve essentialism within a materialist setting, and to avoid presenting essences as some kind of spiritual reality, or as merely subjective and relative products of the human brain, or as arbitrary standards of comparison and value imposed by the philosopher, led him into insoluble difficulties. Likewise Marx, when he reproduced Feuerbach's metaphysics in the *Manuscripts*.

Marx's version of this doctrine differed from Feuerbach's in his more lavish use of the language of estrangement and alienation. Here there was a direct linguistic influence of Hegel. When Marx wrote his critique of Hegel's system in the *Manuscripts*, he turned to the *Phenomenology* as 'the true birthplace and secret of Hegel's philosophy'.[10] This was typical of the Young Hegelian approach to Hegel, which was naturally overshadowed by the formidably articulated systematics of Hegel's later works, the absolute idealism that had dominated the philosophical scene in Berlin. Thus Marx interpreted the *Encyclopaedia* and *The Philosophy of Right* as parts of a single consistent argument whose 'quintessence' was to be found in the last chapter of the *Phenomenology*. Here Hegel had tried to draw together into a monistic idealism the complex and equivocal tendencies of his great work – its valedictions to the past as well as its adumbrations of the future, all vaguely and incoherently orchestrated as they are. For this purpose, spirit was described as self-alienated in the imaginary world of faith, and as returning out of estrangement into self-consciousness by the re-appropriation of this world through human culture. And in the *Logic* the same terminology was employed to implicate the categories of logic with the existence of an external world by positing the self-estrangement of spirit in nature. Marx, in order to characterise Hegel's system with a phrase and to contrast it with Feuerbach's, seized on these passages:

> For Hegel the *essence of man – man –* equals *self-consciousness*. All estrangement of the human essence is therefore *nothing but estrangement of self-consciousness*. The estrangement of self-consciousness is not regarded as an *expression* of the *real* estrangement of the human being . . . etc.[11]

Thus Marx seems to have adopted the metaphysical language of estrangement and alienation from Hegel as a way of expressing his Feuerbachian philosophy, at a moment when he was also adapting Hegel's more sociological usages to a critique of political economy. Because of his own metaphysical approach, he overlooked discontinuities between these more detailed and empirical usages and those in Hegel's sweeping summaries, which were part of a strategy of synoptic integration and system-building.

Marx repudiated the metaphysical elements in Feuerbach's thought in his writings of 1845 – 6. The *Theses on Feuerbach* and *The German Ideology* contain two major, connected criticisms which are aimed at his own earlier ideas no less than at Feuerbach.

First, as stated in the sixth *Thesis*, Feuerbach's conception of 'man' was unhistorical, the personification of an abstraction, 'of Man in general, who belongs to no class, has no reality, who exists only in the misty realm of philosophical fantasy.'[12] He had explained away religion as a perversion of the human essence, but he conceived of this merely as an 'abstraction inherent in each single individual' – his humanity. He recognised no historical types of men with specific common traits, but only characteristics common to the species in general. 'The human essence, therefore, can with him be comprehended only as a "genus", as an internal, dumb generality which merely naturally unites the many individuals.'[13] Similarly, though he explained religion as a result of contradiction in human life, he recognised no historically specific contradictions but only that between the individual and the species, the particular and the universal. Consequently, he had to 'abstract from the historical process and fix the religious sentiment as something by itself and to presuppose an abstract − *isolated* − human individual' as its unexplained subject. Whereas 'the "religious sentiment" is itself a *social product*' and likewise, the abstract individual whom he analyses 'belongs in reality to a particular form of society', situated in history.

Marx credited Feuerbach with having demonstrated that Hegel's speculative philosophy was 'nothing but religion conceptualized and rationally developed.'[14] Yet his own philosophy, by separating existence and essence, also involved a conceptual duplication of mankind's real existence. Like religion, it divided man in half only to reidentify him, teleologically and normatively, with his separated essence. Thus the conditions of existence of an animal or human species were, Feuerbach had argued, 'those in which its essence feels itself satisfied.'[15] This idealisation of nature and mystification of the notion of environmental adaptation could lead, as Marx pointed out, to an uncritical acceptance of average conditions, in which social inequalities and human sufferings were treated as chance differences between persons, compensated for in the life of the species as a whole.[16] Thus Feuerbach was apt to relapse into idealism − a speculative message of comfort − at the very point where a factual grasp of social conditions and their historical causes might enable them to be changed.

But this doctrine of compensation could also take a more futuristic form. Since human development was unlimited, and the 'philosophy of the future' would enable man to reappropriate the essential powers that hitherto had been sacrificed to the gods, it was mainly the future of the species that would truly realise the human essence. Existence and essence would then coincide, for men would relate 'humanly' to nature, to each other and to themselves. It was this implication of Feuerbach's essentialism, with its more critical slant, that had particularly attracted Marx; and it was his own version of it that he disowned in *The German Ideology:*

> The individuals, who are no longer subject to the division of labour, have been conceived by the philosophers as an ideal, under the name 'Man'. They have conceived the whole process which we have outlined as the evolutionary process of 'Man', so that at every historical stage 'Man' was substituted for the individuals and shown as the motive force of history. The whole process was thus conceived as a process of the self-estrangement of 'Man', and this was essentially due to the fact that the average individual of the later stage was always foisted on to the earlier stage, and the consciousness of a later age on to the individuals of an earlier.[17]

Such a view was compatible either with fatalistic inactivity − 'Man' being left to transcend his own self-estrangement, merely contemplated by the philosopher − or with idealistic voluntarism, if the philosopher hubristically identified 'Man' with himself—imagining, for instance, that 'the head of this emancipation is philosophy, its heart is the proletariat.'[18] If Feuerbach's life exemplified the first of these alternatives, Marx's ideas up to 1845 expressed the second.

In this way, Marx's first major criticism was closely related to his second, which was that Feuerbach, like other philosophers, was content merely to interpret the world and offered no guidance for changing it. If he had been satisfied with postulating 'Man' as an abstract and imaginary subject of history, it was because he felt no compulsion to discover the concrete causes that made real men act as they did. As long as theory remained purely contemplative, aiming merely 'to produce a correct consciousness about an existing fact',[19] it would not feel the discipline of the real world's recalcitrance, and hence would not become scientific. By 1845, Marx no longer believed, as he had in 1843, that 'As philosophy finds in the proletariat its material weapons, so the proletariat finds in philosophy its intellectual weapons.'[20] Philosophy needed no material weapons, for it did no violence to reality. Successful revolution—like industry, which destroys nature to create artefacts—depended on accurate knowledge of the constitution of what it sought to transform. Indiscriminate destruction would by no means yield the raw materials for a new social order. Revolutionary leadership of the proletariat therefore had to be based on social science, and conversely, social science would only progress from the standpoint of the revolutionary. For he alone was sufficiently detached from present society, yet also sufficiently motivated, to pierce the illusions which protected it, get outside the subjective viewpoints of its component groups, and search seriously for an Archimedean point on which its structures rested, and from which they might be toppled. Thus

> Where speculation ends—in real life—there real positive science begins . . . Empty talk about consciousness ceases, and real knowledge has to take its place. When reality is depicted, philosophy as an independent branch of knowledge loses its medium of existence.[21]

In this the ascendant influence of Engels is plainly visible. But it also reflects Marx's final transition from student to agitator. His rejection of his own Feuerbachian past, along with the whole German dreamland of professorial ideology, completed the *rites de passage* out of the academy and no doubt also reconciled him to losing all hope of a university career.

Marx's rejection of essentialism, and the philosophical anthropology that depended on it, though complete, was not undiscriminating. He retained some important insights that he could hardly have acquired otherwise than from idealism.

First, he retained part of the phenomenological approach that accompanied essentialism. Essentialism involved reifying concepts, by treating similar things as though they shared a common nature over and above the properties that made them similar—a nature corresponding to the class-concept under which the things could be referred to individually as instances, or generically as a category. Thus the world would seem to contain both 'Man' and men, for individual men were members and representatives of the species, man. An interesting passage in *The Holy Family*, written when Marx was on the brink of rejecting essentialism, contains an excellent criticism of the fallacy of misplaced concreteness as committed by idealists:

> If from real apples, pears, strawberries and almonds I form the general idea *'Fruit'*, if I go further and *imagine* that my abstract idea *'Fruit'*, derived from real fruit, is an entity existing outside me, is indeed the *true* essence of the pear, the apple, etc.; then, in the *language of speculative philosophy* I am declaring that 'Fruit is the *substance* of the pear, the apple, the almond, etc. . . . I therefore declare apples, pears, almonds, etc. to be mere forms of existence, *modi*, of 'Fruit'.[22]

This argument was not aimed at essentialism directly, but at the notion of 'substance'—a special second-order essence attributed to class-concepts of an abstract kind. What Marx condemned in idealism was the artificiality of trying to 'return' from an imaginary reality composed of such substances—not, however, to a perceived reality of individual fruits, but to a perceived reality of apples, pears, almonds, etc., i.e. of different *kinds* of fruit. Thus Marx at this stage was apparently an epistemological and ontological realist, supposing that reality is ordered into real sorts or species of things, and that we can have direct perceptual acquaintance with these real species. This was indeed the doctrine to which essentialism committed him. It enabled him still to maintain, in *The Holy Family*, that Feuerbach had said something significant in positing 'man' as 'the essence, the basis of all human activity and situations'.[23] No doubt he would have agreed that 'apple', 'pear', etc., could denote the essences of the corresponding real species, just as in the *Manuscripts* he had claimed that man, freed of estrangement, would appropriate objects in a manner that 'depends on the nature of the object and on the nature of the essential power corresponding to it.'[24]

Marx abandoned epistemological realism along with essentialism. But his epistemological realism had always been *critical*. Only the crucial postulate of man's self-estrangement depended on a metaphysical, *a priori* claim to direct knowledge of 'Man' and hence of the inadequacy of his incarnation in historical men. Otherwise this doctrine entailed a merely phenomenological view of the knowledge and self-knowledge claimed by men other than Marx himself. Since they were claims made by men caught up in the forms of human self-estrangement, they necessarily involved partial or distorted views of the essences of things, or of the pseudo-essences created by men themselves out of their estranged condition. This critical, negative side of his epistemological realism survived the dropping of its *a priori* premise. He continued to hold that men do, in fact, perceive things directly as belonging to different kinds. Epistemological realism gave way to a social-psychological type of *Gestalt* theory. Human sensory experience is directly meaningful, because human senses function as part of socialised consciousness. So reality for men is necessarily a significant reality. As social language-users, men perceive and live their reality as a world of meanings. Its structure, though determined by its extra-linguistic properties, is mediated through what phenomenologists have called 'typifications'. Not only this, but in their social relationships and social organisation, men create a level of material reality whose structure is *wholly* derived from shared meanings. Thus Marx's materialism never denied the fundamentally 'meaningful' character of human social reality, because it incorporated a phenomenology of social knowledge which remained as the *caput mortuum* of his former idealism of the human essence.[25]

Secondly, the misplaced reification of abstract concepts, though the besetting vice of philosophers, was no less a weakness of the man in the street. Indeed, philosophy, by relentless self-criticism, had finally purged itself of the tendency to fetishism which still remained deeply embedded in practical life. What Hegel had called the 'honest consciousness' was always apt to ascribe mythical existence and agency to ideas as a way of comprehending and dealing with puzzling phenomena. Thus, men having defined their social reality in terms of such mythical agencies, might act successfully on their definitions and so confirm their initial assumptions, false though they were. In this way reified abstractions could come to play an active and dominating role in society, so long as things and persons were treated as their representatives or incarnations. Social structure itself – especially the historical persistence, development and spread of those macrostructures which Marx called 'totalities of production relations'[26] – could only be understood and explained in these terms. Only Feuerbachian essentialism, with its insistence that man, though estranged from his true essence, is nevertheless an essence-conscious and essence-creating being who alienates his powers to imaginary abstractions, could have led Marx to such a clear view of this aspect of society. Thus his early essentialism made possible his analyses of money as the 'real god' of bourgeois society, or of capital as the 'totalizing subject'[27] of the industrial economy.

Thirdly, this view of society as structured by meanings, and even having some of the structural characteristics of metaphysical theories, justified the application of dialectical method, derived from logic, to the elucidation of matters of fact.[28] In the *Manuscripts* and *The Holy Family*, Marx sketched out dialectical developments of the antithesis of capital and labour, as the movement of private property, in strict Hegelian form. By the time he wrote *The Poverty of Philosophy*, Marx's attitude to dialectic had become somewhat satirical. In the 'fifties, however, having reread Hegel's *Logic*, he began 'to discover the rational kernel within the mystical shell'[29] and, in the *Grundrisse*, to adapt dialectics to social and economic analysis. The result was 'not only different from the Hegelian dialectical method, but . . . its direct opposite' (even if not exactly in the way that Marx himself claimed) – and therefore also differed from the dialectical method employed in Marx's own early writings.

Of the many problems that come into view here, I shall mention only that of *contradiction*. In Marx's early works, the contradictory character of human history and institutions was deduced as a *result* of the self-estrangement of man. It is because history's 'subject, man, is a self-estranged being' that his 'activity appears to him as a suffering, his own creation appears as an alien power, his wealth as poverty, the natural tie that binds him to other men appears as an unnatural tie and the separation from other men as his true being. . . .' (etc.)[30] The critique of political economy in the *Manuscripts* consisted in applying such a deduction to its categories and findings, showing them up as a mass of paradoxes explicable by the fundamental diremption between men and their human essence. But at this stage Marx avoided the actual terms 'contradiction'; 'negation', etc. This was because, in his view, the *logical* character of Hegel's dialectical metaphysics was a symptom and consequence of his idealist bias. Because of this bias, 'The full, living, sensuous, concrete activity of self-objectification, therefore, becomes its mere abstraction, absolute negativity.'[31] Hegel's vitiated, intellectualised starting-point meant that his philosophy necessarily culminated in 'forms of thought, logical categories, detached from real mind and real nature.'[32] In place of this dialectic, which portrayed the world-process as a logical evolution because it was ultimately the process of spirit, Marx searched for a concrete, non-logical dialectic that would present history as a process of man's interaction with nature and himself. The search was mistaken, for however concrete the terms in which Marx described the oppositions, the use of any sort of dialectical model still depended on the fundamentally logical idea of an essence, or true meaning, estrangement from which implied negation and contradiction. Without this, there would have been no reason to suppose that reality moved through processes of opposition, *Aufhebung*, etc., at all. Consequently, when Marx threw over essentialism, he also dropped the dialectic.

When he took it up again in the following decade, it was as a logical and methodological tool stripped of metaphysical connotations. He needed a logical method for the analysis of 'economic forms', for they consisted wholly of meanings. Here, 'neither microscopes nor chemical reagents are of use. The force of abstraction must replace both.'[33] He was clear that this was scientific, not philosophical, theorising. (He was clear, also, that logical analysis of economic forms did not exhaust the task of the economic theorist, who was ultimately concerned with structured *processes*, form and content together. And content was by no means determined only by meanings, but also by 'the material transformations of the economic conditions of production, which can be determined with the precision of natural science.'[34]) Since he was employing an overtly logical method as part of a scientific inquiry, and not a covertly logical model as the basis of a metaphysical critique, he used the term 'contradiction' freely. And whereas previously the contradictory trends had been dependent on human self-estrangement, it was now a matter of establishing the factual connections between contradictions of structure and social relationships of estrangement. As we shall see later, Marx usually envisaged reciprocal causation. A situation of estrangement could permit or facilitate the development of contradictory practices, while contradictions, once established, produced, reproduced and sometimes intensified relationships of estrangement. Depending on the nature of the contradiction, these might range from mere indifference to acute conflict.

The fourth and final debt to idealism that will be considered here concerns Marx's humanism. His revolutionary activism no less than his view of history would be incomprehensible but for the continued importance he attached to the idea and ideal of 'humanity'. No longer a metaphysical essence, but an ideological product of history, men's notions of what human existence is and might become have been broadened and enriched by the transformation of the globe and the integration of races through the ever-accelerating development of productive forces. What people regard, and treat in practice, as more or as less human is a function of their social relationships, in which it is always human beings that are immediately present as the representatives of whatever collectivities or cultural powers society may contain. Because of this, whatever a society contains cannot help but be recognised as an attribute of humanity, whether it be considered good or bad, normal or eccentric. But, on the other hand, societies are ruled by the ideas of their ruling class, which will prescribe more restrictive and flattering standards of what it is to be 'fully' human. Thus the ideological contradictions that flow from contradictions of social structure confront each generation with some version of the humanist's challenge: *nihil humanum alienum a me puto*. Marx's championing of the proletariat, and his adoption of the proletarian position as his point of entry into social science would both be unintelligible without this justification, even though it had no *point d'appui* beyond the historical process.

2 MAN AND SOCIETY

In rejecting essentialism as unhistorical and unscientific, Marx's criticisms of Feuerbach in 1845 were also aimed at the assumptions of his own previous writings. Other criticisms made in the *Theses*, however, were not self-criticisms but restated arguments already worked out in the *Manuscripts* or even earlier texts. Two of these concerned the actual content of Feuerbach's conceptions of man and society, and were not directly related to the metaphysical form of those conceptions. In both cases, Marx had concluded that Feuerbach's assumptions were inadequate and had developed them further. When the metaphysical form was discarded, these developments remained as valid theoretical acquisitions in search of a scientific formulation and role.

The first of these criticisms appears in the first and second *Theses*. Partly, this was an epistemological argument. Marx pointed out that Feuerbach, like other materialists, believed that the external world was directly given in sense-perception, and not constituted by the mind and somehow projected outwards, as idealists held. Both materialists and idealists were in Marx's opinion partly right and partly wrong. Feuerbach had correctly stressed the natural and material link between man's senses and his environment. But he had falsely isolated the passive, perceptual attitude from the rest of men's practical interaction with their surroundings, giving it a specious epistemological priority. Hegel, amongst idealists, had correctly seen that men acquire certainty about the world and their own existence through labour, coming to know reality as they constitute it by their own purposive activity. But he had construed this one-sidedly, as mental and incorporeal labour. In correcting each of these views by the other, Marx was repeating a synthesis that he had already developed in his critique of Hegel in the *Manuscripts*. Men's knowledge of the external world is inseparable from their consciousness as human, corporeal subjects continuously involved in practical, material and purposive relationships with an environment of objects. The truth or falsity of this consciousness is itself a pragmatic question.

This epistemological argument had two implications in the evolution of Marx's ideas.[35] The first is obvious enough: it already implied the rejection of a contemplative, philosophical approach to history in favour of a practical and scientific one. As we have seen, however, this was an implication that Marx only drew *after* 1844. In the *Manuscripts* themselves he did not yet apply this insight to his own activity as theorist. The second implication, however, was made fully explicit in the *Manuscripts*. This concerned the image of man as an *object* for theory. The only adequate anthropological model was that of a self-consciously active and purposive material being; a practical agent engaged in production to satisfy needs under given conditons, reproducing and changing both himself and his relationship to the world in the process; formed by circumstances but also, to some variable degree, transforming them by his own activity. Existing images of man in philosophical anthropology were biased towards the epistemological concerns of traditional philosophy. He was seen either as a passive observer, a recipient of impressions, or else, if active, only as active intellectually, as a knower. In either case the image was extrapolated from the philosopher's professional role, and ignored the greater portion of human life.

In the *Manuscripts*, Marx presented his active view of man as *homo faber* in terms of the human essence, so that man's self-estrangement arose through the alienation of his labour and his resulting estrangement from the product, from nature, and from his fellow-producers. History was therefore the history of man's self-creation as a material, cultural being, but occurring in the form of self-estrangement and requiring completion by the reappropriation of his alienated world. When this metaphysical framework had been dropped, however, a basic theoretical acquisition still remained – a model of man for use in scientific theory: the model described in *The German Ideology* and employed, for example, in the chapter on the labour process in *Capital*. The status of all such generalisations, of course, was no longer what it had been in philosophical anthropology. When philosophy gives way to science,

. . . its place can only be taken by a summing-up of the most general results, abstractions which arise from the observation of the historical development of men. Viewed apart from real history, these abstractions have in themselves no value whatever. They can only serve to facilitate the arrangement of historical material, to indicate the sequence of its separate strata. But they by no means afford a recipe or schema, as does philosophy, for neatly trimming the epochs of history.[36]

Substantially the same views were repeated in the *Introduction* of 1857 and the *Preface* of 1859.

The second of the criticisms of Feuerbach which had already been developed in the *Manuscripts* concerns the inadequacy of Feuerbach's conception of society. In the *Manuscripts* Marx had counted it a 'great achievement' of Feuerbach 'to have founded true materialism and real science by making the social relationship of "man to man" the basic principle of his theory.'[37] Already, the inverted commas indicated a reservation, which was made explicit in *The German Ideology:* 'he knows no other "human relationships" of "man to man" than love and friendship, and even then idealised.'[38]

Marx recognised that Feuerbach had made an important advance over eighteenth-century materialists by insisting that other persons are not perceived simply as external objects from which we have to infer the presence of another consciousness, personality and will. Feuerbach had claimed that other persons are directly present to human feelings as other human beings, most obviously so in the case of sexual attraction. Solipsism is thus an untenable position for a sexually differentiated species, and the problem of other minds vanishes before the evidence of the heart. By giving epistemological credence to sensuous experience of other persons besides that got from the specialised organs of perception, Feuerbach placed himself in a tradition reaching from Pascal to Sartre. All this Marx accepted and profited by, but he found it insufficient for reasons that are by now familiar – the epistemological relevance of Feuerbach's insight mattered less to him than its implications for the model of man as an object of anthropological theory, and Feuerbach's own anthropological model was still biased towards epistemology. When men were observed in the round, the material connections between them extended far beyond the bodily and emotional bonds of love and friendship, and in three different directions.

First, since men were productive creatures governed by their needs, there were direct material connections between them wherever the labour of one supplied the needs of another, whether cooperatively or commutatively. The 'metabolism of man with nature' was also a social metabolism, through which production and consumption effected continuous transfers of energy from one person to another. This was no less basic a manifestation of the material unity of the species than copulation and generation. Likewise, the degree of material unity of the species, at any moment, was no greater than the range of unification of such networks of interconnection.[39]

Secondly, however, men being more effective producers than other species, produced more efficient means of communication, and thus of auto-communication, thought. Because of this, men were engaged in continuous symbolic interaction, that was none the less material for being also symbolic. Thus a second material connection between men – typically consisting of 'agitated layers of air, sounds, in short, language'[40] – also formed the species into supra-individual systems. But these were simultaneously systems of meanings, and as such qualified all other connexions and experiences of men according to the meaning, or lack of it, which they had within the collective and individual consciousnesses produced through social communication. Hence, for example, the satisfaction of needs through social production was not *solely* a transfer of energy, but also a communicational process, a cultural interconnection as well as a material one.

Thirdly, inasmuch as human beings were directly present to one another in their social sentiments, it was not only through love and friendship. Besides solidarity – the communication and sharing of mutual attraction – there was also estrangement, the communication and reciprocation of indifference and hostility, which was none the less human for being painful. Feuerbach was therefore guilty of idealising man's social nature by restricting his conception of it to a narrow range of 'personal' and pleasing relationships. Marx had a sociological explanation of how this idealisation of private life came about in bourgeois society, but the theoretical point was that social structure as a whole, and its development, could never be understood by beginning from primary groups, face-to-face interaction, and relationships steered by the will and consciousness of the participants. Such phenomena were subsidiary moments, enclaves in systems which were 'continually evolving out of the life-process of definite individuals, but of individuals, not as they may appear in their own or other people's imagination, but as they *really* are; i.e. as they operate, produce materially, and hence as they work under definite material limits, presuppositions and conditions independent of their will.'[41] In the *Manuscripts* Marx had criticised estrangement in economic life in the light of an ideal model of economic solidarity, which his humanistic teleology led him to see as man's future state latent in the present. But he did not deny that estrangement was a 'natural' feature of the evolution of human society. Where Feuerbach saw it as the result of an arbitrary perversion of the human essence through religion, for Marx it was an inevitable limitation, but a barrier that human progress could transcend.

As with *homo faber*, so Marx's image of social man received a metaphysical formulation in his manuscripts of 1844. With respect to social metabolism:

> Exchange, both of human activity within production itself, and also of human products with one another, represents the activity and enjoyment of the species, whose real, conscious and true being is *social* activity and *social* enjoyment. Since human nature is the true common essence (*Gemeinwesen*) of men, men produce and create the human community (*Gemeinwesen*), their social essence, through the activation of their nature. This social essence is not an abstract, universal power over against the single individual, but the essence of each and every individual, his own activity, his own life . . . Therefore this true community does not originate in reflection, but takes shape through the need and egoism of individuals, that is to say, it is produced directly through the activation of their very being. It does not depend on man whether this community exists or not; but so long as man has not recognized himself as man, and hence has not organized the world in a human way, this community appears in the form of *estrangement*. Because its *subject*, man, is an essence estranged from itself. Men, not abstractly, but as real, living, particular individuals, *are* this essence. It is therefore as they are. So to say that *man* estranges himself is the same as to say that the *society* of this estranged man is a caricature of his *real community*, his true species-life.[42]

Here it is the actual economic interdependence of men, brought about on a widening scale by the division of labour, that is represented as their 'true community', where the social nature of the species develops and shows itself. But this interdependence is not consciously willed as a cooperative recognition of mutual need. It grows haphazardly with the extension of markets, as a by-product of private producers competing to satisfy their own needs as cheaply as possible at one another's expense. Thus 'It is precisely the *unity* of human labour that is viewed only as its *division*, because man's social essence only comes into existence as its opposite, in the form of estrangement.'[43] Hence the economic connections between men that arise as unintended consequences of historical development present both a standard by which to condemn their actual social organisation, and a basis from which to transcend it. For they comprise a measure of man's unrecognised potentiality for socialised existence, his social essence latent within his collective material life – just as, for Hegel, the material world of nature represented the self-estranged latency of spirit.

This historical teleology had a somewhat Rousseauesque starting-point. Society comes into existence in a blind, unconscious way as a result of the natural egoism and self-sufficiency of primitive man. Originally, 'The aim of production is possession . . . the objectification of immediate, selfish need. Thus, in his savage and barbaric condition man's production is measured, is limited by the extent of his immediate need, whose immediate content is the object produced. . . . His need is limited by his production . . . His production is measured by his need. In this case there is no exchange . . . '[44] Hence, human production can develop only within the bounds of private property, for 'the basic presupposition of private property' – that man 'only produces in order to have' – is also the initial condition of human history. Hence 'private property is historically necessary.'[45] Production develops only with the growth of exchange between private owners, egoistic individuals who produce a surplus to their needs only to satisfy other needs by obtaining the surplus produced by others. Hence society itself evolves as a solely material connection in which man's social essence is estranged from him in the movement of commodities. Individuals do not interact as men but only as means to their several ends.

Far from glorifying the initial condition of self-sufficiency, Marx only invoked it as a conceptual starting-point for a historical dialectic that would end with the supersession and annulment of private property and 'the whole estrangement' built upon it. Man would then take command of the world he had produced, including his social world, and organise it 'in a human way'.

Furthermore, Marx held that the initial condition of isolated, egoistic production was really a form of society, though unrecognised as such. For social life is not necessarily or always group activity.

> Social activity and social enjoyment by no means exist only in the form of *directly* communal activity and directly communal enjoyment, i.e. activity and enjoyment which express and confirm themselves directly in *real association* with other men. But this will occur everywhere

where this *direct* expression of sociality arises from the essential content of the activity and is adequate to its nature.

However, even when I am active as a scholar, etc. – when I am engaged in activity which I can seldom perform in direct community with others – I am still acting *socially*, because I am active as a *man*. Not only is the material of my activity given to me as a social product (as is even the language in which the thinker is active) but my *own* existence *is* social activity; therefore what I make out of myself I make for society, conscious of myself as a social being . . . The individual *is* the social essence . . . Man's individual and species-life are not two different things . . .[46]

Thus the isolation of one task from another does not in itself constitute estrangement, though it may cause it by obliterating awareness of man's social essence. The isolated individuals postulated by social atomism are a fiction, for even a society of self-sufficient individualists is a socially structured population of a kind. Even where economic interdependence is lacking the genetic bond must still exist, and the cultural bond of thought itself involves a material connection, for 'The element of thought itself, the element of the vital manifestation of thought, language, is sensuous in character.'[47]

All of these were important insights which Marx retained after he had renounced essentialism, roundly declaring that 'in its reality [the human essence] is the ensemble of social relations.'[48] But since historical teleology was abandoned with essentialism, the postulate of man's primitive egoism could also be dropped. In the 1857 *Introduction* Marx criticised 'the individual and isolated hunter and fisherman, with whom Smith and Ricardo begin', and all other such 'eighteenth-century Robinsonades', as retrospective ideological projections of the assumptions of bourgeois society. Not the isolated producer, but 'Individuals producing in society – hence socially determined individual production – is, of course, the point of departure.' In fact, Marx said, 'The more deeply we go back into history, the more does the individual, and hence also the producing individual, appear as dependent, as belonging to a greater whole . . . ' Private property was itself a historical product, whose origins had to be explained, not assumed as coeval with 'Man'.[49]

3 ESSENCES, SOCIAL MEANING, AND SOCIAL COGNITION

We have seen that Marx did not just dismiss essentialism as nonsense, for he remained aware of the importance of reified concepts in social life. And his debt to Feuerbach included not just this insight, but also a critical method of approaching these abstractions. The point of Feuerbachian criticism had always been reductionist, but in a special way. Its message was not that men succeeded in saying nothing when they talked about God, but that what they were really talking about was not what they thought they were talking about. So their assertions were not necessarily meaningless or false. They had meaning in terms of their own code, and might be partially true in ways that only explanatory criticism could reveal. What it did reveal, however, were new truths which, in a sense, men did not know they knew: 'secrets' (as Marx often put it) which men had kept from themselves. Thus Feuerbachian criticism was like translating out of a mystifying esoteric language.

Marx retained this approach, applying it to Feuerbach himself. Where Feuerbach had translated religion into anthropological terms, Marx translated the philosophical content of Feuerbach's anthropology into sociological terms. Thus the thesis that the human essence 'in its reality' is 'the ensemble of social relations' was, as *The German Ideology* makes plain, intended in this reductionist sense:

> This sum of productive forces, capital funds and social forms of intercourse, which every individual and generation finds in existence as something given, is the real basis of what philosophers have conceived as 'substance' and 'essence of man', and what they have deified and attacked.[50]

Thus, like Durkheim, Marx held that the idea of God, or its secularised metaphysical equivalents, referred to society – but to society as a productive totality. Social science thus usurped the traditional place of philosophy as knowledge of essences, inasmuch as it too claimed to reveal a hidden reality beneath the superficial appearance of human ideas.

But this legacy of essentialism was not confined to the supersession of pseudo-theories by scientific theory. For, as already noted, men build ideas both true and false into social structure itself in the form of institutions, whose rules – no matter how self-evidently valid they may appear with the passage of time – depend for their meaning on the beliefs which they presuppose. Thus religious behaviour and religious institutions would be largely meaningless without religious beliefs, and do not survive for long if belief fails and cannot be revived. Marx argued (from his *Critique of Hegel's Philosophy of Right* onwards) that in the same way as the existence of the visible church presupposed belief in a Church Invisible, with God at its head, so the existence of the state apparatus and legal procedures also presupposed belief in the existence of reified abstractions – 'the state', 'the sovereign people', 'the public', a *Volksgeist*, 'the law'; or more simply, 'France', 'Britain', etc. – lurking behind the institutions and active through them. As with God, so these concepts too had to be construed as referring in oblique and contradictory ways to society. But their ostensible reference, accepted by commonsense, was to illusory entities with which were connected webs of false beliefs about society – that the state was

somehow 'above' it and held it together, for example; or that law was what
ensured the regularity of social behaviour. Thus the actual institutions and
conduct which depended on these ideological premises, though no less real
than any other part of society, were in a sense also delusive, shot through
with false assumptions. This was the more the case, the more abstract,
idealised and remote from the actuality of daily life were the illusory
entities whose existence they presupposed. In this sense, churches were
more ideological components of the social superstructure than states, and
states than legal systems.

In emphasising that it is not just ideas that may refer in a mystifying way
to social realities, but that some social realities themselves, as immediately
given, are structured in terms of esoteric ideological meanings, Marx was
developing a distinction that Feuerbach had failed to clarify. Feuerbach's
critique of religion was aimed indiscriminately at theology, faith and
institutions. When Marx applied the same method to Hegel's political
philosophy (i.e. the 'theology' of the state) he awoke to the difference
between criticising beliefs embodied in institutions and social practice, and
criticising ideological theories designed to systematise these beliefs and
justify the practices. Thus in moving from 'the criticism of heaven' to 'the
criticism of earth' he was making a double transition: from criticising ideas
about another world to criticising ideas about this world, and from
criticising ideological speculative theory to criticising ideological beliefs
present in social consciousness and expressed in the corresponding
practice.

In his introduction to the *Critique*, Marx confessed that it 'does not deal
with the original but with its copy, the German *philosophy* of the state and
law.'[51] If it could nevertheless contribute to the criticism of the contemporary state, this was because of the peculiarity of Germany's
development. 'In politics, the Germans have thought what other peoples
have done.' Hence, 'The German philosophy of law and of the state is the
only theory in German history that stands *al pari* with the official modern
present.' And so, Marx hoped, 'The criticism of the German philosophy of
the state and of law, which was given its most consistent, richest and final
version by Hegel, is both the critical analysis of the modern state and of the
reality that depends upon it.' The underlying assumption here is that this
philosophy also contains the 'most general expression, raised to the level of
a science' of 'the German political and legal mind'. In other words, Hegel
had not only philosophised, but had also reproduced 'scientifically' – i.e.
described in an abstract, simplified, general and systematic way – the
social consciousness of the bureaucrats and jurists who manned the state
machine. And although the Prussian state, objectively, was a travesty of
English or French constitutionalism, the subjectivity of its officialdom was
steeped in modern political ideas, which matched the objective political
process in *other* countries.[52]

A similar assumption guided his approach to political economy in the *Manuscripts*. In his preface, he confessed that preparing his critique of *The Philosophy of Right* for publication had taught him the inappropriateness of 'intermingling criticism directed only against speculation with criticism of the various subject-matters themselves.'[53] He had therefore decided to produce separate critiques of law, morals and politics, and 'afterwards try in a special work to present them again as a connected whole showing the interrelationship of these separate parts, together with a critique of the speculative elaboration of that material.' It seems clear from this that he saw philosophical anthropology as a critical weapon that could be turned against the ideas actually present in society as well as against speculative theory, and also as a tool of synthetic construction. So far as economics was concerned, he claimed that his results had 'been attained by means of a wholly empirical analysis based on a conscientious critical study of political economy.'[54]

By this he seems to have meant two things. First, he had used the works of the classical economists as a source of empirical generalisations and theoretical hypotheses, of an empirical kind, about economic life. He had 'critically' separated these from mere speculation in order to get an account of how the capitalist system worked. But secondly, he had used the same sources as evidence for a generalised account of how 'political economy' *interpreted* capitalism, and therefore also the type of human society in which it belonged. And here he critically isolated crucial limitations in the assumptions with which economists had approached and classified their data. He did not necessarily regard these limitations as invalidating their findings or hypotheses. The assumptions built into the categories of political economy were, in Marx's view, also present in the meanings by which economic life was lived. The economists had merely refined and simplified them into what we might nowadays call ideal-types. 'Political economy – like the actual process – starts from the relationship of man to man as that of private property-owner to private property-owner.'[55]

Once again, therefore, Marx was criticising ideas present in social life through the medium of descriptions which 'raised them to the level of a science'. In this case, however, the meanings systematised by political economy were not, like those underlying Hegel's political philosophy, merely present in a social consciousness that failed to match its objective process. Here, political economy 'expresses in general, abstract formulas the material process through which private property actually passes, and these formulas it then takes for laws.'[56] Its categories thus reflected meanings present in the actual system, and its generalisations described collective processes to the extent that 'capital', 'wage-labour' etc. actually structured them.

In Marx's view, the 'abstract formulas' of classical economics fell short of being laws in any strong sense for three reasons.

First, to abstract economic meanings alone and systematise them in isolation was an inevitably one-sided approach. It was rather like abstracting everything blue from nature in order to create a science of blueness. However important the economy might be in society, and however differentiated and specialised its roles and institutions might become, it remained part of a social system which affected it at every moment. The relative success with which political economy could actually describe society on its artificially restricted assumptions testified less to its general validity than to the degree to which society itself had come to be dominated by economic meanings that allowed only restricted social expression for human capacities and interests incompatible with capitalism.[57] Thus, to criticise the assumptions of the economists it was necessary 'to rise above the level of political economy' and to situate its abstractions in the broader context of society as a whole. Or, as Marx put it from the standpoint of philosophical anthropology, to ask: 'What significance in the development of mankind has this reduction of the greater part of mankind to abstract labour?'[58]

In this way, a critical approach intervenes at just those points where political economy fails to explain. Thus political economy 'does not disclose the source of the division between labour and capital', but 'takes for granted what it is supposed to explain': this was to be Marx's main point of attack and the area of his major contributions. 'Similarly, competition comes in everywhere. It is explained from external circumstances. As to how far these external and apparently accidental circumstances are but the expression of a necessary course of development, political economy teaches us nothing.'[59] Here again, Marx was to make original, and basically sociological, contributions. A critically self-conscious economics would thus not only admit and carefully delimit the restricted validity of its laws. It would also allow that the constitution of the historically determinate reality, whose laws they were, could itself be explained by other, more general laws of the development, functioning, and decomposition of social systems.

Secondly, the formulas of political economy fell short of being laws because, in the pursuit of abstract consistency, its practitioners ignored contradictory implications of the meanings present in economic institutions. Hence, economics failed to take account of real processes flowing from the contradictoriness of these meanings, especially class conflict and its effects; or else took account of the processes but failed to explain them, as with competition; or else explained them by incorporating assumptions about human nature and social life that were so cynical as to be in flagrant opposition to those of daily life; or else the contradictions of reality emerged as polemical differences between rival schools of economic doctrine.[60] Once again, a critical approach proceeds from discrepancies within economic theory, or between the predictions of theory and the facts as reported, to uncover the ways in which real processes are shaped by contradictory meanings present in society. In this way, Marx's first step was to put himself 'wholly at the standpoint of the political economist, and follow him in comparing the theoretical and practical claims of the workers.'[61] The discrepancies that appeared here were paralleled in reality by trends in opposite directions – 'The worker becomes all the poorer the more wealth he produces', etc.[62] Both, Marx suspected, reflected basic contradictions in the meaning of private property within capitalism, and so 'from an economic fact of the present'[63] he moved, through the metaphysical analysis of estranged labour in the *Manuscripts* and the transitional theory of 'relative wages' in *Wage Labour and Capital*, to the theory of exploitation in his mature works. All three turned on the notion that capital and wage-labour are opposite poles of a contradictory production relation.

Thirdly, the economists' generalisations remained less than laws because, by situating themselves at the level of everyday economic conduct, they shared the social ignorance of economic agents. Thus the actual mixture of ignorance and knowledge about the system with which agents perform in it, which should form part of a theory of how the system works, was beyond their horizon. Its place was taken by arbitrary assumptions, such as that of perfect knowledge. Whereas the supply of knowledge in a social system is not arbitrary, but depends on the cognitive functions that the structure of the system itself performs for social consciousness.

Marx had claimed that religious and political abstractions referred to society, but negatively, by contradistinguishing themselves from society as a sacred or public realm within which developed a form of collective self-consciousness. This was a false consciousness, to be sure, but was nevertheless a consciousness of society. Processes otherwise unrecognised in social consciousness became visible, as through a distorting lens, in religious or political guise. This is easiest to illustrate with law. Legal codes and records of cases provide socially accessible indices of what kinds of transactions are going on in society – transactions which in their quantitative extent and qualitative variety remain unrecorded and unknown. Law, obviously, is a *selective* indicator of social processes – not only in what it neglects, both qualitatively and quantitatively, but through its special perspective on social facts, that of 'legality'. Unhelpful and unreliable as knowledge of a country's laws may therefore be for an ethnographer or statistician trying to find out what actually happens there, it is nevertheless better than no information at all. Everyday social action too typically proceeds on this kind of imperfect information, and its imperfections result systematically from the selectivity of its supply. For every supply of knowledge is simultaneously a supply of ignorance. When Marx called religion 'the general theory of this world, its encyclopaedic compendium, its logic in popular form'[64] he was referring, amongst other things, to the way in which religion can stimulate and codify knowledge of social relations, but in ethical terms; or allows social causation to be recognised, but under the guise of providential teleology; and thus also *prevents* the recognition of society itself as the object known.

In the *Manuscripts*, Marx argued that 'private property' and the categories of private law, which dominated both economic life and economic theory, referred in this way to the economic process of society. In reality, this involved men in continuous production and reproduction of their being – that of others as well as their own – through labour. Private property referred to this negatively, by denying its dynamic and collective aspects. The process was grasped as a static condition of 'having'. Its elements were only recognised and given an identity in social consciousness as things held apart from society, in the hands of individuals. So that whereas labour necessarily implied movement, the economists would only set their conceptual system in motion by introducing movement from outside, from the volition of individuals. Production and exchange and all the phenomena of economic life were therefore construed as means to the end of private possession. Values were seen as resultants of supply and demand, of individuals' desires and estimates, whereas in reality – so Marx was to argue – they were social facts transmitted through the system as institutionalised information, providing the framework of knowledge within which desires and effective demand came into play.

In the *Manuscripts*, the fact that private property 'really' referred to labour and production had been deduced from Marx's *a priori* conception of the human essence as creatively productive. When the 'ensemble of social relations' replaced 'human essence', this precipitated the more obviously valid assumption that reproduction (and hence the associated structures) has functional primacy in a theory of persistence of social systems.[65] Marx developed his original critique of private property into his theory of value. *Capital* sought to demonstrate that commodities were, *inter alia*, materialised messages referring to something beyond themselves: namely, the proportion of socially necessary labour-time needed to reproduce them. As such they exemplified the way in which private property referred contradictorily to the social production process. For as commodities, products were defined as having value on condition of becoming private property, things set apart from society; while the value they possessed depended wholly on their representing classes of products having a definite place and ordering *within* society, in the social distribution and organisation of labour-time. Thus, the structure of private exchange determined the way in which information was supplied to participants in the market system, as a basis for action. The commodity, as means of exchange, was also an indicator of social interconnexions beyond the horizon of the market. Whether the law of value 'held', and why it generally did not, were therefore questions of substance about how social structure functioned for social cognition, and not just questions about economic theory, or the theorist's cognition.

Thus Marx never gave up the basic idea that social structure itself contains different levels of meaning, interrelated somewhat as Feuerbachian criticism had claimed that the false essences of traditional metaphysics were related to the true human essence. Pretended essences — ideological abstractions and institutions — referred in oblique and contradictory ways to a more fundamental reality — at first, man's species-being; later, the process of social production. And throughout his life, Marx continued to develop his critique of political economy on the assumption that criticising the presuppositions and categories of economics was the way to win critical access to the practical abstractions contained in economic life itself. And that to criticise these — to reveal their latent contradictions — was the way to discover how visible structures referred to the invisible processes which they also concealed, and thus how society functioned as a system through the actions of individuals without their knowing or intending the result. Thus the abstract, quantitative relationships of the world of commodities — the sphere of private property, exchange and circulation — both hid and revealed the more concrete, qualitative interconnexions of men in the sphere of production, consumption and division of labour. They did so by making them available as social knowledge for social action, but in the 'opaque' language of value. In this way Marx converted Feuerbach's reductionist critical method into a tool for analysing the reciprocal relationships of social structure and social cognition. The possibility of such analyses, like the use of Hegel's dialectical method, depended on society's being structured by meanings, and not at all — as has been argued by both Hegelianizing Marxists and their opponents — on a philosophical conception of society as an 'expressive totality'.[66]

4 ESSENCES AND SOCIAL CAUSATION

Marx's methodological debt to Feuerbach ended here: the critical reduction of religious beliefs to their mundane point of reference was a method that could be extended, by analogy, to political and economic abstractions. But Marx's extensions were not haphazard. The movement from religion to politics to economics seems to have been a sequence of phases within a single developing analysis of the self-estrangement of man, in which the precipitate of one stage provided the starting-point for the next (see Figure 1). We have seen how this generated a series of semiotic and functional ideas about the interrelation of levels of social structure, and of social consciousness. We should also ask, however, whether this sequence had any causal significance with regard to historical and social reality — and if so, how? — or whether it merely records the intellectual route followed by Marx from his Feuerbachian point of origin? In other

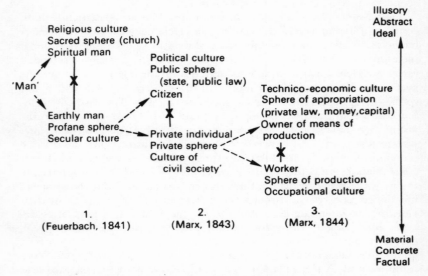

Figure 1 The Phases of the analysis of 'Human Self-estrangement'
The broken lines represent processes of self-estrangement; the crossed lines, the contradictory relationships that result. Each phase is characterised as a dichotomisation of culture, spheres of social life with their corresponding institutions (in brackets), and social roles. The resulting levels are situated against a scale relating to the illusoriness, etc., of the beliefs about society which their existence presupposes.

words, did the doctrine of man's self-estrangement bequeath anything in the way of causal explanation to Marx's later theories?

The answer to this question tended to be obscured so long as Marx himself thought in terms of philosophical anthropology. For since each phase logically depended on the one before, 'Man', as subject of a single historical process, must have gone through them in the same order. Thus there was a strong temptation to interpret them as the historical stages or epochs of human self-estrangement in a way that we have seen Marx disowned in *The German Ideology*.

Marx himself made the analytical transition from phase 1 to phase 2 in his *Critique of Hegel's Philosophy of Right*. In *On the Jewish Question*, shortly afterwards, he suggested that this change in the character of human self-alienation marks the transition from feudalism to the modern period. Under feudalism, the public and private spheres were still undifferentiated aspects of secular life. 'The old civil society had a directly political character.'[67] Then the 'political revolution' of the seventeenth and eighteenth centuries broke up the segments of feudal society into individuals on the one hand, and on the other 'the material and spiritual elements that make up the life experience and civil position of these individuals' (the 'culture of civil society' in Figure 1). Simultaneously, it abstracted, universalised and centralised the 'political spirit' that had been dispersed amongst these segments. Thus was perfected the contradiction between 'the idealism of the state' and the 'materialism of civil society'. The apparent realisation of man's species-being in the democratic state based on liberty, equality and fraternity was belied in the daily life of civil society, where men were unequal, egoistic and dominated by inhuman conditions. As the new dichotomy of public and private became dominant, the older contradiction of sacred and profane was subordinated to it: religion was redefined as a voluntary part of private life, and multiple religious associations superseded the single universal church.

There is clearly much to be said for this interpretation; indeed, I have myself drawn upon it in Chapter 1 in interpreting the transition in ideology from religious to political alienation. But, equally clearly, its merits have nothing to do with the logic of man's self-alienation. And the fact that Marx himself proceeded from the critique of religion to the critique of politics is relevant to the supersession of sacred-profane by public-private in European history only because Germany's delayed development had just reached this transition by the early nineteenth century. So Feuerbach and Marx, in the vanguard of German ideology, reproduced in the form of successively more 'advanced' critiques, and from the standpoint of a single imaginary subject,[68] the actual transition on which European history had slowly pivoted during the past three hundred years.

Besides this diachronic relationship between 1 and 2, the essay *On the Jewish Question* also envisaged a synchronic one. Though the *dominance* of sacred-profane gives way to that of public-private, Marx emphasised that this does not mean the disappearance of religion. 'Political emancipation from religion leaves religion intact even though it is no longer a privileged religion.'[69] The emancipation of religion from politics may even mean that 'the religious and theological consciousness has all the more religious and theological force in the complete democracy.' It becomes purer, 'a really other-worldly life'. But this persistence does not come about by religion's own momentum. On the contrary, religion persists precisely because of the new rift in secular life: 'What makes the members of the political state religious is the dualism between their individual and their species-life, between life in civil society and political life . . . Religion is here the spirit of civil society, the expression of separation and distance of man from man.'[70]

Here Marx drew on Hegel's idea that the unhappy consciousness projected an idealised community into an afterlife, to compensate men who lived in mutual estrangement and had alienated their political sovereignty. But he also combined this with a Feuerbachian image of man politically estranged from his human essence, and the combination was an uneasy one. The 'Feuerbachian' hypothesis that democratic citizens take to other-worldly religion to compensate for the gap between their theoretical popular sovereignty and their limited power in practice is much less plausible than Hegel's view that men are driven to it by despotism. Later on, Marx always took the more sensible line that the shortcomings of democracy would stimulate political and social reform or, in extreme conditions, revolution – but not religiosity. On the other hand, the 'Hegelian' part of Marx's hypothesis – that religion compensates for lack of community in civil society itself, expressing 'the separation and distance of man from man', regardless of the form of the state – is much more plausible. But this, unlike the other, is a sociological hypothesis about estrangement amongst men, and does not depend on man's self-alienation. When Marx wrote *On the Jewish Question*, of course, he still had not embarked on the analysis of civil society that would have illuminated the mutual estrangement of men under capitalism.

But the important point about this attempt to show the dependence of the religious 'superstructure' on its political 'base' is one of method. For it implied that Marx's transition from 1 to 2 had another significance besides coincidence with a transition in history. It now appeared as a move from the theory of one level of social and cultural life to the theory of another level, more basic than the first, and determining its persistence, change, content and institutional form. Thus the persistence of religion with a purified content, and its change of institutional form through pluralistic adaptation to civil society, were explained as effects of social life coming to be dominated by the cleavage between public and private. At the same time, the abstractly psychological contradiction by which Feuerbach had tried to explain man's recourse to religious fantasy was replaced by Hegelian social psychology. The psychological need which religion 'expressed' – reformulated and then 'satisfied' in other terms – was the effect of the estrangements specific to particular types of social structure. For the societies so structured, therefore, religion also had functions: it provided ideological compensations and justification, and reinforced cohesion through its symbolic idealisation of the unity of the whole. This theory implied, of course, that the previous existence of religion, under feudalism, had also been determined by its specific secular basis. Marx hinted at such an explanation in describing how the various segments of feudal society – 'seignorial right, estates and corporations' – constituted 'the relationship of the single individual to the state as a whole . . . [as a] . . . relationship of separation and exclusion from the other parts of society.'[71] Thus the particularistic fusion of public and private life implied the mutual estrangement of its various segments. This fragmentation of feudal society, perpetually threatening disintegration and anarchy, had its counterpart and complement in the coercive unity of a religious monopoly.

In his fourth *Thesis*, Marx apparently referred to this 'political' theory of religion advanced in 1843. Feuerbach, said Marx, 'started out from the fact of religious self-estrangement' and dissolved the imaginary world of religion into its secular basis. But he went no farther, whereas the main task was still to be done: to explain this duplication into sacred and profane by the 'self-cleavage and self-contradictoriness of this secular basis.'[72] This can of course be read as an early statement of economic determinism, but the real point is that what Marx's 'political' and 'economic' theories of religion have in common is their *sociological* character. The determinants, in each case, are specific modes of estrangement, social relationships, established in the first case by the structure of the political realm, in the second by that of the economy. In effect, since the 'political' explanation of modern religion boiled down to an explanation in terms of the estrangement specific to 'civil society', it was really already an explanation in 'economic' terms. For when Marx made the transition from 2 to 3, in the *Manuscripts*, his aim was precisely to dissect civil society and expose its inner contradictions.

The significance of *this* transition was almost entirely that of a shift from one theoretical level to another more fundamental one. True, there was a sense in which it also corresponded with a historical transition. For, in *The Communist Manifesto* and elsewhere, Marx foresaw that the unification of world markets and international capitalism would supersede the political division of the globe into nation-states. National governments would be subordinated to class conflict and to the struggle between capitalism and socialism. But this was not the aspect of economic life that Marx analysed in 1844. His objective in the *Manuscripts* followed on logically from what he had already accomplished. Having successfully applied Feuerbach's critical method to politics, he had established two results. First, that Feuerbach had not gone far enough, for the religious cleavage could itself be explained by the cleavage in the secular basis; but secondly, since the state was the 'heaven' of civil society, the political cleavage also required explanation in terms of its own 'secular' basis. Thus the *Manuscripts* applied to private property and political economy – respectively the major institution and the theoretical expression of civil society – the same analysis as before. This was a conscious deepening of the previous inquiry, the search for a theoretical level corresponding to the rock-bottom of social causation.

In the *Manuscripts*, Marx gave a reason in terms of human self-estrangement for thinking that the shift from 2 to 3 had brought him to the 'theoretical basis' of both history and the revolutionary movement:

> . . . private property is the material perceptible expression of *estranged human* life. Its movement – production and consumption – is the perceptible revelation of the movement of all production until now, i.e. the realization or the reality of man. Religion, family, state, law, morality, science, art, etc. are only *particular* modes of production and fall under its general law. The positive transcendence of private property, as the appropriation of *human* life, is therefore the positive transcendence of all

estrangement – that is to say, the return of man from religion, family, state, etc. to his *human*, i.e. *social* existence.[73]

This relies heavily on Marx's *a priori* view of human nature. As it stands it is hardly convincing, and in the *Introduction* of 1857 Marx actually rejected the idea that 'production in general' could have a 'general law'. In fact, the passage appears to be largely tautological: to the extent that religion, state, etc. have the form of private property, they can be understood in terms of the analysis of private property as self-estrangement, and transcended by the abolition of private property. No doubt there is an important analogy between the appropriation of religious and political powers and the appropriation of productive forces, but this does not explain the first in terms of the second, or allow us to assert that the state, for example, cannot exist without private property as its basis. This latter point, which is crucial for the question of whether Marx's transition from 2 to 3 had any theoretical significance, was not illuminated by Marx's further statement, in elaboration of this passage, that 'Religious estrangement as such occurs only in the realm of *consciousness*, of man's inner life, but economic estrangement is that of *real life*; its transcendence therefore embraces both aspects.' We might be inclined to accept this, for reasons already contained in Hegel's account, yet still remain sceptical about a similar inclusion of political estrangement in economic estrangement.

What this passage really indicates, I think, is that in the transition to economic life Marx had reached the limit of usefulness of his metaphysical model. The idea of man's self-estrangement, no doubt, could be applied in any social context, but in the Feuerbachian model it was logically dependent on that of man's self-alienation. It was by externalising or alienating his essential powers that man became a stranger to them and to himself. And the concepts of externalisation, alienation, reappropriation, etc., were metaphors originating in economic life. When reapplied to their original subject-matter, they seemed to yield a literal description of economic processes, yet one which also invested them with a general philosophical significance: 'As man estranges his activity from himself, so he hands over to an alien person an activity that does not belong to him. . . . ' (etc.)[74] Thus the fact that these concepts relating to transfers of property had previously been *over*-generalised as a metaphysical terminology for describing men's relation to their common 'property' of humanity now seemed to confer a spurious generality on an analysis of transfers of economic property. Because Marx had reduced private property to estranged and alienated labour, and labour was seen as an expression of man's social essence, he rashly concluded that all social forms of human self-estrangement could be comprehended as private property and superseded in one movement.

In the *Manuscripts* themselves Marx remained stuck at this point. When he realised that 'human essence' was a philosophically inflated way of

talking about social relations, he also understood that the self-alienation
and self-estrangement of man were philosophically inflated ways of talking
about processes of alienation and estrangement in social life. Then the real
theoretical gains from the analysis of economic self-estrangement became
apparent. First, as outlined in *The German Ideology* and developed later in
The Poverty of Philosophy, all cultural phenomena, whether material goods,
ideas or social organisation, could be analysed as human *products*,
originating in specific modes and processes of production. (However, as
argued in the *Introduction* of 1857, nothing could be inferred, merely from
this, about the actual relationships between these different processes: those
had to be established on other grounds. Nor did the functional priority of
reproduction have obvious causal implications.) Secondly, as developed in
the *Grundrisse*, the concepts of estrangement, alienation and appropriation
remained as tools of sociological analysis, enabling the abstractions of
political economy to be critically situated in a context of social relations.
Thirdly, by revealing the outlines of what was to become Marx's theory of
exploitation, the analysis of estranged labour pointed towards a theory
that eventually was to link the political and economic levels: the theory of
the ruling class presented in *The Communist Manifesto*.

So just as Marx had hit on a 'political' explanation of religion while
moving from the first to the second phase of the analysis of human self-
estrangement, but one which stemmed from Hegel's sociology, not
Feuerbach's metaphysics; similarly, in moving from the second to the
third, he discovered the basis for an economic theory of politics, but one
which owed more to Hegel's dialectic of master and slave than to
Feuerbach's metaphysics. Read backwards, the sequence of phases in
Figure 1 can indeed be seen to prefigure the model of an economic base,
divided into productive forces and relations of production, upon which
depend political and ideological superstructures. This was what Marx, in
his 1859 *Preface*, referred to as the 'general result' of the studies he had
undertaken in Paris and Brussels in 1844-6. In this way, the sequence
through which Marx's ideas moved from 1842-4 was indeed significant as
a discovery of increasingly basic levels of social structure, but this seems to
have owed nothing to the concomitant idea that it represented a disclosure
of ever more general and comprehensive levels of human self-
estrangement.

5 A THEORY OF SUPERSTRUCTURES?

I shall close this chapter by pulling together the methodological themes of
the last two sections. I suggested, first, that Marx adopted and developed
Feuerbach's method of reductionist criticism as a tool for analysing
meanings contained in social processes. In this way, institutionalised
abstractions were shown to refer obliquely to an 'underlying' social reality.

But, secondly, Marx was also dissatisfied with Feuerbach's explanation of how this came about, and sought its causes in more 'basic' levels of social structure. How were these semantic and causal inquiries interrelated, and what was their valid residue?

Marx himself, of course, barely distinguished them apart at first. His metaphysical approach encouraged him to construe man's social essence as both the inner meaning and the hidden cause of more superficial phenomena. But we have seen that he eventually discarded 'human essence' as a philosopher's abstraction which really referred to the social system; and also that the causal theory he retained did not involve man's estrangement from his essence, but sociological estrangement between men. Once the identity of meaning and cause was dissolved with the abandonment of essentialism, the relation of 'reference' between super-structure and basis could be reinterpreted in terms of the cognitive deficiencies and functions of social structure.

The sociological theory of religion in Marx's political writings leaned heavily on Hegel. Different types of social structure involved specific sorts of estrangement between their component groups or individuals, generating emotional needs for less conflict and a greater sense of community. To the extent that these needs could be satisfied at another level of social structure, within a different institutional setting that could coexist with the first, compensation would be provided for the deprivations caused by the latter, which would thereby be stabilised. Thus the persistence of the second level was explained by the presence of the first and by the interlocking effects of the two levels on the psychological plane; while the persistence of the first was reinforced by the persistence of the second. The initial existence and form of the second level are not explained at all by this theory, but have to be assumed. However, if we add in a cognitive dimension – derived from Marx's relation of 'reference' – this weakness can to some extent be remedied. All that then needs to be assumed is the availability of a suitable ideological theory as part of the historical input which a new social system receives from its predecessor.

The theory can then be enlarged and generalised as a theory of superstructures, as follows – and as indicated in Figure 2. A new mode of production ($P2$) causes the appearance of a new type of social structure ($S2$, Level I) which is also partly the effect of the previous social structure ($S1$) and which is characterised by a specific mode of estrangement between units. This causes changes in social consciousness: emotional needs appear, corresponding to the emotional deprivation entailed by the new type of estrangement, and also cognitive needs arising from the mutual unacquaintance and ignorance of the units which this new structure separates and keeps apart. Each needs some knowledge of the actions of others and the properties of the system as a whole in order to act effectively, yet the structure prevents them from having it. These new emotional and cognitive needs are both included in $C2$ (I) in the diagram.

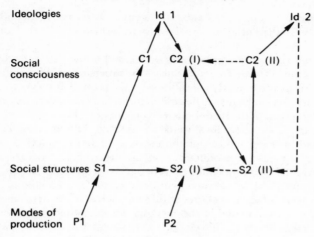

Figure 2 Marx's early theory of superstructures
(Unbroken arrows indicate causal relationships, broken arrows functional relationships.)

The only resources to meet these needs are received ideologies (Id 1): men therefore deliberately create a new level of social structure (S2, Level II) defined in terms of Id 1 and in opposition to what already exists, comprising a known, rationalised institutional order and a specific mode of solidarity, thus providing a substitute satisfaction (C2 (II)) for the cognitive and emotional needs aroused by S2 (I). A new level of social structure entails a new level of social identity for all the individuals in society, defined by exclusion of the old identity from the new sphere of action. Thus, compensation for the estrangement existing in S2 (I) can be had only at the cost of some degree of internalised estrangement, or role-conflict, for the individuals. However, the cognitive deficiencies of S2 (I) are an actual impediment to effective action, and its emotional costs are potentially disruptive. Hence, if cognitive deficiencies in Level I can be overcome by interpreting Level I experience in terms of the rationalised meanings of Level II, and if emotional gratifications generated by the solidarity of Level II can reinforce motivation at Level I, Level I will tend to be integrated and stabilised. If we further suppose that an indefinitely large variety of experimental Level II's are produced, we can also hypothesise that only those survive which adequately fulfil these structural functions for Level I. The struggle for survival against its rivals, and to impose its definitions on Level I, causes a new ideology of Level II (Id 2) to emerge through the professional elaboration and systematisation of the ideas and sentiments in C2 (II) – or more precisely, in the social consciousness of those for whom Level II is a specialised occupation. This new ideology, in turn, will reinforce the interpretation of Level I in terms of

Level II, justify the opposition and estrangement between them, and thus tend to stabilise the entire new social system formed by Levels I and II together.

Let us now run an example through this tediously abstract schema. Marx's example in *On the Jewish Question* – the supersession of feudalism by capitalism – is inconveniently complicated since it really involves a three-level structure, so I shall choose the emergence of feudalism itself in western Europe. The spread of the feudal mode of production (P_2 – i.e. small-scale agriculture in self-sufficient local units, with surplus labour owed directly to a personal overlord who owns the means of defence as well as mills, herds, or other means of production) replaces the social structure of the Roman world (S_1) with the 'political economy' of feudalism (S_2 (I)). The latter is characterised by estrangement between local, occupational, etc., segments as well as between classes within and across segments. The main ideological resource available for meeting the resulting cognitive and emotional needs (C_2 (I)) is religion, and Christianity (Id 1) rapidly eliminates its principal pagan rivals, creating a monopolistic ecclesiastical organisation (S_2 (II)). By enabling Level I to be interpreted as a profane sphere in which all unknown and unfamiliar social elements have a known ethico-religious position *vis-à-vis* the single church, this provides a cognitive framework for conduct, a system of social landmarks in which the cellular multiplication of parishes reproduces in miniature the global relation of spiritual and temporal powers. At the same time it legitimates and supports the feudal hierarchy, offers sentimental and otherworldly rewards to the oppressed, and ritually reasserts the brotherhood of man in Christ. Thus C_2 (II) provides substitute satisfactions for the emotional needs in C_2 (I), but at the cost of a conflict between the values associated with each, which the individual is supposed to resolve by a renunciation in favour of the 'higher' level. In the struggles against paganism and secularism, a new Christian ideology (Id2), that of the medieval monks, mystics and schoolmen, is elaborated as a professional systematisation of C_2 (II) which reinforces the stability and identity (e.g. through Crusades) of the entire European feudal system.

The use of this example implies no judgement on the goodness of the theory, but merely illustrates how it would work. (It is, after all, not an unfamiliar set of ideas.) The example is perhaps a favourable one: the emergence of the modern nation-state from the sixteenth century onwards, in response to capitalism, might pose other problems. But the exposition immediately shows that, good or not, it is certainly an incomplete theory. For it is not enough, in order to create a new level of social structure, to have the need, the will and the ideas. The new order, defining itself in opposition to the existing level, must also succeed in occupying specific times and places set apart from ordinary life. Thus by encroaching on the organisation of labour-time and landed property, its establishment is likely to involve conflicts of material interest. Furthermore, material and human resources have to be permanently diverted into its maintenance. Every superstructure has its *own* infrastructure, and therefore can arise and persist only to the extent that this is compatible with the prevailing mode of extracting and distributing the economic surplus. Similarly, the recruitment of its personnel and their occupational interests must be compatible with the prevailing class system. These were considerations that Marx was aware of in his early writings, but only formulated theoretically later on. As it stands, therefore, the theory of superstructures in Marx's early writings, while promising, is still biased by its idealist origins.

6 CONCLUDING SUMMARY

Before passing on, in the next chapter, to examine the continuity between Marx's sociological uses of estrangement and alienation in his early and later writings, a summary of the argument so far is called for.

I have claimed that two threads are discernible running through Marx's early work, corresponding to a Feuerbachian metaphysic of man's self-alienation and self-estrangement, and a Hegelian proto-sociology of estrangement and alienation amongst social agents. Because they are inextricably intertwined, it would be a tedious and artificial task to separate them out in detail. Their entanglement is due to the fact that Marx, in borrowing sociological models from the *Phenomenology*, also took over Hegel's terminological conflation of the sociological and metaphysical senses of estrangement and alienation, but gave them a Feuerbachian basis. The result was a synthesis in which the language and form of Marx's arguments were largely Hegelian, while their metaphysical content derived from Feuerbach. The factual material on which this critical apparatus was exercised was mainly drawn from Hegel's political theory and the classical economists.

In 1845, Marx discarded Feuerbach's philosophical anthropology in favour of a more scientific and historical approach. By dissolving 'human essence' into the social factors that determine the various historical forms of individuality, 'Man' was turned into a mere abstract universal of no explanatory value. But the Feuerbachian idea that reality for man is essentially a human reality, peculiar and relative to his species-character, survived in the recognition that men experience their environment and activity as directly meaningful, because of the high development of human symbolic communication. Through their social relations, men structure their reality in terms of shared meanings. They reproduce this social structure along with the reproduction of society's demographic and economic material substance, as part of the meaning of that substance. As men personify to each other abstract meanings present in social structure, reified concepts can become powerful social agents, both sacred and profane. This phenomenon allowed Marx to adapt Hegel's dialectical logic to social analysis.

By the time he forsook philosophical anthropology, Marx had already developed Feuerbach's conceptions of man and society in various ways. These developments were expanded in the *Paris Manuscripts* into a mythical history of *homo faber's* self-creation, the coming-to-be of genuinely productive and social man. Necessarily beginning from a primitive poverty and isolation and therefore in the egoistic form of private property, man had nevertheless elaborated the full compass of his latent powers in the worldwide economic community of the division of labour. Yet all had been accomplished as a sacrifice and burden, production and reproduction of a reality alienated from the producing individual. The wealth of civilisation could be appropriated only at a cost and at others' expense, if at all, instead of being enjoyed as an affirmation of man's collective efficacy and solidarity. By the final reduction of the mass of mankind to the condition of abstract labour, this historical estrangement had approached its extreme point: revolutionary annulment of private property would usher in the phases of man's return to the fullness of his potential species-life. Communism is thus 'the solution to the riddle of history and knows itself to be this solution.'[75] By the time he abandoned this teleology Marx had consolidated a number of important and original insights, advances on Feuerbach and his other contemporaries, which re-emerged as guiding assumptions for a scientific approach.

Methodologically, Marx developed Feuerbach's critical approach in extending it, by analogy, from religion to politics, and eventually to economics. In the process, he made important distinctions and innovations. He separated out the criticism of speculative or ideological theories from the critique of institutionalised beliefs. Just as the reified abstractions of theology or metaphysics could be interpreted as mystifying references to social life, so the 'higher' levels of social life itself could be interpreted as referring obliquely to 'lower' levels which, partly in consequence, lacked definition in social consciousness. In this way social structure could be seen to perform cognitive functions in social action despite its cognitive deficiencies. Thus private property was analysed as the mode of social appearance and social cognition of alienated labour, and therefore the level from which political economy generalised about economic processes. By embarking on a simultaneous critique of political economy and the capitalist system, Marx tried to show how the limited assumptions of the former reflected the contradictory structural basis of the latter. This basis also determined the practical limitations and obstacles to its development, and provided opportunities for disrupting and destroying it, and pointers towards an alternative society. Although in the *Manuscripts* this critique was conducted from a metaphysical standpoint, it still involved situating economic man, as he appeared both in reality and in theory, in a broader social and historical context. And Marx retained this approach to political economy after he had abandoned the doctrine that labour was the existential manifestation of the human essence, through whose alienation man failed to recognise himself in a world of his own making.

In addition to pursuing this type of hermeneutic, Marx tried to make good Feuerbach's failure to offer causal explanations for the phenomena of religious estrangement which he described. In extending Feuerbach's mode of analysis from religion to politics and economics, Marx was seeking, with increasing deliberation, a level of social facts that would be theoretically fundamental in a causal sense. In this he was only partially successful, and his reasons for espousing economic determinism were not very convincing until the theory of social classes made its appearance in *The German Ideology*. On the other hand, he had made good use of Hegel's concept of social estrangement as a causal factor, operating at the levels of political and economic structure, and this was the principal valid residue of the inquiry. By combining this type of causal factor, together with a Hegelian emphasis on psychological functions, with the more Feuerbachian view that reified abstractions could supply the cognitive deficiencies of social structure, and could themselves become personified as social entities, Marx's early writings can be shown to contain quite a complex theory of superstructures. Though still biased towards its idealist origins by what it omitted, this remained as a permanent theoretical acquisition.

We now leave Marx the metaphysician behind and enter the company of Marx the social scientist.

Part II

Estrangement as a Sociological Concept

Part II

Interpretation of
Sociological Concept

4 Marx's Hegelian Sociology: Statics and Dynamics of Estrangement

It is usually held that the empirical content of Marx's concept of estrangement, or 'alienation', consists in *attitudes*. The concept has therefore become domiciled in social psychology. It has interested sociologists mainly as an effect of social, economic or technological causes; or has been invoked as a cause of behaviour by those who favour subjective explanations. That is not at all the position taken in this book. I wish to argue that estrangement should be treated as a sociological concept: that it refers primarily to social relationships, social facts in Durkheim's sense, and only secondarily to concomitant attitudes; that it is a genuine sociological universal, indispensable for describing the dimensions of social structure; and that Marx himself, in his later works, was using it in this way. These are large claims, involving a particular conception of sociological theory as well as an unusual interpretation of Marx. The reader can hardly be expected to accept either at first sight.

This chapter tries to substantiate the claim made in the last, that a sociological use of estrangement was already present in Marx's early writings, where it derived from Hegel. The first two sections elucidate the two main contexts where it appears in his youthful writings, and also introduce the two major models that Marx used and combined in his analysis of modern society – capitalist production and commodity circulation. The sense in which these were characterised by specific relationships of estrangement is discussed. Then, in a third section, some other historical applications of the idea in Marx's later works are presented, showing especially how he used it to explain aspects of the genesis of new socio-economic formations.

I ESTRANGEMENT IN CAPITALIST PRODUCTION

The conventional psychologistic interpretation of estrangement has been extracted from the chapter on 'Estranged Labour' in the *Manuscripts*, and especially from the first part of it. The four modalities of estrangement – from the product, the process of production, man's species-being, and other men – are seen as different expressions of a single attitude: the 'sense of estrangement' from nature, self, culture and society. This view is not without textual support. Marx does speak of how the worker 'feels', and how he 'relates to' the external world 'as an alien world inimically opposed to him'. But there are also statements that cannot be reconciled with it. For example, estrangement is identified by a number of undoubtedly objective and external features of the worker's situation – that his product does not belong to him, that it confronts him as an *independent* hostile power; that he himself is not his own master, and works only under external compulsion; that 'the worker loses realisation to the point of starving to death', etc. But, more decisively, this interpretation ignores the fact that the four modalities of estrangement constitute four steps in an *argument*, which has a conclusion; and that it is not a psychologistic conclusion. At the risk of seeming pedantic or labouring the familiar, I shall begin by rehearsing this argument, for its drift seems not to have been always fully appreciated.

Marx began 'from an economic fact of the present' – the role and economic predicament of the wage-labourer under capitalism. He 'formulated this fact in conceptual terms as estranged, alienated labour.' So the first step, claiming that 'the worker is related to the product of his labour as an alien object',[1] was little more than a way of defining the situation of the wage-labourer in a regime of private property – that he must win subsistence otherwise than by appropriating the products of his work. But it *was* a little more than this, for by 'conceptual terms' Marx meant terms amenable to analysis with the aid of the Feuerbachian model of human self-estrangement. The worker therefore became implicitly 'man as worker' or, if you prefer, 'the worker as "Man"'.

The second step was to ask how – in terms of Hegelian logic, where presuppositions are also causes – this came about? 'How could the worker come to face the product of his activity as a stranger, were it not that in the very act of production he was estranging himself from himself? The product is after all but the summary of the activity . . . In the estrangement of the object is merely summarised the estrangement, the alienation, in the activity of labour itself.'[2] Here, quite clearly, Marx was applying the model of 'spirit in self-estrangement' from Hegel's *Phenomenology*, although the worker was not treated as an embodiment of 'spirit', but as an instance of the Feuerbachian 'human essence'. Thus the condition identified in the first step was explained as the outcome of a process both temporally and logically prior.

Next, there was 'still a third aspect of estranged labour to deduce from the two already considered.'[3] The first two steps were reformulated as the worker's estrangement from nature and from himself – i.e. from the material and the labour that are the elements of production. But this combination amounts to nothing less than the estrangement of 'the species from man'. The life of the species is estranged from that of the individual, and becomes (in an abstract and estranged form) mere means to individual survival. This individualisation was precisely the condition that Feuerbach had defined as the self-estrangement of man, or man's estrangement from his essence – the situation which gave birth to man's historical failure to recognise himself in the world he had created, especially the sacred world of religion. Thus by modifying the *definiens* of the human species, and then analysing the role of the wage-labourer as an instance of human existence, Marx sought to show that private property, even more than religion, involved a fundamental estrangement of man from his essence.

But the most important step was the fourth and last. As Marx put it:

> An immediate consequence of the fact that man is estranged from the product of his labour, from his life activity, from his species-being is the estrangement of man from man.

Then he elaborated:

> In fact, the proposition that man's species nature is estranged from him means that one man is estranged from the other, as each of them is from man's essential nature.
>
> The estrangement of man, and in fact every relationship in which man stands to himself, is first realized and expressed in the relationship in which a man stands to other men.
>
> Hence within the relationship of estranged labour each man views the other in accordance with the standard and the relationship in which he finds himself as a worker.[4]

Still applying the Hegelian model with Feuerbachian content, the collective estrangement of the species from its essence was equated with a distributive and reciprocal estrangement amongst its individuals. But man's estrangement from his essence was a philosopher's concept, referring to an 'object of reason': it was not the plain man's mode of self-consciousness. Consequently – and this is the significant point – it only appeared, phenomenally, in the distributive form, in the social relationships of man to man. By this fourth step, Marx had explained the alien relationship of the worker to production (and hence to nature and to himself) as presupposing, and resulting from, a metaphysical condition whose positive and observable manifestation was mutual estrangment between men. Economic and psychological facts were 'explained' as effects of a metaphysical state that was expressed in social facts.

The pronouncedly sociological, even sociologistic, character of this conclusion resulted in part from the roundabout and metaphysical route by which it was reached. For as manifesting an *essential* relation between 'man' and the species, it had to have a form that would be objective and universal with regard to any particular individual. Hence 'each views the other in accordance with the standard and relationship in which he finds himself' —i.e. finds himself as a result of being so viewed by others. In *Capital*, Marx confirmed the importance (and the Hegelian origin) of this way of formulating the logical circularity of processes having this empirical form:

> Such expressions of relations in general, named by Hegel 'reflex categories', are of a peculiar kind. For example, here is a man who is only king because other people behave as his subjects. Yet they, for their part, believe themselves to be his subjects because he is king.[5]

This appears to be, in fact, a more elegant and accurate way of representing that peculiarity of social facts which Durkheim expressed more clumsily by the criteria of externality and constraint.

Having arrived at this point, Marx summarised:

> We took our departure from a fact of political economy—the estrangement of the worker and his production. We have formulated this fact in conceptual terms as estranged, alienated labour. We have analyzed this concept—hence analyzing merely a fact of political economy.[6]

Here Marx recognised the limitation of what he had so far done. He had taken a fact as reported by economics—a fact that appeared to be central to the economists' view of society—and had expressed it 'in conceptual terms' (i.e. metaphysically, in terms of the appropriate essence—man's) and he had analysed its logic with the aid of a philosophical model of self-estranged essence drawn from Hegel. Since this uncovered a presupposition—mutual estrangement—that the economists had ignored, then (assuming their interpretation of the initial fact to be correct) something in reality must correspond to this presupposition—something that the economists had also ignored. For knowledge of essences could yield knowledge of reality. Hence Marx's next question, moving beyond the confines of political economy:

> Let us now see, further, how the concept of estranged, alienated labour must express and present itself in real life.

And his answer:

> We must bear in mind the previous proposition that man's relationship to himself only becomes for him objective and actual through his relation to the other man. Thus, if the product of his labour, his labour objectified, is for him an alien, hostile, powerful object independent of him, then his position towards it is such that someone

else is master of this object, someone who is alien, hostile, powerful, and independent of him. If his own activity is related to him as an unfree activity, then he is related to it as an activity performed in the service, under the dominion, the coercion, and the yoke of another man.

Every self-estrangement of man, from himself and from nature, appears in the relation in which he places himself and nature to men other than and differentiated from himself. For this reason religious self-estrangement necessarily appears in the relationship of the layman to the priest . . . The relationship of the worker to labour creates the relationship of it to the capitalist (or whatever one chooses to call the master of labour).[7]

In other words, what the economists blandly ignored, or subsumed under the general idea of private property and wage-labour, were social relationships of estrangement, hostility and domination between capitalists and workers.

This led to Marx's early accounts of class oppression and exploitation in *The Communist Manifesto* and *Wage-Labour and Capital*, and thus to the fully developed model of a capitalist system in the *Grundrisse* and *Capital*. Consideration of this will be postponed until alienation as well as estrangement has been discussed. However, two significant long-run implications of the argument in the *Manuscripts* are already clear.

First, the metaphysical critique of political economy had led Marx in a roundabout way to a sociological level of inquiry. Or rather, Marx's Feuerbachian metaphysics had made Hegel's implicit sociology explicit. Class structure and class antagonism, to be defined as forms of estrangement, were seen to be preconditions of the 'movement of private property' described by economics, as well as of the psychological attitudes, needs, deprivations, etc., that this implied.

Secondly, the metaphysical ladder that had enabled Marx to 'rise above the level of political economy' could now safely be kicked away. If 'the proposition that man's species nature is estranged from him means that one man is estranged from another'; if 'man's relationship to himself only becomes objective and actual for him through his relation to the other man'; and if 'every self-estrangement of man, from himself and from nature, appears in the relation in which he places himself and nature to men other than and differentiated from himself' – then the concepts of a human essence and of man's metaphysical estrangement from a metaphysical species nature have become redundant. As Marx was shortly to proclaim, 'In its reality [the human essence] is the *ensemble* of the social relations'; and – we may add – sociology is its study. The logic of meanings present in social life could be analysed directly, and not by reference to their 'essence'.

2 ESTRANGEMENT IN THE CIRCULATION OF COMMODITIES

The analysis of 'Estranged Labour' appears to have been a deeper elaboration of a paragraph in the notes which Marx wrote early in 1844, while excerpting James Mill's *Elements of Political Economy*.[8] Admittedly, there seems little likelihood that the chronological relationship of the notes on Mill and the *Manuscripts* can be settled beyond doubt. But if the former do not antedate the latter – as seems most probable, from internal evidence – they certainly precede it logically. Dealing as they do with exchange, money and commodity production, the notes bear the same relation to 'Estranged Labour', which deals with wage-labour and capital, as the first chapter of the *Grundrisse* bears to the second, or the first two parts of *Capital* to the next four. In each case, the second presupposes the first, but also carries the analysis to a deeper level of causation. In fact, these two texts can be read as successive stages in Marx's analysis of civil society as the sphere of man's economic self-estrangement. Phase 3 in Figure 1 (on p. 72) telescopes these two sub-phases in the early writings, which correspond to the two levels of analysis in the later works. They are separated out in Figure 3, as phases 3A and 3B.

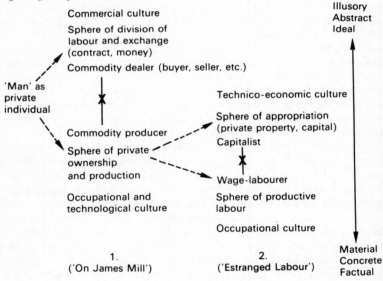

Figure 3 The Two Phases of the Analysis of 'Human Self-Estrangement' in Economic Life
(symbols as in Figure 1)

The notes expose the social estrangement endemic in market relationships, just as 'Estranged Labour' exposed antagonism and domi-

nation between capitalist and worker as the suppressed presupposition of
the economists' treatment of wages and profit. The latter dealt with an
estrangement specific to the sphere of production, the former with the
estrangement specific to the sphere of circulation. Since circulation
includes the labour market, the antagonism of worker and capitalist in
production itself presupposes and is added to their initial mutual
estrangement as sellers and buyers of labour-power as a commodity. Thus
workers are also mutually estranged, as sellers of their labour-power in a
competitive market, although jointly subject, as employees, to the
estrangement and domination prevailing in the sphere of production. And
capitalists, though they too have in common their antagonistic domination
of their employees, are also mutually estranged as competitive sellers of
their employees' products. However, in his analyses of the sphere of
circulation, in the notes on Mill and in the initial sections of his later works,
Marx assumed that the differentiation and estrangement of capital and
labour (in production) did not exist. He used a model of simple commodity
production, to which capital and wage-labour were added at a later stage.
The owner of a product for sale in the market was therefore assumed to be
its producer, so that the 'individual' who figures as the unit of private
ownership in these passages is the *representative* of a productive unit that
might be either a one-man outfit or a capitalist enterprise.

A great many of Marx's early economic ideas came from Engels'
pioneering article 'A Critique of Political Economy', and here, couched in
somewhat moralistic language, appeared the first Young Hegelian sketch
of the estrangement of the marketplace:

> The immediate consequence of private property is *trade* – exchange of
> reciprocal demand – buying and selling. This trade, like every activity,
> must under the dominion of private property become a direct source of
> gain for the trader, i.e. each must seek to sell as dear as possible and buy
> as cheap as possible. In every purchase and sale, therefore, two men
> with diametrically opposed interests confront each other. The con-
> frontation is decidedly antagonistic, for each knows the intentions of the
> other – knows that they are opposed to his own. Therefore, the first
> consequence is mutual mistrust, on the one hand, and the justification of
> this mistrust – the application of immoral means to attain an immoral
> end – on the other. Thus, the first maxim in trade is 'discretion' – the
> concealment of everything which might reduce the value of the article
> in question. The result is that in trade it is permitted to take the utmost
> advantage of the ignorance or the trust of the opposing party, and
> likewise to bestow qualities on one's commodity which it does not
> possess. In a word, trade is legalized fraud.[9]

This was probably in Marx's mind when he interrupted his notes on Mill to
launch a denunciatory analysis of the credit system. Here again were

echoes of Hegel's discussion of wealth in the *Phenomenology*, and an attack on the Saint-Simonian policy of nationalised credit as an economic regulator. But also, Engels' moral paradoxes were sharpened up. Not just the permitted conduct, but the actual *morality* of the marketplace, was seen as symptom and systematisation of human self-estrangement:

> Credit is the economic judgement on the morality of a man . . . Here there is still plain in all its clarity the mistrust that is the basis of economic trust, the mistrustful consideration of whether to give credit or not, the spying into the secrets of private life, etc., of the person seeking credit; the betrayal of temporary difficulties in order to ruin a rival through the sudden shaking of his credit. The whole system of bankruptcy, ghost companies, etc. . . .[10]

Not content with this superficial criticism, Marx then plunged into a Feuerbachian-Hegelian analysis of the assumptions underlying the entire market system.

> Economics, as does the actual process, starts from the relationship of man to man as that of private property owner to private property owner. If man as private property owner is presupposed, i.e. man as an exclusive possessor who maintains his personality and distinguishes himself from other men by means of this exclusive possession (private property is his personal, *distinctive* and thus essential being), then the loss or surrender of private property is an alienation of man and of private property itself.[11]

Just as wage-labour was submitted to conceptual analysis as the self-estrangement of 'man as worker', so here commodity exchange was analysed as the self-alienation of 'man as private proprietor.' From this, Marx derived exchange-value, as the alienated form of private property itself, and also the fact that what appears under the form of exchange-value, in commodities, is their use-value. This is the alienation of man implicit in the alienation of private property. For just as in market relationships the real needs and capacities of men appear only behind their roles (or masks) as private owners, so the character of commodities as products of human capacities, with the power to satisfy human needs, is concealed beneath their pecuniary mode of existence.

We shall not follow this argument, but simply note the character of the social assumption said to underlie private property. It was a formula reminiscent of Fichte and Hegel, and Marx reproduced it in several forms in the *Grundrisse*. The basic idea was the model of a society where the social identity of units (individuals) consisted solely in their mutual exclusion and differentiation, and where this is established and secured solely by their command over different and distinctive objects. Here, 'the situation is

such, that man as an isolated person has relation only to himself, [and] the
means of establishing himself as an isolated individual have become what
gives him his general social character.'[12] Individuals regard one another as
merely anonymous and indeterminate others, bound by no affection,
personal recognition or moral ties. But in so far as their respective interests
in what defines their individuality cause them to interact, they are
compelled to recognise one another, either as a potential threat or a
potential obstacle to self-fulfilment. The market is not the only application
for such a model, and we shall see later on that Marx used it in another
context as well. To arrive at a market model, it was necessary to add a
second assumption: all-round division of labour, and hence all-round
interdependence through the medium of products. The result is that 'The
mutual and universal dependence of individuals who remain indifferent to
one another constitutes the social network that binds them together.'[13]
And in *Capital* Marx claimed that this approximated to situations where
'private individuals or groups of individuals . . . carry on their work
independently of eath other . . . and do not come into social contact with
each other until they exchange their products'[14] – in practice, seldom then
either.

In the notes on Mill, Marx argued that interdependence between units
who define their identity by mutual negation must eventuate in all-round
antagonism. Each produces not to meet the known needs of determinate
others, but as a means of obtaining the satisfaction of his own needs at the
expense of any other.

> Exchange can only set in motion and activate the attitude that each of
> us has to his own product and thus to the product of another. Each of us
> sees in his own product only his own selfish needs objectified, and thus in
> the product of another he only sees the objectification of another selfish
> need independent and alien to him.

Mutual needs are therefore only a source of reciprocal power in the conflict
of interests:

> An intention to plunder and deceive is necessarily in the background,
> for since our exchange is a selfish one both on your side and on mine and
> since each selfishness tries to overcome the other person's, of necessity
> we try to deceive each other. Of course, the measure of the power that I
> gain for my object over yours needs your recognition in order to become
> a real power. But our mutual recognition of the mutual power of our
> objects is a battle in which he conquers who has more energy, strength,
> insight and dexterity. If I have enough physical strength, I plunder you
> directly. If the kingdom of physical strength no longer holds sway, then
> we seek to deceive each other and the more dextrous beats the less. Who
> defeats whom is an accident as far as the totality of the relationship is

concerned. The ideal intended victory is with both sides, i.e. each has, in his own judgment, defeated the other.[15]

Having begun with a model borrowed from Hegel's 'soulless community', Marx now developed it along the lines of the 'dialectic of master and slave'. Only, unlike Hegel, Marx concluded the struggle for recognition with the enslavement not of one party but of both. Each became the slave of his own product by turning his activity into the means of obtaining objects that enslave him to his desires. 'If this mutual enslavement to an object also appears, at the beginning of the process, as an actual relationship of lordship and bondage, that is only the crude and open expression of our true relationship.'[16]

Thus, far from the growth of private property and culture eventually dissolving primitive slavery into personal freedom, as Hegel held, Marx argued that 'they are rather the dissolution of these [primitive] relations into a general form; they are merely the elaboration and emergence of the general *foundation* of the relations of personal dependence.'[17] Personal subjection through slavery and serfdom, in the past, Marx implied, was not the result of a struggle for recognition between pure egos. Rather, in violent struggles over land and resources, men could recognise one another only as negatively related through the objects of their contention, so that the vanquished were appropriated by the victors along with other material spoils of conquest. Pecuniary competition among private owners of means of production was merely a 'peaceful' and universalised form of the same phenomenon. In so far as there was a permanent winner, it was no longer this or that victorious tribe or nation, but the impersonal worldwide force of capital itself and the class of its representatives, the bourgeoisie. Implicit in this use of Hegelian models to elucidate contemporary society was a criticism of Hegel: that his models were originally themselves abstractions from bourgeois society that had been projected into the past to yield a philosophical interpretation of history as a preparation for the present.

Thus Marx's economic manuscripts of 1844 applied and developed Hegel's sociological concept of estrangement. By the end of the chapter on 'Estranged Labour' it had been explicitly distinguished from metaphysical estrangement, and the latter had become fairly obviously redundant. With its aid, Marx elucidated two social relationships underlying the categories of private law and political economy. First, there was the estrangement that found legal expression in private property and structured the economic processes of production and circulation of commodities. Secondly, there was a more markedly hostile and antagonistic estrangement concealed beneath the form of the wage contract and the economic facts of capital accumulation and profit. The first was not necessarily accompanied by any specific distribution of power amongst the competing parties except in the labour market, where it was one-sided. In capitalist production itself, this one-sided power relation was even more marked.

Both these estrangements were institutionalised. That is to say, whatever the initial situations of estrangement that allowed markets or capitalist production to arise and spread, once installed they tended to reproduce their characteristic patterns of self-other orientation. Market norms of neutrality, impersonality, etc. reinforced the tendency of the circulation process itself (its anonymity, etc.) towards mutual estrangement; in industry, the generally aggressive authoritarianism of entrepreneurs and the resistant compliance of workers reinforced the objective tendency of the production process—which Marx was later to analyse in detail—to evoke conflict on a broadening and intensified scale.

These models of market circulation and capitalist production are specific applications of much broader and more general sociological models. These may be called, respectively, models of 'horizontal' and 'vertical' estrangement. The first consists simply of similar, juxtaposed social units between which estrangement prevails. The units may be either distinct social systems, such as neighbouring tribes or nations, or segments of a single social system, such as families, lineages, villages, productive units of any kind, or even branches of a single dispersed organisation. The second can only occur within a single social system, and refers to its character as a stratified system. Once again, the estranged strata may be of any type—castes, status-groups, classes, élites and masses, or levels in a hierarchical organisation. Segmentation and stratification are, without doubt, the two major types of division in social systems, and estrangement, it is suggested, is the general medium by which social division is created and maintained. Looked at from the opposite point of view, the addition and replication of segments and the imposition or deposition of new strata are the principal processes by which social systems expand and complexify: hence the incorporation of horizontal and vertical estrangements into a system requires a simultaneous development of integrating factors. The latter cannot be discussed here, but the concept and varieties of estrangement are examined more closely in Chapter 5; in the final section of the present chapter some examples of how Marx used this idea in precapitalist contexts are briefly presented.

3 ESTRANGEMENT IN PRE-CAPITALIST SOCIETY

In his later works, Marx used the concept of estrangement in three pre-capitalist contexts. All three were concerned with showing how estrangement could have been present as a structural precondition permitting the genesis of economic formations which required and institutionalised some mode of estrangement in their production and circulation processes. I shall look briefly at the role of estrangement in Marx's account of the origins of commodity production, of slavery and serfdom through conquest, and of feudal and capitalist class relations through migration.

We have seen that Marx analysed market society (as I shall, for short, call the abstract model of a social system presupposed in the analysis of the circulation of commodities) as a system in which highly developed occupational specialisation, hence general interdependence of all producers and consumers, was combined with general estrangement as the dominant social relationship. This mutual estrangement is (to use a formula frequent in Marx and distinctive of his approach) both prerequisite and result of the process of circulation of commodities. Once exchange, division of labour and private property become institutionalised in society, this mutual estrangement is self-reproducing, merely becoming the more ingrained as long as the productive processes which are its bearers remain sufficiently unchanged. However, for commodity exchange with its concomitant forms of production and property to establish itself in the first place, it was necessary that the situation of mutual estrangement should have been in some way structurally given, as historical starting-point. And as we have seen Marx frequently emphasised, it was never historically given as a 'natural' relationship between individuals. On the contrary, 'man is only individualized through the process of history'[18] and 'Exchange itself is a major agent of this individualization. The further back we go into history, the more the individual and, therefore, the producing individual seems to depend on and belong to a larger whole.'[19]

Marx conceptualised this original collective personality, and the various types of modified tribal society that issued from it, in his model of the primitive community. It is a corollary of this model that the external situation of primitive communities is precisely one of mutual estrangement. Intensely solidary within, they constitute collective subjects regarding each other as aliens. Juxtaposed·communities thus compose a pattern of horizontal estrangement. In so far as their surplus products differ and are useful to one another, they also potentially constitute a social system in which the identity of the units, for one another, would consist in their mutual differentiation and exclusion, established by their command over distinctive, valued objects. Here, consequently, is a formal analogue of the mutual estrangement of individuals in market society, which can also be hypothesised as a historical starting-point for commodity exchange. As Simmel put it, 'the stranger everywhere appears as the trader, and the trader as the stranger.'[20]

Marx recognised the analogy, and the implied possibility of barter and trade originating in this way:

Objects in and by themselves exist apart from man, and are therefore alienable by him. If this alienation of objects is to be reciprocal, all that is requisite is that human beings shall tacitly confront one another as the individual owners of such alienable commodities, and shall thus confront one another as mutually independent persons. But no such relation of mutual independence exists for the members of a primitive

community . . . Commodity exchange begins where community life
ends; begins at the point of contact between a community and an alien
community, or between the members of two different communities. But
as soon as products have become commodities in the external relations of
a community, they also become, by repercussion, commodities in the
internal life of the community.

And also,

Nomadic peoples are the first to develop the money form, because all
their possessions are of a moveable kind, and are therefore directly
alienable; and because their mode of life is continually bringing them
into contact with alien communities – a contact which invites the
exchange of products.[21]

In this way, and depending also on the resilience of the structural type of
community concerned and other factors, 'the continual repetition of
exchange, makes of exchange a habitual social process'. Alongside
traditional production for use grows up regular production for exchange.
Eventually, with the advent of capitalism, both the internal solidarity of
the different communities and the mutual estrangement between them are
(economically if not politically) dissolved in the pervasive mutual
estrangement of market society. Individuals, instead of communities – or
at least the individual representatives, as private proprietors, of households, farms, firms and other productive units – now compose an open-
ended network of neutral reciprocations.

The mutual estrangement of individuals in market society involves
latent hostility, and the same is true of primitive communities. And so it
remains, theoretically, an open question whether trade or warfare
develops as the more normal mode of interaction between them. A wide
range of further conditions clearly enters at this point. Exchange cannot
occur unless there is surplus production and a corresponding need on both
sides (differences of geographical environment are obviously of importance
here.) Marx – like Max Weber, who also stated that 'the oldest commerce
is an exchange relation between alien tribes' and that everywhere the
'alien trader' precedes the 'resident trader' – emphasised the close connection between war and trade among peoples specialising in piracy, slave-
raiding, etc.[22] Mandel provides further illustration of the argument,
showing incidentally how the institution of 'silent barter' allows the latent
hostility of alien tribes to be circumvented.[23] Thus Marx's model of
mutually estranged communities allows two outcomes; both are of
historical importance, for war can lead to conquest and the foundation of
new, antagonistic types of community on the basis of stable domination.

Marx advanced the theory that, just as trade between communities
might give rise to commodity production within them, so warfare between

them might lead to their transformation into a system based on slavery or serfdom.

> The only barrier which the community can encounter in its relations to the natural conditions of production *as its own* – to the land – is some *other community*, which has already laid claim to them as its inorganic body. War is therefore one of the earliest tasks of every primitive community of this kind, both for the defense of property and for its acquisition . . . Where man himself is captured as an organic accessory of the land and together with it, he is captured as one of the conditions of production, and this is the origin of slavery and serfdom . . . The fundamental condition of property based on tribalism is to be a member of the tribe. Consequently a tribe conquered and subjugated by another becomes *propertyless* and part of the inorganic conditions of the conquering tribe's reproduction, which that community regards as its own. Slavery and serfdom are therefore simply further developments of property based on tribalism. They necessarily modify all its forms.[24]

Trade and warfare thus lead in contrary directions – but not quite in the way advertised by nineteenth-century liberals, towards peacefulness or violence, industrialism or militarism. Marx was rightly sceptical of this view, and well aware of the bellicosity of capitalism. The bifurcation in his model was rather that trade transformed the mutual estrangement inherent in the contact of closed communities into the predominating orientation of an open society; while warfare and domination suppressed it, but only by absorbing it as a contradiction within the structure of the resulting community. As a result of slavery or serfdom:

> . . . the simple structure is thereby determined negatively . . . they constitute a necessary ferment of the development and decay of all primitive relations of property and production. At the same time they express their limitations.[25]

A tribe deprived of its property and collective personality by conquest and subjugation is no longer an independent subject, and can strictly speaking no longer be an *alien* subject. Its former members, having lost their collective identity, lose in some measure their human identity also and are appropriated directly by the victors as 'labour-machines' or 'accessories to the land'. However, conquest seldom deprives a people of its collective personality so completely as this suggests. Consequently, rulers and subjects retain attitudes of mutual estrangement, and the formerly alien character of the two communities is usually institutionalised as some kind of status division, which may range from the semi-human status of the slave to a political independence limited only by exactions of tribute and loyalty. When Marx turned to the question of servile tenures in the context of labour rent, in the third volume of *Capital*, he recognised that the conquest of a free petty peasantry could be either more or less complete, and might leave the producers a smaller or larger amount of personal independence.[26] Thus the model of total expropriation is to be regarded as stating the limiting case. In fact, domination stemming from conquest is more likely to exhibit highly variegated patterns of exploitation and estrangement institutionalised as inequalities of power and status.

Marx also recognised that just as commodity exchange, once established, promoted its own orientations of neutrality and privacy and ceased to depend on those fortuitously provided by the contacts of alien communities, so also communities based on domination, as they achieved stability, developed their own supply of individuals who had lost their civil status, and so ceased to rely wholly on warfare and the natural increase of the servile population for their labour-force. And of course the symbiosis of these two institutional developments out of primitive mutual estrangement, in the shape of *slave-trading*, has been of the first historical importance.

In the mutual horizontal estrangement of primitive communities, therefore, Marx presented a simple but powerful theoretical model. From it could be deduced both primitive warfare, and thus the possibility and the main structural features of antagonistic socio-economic formations based on domination and vertical estrangement; and also simple exchange, and thus the possibility of developed exchange, market society and capitalism.

The third and final example I shall mention is Marx's emphasis on the role of the migrant, as a stranger, in the rise of new and exploitative relations of production. In treatments of the role of the stranger, from Simmel onwards, emphasis has been placed on his freedom from community prejudice, and migration has been viewed very much from the standpoint that *Stadtluft macht frei*. Park, in his essay on 'Human Migration and the Marginal Man' asserted that 'The effect of mobility and migration is . . . the secularization of society and the individuation of the person.' And Park cited Gilbert Murray's introduction to *The Rise of the Greek Epic* as an account of the origin of the *polis* which, while resembling that given by Marx, also stressed the estranging effects of migration following social breakdown after the Nordic invasion of the Aegean. For these fugitive settlers

> Household and family life had disappeared, and all its innumerable ties with it. A man was now not living with a wife of his own race, but with a dangerous strange woman, of alien language and alien gods, a woman whose husband or father he had perhaps murdered . . . And he lived on the beasts of strangers whom he robbed or held in servitude. He had left the graves of his fathers, the kindly ghosts of his own blood, who took food from his hand and loved him. He was surrounded by the graves of

alien dead, strange ghosts whose names he knew not, and who were beyond his power to control, whom he tried his best to placate with fear and aversion. One only concrete thing existed for him to make henceforth the centre of his allegiance, to supply the place of his old family hearth, his gods, his tribal customs and sancities. It was a circuit wall of stones, a *Polis*; the wall which he and his fellows, men of diverse tongues and worships united by a tremendous need, had built up to be the one barrier between themselves and a world of enemies.[27]

Many of the characteristics of Greek culture can be explained in such terms. Marx, who had a keener eye for the dark side of liberalising movements than for their virtues, laid more stress than these writers did on the negative aspect of the migrant's role. For the immigrant into an existing society, 'freedom' could simply mean vulnerability to exploitation. If migration could create the *polis* as a political bond between horizontally estranged family units, it could also be a source of hierarchical subordination of vertically estranged strata.

Thus besides the contribution of war and conquest to the rise of feudalism, Marx also described a more piecemeal evolution of inequality through the migratory movements of propertyless men. In the ethnological notebooks which he kept towards the end of his life, Marx interrupted his excerpting of Maine's account of ancient Irish institutions to summarise his conclusions on the growth of a dependent class, exploited by the chiefly families.

> The major part of these classes were those settled by the chief on the unappropriated tribal lands. These were *Fuidhirs*, otherwise strangers or fugitives from other territories, in fact men who had broken the original tribal bond which gave them a place in the community. It would appear from Brehon law that this was a numerous class; it speaks on several occasions of the desertion of their lands by familites or portions of families. Under certain circumstances the rupture of the tribal bond and the flight of those who break it are treated by the law as 'eventualities'. The responsibility of tribes, subtribes and families for crimes of their members, and even to some extent for their civil obligations, might be prevented by compelling or inducing a memeber of the group to withdraw from its circle; and the Book of Aicill gives the legal procedure which is to be observed in the expulsion . . . Result, probably, to fill the country with 'broken men' and these could find a home and protection by becoming *Fuidhir* tenants.[28]

He went on to point out that 'the chief had a great interest to encourage these *Fuidhir* tenants' on account of the rackrent extorted. 'The interests really injured were those of the tribe, which suffered as a body by the curtailment of the waste land available for pasture.' The process was compared by Marx with another in contemporary India, through which 'the "hereditary peasantry" of Orissa were ruined through the broken "migratory husbandmen" ', etc.

There is no doubt that Marx here detected one of the formative processes through which estrangement fostered feudal dependence. Similar changes occurred in Europe after the breakdown of the Roman empire. Much earlier in his life, Marx had used a similar model to explain the genesis of medieval towns within the settled and feudalised countryside. Under feudalism, the relation to the land was the basis of solidarity, and the major line of estrangement was the cleavage between town and country. Marx presented this division itself as largely a result of the migration of strangers from the country to the nuclear towns, where they either formed themselves into an armed bourgeoisie, somewhat as in the case of the *polis*, or were confronted by one already formed:

> The flight of the serfs into the towns went on without interruption right through the middle ages. These serfs, persecuted by their lords in the country, came separately into the towns, where they found an organized community, against which they were powerless and in which they had to subject themselves to the station assigned to them by the demand for their labour and the interest of their organized competitiors . . . The rabble of these towns were devoid of any power, composed as it was of individuals strange to one another who had entered separately, and who stood unorganized over against an organized power, armed for war, and jealously watching over them.[29]

This only delineates the most general terms of an explanatory model, containing the following variables: estrangement based on domination between lord and serf; estrangement between town and country; estrangement between occupants and immigrants; estrangement between competitors in urban markets; estrangement between classes. Marx applied this to three stages of urban growth: first, to explain the original settlement of medieval town populations at trade centres, etc; secondly, to explain the formation of the feudal urban class system of masters, journeymen and labourers; and thirdly (with the break-up of guilds through extended trade and finance, the national consolidation of the burgeoisie as a third estate in opposition to the landed nobility, and mass migration following the crisis of medieval agriculture) to explain the appearance of capital and wage-labour. In other contexts also, Marx and Engels stressed the significance of the migrant worker as a stranger at every stage in the spread of capitalist industry – the Irish in Lancashire, the Europeans in America, or transported slave and coolie labour throughout the European colonial dependencies.[30]

Marx's models of capitalist society and commodity production, together with the historical applications just discussed, indicate how Marx turned Hegel's somewhat vague sociological concept of 'estrangement' into a tool of analysis and theory construction. But he never systematically defined it or explored its implications for general sociological theory, since his interests lay elsewhere. In the next chapter an attempt is made to link it up with the mainstream tradition that has grown up since his day.

5 Estrangement and Solidarity in Sociological Theory

I have already suggested that the opposite of estrangement is best expressed by 'solidarity'. As a critical analyst of his society, Marx had much less to say about solidarity than about estrangement. There is of course the well-known passage in the *Manuscripts* pointing out that

> When communist artisans associate with one another, theory, propoganda, etc., is their first end. But at the same time, as a result of this association, they acquire a new need – the need for society – and what appears as a means becomes an end . . . whenever French socialist workers are seen together . . . Such things as smoking, drinking, eating, etc., are no longer means of contact or means that bring together. Company, association, and conversation, which again has society as its end, are enough for them; the brotherhood of man is no mere phrase with them, but a fact of life . . . [1]

This observation, which Marx certainly recorded as much for its general indicativeness about the social possibilities of the future as for its topical and organisational relevance, is also a familiar finding for students of group dynamics. Homans formulated it as follows: 'If the interactions between the members of a group are frequent in the external system, sentiments of liking will grow up between them, and these sentiments will lead in turn to further interactions, over and above the interactions of the external system.'[2] Marx incorporated this and other insights into his accounts of how working-class solidarity would develop through the evolution of capitalism and the class struggle. But rather than examine these, which raise questions about the causes of solidarity under varying conditions, I shall consider more generally the sociological significance of estrangement and solidarity, and try to justify resurrecting these hoary concepts.

I IN SEARCH OF SOCIAL SENTIMENTS

If Marx is the theorist of estrangement, Durkheim is the theorist of solidarity.³ Nevertheless, Durkheim was reluctant to venture a general definition of solidarity, which he feared would only be taken as an invitation to substitute philosophical or psychological speculation for sociological inquiry. For, as he argued:

> What remains of it divested of its social forms? What gives it its specific characteristics is the nature of the group whose unity it assures; that is why it varies according to social types. It is not the same in the family and in political societies; we are not attached to our country in the same fashion as the Roman was to his city or the German to his tribe. But since these differences are related to social causes, we can understand them only with reference to the differences that the social effects of solidarity present. If, then, we neglect the latter, all the varieties become indistinguishable and we perceive only what is common to all of them, that is, the general tendency to sociability, a tendency which is everywhere the same and is peculiar to no particular social type. But this residue is only an abstraction, for sociability in itself is nowhere found. What exists and really lives are the particular forms of solidarity, yesterday's, today's, etc. Each has its proper nature; consequently, these general remarks, in every case, give only a very incomplete explanation of a phenomenon, since they necessarily omit the concrete and the vital.
>
> The study of solidarity thus belongs to sociology. It is a social fact we can know only through the intermediary of social effects. If so many moralists and psychologists have been able to treat the question without following this procedure, it has been by circumventing the difficulty. They have eliminated from the phenomenon all that is peculiarly social in order to retain only the psychological germ whence it developed. It is certainly true that solidarity, while being a social fact of the first order, depends on the individual organism. In order to exist, it must be contained in our physical and psychic constitution. One can thus rigorously limit oneself to studying this aspect. But, in that case, one sees only the most indistinct and least special aspect. It is not even solidarity properly speaking, but rather what makes it possible.⁴

This argument is formally similar to that which made Marx chary of defining 'production' in general terms. For 'Whenever we speak of production, what is meant is always production at a definite stage of social development' and 'it is always a certain social body, a social subject, which is active in a greater or a sparser totality of branches of production'.⁵ Just as Durkheim deprecated the shallowness of psychologists who abstracted from all social specificity, so Marx satirised 'The whole profundity of those modern economists' whose demonstrations relied on forgetting the essential differences between historical or social forms of production. Marx also argued that the general definition of production could contain only what made its concrete varieties possible, not the phenomena themselves.

But in addition, Marx recognised that '*Production in. general* is an abstraction, but a rational abstraction in so far as it really brings out and fixes the common element and thus saves us repetition.'[6] And similarly, Durkheim recognised in practice that solidarity in general consists in the sentiments of attachment which bind individuals into social wholes and thereby structure social action.[7]

My purpose in focusing on estrangement and solidarity is to recover two important aspects of social life which sociological theory seems to have lost sight of. The first is emotion, especially shared emotion and more particularly the social sentiments that form a distinctive and necessary element in every social relationship. The influential Weberian emphasis on rationality, and even more the Parsonian emphasis on the means-end schema and on norms and values, have deflected attention away from this aspect of social order. In the process, Weber's own considerable stress on affect as a type of social meaning that can be communicated and shared has been neglected.

Following Toennies, Weber distinguished between 'communal' and 'associative', relationships, according to whether they were based 'on a subjective feeling of the parties, whether affectual or traditional, that they belong together' or on 'a rationally motivated adjustment of interests or a similarly motivated agreement', whether of an instrumental or an obligatory nature. While recognising that emotional bonds were more characteristic of some relationships than others ('a religious brotherhood, an erotic relationship, a relation of personal loyalty, a national com- munity, the *esprit de corps* of a military unit'), Weber also pointed out that 'the great majority of social relationships has this characteristic to some degree, while it is at the same time to some degree determined by associative factors . . . Hence in such cases as association in the same military unit, in the same school class, in the same workshop or office, there is always some tendency in this direction . . .'[8] Though Parsons, as translator, footnoted his approval of this passage and cited the Hawthorne findings as confirmation of Weber's hunch, it remained undeveloped by both Weber himself and Parsons.

The reason for neglect, in both cases, was presumably their overriding interest in macroscopic problems. Solidarity seemed to be important only in primary groups, whereas the need to explain the cohesion of larger systems arose from the 'Hobbesian problem' of a general conflict of interests in economy and polity. For lack of a concept of estrangement, which would have allowed these secondary associations to have been seen as areas in which negative social emotions prevailed, they were taken as devoid of social emotion. The Protestant ethic, for example, was interpreted as an ideology which nullified emotion in social life, rather than one which promoted a specific moralistic mode of estrangement between individuals. The tone of modern life was regarded as pre- dominantly neutral, calculative and impartial; although Simmel, for instance, perhaps thanks to the greater social sensitivity of a Jew, had already described the impersonality of the modern metropolis as depending on pervasive, latent interpersonal hostility:

> Without such aversion, we could not imagine what form modern urban life, which every day brings everybody in contact with innumerable others, might possibly take. The whole inner organization or urban interaction is based on an extremely complex hierarchy of sympathies, indifferences and aversions of both the most short-lived and the most enduring kind. And in this complex, the sphere of indifference is relatively limited. For, our psychological activity responds to almost any impression that comes from another person with a certain determinate feeling. The subconscious, fleeting, changeful nature of this feeling only *seems* to reduce it to indifference. Actually, such indifference would be as unnatural to us as the vague character of innumerable contradictory stimuli would be unbearable. We are protected against both of these typical dangers of the city by antipathy, which is the preparatory phase of concrete antagonism and which engenders the distances and aversions without which we could not lead the urban life at all.[9]

Similarly, Durkheim's idea of social integration through moral consensus and normative regulation has been allowed to eclipse almost entirely his complementary idea of integration through social sentiments of solidarity. Indeed, the latter was perhaps not just complementary but fundamental, being the point from which Durkheim started in the *Division of Labour in Society*, and the point to which he returned in *The Elementary Forms of the Religious Life*, where the sanctity of moral values was explained by the 'collective effervescence' engendered through interaction on occasions of shared activity, joy or stress. In the same way also, I would argue, Marx's rational models of market economy and class interest have been largely abstracted from the context of affective relationships in which they were embedded: the estrangement of the marketplace and the capitalist enterprise, and the solidarity of class membership. In these selective interpretations a deep-seated tendency towards intellectualistic distortion is apparent, which the most recent developments in sociological theory – structuralism, phenomenology, and other less well-marked new departures – carry even further. For despite all the differences among them, these new developments have been seen as amounting to nothing less than a 'cognitivist revolution'.[10] As a rebellion against excessive emphasis on the normative dimension of social life, this is an advance. But by retreating even further from a concern with social sentiments it diminishes the chances of rebuilding a unified theory of society. This cerebral bias is perhaps to be attributed to the ethos of academic scholarship, whose intellectualism is of course abetted by many conspicuous and well-known features of modern society.

The second aspect of social life that I hope to recover for sociological theory is its character as an interplay of opposed forces. In the history of sociology, it was the 'formal' school of Simmel and Von Wiese which made most of this. They had a clear vision of social processes as oscillating between poles of approach and withdrawal, association and dissociation, harmony and conflict. But they were unsuccessful in reducing these oppositions to a systematic theory, and their vision formed no part of the theoretical traditions that have dominated sociology for the past half-century. In Weber's work, because of its atheoretical orientation, the use of polar concepts became little more than a general methodological device, in which no particular emphasis was placed on the polarised nature of social life itself. Durkheim conceptualised the polarity of social life along the dimensions of altruism-egoism and fatalism-anomie, in *Suicide*, hypothesising that every 'social type' rested on some balance of these forces. Thus fatalistic or altruistic currents might become 'excessive' or 'pathological', relative to the type, and some degree of egoism and anomie was 'normal' and functionally requisite, ensuring a sufficient amount of individual specialisation, and adaptability of the system. Though this was an important insight, his prevailing concern with social integration and normal functions gave his approach a one-sidedness that was carried over into later structural-functional schools. To be sure, in the work of Radcliffe-Brown, Evans-Pritchard and Gluckman stabilities of social structure were construed as a balancing of opposed forces, in which divisions between solidary groups were maintained by conflict.[11] Parsonian theory, however, remote from the affective immediacy of primitive life, carried Durkheim's one-sidedness to an extreme. As Coser has pointed out, Parsons' treatment of 'boundary-maintaining mechanisms' ignores functions of external conflict that had been evident to Sumner, Sorel and many other writers.[12] Coser's own reworking of Simmel's essay on *Conflict*, though a valuable corrective, remained within a functionalist frame of reference and concentrated on problems of stability. Because of the one-sidedness of the dominant systems-theory approach, the revival of interest in Marxian theory took the form of an almost equally extreme and one-sided emphasis on its character as a theory of conflict and change. Dahrendorf's desperate notion that sociology might need to employ two radically disjoined and logically opposed bodies of theory to deal with the two equally ubiquitous and fundamental aspects of social life, integration and conflict, was symptomatic of the distorted state of macro-theory, which by the late 1950s had lost grip on the reality of social processes.[13]

Since then, theorists have become more realistic, but less and less unanimous. The structuralists' emphasis on binary oppositions, especially, has reintroduced a kind of dialectical awareness into discussions of social structure. However, structuralism regards polarity as a product of logical necessity inherent in all human thought (perhaps, even, determined by the structure of the brain) and therefore only evident in social life as a consequence of *culture*. Hence, it has no place for Durkheim's idea of the social *milieu* as a field of *sui generis* forces, nor for Simmel's conception of polar oppositions present in the form of sociation itself, independent of any cultural content. In this sense, the structuralists' reduction of social life to the opposition of culture and nature is profoundly anti-sociological.[14] To recover a fruitful sociological perspective, I would argue, we have first to recognise social emotions as comprising a distinct stratum of social meanings and an irreducible social reality; and secondly, to recognise within this reality an autonomous source of polarity in the opposition of sympathy and antipathy, positive and negative social sentiments. Given the positional and communicational features of a *social milieu* (what Durkheim often referred to as its 'substratum') and relevant inputs of cultural meaning, the flow of social emotions between persons provides the medium in which exist both the configurations of social structure and its tendencies to be rigid or labile, stable or unstable. My contention is that this reality can be conceptualised by combining the Marxian concept of estrangement with the Durkheimian concept of solidarity.

2 MORENO AND THE SOCIOEMOTIONAL MATRIX

This original component of the sociological perspective, largely banished from macro-theory, has survived better in micro-theory. Indeed, this circumstance has contributed not a little to the divorce between the two fields, from which both have suffered. As a result of it, micro-sociology has been developed more by researchers trained in psychology than by sociologists. The sociological emphasis on meaning has, in consequence, sometimes been sacrificed to behaviourism, and the autonomy of the social has been weakened in the direction of psychological reductionism. Even where an emphasis on social facts has survived, as in group dynamics, it is often recognisable mainly as a residual tendency to reify the concept of 'group'. When the study of interpersonal processes gives way to a focus on relationships between 'the individual' and 'the group', this easily collapses into a study of individual perception, cognition, motivation and other processes internal to the psyche. For these reasons it is not sufficient, in order to remedy omissions in macro-theory, simply to have recourse to the separate developments that have occurred in micro-theory. Even though much that is relevant to restoring estrangement and solidarity to their places in macro-theory is to be found in micro-theory, the divorced and antithetical evolution of the two has meant perversion on *both* sides. The attempt to bridge the gap in its immediacy can lead only to an uncritical synthesis like that of Homans' more recent work, where extreme versions of the abstract individualistic approaches that have invaded either side – behaviourism and economic rationalism – are conflated into an amalgam which has been misleadingly presented as a new standpoint for sociology.

Therefore micro-sociology too must be approached in a critical and historical spirit. To rediscover within that tradition a full appreciation of the sociological importance of social emotions we have to return to the work of J. L. Moreno, the founder of sociometry, from whom Kurt Lewin's disciples borrowed (or pirated, according to Moreno) some of the leading themes of group dynamics. In Moreno's somewhat grotesque book *Who Shall Survive?* (the idiosyncrasies of which were, so the author alleges, a deliberate precaution against fraudulent claims to authorship by others) there are indeed more than traces of the genius to which he unhesitatingly laid claim. But isolation from academic life at a period when sociology was undergoing rapid professionalisation buried most of Moreno's ideas in oblivion. Whatever may remain of his techniques of group therapy and community planning within psychiatric and social-work contexts, in social science he is now remembered for little other than the method of sociometric testing. There can be no doubt, however, that he deserves more recognition, if only as a pioneer of role theory, network analysis, and what has come to be known as the 'dramaturgic approach'.

In Moreno's words, 'The sociometric test is an instrument which examines social structures through the measurement of the attractions and repulsions which take place between the individuals within a group.' For readers who are unfamiliar with it, the test consists in asking each of a population to name one or more of the others whom they would most and least prefer as companions for various purposes – to room with, work with, etc. Standard safeguards are prescribed to maximise the spontaneity and realism of replies. The resulting choices are then usually mapped on a 'sociogram'. This is a scatter of triangles and circles representing male and female respondents, joined by lines of several kinds which denote the possible permutations of mutual or one-sided choice or rejection. Alternatively, the results can be presented in the form of a matrix, in some ways a more elegant device and one which can be manipulated algebraically to yield information. However they are analysed, various structural possibilities are present: isolates, unchosen, non-choosers, rejects, incompatible pairs, mutual rejects; pairs, chains, triangles, squares, etc. of mutual attraction; stars of attraction and repulsion. The more important findings turn on the regularity with which certain patterns occur more often than chance would dictate – especially mutuality of attraction, triangles and other clusters of mutually attractive pairs, and stars of attraction or rejection. By these means a way of discovering, describing and generalising about a certain sort of group structure is obtained. Its variations can be investigated – e.g. with sex or age, or with differing criteria of choice – and it becomes feasible to predict the behaviour of individuals from their sociometric positions, or of groups from their sociometric configurations.

Though Moreno is remembered as a technical innovator, I want to recall briefly some of the ideas that lay behind the technique. His *idée maîtresse* reveals a starting-point close to that of Simmel and Von Wiese, but also having points of contact with Feuerbach and the early Marx:

> It helped us in the beginning to think, although we had no definite proof of it, that mankind is a social and organic unity . . . If this whole of mankind is a unity, then tendencies must emerge between the different parts of this unity drawing them at one time apart and drawing them at another time together . . . These tendencies may become apparent on the surface in the relation of individuals or of groups of individuals as affinities or disaffinities, as attractions and repulsions. These attractions and repulsions must be related to an index of biological, social, and psychological facts, and this index must be detectable. These attractions and repulsions or their derivatives may have a near or distant effect not only upon the immediate participants in the relation but also upon all other parts of that unity which we call mankind. The relations which exist between the different parts may disclose an order of relationships as highly differentiated as any order found in the rest of the universe.[15]

As a rather religious-minded existentialist whose deeper affinities lay with Kierkegaard and Buber, Moreno was rootedly opposed to much of Marxism, yet he saw some merit in dialectical method. He viewed it as a necessary supplement to Mill's logic of science, for Marx 'was unconsciously following a model of experimental method more indigenous to the social sciences, a model of social actors in a world of action.'[16] Thus social reality, for Moreno – 'the historically growing, dynamic groupings of which the actual social universe consists' – was a 'dynamic synthesis and interpenetration' of two 'dialectic opposites':[17] outer, external society, on the one hand, – all visible, overt and observable groups and categories, whether formal or informal, legitimate or illegitimate – and on the other, the hidden 'socioemotional matrix' of which the sociometric test was the prime indicator.[18]

Moreno therefore sought to devise methods of revealing what might nowadays be called a 'deep structure' underlying the systems of visible social and cultural relations. This was an exploration of the social unconscious, and indeed Moreno saw himself engaged in a lifelong rivalry with his fellow-Viennese Freud. In contrast to the psychoanalyst's detachment from his patient and his concentration on the past and on individual biography, Moreno advocated participant observation and even a dialectical identity between researcher and subject. He stressed the importance of seizing the newly emerging patterns of the present moment – their 'becoming' – and the total social situation in which individuals were immersed. He was perhaps the first to make the now fashionable call for a reflexive social science. In his attempt to expose unconscious structures in social life he had something in common with modern structuralism, but differed profoundly in the significance he allowed to emotional bonds. Closer to Durkheim in this repsect, he nevertheless thought that what 'had started under the leadership of Emile Durkheim as a good road developed into a blind alley' on account of excessive holism.[19] The sociometric approach, he claimed, was 'free from preconception of the contrast between individualism and collectives or corporate bodies. It takes the attitude that beyond this contrast there is a common plane, as no individual is entirely unrelated to some other individuals and no individual is entirely absorbed by a collective.'[20] Thus Moreno appears to have held, as Marx did also, that 'individuals' and 'collectivities' are both alike relatively stable socio-cultural phenomena created, maintained and changed by networks and processes of interaction.

The 'socius', as he called this dynamic aspect of social reality, is only normally perceptible in a very fragmentary and unsystematic way, through intuition or by sharing a collective mood, and hence requires special instruments for its observation and measurement. This is because it exists '*between* individuals',[21] whose perceptions inevitably have a limited range and egocentric perspective.

The dynamic logic of social relations is particularly intricate and has remained unconscious with Man because of his maximal proximity and involvement in his own situation. For millennia, therefore, the activities of human society have been a greater mystery to him than every other part of the universe. Because of their greater distance from him he could see the movement of the stars and planets, or the life of the plants and animals more objectively. It takes enormous sacrifice and discipline to view and accept himself as he is as an individual man, the structure of the individual psyche, its psycho-dynamics; but the degree of invisibility of the structure of human society, of its sociodynamics, is much greater that that of the single individual. The effort of becoming objective toward the socius encounters many more obstacles than to be objective toward his own individual mind. The involvement of the ego he can still grasp, perhaps he can pretend to know it because it operates within him. The involvements of the socius, however, he cannot pretend to know as it operates outside of him, but it is an outside to which he is inescapably tied.[22]

To this, Moreno should perhaps have added that, if we can perceive the individual psyche more easily than the social matrix, it is because each sees himself reflected as an individual in the actions of *others*, whereas the interaction through which this occurs passes largely unrecognised by all and is therefore never clearly presented to any one through awareness of another.

Moreno developed a special vocabulary to conceptualise his hypotheses and discoveries about the socius. It has long been ousted from group dynamics by Lewin's topological terminology and has become little more than a historical curio. However, since I am embarked on the recovery of a lost tradition it is worth mentioning as illustrative of how Moreno conceived his elusive subject-matter. Claiming that human society has an atomic structure, he defined the 'social atom' as the total configuration of positive and negative relationships to others which is centred upon a given individual. Its volume expands continuously from birth, and contracts with ageing. The social atom forms the nucleus of emotionally related persons at the centre of a much larger 'acquaintance volume' centred on the same individual. The transition from this outer sphere to the social atom involves crossing social thresholds of wished and then consummated relationship. Social atoms link up and interpenetrate to form interpersonal networks, which, because of the selective character of atom-formation, are 'more or less permanent structures which bind individuals together into complex lines of transportation and communication' either within or across the boundaries of particular groups. A slightly different sort of configuration is the 'socioid' – the sociometric counterpart of the external structure of a social group, and related to it somewhat as the social atom is to the individual.

The radiating aura of choices and rejections which indicates the existence of a social atom involves processes of attraction and repulsion, of which atoms and networks are composed. To designate the generic character of these processes, Moreno coined the term *tele* to emphasise that social emotions could flow across physical distance. The barrier imposed by individualistic and physicalist views against conceiving emotions as 'leaving' the organism where they originate, and as residing outside it, was lifted, Moreno argued, once it was found experimentally that social atoms and networks existed as persistent extra-individual structures. Interpersonal and especially mutual feeling no longer has to be conceptualised psychologistically as 'empathy', 'transference', 'projection', etc., for it could be treated as flowing through the structures of the socius, which it also determines. *Tele* is 'a sociological phenomenon', for it refers to the reciprocating aspect of emotional relationships. The best definition probably relates to its experimental function: it is the factor responsible 'for the increased mutuality of choices surpassing chance'.[23]

The relationship between *tele* and attraction and repulsion is not entirely clear. On the one hand, 'When we say *attraction*, we indicate that a certain emotion spreads through a certain geographical area in respect to a certain criterion to *join* with a certain individual.'[24] *Repulsion* indicates the same, with respect to *separation*. This suggests that the *tele* factor is a property of these flows. Moreno also says that 'Attractions and repulsions are not emotions, they are their *end* products' – of '*all* emotions that bind or separate people, like love and hate, pity and compasion, jealousy and envy . . .' (etc.)[25] Thus *tele* seems to be a composite concept. On the one hand, it is just a general and neutral way of conceptualising attraction—repulsion phenomena, and in this sense resembles Lewin's term *valence*. Thus 'any object has positive valence for any other object to the degree that there are forces acting upon the latter that impel it (either physically or psychologically) toward the former.'[26]—and the reverse for negative valence. But on the other hand, it also contains a double hypothesis. First, that the bonding and separating force in social life is social emotion; and secondly, that there exists some extra force or factor in the interpersonal *milieu*, somewhat analogous to magnetism, which regularly imposes certain patterns on the confused and heterogeneous manifold of social emotions. Activated by social interaction, this factor reduces and converts the potentiality of polarisation between positive and negative values—which is merely inherent in these emotions—into a single, relatively coherent and more or less strongly polarised field of interpersonal attraction and repulsion. Partly, this factor would seem to operate through the mutual suggestibility of social emotions. Thus Simmel also spoke of 'the easy reciprocal stimulation of hostility', pointing out that within a group 'which feuds with another, all kinds of latent or half-forgotten hostilities of its members against those of the other group come to the fore.'[27] Though *tele* requires certain psychological assumptions, it does not contain any directly psychological hypothesis. Moreno himself stressed that '*Tele* is an abstraction . . . It has to be comprehended as a process within a social atom.'[28]

Before leaving Moreno's ideas, there are two misconceptions that need to be averted. Both have arisen from the ways in which sociometry has been incorporated into group dynamics and social psychology. The first concerns the intended scope of the concepts of attraction and repulsion. Moreno's comment in 1953, that 'The misunderstanding that attraction and rejection as defined by sociometrists is exclusively "private" or "emotional" or "liking" and "disliking" has not been entirely dispelled', remains true.[29] Social psychologists studying interpersonal attraction have tended to treat sociometry as a special technique for eliciting one particular, 'informal' kind of bond—that of friendship, personal admiration, etc.—and for measuring attributes like popularity.[30] Sociometrists themselves have mainly employed the method in this way, using very diffuse criteria of choice, and upon groups that were already strongly defined by external, specific criteria—inmates of corrective, educational and military establishments especially. But whatever the limitations of the method, in practice or in principle, Moreno intended it to allow the application of any criterion. He theorised that a pattern of emotional bonds (including indifference) would be found between persons linked by any criterion present in their frame of interaction and joint activity.[31]

Moreno tried, not altogether successfully, to allow for the differentiation of choices according to varying cultural criteria by introducing the notion of a 'cultural atom', a term corresponding to Merton's 'status-set'.

Analogously to 'social atom', this designated the 'focal pattern of role-relationships around an individual'. Since Moreno defined 'role' very widely, to include even 'psychosomatic roles' such as 'walker', 'sleeper', etc.; and since all socioemotional currents within the social atom are related to some such culturally defined traits, it followed that 'The socio-atomic organization of a group cannot be separated from its cultural-atomic organization. The social and cultural atom are manifestations of the *same* social reality'.[32] In much the same strain, he claimed that *tele* had a cognitive as well as conative aspect.

The weakness of this formulation is apparent when we place two of Moreno's statements side by side: 'The tangible aspects of what is known as "ego" or "self" are the roles in which he operates' and 'The use of the word "atom" here can be justified if we consider a cultural atom as the smallest functional unit within a cultural pattern.' The first indicates that the ego or self and the cultural atom are virtually identical; but it is by no means obvious that the various forms of individuality are the smallest functional units in cultural patterns. An excellent counter-example is Marx's analysis of the commodity form as the 'economic cell-form'[33] of bourgeois society, logically prior to the corresponding type of bourgeois individuality or its component roles. Another is Lévi-Strauss's analysis of the basic kinship unit consisting of brother, sister, sister's husband and son – the core of a role-set.[34] Nadel's theory is representative of the various attempts to treat 'role' itself as the atom of that part of culture which is articulated as social structure.[35] In short, while the social atom is inevitably centred on concrete individuals as source and reciprocating objects of emotional particularity, 'cultural atoms' are logically elementary units of the institutionalised conceptual patterns, linguistic and other, that impart some degree of universality to social action. These same patterns produce generalised models of individuality or selfhood, varying from one culture to another, but these are unlikely to be their elementary particles. Thus in exploring the deep structures that lie beneath the surface of ongoing social life, a clear distinction should always be made between socioemotional structures, which are logically tied to some particular substratum of spatio-temporally located psychic centres, and cultural structures, which are purely conceptual in nature and have only a contingent connection with the collective consciousness through which they become operative. If Lévi-Strauss is the theorist *par excellence* of the latter, Moreno is the most penetrating theorist of the former. Both are unreliable guides outside their chosen terrain.

The second misunderstanding is related to the first, and also derives from the research contexts in which sociometry has been applied. It is the view that the socioemotional matrix which the test measures is only a phenomenon of small groups, small numbers, and face-to-face interaction. We have already seen that network analysis transcends these limits, and Moreno went to the length of claiming that all 'social systems are attraction-repulsion-neutrality systems.'[36] He hoped that with 'the devising of new sociometric techniques . . . the more subtle and more mature processes – the economic milieu, the religious milieu, the cultural milieu, which operate within social aggregates – will be made increasingly comprehensible', for 'the interweaving of emotional, social, or cultural factors eventually takes the form of attraction, rejection or indifference on the surface of human contact.'[37] He advanced speculative descriptions of some of the sociometric features of German and American society as entire systems, and recognised the probable existence of 'large sociodynamic categories which are frequently mobilized in political and revolutionary activities; they consist of the interpenetration of numerous socioids and represent the sociometric counterpart of "social class" as bourgeoisie or proletariat; they can be defined as sociometric structure of social class or as "classoids" '.[38] Similarly, though in many contexts the social atom is numerically small, 'For a powerful individual attractive and attracted to thousands of individuals the number of participants forming an immediate network of emotions may be thousands, but the pattern of relationships is still also in this case the smallest imaginable under the circumstances.'[39]

Thus, in principle, Moreno's concepts apply equally well to factors affecting the division and cohesion of large aggregates and macroscopic social systems, resembling Durkheim's 'solidarity' and Marx's 'estrangement'. However, as we begin to return from micro-levels to macro-levels a contrast between the two approaches also becomes apparent. Moreno's concentration on the moment-by-moment resuscitation of society through interaction caused him to neglect one side of the two-way dynamic interrelationship that he postulated between the visible system and its socioemotional structure. For he ignored the fact that social emotions can become institutionalised and collectivised, part of the culturally prescribed response to others in standard situations. Thus, while it remains true that the socioemotional structure underlying a social class, for example, must relate to an aggregate of particular individuals, and exists only through the social emotions they exchange in class situations, it is also legitimate to refer to an abstract type of 'class solidarity' of 'class antagonism', etc. This is not just because as scientists we can generalise from a number of similar 'classoids', but also because class members themselves learn to exchange 'appropriate' and 'typical' emotions, or signs of emotion, in recurrent types of encounter. Thus to bring macro-sociology and micro-sociology closer together through the recognition and exploration of socioemotional structures involves admitting a major dimension of variation as between prescribed and spontaneous valence or *tele*. (Moreno's fetishism of spontaneity, which would have made him resistant to such an admission, derived from his religious and philosophical ideology and chimed with a number of tendencies in American inter-war liberalism glorifying the primary group.) Such a dimension was recognised by Weber, for example, and used for a similar purpose in his sociology of authority. For between the disciplined neutrality of the bureaucrat, acting *sine ira ac studio*, and the spontaneous charismatic enthusiasm of a band of disciples, lies a hidden hypothesis about the different socioemotional bases of social cohesion in large and small groups.

It seems reasonable to conclude this section by asserting continuity between Moreno's concepts and those of Durkheim and Marx. There would seem to be no difficulty about defining solidarity and estrangement in terms of attraction and repulsion – which is also consistent with Hegel's view of estrangement as the human analogue to forces of repulsion in nature. If we drop certain limitations due to sociometric measurement being in terms of preferential ratings, a number of theoretical assumptions might be made at this point. Attraction and repulsion may be conceived as distinct socioemotional interpersonal forces, varying inversely on any given criterion, whose intensities are in principle measurable on an absolute scale. They should be thought of as normally in a process of flux and change, either slow or rapid. Every relationship in a social milieu, no matter how indefinite its boundaries or mutually anonymous its inhabitants, could in principle be assigned a position and value in a field of forces of attraction and repulsion. Since attraction and repulsion exist as a complex interpersonal resultant of social emotions, which are always evoked by some definite criterion or attribute of the other, and since most relationships involve numerous attributes on both sides, ambivalence is normal and pure types of attraction and repulsion are mere conceptual idealisations. Relationships in which mutual attraction predominates we may call solidary, while estrangement refers to those where mutual repulsion predominates. Something akin to the *tele* factor appears to operate, favouring the emergence of matched orientations. It is in line with much standard theory to suppose, with Durkheim and Simmel, that the intensity of social emotion, and hence strength of attracting or repulsing forces, increases with the diffuseness and diminishes with the specificity of the complex of criteria evoking them. Indifference or neutrality may be conceived as a position of relative equipoise between the two forces, which will presumably be the less likely to occur, or harder to maintain, the greater the strengths of the forces in balance. Thus we should expect to feel most indifferent towards those about whom we need to know very little in order to interact with them – either because of institutional specialisation or the minimal nature of the interaction – and therefore that neutrality would appear more often in large, differentiated social systems. Consistent with this, the maxim 'He that is not with me is against me' is characteristic of small charismatic groups. And Lévi-Strauss, citing Susan Isaacs, has emphasised the absence of a middle point between love and hate, friendship and enmity, in the social relationships alike of children and primitive peoples, who both inhabit highly condensed social milieus and must relate to their others through correspondingly diffuse criteria.[40] These considerations all point towards the possibility of describing and analysing socioemotional 'deep structures' underlying groupings and institutional processes in society.

The justification for Marx's view of class relations as externally estranged and internally solidary emerges from this discussion clearly enough. But the estrangement of the marketplace is less obviously appropriate. Indeed, Marx allowed that a degree of consensus over the rules of competition was necessary, for it was a prerequisite of exchange that

> . . . the guardians of the commodities must enter into relation one with another as persons whose wills reside in these objects, and must behave in such a way that neither appropriates the commodity of the other, nor parts with his own, except by means of an act performed with mutual consent. They must, therefore, reciprocally recognise one another as private owners. This legal relation, which secures outward expression in a contract, is (whether legally formulated or not) a voluntary relation . . .[41]

This is what Durkheim, in his critique of Spencer, called 'contractual solidarity', and it is evident that this aspect of market behaviour involves not just adherence to rules but some minimum of mutual attraction, or maximum of mutual repulsion, within which such a consensus can take effect. What is involved here is, in fact, a typical case of ambivalence, where some mutual attraction is likely to arise out of one aspect of the role-set (interaction as fellow members of a market) and mutual repulsion out of another (relationships as competing buyers and sellers). Parties to exchange may be indifferent to one another as private persons, not unfriendly as fellow marketeers, but are antagonists in so far as each appears as the self-interested guardian of commodities desired by the other. Since acquisition of commodities is the point of their encounter, it contains, as Engels originally pointed out, an inherent tendency towards hostility. Hence, norms of neutrality and consensus over private property and other rules of the game are institutionalised ways of *neutralising*, bringing back to indifference, the potential estrangement caused by mutual withholding of what is mutually desired. Marx was probably justified therefore, in expecting the socioemotional tone of market behaviour to fall, on balance, on the side of estrangement.

3 CAUSES OF SOLIDARITY AND ESTRANGEMENT (I)

The question of what causes interpersonal attraction has received a good deal of attention from both experimentalists and theorists. Causes of repulsion have been less investigated, but are often assumed — and sometimes found — to be the obverse of the causes of attraction. If experimental research has tended to catalogue factors, theory has looked for broad and simple categories of cause to match the very general character of the effect. Without neglecting the results of the former, I shall follow the example, and the ideas, of the latter.

The simplest suggestion is probably that of the interactionist school, which Homans made the basis of the system elaborated in *The Human Group*. This states simply that 'persons who interact frequently with one another tend to like one another' — or more precisely, 'If the frequency of interaction between two or more persons increases, the degree of their liking for one another will increase, and vice versa.'[42] Although formulated as a relation between mutually dependent variables, Homans gave some causal priority to interaction. The difficulty with the hypothesis, as he admitted, was the obvious need to support it with a large *ceteris paribus* qualification. There are so many circumstances in which it seems not to hold, that its universality becomes suspect. The presence of authority, especially, tends to nullify the relationship. Homans attempted to deal with this by treating authority as a question of who initiates interaction. Thus 'when two persons interact with one another, the more frequently one of the two originates interaction for the other, the stronger will be the latter's sentiment of respect (or hostility) toward him, and the more nearly will the frequency of interaction be kept to the amount characteristic of the external system.'[43] The first hypothesis, in fact, holds only to the extent that interaction is initiated equally. However — as Homans himself says in connection with filial relationships in Tikopia (the example of authority under analysis) — 'the crucial point in establishing the attitudes we are describing is not the mere fact that the father originates interaction but that the son's response to the origination is in accordance with the father's wishes: his orders are obeyed.'[44] But why then frame a hypothesis which ignores 'the crucial point'? More generally, the attempt to abstract wholly from the content of interaction seems doomed to failure. Interaction, after all, includes all types of conflict, and it seems unrealistic to suppose that increasingly frequent conflict, equally initiated, will make persons more and more mutually attractive.[45]

Empirical research also justifies some scepticism about a purely interactionist hypothesis. Hare notes that liking 'has complex determinants, as does the amount of interactive contact. Neither is a simple function of the other.'[46] On the other hand, the effect of sheer interaction certainly cannot be ignored. Experimental evidence seems to suggest that mutual attraction promotes both frequency of interaction and equal initiation, and these in turn probably reinforce the original attraction. Similarly, numerous studies indicating that likelihood of attraction increases with spatial proximity, and decreases or turns to a likelihood of hostility with physical distance, show that interaction opportunities and frequencies are important intervening variables. So a tentative conclusion might be that frequency and reciprocity of interaction combine with other variables relating to its content or meaning, to produce attraction-repulsion effects.

The relevant area of meaning is obviously the meanings which actors have for each other in their various relationships. But any aspect whatever of a situation or activity can be construed as an attrubute of the actors involved, and it would seem to be the case that self-other orientations are largely constructed in just this way. Thus a rainy day evokes self-other orientations in which people see one another as sharing the attributes 'likely to get wet', 'sheltering', etc. and adds a new dimension of meaning to the differentiation between car-drivers and pedestrians. What is involved here is the *salience* of attributes in varying situations and relationships.[47] Sociometry has already shown that preferential ratings in the same population vary depending on the criteria of choice, and the intervening factor here is clearly variation in the attributes of others which become salient in relation to differing criteria of choice and different hypothetical situations of contact. It was this aspect of sociometric data that Moreno tried to convey with the idea that *tele* had both a conative and a cognitive dimension.

Of course, as soon as we bring in variables relating to mutual cognition we touch on a range of problems connected with perceptual accuracy. The distinction, dear to many social psychologists, between the 'phenomenal' and 'objective' levels demands to be considered. I propose to cut this knot by simply following the example of those theorists in the field who 'make the relatively simple assumption that the perceptions and expectations of an individual are likely to be veridical to his environment if he has had enough experience of the situation, if he has intelligence, and if the situation is simple enough.'[48] After all, the aim (or function) of compartmentalising our experience under selective and abstract headings such as 'rainy day' is precisely to simplify it to the point where it *can* be conceptually shared and manipulated with sufficient accuracy for everyday purposes. 'Rainy day' is a model of sorts, one of thousands that we use, having their own tacit assumptions and standards of exactitude. We know fairly well when it begins and ceases to be applicable to our situation, even though the appropriate application of other models, such as 'middle age', may typically be more problematic. By insisting that cognition is the servant of praxis, we can subordinate the problems of perceptual accuracy to the truism that social man, on the whole, adapts very successfully to his environment. That he does so, in large part, through social mechanisms of which he is unconscious is a major hypothesis of this book; but identifying these is a quite different problem from establishing the accuracy of his conscious perceptions.

The simplest explanation of mutual attraction in terms of meaning is Durkheim's hypothesis that there is a 'mechanical' type of solidarity based on *similarity*. 'Everybody knows that we like those who resemble us, those who think and feel as we do.' He was able to cite Aristotle, who in turn recalled proverbial wisdom to the same effect. Durkheim argued that

> there can be no solidarity between others and ourselves unless the image
> of others unites itself with ours . . . when the union results from the
> resemblance of two images, it consists in an agglutination. The two
> representations become solidary because, being indistinct, totally or in
> part, they become confounded with each other, and become no more
> than one, and are solidary only to the degree that they are confounded.[49]

Empirical findings are mostly consistent with this view. 'The general-
ization that "birds of a feather flock together" is supported by most of the
studies of friendship.'[50] Hare suggests that the process of attraction from
acquaintance to friendship can be represented as a funnel with a series of
filters consisting of modes of resemblance. Important filters seem· to be
proximity (those who live near each other, or are close together in school or
at work, more often become friends than those farther apart), similar
individual characteristics (widely 'confirmed' for such variables as age,
sex, intelligence and athletic ability), common interests or values
('verified' for religion, ethnicity, social class, professional ideologies, and
community of experience and interests arising out of long occupancy of
similar situations), and similar personality (spouses with similar personality traits are found to be more satisfied with each other; on other
criteria of choice there are somewhat conflicting and varied findings in
relation to personality).[51] Newcomb, classifying varieties of attraction in
terms of the rewards they offer, has proposed three main categories. The
first, 'admiration', simply involves attraction to some attribute of the other
which gives pleasure. The two others – 'reciprocation', where A is
attracted to B because he is himself attractive to B; and 'support', where A
and B have similar attitudes to some third object – both involve perceived
resemblances. Newcomb's approach is primarily psychological; however,
he found that 'The most "solid" and enduring attraction-pairs were those
in which both members perceived both reciprocation and support, though
not necessarily admiration, on the part of both'.[52] So far as solidarity is
concerned, therefore, mutual attraction through resemblance appears to
be a fairly well-established correlation. It is also consistent with the initial
description of the self-other orientations entering into solidarity and
estrangement which was ventured in the Introduction. There it was
suggested that a key variable was the familiarity or unfamiliarity of the
other, in so far as the first guaranteed that he was not hostile or dangerous,
and the second suggested that he might be.

Moreover, in so far as sheer interaction may cause solidarity it is perhaps
because interaction itself is a *shared* process, producing a stock of common
experiencè in the exclusive possession of which the parties to interaction
come to resemble each other and differ from outsiders. This is probably
sufficient to explain the familiar fact that enemies may find a bond in their

very enmity, and afterwards may unite to look back with nostalgia at the risks and passions they shared. Thus the interactionist hypothesis can be accepted as a special case of the similarity hypothesis. The apparent variability of its effects becomes a matter of its varying salience compared with that of the similitudes and differences which it mediates.

An obvious corollary of the similarity hypothesis would be its converse: that estrangement arises out of *difference*; a hypothesis that is readily suggested by the fact that 'difference' itself can mean either 'unlikeness' or 'disagreement in opinion or a quarrel arising out of it.' It is suggested also by the Hegelian dialectic, where estrangement appears as a social and historical vehicle of negativity, and negation itself covers the entire logical range fron non-identity to contradiction. It was characteristic of Durkheim's lack of interest in the negative pole of social relationships that, having cited Bain's view that there is a type of difference which repels, and characterised it as those differences which 'oppose' and 'exclude' each other, he left the matter on one side.[53] And it was characteristic of his undialectical approach that he failed to see, or develop, the implication that since resemblance between A and B entails their difference from C, the solidarity of A and B is likely to be associated with their estrangement from C. Weber, a more dialectical thinker, used the example of language to point out that 'it is by no means true that the existence of common qualities, a common situation, or common modes of behaviour imply the existence of a communal social relationship.' But he added

It is only with the emergence of a consciousness of difference from third persons who speak a different language that the fact that two persons speak the same language, and in that respect share a common situation, can lead them to a feeling of community and to modes of social organization consciously based on the sharing of a common language.[54]

We may doubt whether the salience of a difference is always the cause of a resemblance becoming salient and thus promoting solidarity, rather than the reverse. Nevertheless, Weber's comment is appropriate to everyday, taken-for-granted similarities. The important point is the correlativity of similarity and difference with in-group solidarity and hostility toward the out-group – to use Sumner's terms. Weber, like other sociologists, made much unsystematic use of this insight, but no more.

Although the assumption that similarity causes group affiliation and differences provoke hostility underlies much of Simmel's treatment of these themes, he never formalised a hypothesis to that effect. Thus he argued that historically, solidary groups based on similar location preceded those based on similar occupation. He analysed alternative bases of alliance between a mother and her son or her daughter-in-law, according to whether kinship or sex was the salient similarity. He devoted considerable attention to social organisation through age-groups, and to the 'republic of scholars' as a solidarity based on common intellectual and educational interests. The solidarity of wage-labour he saw as presupposing a peculiarly abstract type of social consciousness: 'The worker's identical relation to capital constitutes the decisive factor, i.e. wage labour is in a similar condition in the most diversified activities'. The emergence of working-class organisation thus required social developments which made this common situation more salient than local and occupational sectionalism. Of most interest in this context, however, is a passage where he appears to be relating degree of resemblance to intensity not of solidarity but of antagonism:

> Two kinds of commonness may be the basis of particularly intense antagonisms: common qualities and common membership in a larger social structure. The first case goes back simply to the fact that we are discriminating beings. A hostility must excite consciousness the more deeply and violently, the greater the parties' similarity against the background of which hostility arises . . . People who have many common features often do one another worse or 'wronger' wrongs than complete strangers do. Sometimes they do this because the larger area common to them has become a matter of course, and hence what is temporarily different, rather than what is common, determines their mutual positions. Mainly, however, they do it because there is very little that is different between them; hence even the slightest antagonism has a relative significance quite other than that between strangers, who count with all kinds of mutual differences to begin with. Hence the family conflicts over which people profoundly in agreement sometimes break up . . . The break can result from so great a similarity of characteristics, leanings and convictions that the divergence over a very insignificant point makes itself felt in its sharp contrast as something utterly unbearable.
> We confront the stranger, with whom we share neither characteristics nor broader interests, objectively; we hold our personalities in reserve; and thus a particular difference does not involve us in our totalities. On the other hand, we meet the person who is very different from us only on certain points within a particular contact, or within a coincidence of particular interests, and hence the spread of the conflict is limited to these points only.[55]

Whether Simmel was right or wrong in detail, there can be no doubt that the underlying theoretical assumption is that solidarity and hostility are related to salient similarities and differences, respectively. The amount of resemblance determines the *salience* of the differences which produce hostility, not the actual degree of antagonism.

Simmel was sensitive to the dialectical aspects of logic, but was unable to make up his mind about its relation to social facts. Generally, he drew illustrative analogies between logical and social processes, but occasionally hinted at a closer connection. But he failed to exploit the possibility that, since social interaction is structured by meaning, the logical structure of meaning may itself play, paradoxically, a causal role in social processes. Before following up the logic of similarity and difference as bases for attraction and repulsion, however, let us glance at the interactionist account of repulsion phenomena.

It was to Homans' credit, in *The Human Group*, that he emphasised that 'The greater the inward solidarity, the greater the outward hostility.' When he tried to state this generalisation in precise interactionist terms, the result was 'a decrease in the frequency of interaction between the members of a group and outsiders, accompanied by an increase in the strength of their negative sentiments towards outsiders, will increase the frequency of interaction and the strength of positive sentiments among the members of the group, and vice-versa.' And he rightly expressed this as a special case of the general hypothesis that 'the nature of the relationships between A, B, C . . . is always determined in part by the relationships between each of them and other individuals, M, N, O . . .'[56] One difficulty with this is that experimental evidence (e.g. Sherif's well-known findings) shows that increased interaction, if it is of a conflictual character, promotes intergroup hostility and thereby in-group solidarity. A second difficulty is that it introduces the concepts of 'group members' and 'outsiders', which leaves indeterminate the relationships between sentiments and interaction. For although these new terms are perhaps reducible to functions of interaction, the fact remains that they also stand for roles – the elementary roles of all social organisation – which might plausibly be said to contain the hypothesised behaviour (both sentiments and interaction) as social expectations. As such, these roles would be an unexplained yet basic variable. To explain it, it is necessary to show in more detail how such member-outsider relationships are, as is claimed, a special case of the relationships between all the individuals concerned.

But this can best be shown by attending to the *logic of the meanings* of the interaction involved. I have already suggested that inasmuch as re-semblance between A and B entails their difference from C, it is also likely that solidarity arising from the resemblance of A and B will be associated with estrangement between both of them and C. Neither in logic nor in social relationships have we any reason, as yet, to call this a joint or collective estrangement. And it is perfectly sensible to suppose that mutually attracted individuals, made aware through their resemblance of their difference from others (or vice-versa) – and thereby also repelled from others – need not for that reason exhibit any behaviour that would deserve to be called joint or group rejection of the outsiders. But we know that they often do so, exhibiting what Simmel called 'the peculiar phenomenon of social hatred.'[57] And this fact resides in the logic of their position, at least as a possibility. which circumstances tend to actualise.

For in perceiving their original similarity (let us call it their 'primary similitude') they may also see that they form a logical category of similar beings. To the extent that they do so, and ignore all the other respects in which they may differ, they are automatically provided with grounds for a new, superimposed solidarity: their resemblance as 'members' or *representatives* of the same logical category. As a resemblance derived from the logical implication of having primary similitudes, let us call this their 'secondary similitude'. The perception of primary similitudes may obviously be accompanied by the perception of primary differences, both amongst those who share a primary similitude, and amongst them and others. The secondary similitude between the former, however, has as its correlate their secondary difference from non-members of their category, or 'outsiders', likewise derived as a logical implication of primary similitude, and this provides the grounds for a new external estrangement. Let us call attractions and repulsions arising from these logically derived grounds, 'secondary solidarity' and 'secondary estrangement'. Whether they in fact appear, we hypothesise, depends on situational factors affecting the salience of these particular attributes and on whether, and how, interaction develops. We might further suppose that while situational factors will maximally determine the salience or otherwise of primary similitudes and differences, they will determine the salience of secondary attributes much less, precisely because these are logically implicit in the primary attributes. Whether they are 'brought out' as shared meanings, therefore, will depend mainly on interaction. Let us simplify, therefore, and suppose that attraction and repulsion will develop in step with the logical chain of implications, to the extent that continuing opportunities, frequencies and modes of interaction allow or compel the implications to become salient.

Thus to the extent that A, B, C . . . interact exclusively on the basis of their primary similitudes, and each interacts with M, N, O . . . exclusively on the basis of primary differences, A, B, C . . . will become mutually attracted to each other, and severally repelled from M, N, O . . . But simultaneously A, B, C . . . will develop awareness of forming a category and to the extent that this occurs, will develop secondary solidarity as its 'members' and secondary, joint estrangement from M, N, O . . . as 'outsiders'. The degree to which these processes unfold in actual human behaviour is simply what we mean by their forming a *social* collectivity. However, there are certain pitfalls in applying these ideas to real life. One is that the logical structure of social consciousness is rarely explicit in the 'official' language of role or group nomenclature, membership, etc. Thus the assumption of any social attribute, relationship, or role-name carries with it, like a logical penumbra, the implication of membership in a logical category, and hence the possibility of some degree of social concretisation of this collective existence; yet little of this can usually be gleaned from conventional typifications of people's qualities and performances. Wherever a social relationship persists for any length of time, it spontaneously acquires certain characteristics of a group. On the other hand, where membership has become formalised as social membership of a named group, other implications and sentiments tend to be present besides the simple secondary solidarity mentioned above. For example, the mere existence of the group as an entity in the social world – especially if it is a visible, face-to-face group – tends to evoke a new set of secondary similitudes, whereby the members of a logical category become simultaneously parts of a whole (as the etymology of 'members' suggests). Again, the mere fact of *social*, as opposed to logical, membership provides new similitudes arising from the particular circumstances and conditions of membership.[58]

Behind this, too, another factor may be at work. If similarity induces solidarity by psychological mechanisms like those described by Durkheim, involving easy fusion of ideas, then *identity* – similarity in all respects – would very probably induce solidarity to a significantly higher degree than a simple similarity which it includes or implies. If so, then identity as the *content* of secondary similitudes – i.e. that members resemble each other as members of the *same* category, or as parts of the *same* whole – is likely to be a more significant variable than the mere formal similitude between 'members' or 'parts' as such. Unless this were so, it might be difficult to explain why membership of the same group should promote solidarity, but membership in different groups estrangement. In other words, although the discreteness of human beings prevents their total identity, so that identity can only be mediated through resemblances, it nevertheless operates as an amplified similitude in activating solidarity, and will have higher salience than mere resemblances which it subsumes. In this direction, Durkheim's pure type of mechanical solidarity, where clone-like individuals share the greatest possible number of attributes and their life is consequently pervaded by a common consciousness, can be taken to represent the nearest to total identification to be found in a population of discrete beings. The effect attributed to identity here is no more than is contained in the commonsense idea that where people belong to one and the same group, have one and the same goal, or pursue a single common interest, it is this which evokes their solidarity rather than the fact that they resemble each other in these respects.

A group's collective rejection of outsiders as different from itself (secondary estrangement) carries with it a further logical implication of some theoretical importance. For to the extent that rejective interaction actually occurs, the group members come to share a third type of attribute. Besides their primary similitude, and secondary similitude as members of the group based upon it, they are now also similar as being *opposed* to those unlike themselves: they share their secondary estrangement from outsiders. This resemblance can itself become a further source of solidarity. Because of its importance as a reinforcer of secondary solidarity, it is worth referring to this as 'tertiary similitude' and 'tertiary solidarity' — defined as based on the negative implications of secondary similitude.

Those rejected by the group — who may have nothing hitherto saliently in common — also now have a shared attribute in their exclusion from it. If there is no interaction between them, this resemblance is unlikely to become salient for them either. As individuals, they may take the group as either a negative or a positive reference-group. In the first case they may tolerate, avoid or resist its exclusiveness; in the second, they may aspire to membership and try to acquire qualifying attributes, or else submit themselves to its power.[59] But if interaction amongst the rejects occurs, their common exclusion may give rise to solidarity, so that the first group finds itself opposed by a second, which exists and coheres solely on the basis of estrangement from the first. Logically, of course, there is no reason why persons with nothing saliently in common should have to be actually rejected by a group to find a basis for solidarity: their shared difference from some other solidary group (or individual) could be sufficient cause. But it seems much less likely that persons with nothing in common would begin to interact spontaneously *merely* on the basis of a shared difference from some third party, than that they would do so after repulsions had been generated through their severally engaging in interaction with a single excluding agent. In general, abstract relationships between men, such as similarity and difference, are always only presented and perceived through the medium of their concrete attributes and circumstances. Only theory, in seeking to generalise, reduces these to their common abstract form. Similarly, the logical implications of a situation are seldom perceived as such until they become real through socioemotional influences. The polarity of social emotions actualises affirmative and negative implications, so that men apprehend these logical relationships only by standing within them as social relationships with other men.

From this highly abstract discussion we can derive a distinction between two types of solidarity, positive and negative. The solidarity of a group is positive to the extent that it is based on resemblances which exist irrespective of the group's relation to outsiders, and it is negative to the extent that it is based on a common difference or estrangement from outsiders. In that secondary similitudes involve recognition of the group's *in*clusiveness, and tertiary similitudes recognition of its *ex*clusiveness, solidarity will be positive or negative to the degree that secondary or tertiary similitudes are salient in its interaction processes.[60] In addition, primary similitudes may themselves encourage either positive or negative solidarity. The first group discussed above (we may assume) was formed on the basis of some self-regarding attribute — a personal trait or a common taste — and therefore was positively solidary. But the second group, formed by the first group's rejects on the basis of their common repulsion from it, was negatively solidary *ab initio*. Here the tertiary solidarity of one group has provided another with a negative primary solidarity.

The idea of 'opposition' which has been introduced here raises questions not unlike those connected with 'identity'. 'Opposition' is, of course, ambiguous as between logical and social processes, and furthermore covers a range of logical relations, from 'difference' to 'contradiction'. It seems sensible to suppose, as with identity, that where the content of a difference is contrariety or contradiction, this will have higher saliency and also function like an amplified difference in evoking estrangement. Thus if two people differ in upholding contrary views, and this makes them enemies, it is at least accordant with commonsense to say that it is the contrariety of their views that estranges them rather than their difference, even though it does so only by being mediated through such a difference. This applies also to the relations of inclusion and exclusion, implied by a common identity or by being part of a whole, which has an inside and an outside and entails a negation of the form 'If A, then not B'. Inasmuch as A and B differ by virtue of A's belonging to a whole or sharing in an identity which excludes B, this is a higher order of difference than the mere distinction of qualities or performances involved, and no doubt has higher saliency as a source of estrangement. These are Durkheim's differences which 'oppose' and 'exclude'. Similar points can be made about Marx's 'contradiction'. This may refer either to contradictory definitions of social reality – e.g. the worker is a free agent selling his labour-power for a fair price; or, the worker is a captive object of exploitation like any other factor of production, and only employed as such – or it may refer to opposed interests, especially when they arise from such contradictory definitions. A sociologically very important range of phenomena – goal-oriented interaction – comes into view at this point. In so far as this is oriented to a future end-state, anticipated final identities and oppositions will be salient, rather than intermediate similarities and differences. Thus – as has frequently been argued in theory and sometimes shown experimentally – we should expect cooperation to stimulate solidarity because of a common goal, and competition to provoke estrangement to the extent that goals are mutually exclusive and the action dominated by the difference between winning and losing.[61] This is also compatible with the notion advanced in the Introduction, that the most important perceptions entering into the self-other orientations accompanying solidarity and estrangement, where the other is familiar, will be whether or not he is hostile or dangerous.

The foregoing can be summarised by distinguishing between two orders of meaning which are constitutive of social structure at a basic level. One is cognitive, and in this instance relates to the logical structure of self-other orientations in so far as they involve the two modes of similarity and difference – likeness and unlikeness, or identity and opposition. The other is socioemotional, and is the solidarity-estrangement polarity:

The second is dependent on the first, but only in conjunction with interactional and situational variables. Furthermore, it is by no means the

(i)

Similarity (likeness, identity)	Difference (unlikeness, opposition)

(ii)

Solidarity	Estrangement

case that the logical 'extremes' of identity and opposition necessarily evoke more intense solidarity or estrangement than mere likeness and unlikeness, except where the former include or imply the latter. Relative intensities, as Simmel perceived, depend on the total structure of similarities and differences in the relationship.

These two orders of meaning need to be distinguished from a third, consisting of the practices, or techniques of interaction, which usually accompany, and in a sense, express them, of which the following are some of the principal types:

(iii)

Approach, contact, association	Withdrawal, flight, avoidance
Inclusion, group formation	Exclusion, group closure
Sharing, giving	Withholding, taking
Helping, cooperation	Hindering, competition
Agreement, conciliation, forgiving	Dispute, conflict, revenge
Co-determination	Coercion

This table helps us to see how it is that interaction apparently has the effect of 'bringing out' the logical implications of self-other orientations. For operating these techniques of interaction stimulates a range of subsidiary mutual orientations, similarities and differences. Individuals (and groups) build up shared identities or become opponents in a multitude of ways, often exceedingly vague or transient, simply by finding themselves in agreement or dispute, helping or hindering one another, sharing or withholding, in the course of interaction focused on whatever cultural-situational content it is that brings them together and defines their primary similitudes and differences. All this presumably affects the overall socioemotional structure of the relationship, enhancing or inhibiting its polarisation and its likelihood of developing the whole gamut of secondary and tertiary solidarities and estrangements. Furthermore, these techniques of interaction become institutionalised as obligatory practices through which major societal functions are carried on. For this, they require – but may also create and reinforce – an appropriate socio-emotional environment. Later chapters will focus on one set of these – sharing, withholding, giving and taking – as the basic elements from which societies construct institutions of ownership and modes of alienation.

A further, final point can appropriately be made here. It was suggested above that the interactionist hypothesis – that interaction promotes solidarity – can be treated as a special case of the similarity hypothesis. It can now be seen what this would mean. If the similitude involved in the mere fact of interaction as such is more salient than similitudes or differences arising out of the particular *form*, or technique, of interaction, as exemplified in the table above, then it will have a solidarising effect. In general, though, it seems likely that the particular form of interaction would be the more salient. It can be added, also, that the hypothesis that solidarity varies with the tendency towards equality of initiating interaction appears to be a special case of the difference hypothesis. The more equally partners initiate interaction, the more they resemble each other; the less equally, the more they differ. Once again, we may suppose that corresponding solidarities and estrangements will emerge to the extent that these ratios are salient features of the social situation. But this too is only one aspect of the range of similitudes and differences involved in the particular form that interaction takes. That it is likely to become salient in situations of unequal status and authority, however, is suggested by the existence of rules forbidding inferiors to speak until spoken to, and also by the logical structure of 'command' and 'obedience'. For though a subordinate may anticipate his superior's commands, he cannot (logically) initiate obedience without a prior command, either real or imagined. Similarly, in so far as co-determination implies participatory decision-making, it involves a degree of equality in the initiation of interaction.

This section has advanced two related arguments. First, that similarity and difference, combined with interaction variables, can account for some of the familiar connections between attraction and repulsion in social life. Secondly, that the logic of similarity and difference, combined with interaction variables, is sufficient to generate the simplest features of group structure, as the foundation of social organisation, and simultaneously provides a basis for more derived relationships of solidarity and estrangement that maintain these features as factors of cohesion and division in social life. The second argument was made with the aid of a very abstract and schematic model of a process of group formation and intergroup relations, which, despite its extreme simplification, may have some utility as part of a theory of elementary social dynamics. However, the logic of similarity and difference has other facets than those mentioned so far, and the sociological relevance of these must also be considered.

4 CAUSES OF SOLIDARITY AND ESTRANGEMENT (II)

There are several problems connected with the fact that 'similarity' and 'identity' are not themselves identical. The first arises as follows. If similarity causes solidarity and difference causes estrangement, does this not imply that estrangement is the primary phenomenon in social life, or at least that all solidary relationships are simultaneously relationships of estrangement? For if A and B become aware of their resemblance, must they not have been, and remain, also aware of the differences which make them respectively A and B?

We can unpack several different problems from this question. First of all, if A and B are already groups, collective agents, then no difficulties arise. Our model already allows that estrangement from differing outsiders is a logical and likely empirical consequence of their internal solidarity. Should the two groups themselves become solidary, this may or may not go to the length of a total merger in which their separate identities are lost in that of the new group.

But is there a problem if A and B are individuals? This question requires us to look more closely at the nature of the difference which is at issue here. For there are two distinctions, which in practice may not be clearly differentiated. First, if interaction commences between A and B on the basis of a salient similitude, it is likely to become apparent that while they resemble each other in this one way, they differ in others. As a frequent cause of cooling-off, honeymoons ending, or even violent ruptures, this is an important instance of estrangement. It is probably a general factor which tends to stabilise attraction at certain moderate intensities, just as its converse is well-known in pluralist theory as a factor which mitigates hostility and facilitates the compromise or resolution of conflict.

This is clearly a different matter from the mere non-identity of all human beings which makes them discrete entities. We have seen that Christianity, as well as the main tradition of bourgeois thought from Hobbes and Rousseau to Freud and Sartre, has tended to postulate a sort of original estrangement between men as a function of their discreteness. Generally, this has taken the form of a psychological hypothesis. Freud assumed a 'primary hostility of men towards one another', so that the task of civilisation was to inhibit aggressive instincts or channel them into harmless pursuits.[62] Simmel suspected that the tendency to contradict and oppose was universal, and that 'the individual, even when he is not attacked but only finds himself confronted by the purely objective manifestations of other individuals, cannot maintain himself except by means of opposition.' Echoing Hegel and Nietzsche, he surmised that 'the first instinct with which the individual affirms himself is the negation of the other . . . It seems impossible to deny an *a priori* fighting instinct.'[63] Such guesses are inevitably extrapolations from experience of social life, and there would be no need to assume such specificity of instinct if all the perceptible phenomena could be explained by the cognitive and socio-emotional variables hitherto mentioned. As I shall suggest in a moment, something like this elementary hostility between individuals may be involved in the processes by which individual personality is developed through social interaction, but not on account of its being an instinctive drive. The latter view, in my opinion, is the result of conflating mere logical discreteness with human individuality. The latter is the particular meaning which different societies and cultures set upon personality, as the complex resultant of the fact that their structures have practical existence only through the mediation of discrete human entities. It is a type of conflation to which individualistic societies and cultures are, not surprisingly, very prone.

Although the similarity hypothesis relates meanings of which one set is logical and the other emotional, it is intended to be empirical. Sociological theory must try to predict which differences, out of the infinity of those possible, will most likely be salient in social life, and which least. Historical materialism is a theory which attempts the first, suggesting that men's similar or differing relations to the means of production are those which primarily structure their mutual estrangements and solidarities. Clearly this has also to make room for biological and familial attributes at an equally basic level. However, a difference which separates all men without exception from every other would seem to be a strong candidate as the *least* salient difference. There is nothing to prevent us supposing that under circumstances of extreme individuation, reflective and sophisticated individuals may develop estranged relationships through consciousness of their own ultimate isolation within their own skins.[64] More interestingly, estrangement between a dying man and the living,[65] and the enhanced solidarity of those who bury him, may be based on the fact that human discreteness is manifested in a staggered mortality, and to that extent denied by the synchronous existence of a community of the living. But these are extreme situations. Existentialist philosophers may find them significant, but sociological theory begins from the average and the everyday. A fundamental estrangement based on human discreteness seems to be ruled out because discreteness is the basic common circumstance from which the search for similarity begins.

Marx (and others have followed him) strengthens this argument by suggesting that the search for similarities is precisely the way in which human beings seek the meaning of their discreteness. Thereby, through social interaction, they gain the social identity as individuals which they lack simply as discrete units of humanity. The idea, Hegelian in origin and Meadian in its later affinities, was expressed by Feuerbach:

> between me and another human being there is an essential, qualitative distinction. The other is my *thou* – the relation being reciprocal, – my *alter ego*, man objective to me, the revelation of my own nature, the eye seeing itself. In another I first have the consciousness of humanity; through him I first learn, I first feel, that I am a man.[66]

Marx took this up in a footnote to *Capital*:

> Since the human being does not come into the world bringing a mirror

with him, nor yet as a Fichtean philosopher able to say 'I am myself' he first recognizes himself as reflected in other men. The man Peter grasps his relation to himself as a human being through becoming aware of his relation to the man Paul as a being of like kind with himself. Thereupon Paul, with flesh and bone, with all his Pauline corporeality, becomes for Peter the phenomenal form of the human kind.[67]

Since 'humanity' is simply the sum total of whatever any society recognises as consistent with being human, we are justified in taking this as a condensed general theory of social identity. A person comes to have and recognise his identity, in some particular respect, by perceiving another as sharing some attribute with him: an attribute corresponding to a relationship between them. In this respect, therefore, the other is the symbol for him of his own identity, which he represents to him. The corollary — and often no doubt, the cause — of this perception is that he distinguishes the other from any third party. Furthermore, if we assume that he is endowed with self-love, he will feel an attraction for the other as an embodiment of his own selfhood, and indifference or repulsion towards third parties in so far as they differ from himself and form a barrier to this expansion of the ego. It is a psychological commonplace to add that these attitudes will only become effective if they are confirmed by the behaviour of the other, which in this case means that they must be reciprocated. This provides a fairly simple psychological hypothesis to support the one which we have drawn from sociological theory and research, that similarity induces attraction.[68]

It also provides a model of how individual and collective identities — personalities and groups — are both engendered from interaction processes. If we suppose that our subject is engaged in a number of such relationships, both simultaneously and successively, the model suggests a biographical and genetic account of how personal identity is developed through the synthesis of many such reflected partial identities and non-identities into a single more or less coherent self. It tells us nothing about the mechanisms of synthesis, but perhaps we may assume, at least, a drive towards consistency and differentiation.

On the other hand, a collective identity is formed to the extent that (and so long as) each mutually affirms his relation to the other as his *alter ego*, and they form a solidary group — an active 'we' or a passive 'us'—whose identity is, in turn, affirmed by some third party. To the extent that third-party recognition is accorded, the mutuality of the pair is converted into a meaning which has objectivity in their social environment as a single effective reality. It therefore takes on this meaning for them also. Instead of just mutually symbolising the selfhood of the other, each comes to represent, both mutually and externally, the group of which they are members, as parts of a whole. But, in representing the social whole which transcends either, each is nevertheless still representing a part of his own ego. And as this ego develops through participation in many such partial collectivities, it too becomes a whole, transcending its parts – a personality system – and as such re-enters the social process at other levels. Discreteness and plurality are thus basic givens which condition the ways in which both individual and collective selves appear, reappear and disappear upon the socio-historical scene.

Simmel expressed a similar conception:

> There is here a reciprocal relation between the subjective and the objective. As the person becomes affiliated with a social group, he surrenders himself to it. A synthesis of such subjective affiliations creates a group in an objective sense. But the person also regains his individuality because his pattern of participation is unique; hence the fact of multiple group-participation creates in turn a new subjective element . . . The genesis of personality has been interpreted as the point of intersection for innumerable social influences, as the end-product of heritages derived from the most diverse groups and periods of adjustment . . .[69]

This approach can derive attraction-repulsion phenomena from a basic psychological assumption of self-love – or perhaps we should say, from a drive towards defining, securing and enhancing the ego. Similarities with others produce attraction because they expand the identity of the ego; differences arouse repulsion because they restrict it. But does this not lead back to a Hobbesian universal estrangement? If all egos are expansive, will they not limit and restrict each other regardless of qualitative differences, simply on account of their plurality?

It is postulated that the ego-drive communicates its energy to the socially acquired identities, and is only effective through them. These will be of two kinds: collective identities, group selves existing at lower or higher levels of integration, depending on the strength of solidarity and other cohesive factors; and individual identities, the personality that individuals develop over time through participation in many collectivities. The substratum of the latter is the life-cycle of the discrete human being, but that of the former is a human aggregate bound together over time and space by communication flows. If the former, 'the individual' as we so often think of him – Jones, the 'whole person' – could somehow be extracted *in toto* from social life and then set in motion along with all the other Joneses, in competition for some scarce resource, we should have something approaching the Hobbesian war of all against all. But 'Jones' is a biographical fiction, abstracted from the actual relationships in which alone he exists, always sequentially and never wholly present, even to himself.

However, although it is an abstraction, the individual's self or personality is an abstration which is made in real life too. The personalities of individuals become cultural objects in their social world, which they unconsciously represent (and, as Goffman has taught us, consciously strive to 'present') to each other in their interaction. Thus in the style of role performances, in dress and manner and a myriad other ways, personalities are 'expressed'. Inasmuch as this is part of a continuous competition for the esteem of others, it resembles the desire of Hobbesian man for vainglory; but even individuality, in this sense, is a socially formed and recognised role which the bearer, as social actor, unwittingly performs or deliberately stages. The struggle for esteem may produce competitive estrangement, for example in peer-group situations, but not as a simple function of ego expansion.

With regard to any particular identity that is shared with others, the discrete human being is the focus of tension between the demands of collective and individual personality. The former exerts pressure towards uniformity with others, the latter towards consistency with past identities, and hence individual differentiation. Since different persons' similar attributes are seldom exactly the same, this tension is manifest in 'marginal differentiation' between individuals within their shared similitudes. Everyone tries to stamp their role performances with an individual hallmark by exploiting permissible differences. Similarly, young people of the same sex engage in continuous tacit sexual rivalry. (Riesman has treated this marginal differentiation as characteristic of the other-directed type of personality, who is an 'antagonistic co-operator'; but it seems, like other-directedness itself, to be a general dimension of human social existence.)[70] The result of this is that the solidarity of primary similitudes is often accompanied by a degree of interpersonal estrangement based on these minor differences. The more complex and differentiated a society, the greater the scope for tensions between collective and individual personality to develop, and the more individuality itself will be valued. The sum of all these minor estrangements surrounding individuals in face-to-face contact add up to what Laing and others have called their 'private space'.[71] Intimacy, therefore, can be defined as the degree to which particular solidary relationships are unaffected by these minor estrangements, compared with the extent to which the parties' private spaces are developed.

More important than this is the bearing of collective identity on the Hobbesian problem. Obviously, since power, status and wealth tend to be 'scarce' resources, and since plurality translates itself into a plurality of groups, there will be inter-group competition in many areas of social life. The main thing in this regard is not to 'solve' the abstract Hobbesian problem of social cohesion, but to determine, for each type of society, where its main structural cleavages and corresponding estrangements lie, and in consequence what are its cohesive factors and disintegrative tendencies.

All societies are at some level divided into basic cellular units, or similar segments. Complex societies are segmented in several or even many different ways, each individual belonging to several kinds of segment. In principle, the similarity of segments is a basis for their solidarity, but in practice this usually has low salience compared with the minor differences or points of opposition – growing out of simple plurality and discreteness – that separate them. Durkheim distinguished between self-sufficient segments which merely replicate the same pattern, and 'organs', or differentially specialised units which are functionally interdependent, and he correlated the first with the relatively weak social linkage of mechanical solidarity, and the second with the stronger bond of organic solidarity. We must add to this, however, that estrangement between units of the first type is also likely to be relatively weak, while in the second case the bonding force of interdependent needs may well be effaced by the much more powerful estrangement emanating from competition for scarce resources. In other words, we cannot assess the contribution which solidarities make to social cohesion without taking estrangements into account also. In a market system, productive organs are simultaneously segments of private ownership; the society therefore reproduces a structural analogue of the Hobbesian model, and the ego-drives of individuals are channelled into the multiple collective egoisms of businesses, farms, unions, households, etc. Universal anticipation of possible differential competitive outcomes, and the conflictual techniques of interaction required, together with primary differences and tertiary similitudes, are sufficient to maintain high levels of estrangement between such units. As Parsons and Coser have pointed out, the function of representing a group in external competition tends to devolve on specialised roles, often that of the chief. His personal identity comes to be defined, and to some degree psychologically determined, by the obligation, as member, to personify the collective egoism of the solidary group. The individual property-owner of classical liberal theory was such a representative, personifying the collective egoism of families and enterprises in market situations. Small wonder that in an epoch of family businesses and the subjection of women, male family heads in this role should have been conflated, by theorists, with 'man' in general, and the abstract individual endowed with 'natural' interests opposed to his fellows.

Thus postulating a psychological drive towards expansion of the ego does not imply any sort of primary or universal estrangement between men as natural competitors. It is necessary to distinguish between this psychological egoism and social egoism, which is its consequence, but mediated through roles representing the competitive interests either of individual personalities or collectivities. Both of these are socially formed identities and wholes.

5 ALTRUISM AND EGOISM

Social egoism requires more extensive consideration in view of its obvious importance in both social life and sociological theory, and its connection with a range of traditional ethical problems. Its obverse, we may say (following Durkheim and Simmel) is altruism, and we can define the terms as connoting negative or positive orientations of self to other's goal-attainment or need-satisfaction. If such orientations form a continuum, then the extremes will relate to situations where there is a direct conflict of interests, goals being mutually exclusive. Here – the most important case – egoism measures A's readiness to sacrifice B's goal-attainment to his own, and altruism his readiness to sacrifice his own goal-attainment to B's.

Altruism and egoism are subjective manifestations of situations where solidarity or estrangement prevail. As dispositions or motivations having a cognitive component, they are effects of the same logical causes as produce solidarity and estrangement; and their conative component is simply the affective force of the solidarity or estrangement in question, which drives individuals to act as the logic of their group situation demands. Thus, just as the preponderance of salient similitudes over differences within a group causes solidarity, it also provides occasions and reasons for compromising or sacrificing any opposed interests arising from these differences. Similarly, just as the differences separating a group from outsiders breed estrangement, so they also provide occasions when goals conflict, and reasons for pursuing the interests of the group at the expense of outsiders.

Within the context of any particular relationship, the identity and solidarity of the group – its degree of collective personality – is theoretically the absolute standard and determinant of members' conduct. That this is seldom the case in reality is due to the facts that most groups are imperfectly integrated, and none operates in isolation from superordinate or intersecting collective loyalties. Collective personalities are no more Robinson Crusoes than are individual personalities. There is nevertheless a *tendency* towards group absolutism. This seems to manifest itself in three ways: internal universalism, external particularism, and holism.

Simply as group members, and abstracting from any internal or functional differentiation of roles, all have claims to equal mutual treatment, and equal treatment by the collectivity, while none has any reason to prefer himself to others, so that all have equal obligations also. This appears to be simply a logical consequence of what it is to be a 'member', assuming one man, one membership. Yet it is the foundation of all ethical universalism, and probably a necessary element in the functioning and cohesion of all groups, where 'fairness' appears as an elementary value and 'the specific virtue of institutions'.[72] As such, this universalism is more a limitation on egoism than a demand for altruism. It carries within it, however, the particularism implied by the discreteness of group identity *vis-à-vis* outsiders. For in the dealings of members with non-members, the claims of the groups are absolute since none has the right to diminish his own or his fellows' equal claims to their collective stock of benefits, and must therefore uphold the standards of 'my group, right or wrong'.

It is when the universalism implicit in group membership is combined with the holism of group identity that self-denying altruism is likely to be most fully developed. Universalism arises from mere likenesses and the secondary similitudes they entail. External particularism is likely to develop to the extent that external differences actually give rise to inter-group opposition. Self-sacrificial altruism emerges to the extent that group members treat themselves and each other as parts of a whole, and depends on how far the whole is, to them, greater than the sum of its parts. This in turn depends on the salience of their collective identity as the basis of solidarity. (Thus the question which has often been treated under the heading of 'methodological holism' may, in fact, be largely a matter of the inner logic of the assumptions prevailing in actual social life: how far social wholes exist depends on these assumptions and on the corresponding socioemotional matrix.)

Altruism may be directed either towards the other members collectively, or towards another member individually, in so far as he is treated as a *representative* of the whole. In *Suicide*, Durkheim considered mainly the first type of orientation, seeing it as characteristic of primitive peoples, charismatic groups, and military (or 'total') organisations where discipline is aimed at mortifying individuality and forging a single 'organizational weapon'.[73] In each case, the range of relevant similitudes is maximised, either by sheer lack of differentiation, or by deliberately suppressing differences and giving similitudes high salience.[74] Christian morality, however, emphasises the second type, which is also instantiated in intimate dyads such as friendship, mother-love or romantic love, where the other is taken as the representative of the whole. This situation is simply a development from that dyadic mutual identification which was held to be the source of all solidarity. Here it has become a more permanent, many-sided relationship between the pair, where collective identity has grown out of multi-stranded similitudes. It is obvious that the structure of the dyad, forcing each to focus on the single other as representative of the whole, and thus making it difficult to distinguish between the whole and the other, facilitates other-directed altruism rather than group-directed altruism. For this reason it has always provided a model for ethics of charity and chivalry, and is symbolically expressed in such images as the Christian Trinity, consisting of a father, a son and a third – the third symbolising no more than their mutual love and interaction. Feuerbach, we have seen, idealised the dyad for similar reasons, and the young Marx did not escape the influence of this model, as will shortly appear.

Three comments need to be added before passing on to some of the implications of this discussion of altruism and egoism. First, it is evident that, as well as being correlates and effects of solidarity and estrangement, altruism and egoism may also act as reinforcing causes of them. In this capacity, they can be brought within the pale of the similarity hypothesis. Altruism presupposes identity of interest between A and B, and when it appears in A, unites A and B by the new similitude of actually favouring and promoting B's interest.[75] Likewise, egoism presupposes a conflict of interests, and when it emerges in A, estranges A and B further by the new difference that A, unlike B, is seen to be indifferent or opposed to B's interest. Admittedly, B may not care about his own interests, and A would still be altruistic or egoistic depending on *his* attitudes to B's interests. But in that case A's disposition would be unlikely to become salient between them or act as a reinforcer of a pre-existing solidarity or estrangement.

The second point is that 'egoism', in this discussion, corresponds to its use by the young Marx, and also to Weber's notion of impersonal acquisitiveness as a part of the 'spirit of capitalism', but not to Durkheim's 'egoism'. The latter, standing for the degree of detachment, or socio-emotional isolation, of the individual from the group, is closer to one of the meanings often given to 'anomie' in modern treatments of that idea. Conversely, Durkheim's 'anomie' really referred in part to an aspect of what has here been called 'egoism' — namely, the extent to which certain kinds of egoistic role-requirements (the acquisitiveness of 'economic man' or the sexuality of the 'aggressive male') may fail to be held in check by other, higher-order constraints or group solidarities. This also approximates to the sense in which Merton used 'anomie'. As such, 'anomie' does not refer to anything very specific, but simply to a certain pattern of estrangements and solidarities in social structures, and its effects. Its resonance in Durkheim's theory derives mainly from its connection with a spurious individual-society problem and from its evaluative connotations.[76]

This helps to resolve another major problem, which Durkheim tried to solve by introducing the concept of 'organic solidarity'. In doing so, he posed a challenge to the similarity hypothesis underlying his own concept of 'mechanical solidarity', for he claimed that 'Difference, as well as likeness, can be a cause of mutual attraction.' If Aristotle could be cited on the subject of resemblance, Heracleitus was the first to teach the fruitfulness of opposition: 'contrariety is expedient, and the best agreement arises from things differing, and that all things come into being in the way of the principle of antagonism.'[77] Not all differences have positive social effects, Durkheim claimed, but 'those which . . . complement each other' do. From this assumption, of course, it was a short step indeed to his conclusion, that 'we are thus led to consider the division of labour in a new light. From this point of view, the economic services that it can render are picayune compared to the moral effect that it produces, and its true function is to create in two or more persons a feeling of solidarity.'[78]

Complementary differences thus appear to refute the similarity hypothesis. But was this conclusion justified? It appears to have some experimental support. Although most studies of marriage, friendship and other companionship choices demonstrate correlation between similarity and attraction, some do show that 'opposites attract'. But, apart from the obvious preponderance of heterosexual over homosexual attraction, the only widespread evidence of this kind relates to personality. Here, pairings of assertive-receptive or dominant-submissive personality traits have been found as bases of mutual attraction (although some experiments have also failed to confirm even this).[77] The important point, however, is that such evidence as exists agrees with Durkheim's guess that the only differences likely to cause attraction are those which complement each other. Durkheim's explanation of this runs as follows:

> The image of the one who completes us becomes inseparable from ours, not only because it is frequently associated with ours, but particularly because it is the natural complement to it. It thus becomes an integral and permanent part of our consciousness, to such a point that we can no longer separate ourselves from it, and we seek to increase its force. That is why we enjoy the society of the one it represents . . .[80]

Whether or not this is empirically acceptable, it provides weak grounds for abandoning the similarity hypothesis. For what Durkheim says is that the two parties *resemble* each other, in that each sees himself and the other as different but complementary parts of a whole: and that it is this similarity – the emotive force of the shared perception of the whole, or the image of their joint identity – which causes mutual attraction. The only type of case where difference seems to produce solidarity can thus easily be brought within the similarity hypothesis – and on psychologically plausible grounds, not merely by a logical sleight of hand.

In passing, it may be suggested that complementarity is not, after all, a very significant basis of attraction, sociologically. Obviously, the most important and conspicuous instance is heterosexual attraction: romantic love is the form of solidarity corresponding to the idealised image of the whole formed by sexual union. But even here, the mutual selection of particular mates, as well as their subsequent harmony, seems to depend very largely on the presence of other likenesses. As a general feature of social life, the difference between the sexes is a source of mild estrangement, seldom salient (except for children in puberty, and perhaps religious celibates) because ubiquitous, and usually expressed through avoidance, by role segregation. In the absence of solidarity, whether romantic love or attraction through likenesses, the mere *biological* complementarity of the sexes is a difference to be exploited as a source of bargaining power, whether commercially through prostitution or by the mere withholding of legitimate favours in return for concessions and gifts; and thus by no means a solidarising factor in itself. The complementarity of gender roles, so important in European history, to which Durkheim alluded in support of his thesis, was – as Simmel perceived[81] – more a consequence of the subjection of women, and hence of estrangement rather than solidarity. It was a 'complementarity' resembling that of capital and labour, rather than that of pilot and navigator – an effect of unequal power – and solidarity between the sexes has probably increased as it has diminished. Cases of mutual choice between complementary personalities (the other type of evidence cited) also seem to be limited to instances where patterns of dominance and dependence have become internalised as needs, which may often be a consequence of exposure to social patterns of estrangement and domination in early socialisation.

Even if complementarity can be construed as similarity, rather than difference, this by no means allows us to assume that the division of labour makes complementarity a salient enough similitude to create a new solidarity. Complementarity implies that A and B both have the means of satisfying the other, or enabling the other to achieve his goals, while each lacks these means for himself. However, the effects of this will probably differ, depending on whether A and B are altruistically or egoistically oriented. Both may wish to satisfy the other, or feel obliged to do so; or else each may seek to exploit the other's need to his own or his group's advantage. The first case presupposes a solidarity compatible with sharing or mutual giving; the second, no more solidarity than is necessary for competitive exchange. So whether or not integrative effects of the kind which Durkheim called 'organic solidarity' will in fact appear with the division of labour, depends on the existence not just of the latter, but of a sufficient level of altruism in society: Durkheim's view that 'there exists a social solidarity which comes from the division of labour', far from being a 'self-evident truism',[82] was therefore a misleading simplification.

That he was aware of the gap in the argument appears, first, from his insistence that organic solidarity can only emerge within an existing community with mechanical solidarity, and secondly, from his later advocacy of guild socialism as a way of fostering solidarity and altruism in occupational life. He was inclined to transfer the blame for weakness in his argument to society itself, with the notion of social pathology, but the flaw really lay in the basic assumption that complementary differences were enough to engender solidarity. This explains much of the shift in theoretical emphasis, back towards mechanical solidarity and collective consciousness that has been noted in his later works.

Marx's superiority as an analyst of modern society shows in his clear perception that complementarity resulting from division of labour will produce solidarity only if social organisation also fosters altruism; if, like the regime of private property, it consecrates egoism, the differentiated society will be a scene of estrangement.

The nearest to an abstract discussion of solidarity by Marx is addressed to just this question. It occurs at the close of the notes on James Mill. As was seen in Chapter 4, Marx analysed commodity exchange as the consequence of division of labour in a situation of general estrangement, expressed in the egoism of private property:

> I have produced for myself and not for you, as you have produced for yourself and not for me. The result of my production bears in itself just as little relation to you as the result of your production bears directly to me. That is, our production is not a production of men for men as such, i.e. social production. So as a man, neither of us is in a position to be able to enjoy the product of the other. We are not present to our mutual products as men. Thus, neither can our exchange be the mediating movement which confirms that my product is for you, because it is an objectification of your own essence, your need.[83]

He then asked what the opposite situation would be like: 'Supposing that we had produced in a human manner; each of us would in his production have doubly affirmed himself and his fellow man.' Marx distinguished four aspects. First, I would have affirmed my specialised individuality in the product itself, whose usefulness would be my direct concern, irrespective of market considerations. He continued:

> (2) In your enjoyment or use of my product I would have had the direct enjoyment of realizing that I had both satisfied a human need by my work and also objectified the human essence and therefore fashioned for another human being the object that met his need.
> (3) I would have been for you the mediator between you and the species and thus been acknowledged and felt by you as a completion of your own essence and a necessary part of yourself, and have thus realized that I am confirmed both in your thought and in your love.
> (4) In my expression of my life I would have fashioned your expression of your life, and thus in my own activity have realized my own essence, my humanity and community with you.
> In that case our products would be like so many mirrors, out of which our essence shone.[84]

The third of these considerations is the equivalent to that which Durkheim made the basis of organic solidarity, but viewed from the standpoint of the producer rather than the consumer. Like Durkheim, Marx suggested that the producer be 'confirmed in your love' —i.e. an object of attraction to the consumer— through knowing that they both comprise parts of a whole, and that their complementarity mediates a *common* relationship to the human species, or to the cultural community embodied in the division of labour. The second and fourth considerations emphasise this 'mirror' aspect of the relationship even more strongly. Thus solidarity would arise from resemblance, certainly, but not from mere complementarity. It would arise from the common identity through which complementariness was realised – that of fellow-members of the human species – and because this was treated as a basis for altruism.

This connection was spelt out in the *Manuscripts*: 'In so far as man, and hence also his feeling, etc., are *human*, the affirmation of the object by another is likewise his own gratification.' Even, Marx insists, where 'the sensuous affirmation is the direct annulment of the object in its independent form (as in eating, drinking, working up of the object, etc.)'.[85] As an ethical ideal, this combines holism and universalism, and maximises the scope of both by taking 'humanity' as the reference-group within which the criteria of common membership and participation in a common whole are applied. As parts of the human collectivity, no individual can set his own interests before those of the whole, but as a member, no individual has any reason to prefer the interests of another to his own except in so far as the other represents the whole. But as a *man*, each is equally a representative of the whole species: this single similitude is assumed to be more salient than any internal differentiation. The human community is the only collectivity for which the general rule underlying the logic of 'membership' – one man, one membership – equates the demands of universalism with those of holism. Thus each should put every other before himself, participating in the satisfaction of others as though they were his own; and if all do so equally, none is the loser.

As a programme for stimulating the necessary solidarity, this humanism might indeed seem no less utopian than Feuerbach's, and it is not surprising that Marx, like Feuerbach, developed it in terms of a dyadic relationship of 'love'. Very possibly his long courtship provided him with an idealised model of solidarity which he carried over into economic and political ideology. Durkheim, less utopian, sought bases for solidarity and altruism in national and professional loyalties. But the theoretical aim was the same in both cases: to state conditions under which the complementarity of an occupationally differentiated society would be mediated through membership roles guaranteeing sufficient solidarity to impart a degree of altruism to economic life. Marx held that private property was a permanent obstacle to this. Under capitalism, estrangement would prevail, and social cohesion, to the extent that it was attainable, would depend on factors other than solidarity. Although national and occupational solidarities have tempered the Marxian class struggle – and in some capitalist countries, Japan especially, reserves of traditional altruism have been important in facilitating economic growth – events have tended to confirm his view.[85a]

6 APPLICATIONS AND IMPLICATIONS

The aim of this concluding section is to show how the concepts and hypotheses developed in this chapter can be used to derive some of the basic concepts of sociological theory — or at least, how these would be related to solidarity-estrangement models. I shall deal first with social control, deviance, norms and values; secondly, status and authority; thirdly, class and conflict. But the discussion, far from being exhaustive, will be largely indicative of connections that could be worked out in greater detail.

To examine the question of deviance, we revert to the simple model of group membership, where secondary and tertiary similitudes cause the development of superadded levels of solidarity. Parties to interaction, we assume, are constantly monitoring each other's qualities and performances. The greater the number of relevant similitudes, and the more frequent and continuous their interaction, hence also the more marked their solidarity and joint estrangement from outsiders, the greater should be their joint capacity for social control. For they will understand one another better and share a wider range of more accurate expectations about one another's behaviour; they will have more occasion for exercising mutual surveillance, hence of perfecting the means of mutual control, becoming accustomed to it, and taking it for granted; and the motivation to please one another and avoid rejection will be stronger. Now let us assume that primary similitudes may nevertheless weaken or be interrupted over time. If primary similitudes give way to differences, we should expect estrangement to replace solidarity, and the relationship to weaken and perhaps vanish. But this might not be so if secondary solidarity has developed. For although its logical basis (the set of those sharing the primary similitude) depends on the continuance of the primary similitude, the new emotional bond of group membership is separable from the first, and in practice becomes distinct from it as the group, through interaction, acquires a new stock of common experience peculiar to itself. This solidarity may therefore resist and counteract a weakening in the region of primary similitudes, especially if secondary solidarity is also reinforced by tertiary. The monitoring of members' performances by each other therefore acquires a constraining and normative function besides a merely cognitive one. Members seek to secure and maintain the bases of their primary solidarity, as representatives of their secondary and/or tertiary similitudes; and by rewarding and punishing each other for deviations from the modal performance, establish a group norm.

As experiments have shown, a group norm can develop without conscious coordination, as in the case of output rates of contiguous friendship pairs in the Hawthorn plant. But with larger groups and more complex primary similitudes, more elaborate explicit communication is needed. This suggests an explanation of the experimental finding that more communication is directed towards deviants than co formers, that it is reduced as a deviant returns to conformity but continues to mount if he refuses to do so, until a ceiling is reached where he is apparently given up as incorrigible. Thereupon communication with him falls off steeply and, especially in highly cohesive groups, he is rejected by the rest.

The explanation would run as follows. Deviance over a primary similitude weakens the total solidarity of the group at the point of the bond uniting the deviant member to the rest. Increased interaction at this point, on the basis of secondary similitude, counteracts this weakening up to the point where it causes the deviant to move back towards conformity, when it can be reduced again as primary solidarity is repaired. If increased interaction reaches whatever ceiling the group's solidarity permits without affecting the deviant, it will eventually cease; the bond is broken and the member rejected, and the remainder regroup on the basis of a new tertiary similitude as rejectors of the deviant, which restores total solidarity at a new level.

An added hypothesis, which emerges from the discussion in the last section but which has not been tested (so far as I know), would be that the efficacy of interaction (on the basis of secondary similitudes) as a reducer of primary deviance will vary with its tendency to be equally initiated as between the deviant and the remainder. If the rest of the group bombard the deviant with communications it will increase his estrangement from them as a subgroup, diminishing the effect of increased communication. Whereas if he can argue his case fairly (as intended in a law-court) or is allowed to confess fully (as in a religious confessional) he is more likely to be attracted back to the norm. Since this law (if it is one) puts the individual deviant on a footing of equality with the rest of the group collectively, the deviant (or 'maverick') role can be a means of magnifying the individual's status in the group, and may even make him a potential alternative leader. (Political careers, e.g. of Churchill or Bevan, illustrate these hypotheses.) In more theoretical vein, this explanation suggests that there may be both stable levels of solidarity for groups of different sorts and sizes, and some 'law of conservation of solidarity' which operates to maintain it at this level throughout the group, although not necessarily uniformly.

Let us bring our assumptions closer to real life. We shall suppose the group to be indefinitely large, to interact only intermittently, and that its members each have multiple and changeable group memberships with others, outside, on the basis of different primary similitudes. The latter is likely to produce a variety of estrangements between the group members in other, external roles, and since these also modify their personalities they spill over into the original group, becoming 'latent roles' within it. The solidarity of the latter now has to maintain itself over and above internal estrangements and ambivalences. As the group members become more differentiated individuals, chances of deviance and the need for normative communication increase. Intermittent interaction requires effective storage, by the members, of their roles and their understandings of the primary similitudes and state of development of the group. All these circumstances induce pressures towards codifying the criteria of salient similitudes in conceptual terms, and formalising rules for recognising and maintaining them.

By varying the assumptions, in other words, we move from a situation where an implicit group norm suffices to one where an explicit system of values (or ideals) and norms is required. In Weber's terms, the need for an associative aspect of group organisation and for closure on the basis of a normative order is added to the communal aspect. To the self-consciousness of the group which is implied in their secondary similitude, as representatives of a collective identity, is added a collective self-consciousness as representatives of common values. Durkheim's analysis of sacredness suggests that the specifically moral force attaching to values and norms is the reflected counterpart, within the auto-communication of individual thought, of the solidarity which is both evoked and symbolised by their use in group contexts. This individual reflection is itself conceptualised and fed back into the group process, as an 'ought'.

To the extent that 'ought' and 'is' become divorced, verbal or other material symbols of values and norms come to be 'idealized'. They are conceived as a special and privileged sort of existent and, as such, must become objects of displaced interpersonal attraction, capable of evoking altruistic self-denial, if the group is to retain its identity. This necessity arises to the extent that the group members become partially estranged through dispersal, conflict, multiplication of latent identities, or other forms of separation. In that case the idealised symbol of their collective identity becomes a 'fetish' (in a strictly Marxian and non-ethnological sense). Two major forms of this are, obviously, fetishisation of the group identity itself and its primary similitudes (e.g. gods; 'the nation' with its emblems and values; 'sociology', with its demi-deified theorists as symbols of the profession, etc.) and fetishisation of norms, arising from secondary similitude (church ritual and dogma; political constitutions and procedural conventions; law; the Queensberry rules and suchlike; red tape and scientific methodology as fetishised professional norms; etc.) This seems to be the point at which 'sacred' phenomena become distinguishable from merely 'moral' ones.

Durkheim stressed the Janus-faced nature of sacredness and morality. They act both through the attraction of the ideal and the constraint of the obligatory. He saw this as a result of the fundamental dualism between society and the individual. The individual was overawed by society and frightened of its superior force, as well as attracted by all that it gave him. Obligation, however, could have been more easily explained if Durkheim had had a more dialectical view of solidarity and its relation to estrangement. For the constraint of 'ought' may be explicable as a verbal expression of a specific psychic tension between solidarity based on secondary similitude and the anticipated estrangement that would arise from a breach or lapse in primary similitudes, or departure from the group norm.

Similar considerations might improve Durkheim's theory of punishment. Durkheim equated punishment with the repressive sanctions characteristic of criminal law, and interpreted it as an expression of the outrage occasioned in the collective consciousness by any sufficiently precise and visible deed which contradicted unanimously and strongly held convictions. Such denials of collective beliefs would tend to enfeeble them 'if an emotional reaction of the community did not come to compensate its loss, and it would result in a breakdown of social solidarity. It is necessary, then, that it be affirmed forcibly at the very moment when it is contradicted, and the only means of affirming it is to express the unanimous aversion which the crime continues to inspire, by an authentic act which can consist only in suffering inflicted upon the agent.'[86] It is the last clause that contains the most obvious non-sequitur in the argument, and Durkheim's idea of 'expiation' does not illuminate the matter. Why should reaffirmation of collective values take the form of making the offender suffer, instead of a ceremony of purification, a collective pardon, or some other non-instrumental act?

An answer can be ventured if we see criminal laws as prohibiting certain sorts of injury between members of the solidary group, which are not prohibited in the same way against outsiders and may indeed be mandatory or laudable in time of war. With Durkheim, we assume reprobation of such injuries to be general throughout the common consciousness. An offender, therefore, declares himself by his deed to stand outside the common consciousness, and society affirms this declaration by its verdict of guilt and sentence of punishment. It is not the criminal's suffering, therefore, which is the point of the punishment, as though this were a spontaneous and appropriate expression of social wrath (though it may be this). Rather, suffering is inseparable from society's affirmation of the meaning of the criminal's act: namely, that he should be expelled from the group of the likeminded, to which he does not really belong, or 'deserve' to belong. Thus ostracism is the archetype of all punishment, and consists in a process of estrangement by which society withdraws from the offender, rejects him, and classes him with outsiders. As such, of course, he becomes liable to the sorts of injury against which he was protected as a member of society. Hence punishment need not be – and seldom is – limited to simple exclusion or banishment. The offender may be more effectively expelled by death, and either permanently or temporarily by imprisonment. Outlawry and excommunication are forms of internal exile and stigmatisation. Similar considerations are present in branding and mutilation: symbolic maiming also often excluded victims from the occupational or other skills they had abused – forgers from those able to write, etc. Even flogging is perhaps a demotion from the adult community to the status of child, while paying a fine, like penance, is a symbolic fee for readmission to the society of the law-abiding. This is not to deny that penal law has been determined by factors other than modes of exclusion – such as the cruelty of despots and their minions, adduced by Durkheim in 'Two Laws of Penal Evolution' – [87] but it is to assert that Durkheim's perspective should have included this factor.

This raises the important question of the bearing of this whole discussion on the use of violence. For reasons which emerged in the context of Marx's humanism, in Chapter 3, every similitude through which people identify with one another is simultaneously a way in which they treat each other as fellow-humans, while every difference that estranges people causes each to regard the other as, in that respect and to that extent, less than human, and consequently to treat him more like a thing. Since treating another as a fellow-human implies doing to him as you would have him do to you, and acknowledging that he is a reasonable creature, capable of moral choice and of feeling pain and pleasure, solidarity always carries with it an injunction against the use of force, except perhaps for the other's good. Thus interpersonal power, in solidary relationships, can only be exercised through persuasion. Conversely, the greater the scope or degree of estrangement, the less compunction there is about exerting power through the threat or use of violence, since force is the normal means of controlling things and making them respond to the human will. Thus while power is a ubiquitous phenomenon in inter-personal relationships, coercive power, which is what mostly interests sociologists and political scientists, always presupposes – and reinforces – some degree of estrangement. Durkheim's treatment of the absolute power of despots as a distinct type of social force that always tends to increase the inhumanity of penal law is based on this idea; for the despot, as the single commanding will, sees himself as the *only* fully human individual in his universe. (And for that reason – as Hegel indicated in his discussions of the 'soulless community' and absolute monarchy – sees himself and is seen by his flatterers as a god.)

This is a different situation from the case where a *representative* of a god receives altruistic devotion to the point where self-sacrifice involves self-inflicted or willingly accepted violence. In this case the individual to some extent treats himself as a thing, as less than human, because humanity has become an ideal associated with the symbolic representation of the group as a whole, as the perfection of man, of which the believer is merely an imperfect part. This 'Feuerbachian' situation is to be explained in terms of vertical estrangement within the solidary group, for example between priesthood and laity, in a way which will be clearer shortly.

This discussion of how explicit values and norms grow out of an implicit group norm, defining primary similitudes, is still incomplete. What needs to be added also enables status and authority to be introduced. Fetishisation will only occur to the extent that the function of representing the fetish becomes a differentiated role in the group. Conversely, the need for this specialised reinforcement of cohesion, by harping on symbols and procedures of group identity, becomes all the greater if internal diversity increases and contact becomes more intermittent. In principle, this newly differentiated role of keeping the group's conscience could be shared equally amongst the members. In practice, what makes it necessary also renders this improbable – namely, the tendencies towards internal difference and estrangement, which are not likely to be evenly distributed. In fact, primary similitudes are almost invariably unevenly distributed, or unequally present in all, and any collective process generates new, unequally distributed, shared attributes. Thus the invidious differentiation of collectivities with respect to the representation of shared norms and values is rooted in universal facts of group life. This is very close to what Moreno called the 'sociodynamic effect'.

It was a universal finding, Moreno claimed, that the frequency distribution of sociometric choices in a group was skewed, so that the proportion of over-chosen and underchosen individuals always exceeded chance. If the opportunities for choice were extended, by enlarging the group or permitting more choices, 'surplus' positive choices still tended to go to the most chosen, and isolates and rejects remained such. These surplus choices of popular figures were found to have a mainly symbolic rather than personal significance: stars of attraction were apparently chosen as representatives of the group, symbolising the respondent's desire to remain acceptable, and not to become estranged by association with unpopular members. Thus because group members necessarily exhibit a multiplicity of salient attributes, some of which are minoritarian and deviant with respect to its primary similitudes, there is inevitably a degree of internal estrangement. The role of group member is performed unequally, or with varying frequency and success, by different members. Those in whom the greatest number of primary similitudes is concentrated form cliques, which arrogate to themselves the role of representing the norms and values of the group, and become 'influentials', monopolising the monitoring and punitive functions. Dahrendorf has rightly seen in this type of phenomenon the source of status stratification; but whereas he regards it as a derivative of power, the present argument suggests rather that the power to sanction by approval and disapproval – 'moral power' – is a consequence of the pattern of solidarities and estrangements.

Prestige and deference are a deflection from other members in general of the sentiments of attraction aroused by secondary similitude, and their concentration upon those who most fully exemplify the 'essence' of the group. they differ from simple solidarity not just in their strongly focused pattern, but also in their asymmetry, and in their mixture with specific patterns of internal estrangement. Thus the similarity which underlies deference is not between attributes of A and B, but between A's attributes and what is attributed to an idealised B. B defers to the ideal pattern of what he might be, as personified by A. This type of similitude can only become salient given the processes of group disintegration and fetishisation already mentioned, so that B is socialised into a group culture that presents B with an identity which he does not yet possess, or which is other than he is. This situation is formally similar to that confronting an outsider who aspires to join the group and takes it as his reference-group. In both cases there is estrangement present. In the case of the outsider this is self-explanatory. In the case of the low-status insider it is simply the vertical estrangement that appears along with internal differentiation with respect to group values. Usually this is accompanied by sub-group formation and thus differentiation into élite and non-élite nuclei. Thus the gap between reality and the ideal which underlies deference reflects the fact that its reciprocal, on A's part, is disdain: a permanent deflection of the estrangement towards outsiders upon some of the group. Its basis is the difference between them and the 'ideal member', but it may be tempered by the universalism of group membership. This breeds toleration and a sense of responsibility for differences that cannot be helped (*noblesse oblige*, patronage, etc.)

Weber, whose chief contribution to sociology is arguably his theory of status-groups, distinguished between ethnic and status segregation in terms consonant with this account:

> Ethnic co-existences condition a mutual repulsion and disdain but allow each ethnic community to consider its own honour as the highest one; the caste structure brings about a social subordination and an acknowledgment of more honour in favour of the privileged caste and status-groups.[88]

Related to these intermixtures of solidarity and estrangement is the phenomenon of *ressentiment*, named by Nietzsche and discussed by Scheler. This is the 'sour grapes' attitude of subordinate groups in a relatively open status-system towards their superiors. It is a species of envious hostility that does not, however, indicate rejection of élite values or the stratification founded on them. This appears to result when the inequality of different strata is more salient than their common values: hence estrangement predominates; yet it has strong undertones of deferential solidarity based on idealised similarities to which all are encouraged to aspire.[89]

These cases call for some further elucidation of the notions of 'horizontal' and 'vertical' solidarity and estrangement, which were partially introduced in the last chapter. These spatial metaphors, however general and ingrained in social life itself, are not wholly self-explanatory. Their basis seems to be certain fundamental patterns of relatedness found in all social structures.

The secondary solidarity of group members can be considered a case of 'horizontal solidarity' between individuals. It is based, we have said, on their secondary similitude as members of a class of similar beings, and simply as members they have equal rank. By 'horizontal solidarity' a little more is meant than this, however. In addition to being equal by virtue of possessing an attribute in common, they may be equal or unequal in the degree to which they possess it. If they possess it equally, they can be seen – and can see one another – as equal parts of a whole. But, as we have noted, status differentiation can arise from their possessing it unequally, and hence being unequal – greater and lesser, higher and lower – parts of a whole. This is the pattern which underlies 'vertical solidarity'. Horizontal and vertical solidarity do not, however, refer just to the situations where group members see one another simply as equal or unequal parts of a whole, and thus share a common identity. More realistically, they refer to situations where this perception is more salient than its converse: where quantitative equality of common qualities is more salient than the qualitative differences that make separate individuals; or where qualitative resemblance is more salient than quantitative differences in distribution. Horizontal and vertical estrangement refer to the opposite state of affairs, where the differences are more salient than the similitudes.

Reasons have been given for doubting whether estrangement can be the predominant relationship between individuals, except in their capacity as representatives of a collective personality. This holds of both horizontal and vertical estrangement. As between groups, however, this limitation is lifted, and it is here, in the relations of subgroups within a group, or of groups within a larger system, that the concepts have their greatest utility. Collectivities related as equal parts of a whole are what we have called 'segments', and those related as unequal parts, 'strata'. In each case, solidarity or estrangement may prevail between them, depending whether the similitudes that unite, or the differences that divide them, are the more salient. Furthermore, we have already seen that Marx thought these dimensions might vary together. This is because, unless a set of segments composes a total structure, which will then be acephalous, it must compose a stratum *within* a stratified whole. The less the components of that stratum are related as parts of a segmented whole, the less the whole stratum can relate to other strata as parts of a stratified whole. Thus horizontal estrangement may be a sufficient condition for vertical estrangement, and horizontal solidarity, if positive, a necessary condition for vertical solidarity.

However, if horizontal solidarity is negative, uniting segments as a stratum which excludes or opposes another, this will intensify estrangement. Thus a rising class, whose segments unite to exclude those with less access to means of production than itself, will increase vertical estrangement. But class conflict will be less if the segments of the dominated classes fail to unite to oppose their oppressors than if they do. Thus *divide et impera* is a wise strategy for the latter, since it keeps vertical estrangement at more manageable levels by stimulating horizontal estrangement within the lower stratum. This is the situation in which Mosca's law – that an organised minority can always dominate an unorganised mass, because it is able to isolate its parts which, individually, it can outnumber and overpower – would seem to hold; and it was to circumstances of this kind that Marx, before Mosca, used much the same idea in analysing authority.

The difference between prestige and authority parallels that between the attractive and coercive aspects of morality. In status phenomena, the attraction of the ideal group member predominates over the coercive side, but the latter is also present in the sanctions (mainly acts and reminders of exclusion) by which high-status members put down their inferiors. In authority, the coercive side is a specialised outgrowth of these sanctions and is dominant, but the attractive aspect is present in the form of legitimacy. Whereas prestige is the mode of symbolising the unity of the group associated with the formation of an internal elite, authority can be wielded by an outsider who successfully claims to represent its unity. Marx mentions two interesting examples of this phenomenon, both of them being cases where extreme vertical estrangement between ruler and ruled was a function of extreme horizontal estrangement between the segments at the base of the political pyramid.

One is the case of oriental despotism, where because of the extreme dispersion, self-sufficiency, and exclusiveness of village communities, there was complete discontinuity between the base and apex of the pyramid. Hence the function of representing the unity of them all could become the prey of alien conquerors, and could be extended over indefinitely broad areas of empire, without the base changing its character or its relation to the apex. This was a prime characteristic of Asian history.

The second example is Marx's well-known analysis of Napoleon III's ability to consolidate his dictatorship by posing as the protector of the small peasantry. Because of the separation and estrangement of peasant families, 'They cannot represent themselves, they must be represented. Their representative must at the same time appear as their master, as an authority over them . . .' In this case the peasantry, as a class, existed only through consciousness of primary similitudes. No secondary solidarity or sense of unity existed: it was a logical possibility in the situation, yet socially unrealised. Bonaparte sought to realise it by personifying an idealised political version of the peasants' primary similitudes: the myth of his uncle's leadership of an all-conquering peasant army.

The same example can show how distinction between different logical levels of similitude, and between positive and negative solidarity, may be used to elucidate levels of class formation and class consciousness. All solidary groups contain internal estrangements, but group structures vary according to how their inner mix of solidarity and estrangement is arranged. Marx's usual model of class was of a negative solidarity superimposed on horizontally estranged cellular units: 'the separate individuals form a class only in so far as they carry on a common battle against another class; otherwise they are on hostile terms with each other as competitors.' This general pattern also underlay Marx's analysis of the class situation of the French peasantry in *The Eighteenth Brumaire*.

Mode of production, self-sufficiency and poor communications inhibited interaction, preventing the growth of solidarity on the basis of the similarities of peasant familes as 'homologous magnitudes' dispersed upon the French soil. They remained estranged segments, 'a vast mass, the members of which live in similar conditions but without entering into manifold relations with one another.' In so far as bonds existed, they formed 'merely a local interconnection': estrangement prevailed between localities. The celebrated five conditions of class formation introduced by Marx can easily be classified in terms of the theoretical scheme so far developed:

> In so far as millions of families live under economic conditions of existence that separate their mode of life, their interests and their culture from those of other classes, and put them in hostile opposition to the latter, they form a class. In so far as there is merely a local interconnection among these small-holding peasants, and the identity of their interests begets no community, no national bond and no political organization among them, they do not form a class.[90]

Distinctive way of life and culture thus form a primary similitude on which positive solidarity could develop, and common interests opposed to other classes a primary similitude from which negative solidarity could arise. In so far as interaction develops through local to national levels, converting these similitudes into solidarity, a secondary similitude would appear through the emergence of class identity. As class members, individuals may develop a new solidarity as representatives of 'the class'. Finally, in so far as they are members of a negatively solidary interest group and forge a national political organisation to pursue their interests against other classes, tertiary similitudes can arouse further solidarity as protagonists in the class struggle. This is, obviously, part of what 'class consciousness' usually refers to, except that discussions of class consciousness typically focus on cognition rather than sentiments. Research findings that show the strong effect of shared physical danger as a promoter of solidarity tend to justify the Sorelian emphasis on violent struggle as a catalyst of class unity.

Weber's influential contrast between status-groups and classes, based respectively on common life-styles and values, and similar interests against others, is an important instance of the polarity between positively and negatively solidary groups. Weber pointed out that to the extent that social action (and hence interaction) developed on either basis, such groups were likely to move closer together. Status-groups would make exclusive claims to prestige and monopolise economic or political advantages, while classes would acquire common life-styles, values and ideologies. In our language, status-group solidarity becomes more negative as it develops from secondary to tertiary similitudes; while class solidarity, originally negative, becomes more positive as its members acquire secondary similitudes. This suggests that a certain model of social dynamics underlay Weber's typologies and hypotheses – or at least, that they can be interpreted in this sense. Commentators have frequently noted that Weber's typological fluency in *Economy and Society* seems to presuppose quite a complex array of unstated theoretical propositions of high generality, but few attempts have been made to elicit them.

Finally, it may be suggested that the dialectical relationship between solidarity and estrangement that has been proposed might help to bring together 'integration' and 'conflict' approaches in sociological theory. Talcott Parsons' model of a society held together by common values and Dahrendorf's concept of conflict-groups, held together by common interests, are often taken to be wholly opposed to one another, and even to belong to irreconcilable theoretical approaches. This is no longer necessary if we see them as instances of positive and negative solidarity which have been developed in artificial isolation from a dialectical theory of social processes, and thus from each other. Bringing them together in this way, however, is more than a classificatory exercise, for it involves a theoretical claim. It is, that what holds these groups together is not the common values or the common interests, but sentiments. Either interpersonal sentiments of solidarity on the basis of the commonness of the values and interests, or of the similitudes which give rise to them; or sentiments deflected into deference towards elites personifying fetishised values, or into legitimation of obedience to the claims of ruling authorities; or into altruistic or egoistic motivation in self-sacrifice to the collectivity or pursuit of the collectivity's self-interest. It follows that the importance of shared values and explicit norms for social cohesion is always problematic, and by no means offers a general paradigm of social integration. The relative importance of all the solidarities within a society has to be discovered and weighed, and compared with the precise significance and scope of explicit value-consensus and moral integration. The latter would almost certainly turn out to be of lesser significance than has generally been supposed, as Durkheim understood. But, in addition to this, the distribution and strength of estrangement in society has also to be taken into account. And it may very well be the case that solidarities and moral integration together are not sufficient to account for the cohesion of societies high in estrangement. This was Marx's view of capitalist society, and he provided a theory which explained its integration by a third factor, reification. The importance of this theory for understanding the cohesion of macro-systems is, I believe, immense. To understand it, however, means going beyond interpersonal relationships, to which this chapter has been confined, and examining the roles and functions that can be performed in social life by inanimate things, and by people's relationships with them.

Part III

Alienation as a Sociological Concept

6 What is Property?

I have argued that, in order to unearth – or construct – sociological foundations for Marx's economic theories, the two concepts of estrangement and alienation must be kept separate and distinct. In the Introduction, 'alienation' (*Entäusserung*) was said to refer to the renunciation or relinquishment of possession or of a claim to something – usually, but not necessarily, in favour of another person. Its correlative was said to be 'appropriation' (*Aneignung*): taking into possession or assuming new powers of disposal over something – often, but by no means always, from another person. Clearly, neither term refers exclusively to relations involving 'things', since it is possible to alienate and appropriate activities or capacities, such as labour and labour-power, or persons (slaves) or abstract social entities (privileges, offices, freedoms, 'goodwill' etc.) However, it is fair to say that their primary reference is to things, and that these other uses, however common, are secondary, and have a figurative content. Or, to put it another way, that these diverse sorts of object are being assimilated to things and treated accordingly when they are said to be alienated or appropriated. So whereas solidarity and estrangement concerned the social bonding and sundering of persons, appropriation and alienation concern the making and breaking of social bonds between persons and things. Inasmuch as bonds are social, their making and breaking cannot be effected by the person and the thing in solitude, but only through the activation of shared meanings in a third party. These meanings constitute a distinct stratum of social consciousness: that which concerns possessory relations of persons to 'things' – i.e. to non-human entities external to themselves. The present chapter prepares for the analysis of alienation and appropriation in the next, by trying to lay some foundations for a sociology of possession, ownership and property.

Marx's approach to economics, in 1844, was by way of Hegel's analysis of 'civil society' as a system of needs and property rights. From the first, he was searching for better answers than Proudhon had given to the question 'what is property?' In Chapter 4 we saw how the young Marx used the concept of 'estrangement' to construct models of commodity circulation and capitalist production, founded on horizontal and vertical social divisions. These were coupled with analyses of how the alienation and appropriation of products and labour-power occurred within such models.

The purpose was to elucidate the historical meaning and economic function of 'private property' in European society. This was the beginning of the path that led to his definitive dismissal of Proudhon's effort in 1865:

> The question was so falsely formulated that it could not be answered correctly. *Ancient* 'property relations' were swallowed up by *feudal* property relations and these by '*bourgeois*' property relations. Thus history itself had practised its criticism on past property relations. What Proudhon was actually dealing with was *modern bourgeois property* as it exists today. The question of what this is could only have been answered by a critical analysis of '*political economy*', embracing these property relations as a whole, not in their legal expression as *voluntary relations* but in their real form, that is, as *relations of production*. But as he entangled the whole of these economic relations in the general juristic conception of '*property*', Proudhon could not get beyond the answer which Brissot, in a similar work, had already, before 1789, given in the same words: 'Property is theft'. But . . . theft as a forcible violation of property presupposes the existence of property . . . [1]

Marx's methodological criticisms of Proudhon were threefold. First, he cast doubt on the utility of inquiring into the nature of property in general, as he had done with 'production in general', and for the same reasons: the meaning of property varied with different social and historical modes of production. However, Marx did not take a reductionist view of property: there was something – some distinct level of meaning – which actually did vary from one period and one society to another, depending on the character of the relations of production. Accordingly, as with 'production' and 'solidarity', we can frame a 'rational abstraction' corresponding to this 'something' – what I have called, clumsily enough, 'possessory relations between persons and things' – and even try to theorise about it. The second criticism was that Proudhon failed to distinguish between this general substratum of possessory relations and 'modern bourgeois property' – obviously a confusion to be avoided.

Marx's third criticism was that Proudhon failed even to analyse modern bourgeois property relations properly. He did not distinguish their 'legal expression' from their 'real form', and concentrated on the former, more superficial aspect; whereas this could only be understood by investigating the latter, the production relations which determined it. This is a much weightier objection, and raises familiar difficulties often collected under the heading of 'the problem of legality'. In the course of this and the following chapters I hope to provide solutions to most of these difficulties. In the meantime, I want to suggest a reading of Marx's slightly careless wording in his letter to Schweitzer which will hopefully be substantiated by what is to follow. 'Property relations as a whole' is to be seen as referring to the set of possessory relations corresponding to a given mode of production. It has two aspects: voluntary relations between persons, and economically determined relations between things. People enact roles reflecting their production relations, in so far as they interact as 'personifications' of these economic relations between things; yet they do so only by simultaneously entering into 'voluntary relations', which find 'legal expression' in 'the general juristic conception of "property"' and which are in turn influenced by it. This distinction between economic relations and voluntary relations is more relevant to alienation and appropriation, i.e. to the social *movement* of property rather than its existence *qua* property, and therefore will not be elucidated further until the next chapter. Nevertheless, alienation and appropriation, no less than theft (i.e. illicit appropriation) presuppose at least recognised possession. It therefore seems worth while to analyse the framework of assumptions about 'static' possessory relations, within which alienation sets things in motion, before examining the 'dynamic' aspect.

It is obviously true, at the level of historical social systems, that possessory relations have greatest structural significance in the context of the economy, and that economic factors therefore determine the major forms in which they affect social life and hence receive legal codification. Nevertheless, it remains that economic objects are only one area of application of possessory relations, however important, and that as elementary *social* relations between persons and things they can be studied in abstraction from any particular application. There is therefore a distinctive sociological approach to possessory relations, which treats them first and foremost as social facts, *sui generis*, whatever cultural contents they may acquire.

Much that has been written on the question of whether 'property relations' belong to an 'economic base' or a 'legal superstructure' is irrelevant for this reason. All action occurring in the social setting of 'economic institutions' involves assumptions and decisions about owner-ship, and indeed this is true also of societies in which economic and legal institutions are much less differentiated from kinship or other customary settings than in our own. The degree to which any of these assumptions or decisions, whether on particular occasions or in some general way, may or may not 'accord with the law' – or whatever code of rules is recognised as authoritative – is obviously often inquired into and put to the test, both practically and academically. But it does not follow that one and the same transaction is regulated by a special set of norms – legal, superstructural norms – in so far as it concerns ownership, and by other norms in its other aspects. Rather, it is regulated by the norms of ownership current in the social milieu in question, of which the law may or may not be an adequate *résumé*. The fact that the transaction *may* be deliberately regulated by reference to the law, if the parties so design, makes no difference; except that if such is the general custom (e.g. where lawyers are employed to draw up contracts) then law is likely to correspond closely with practice in that area of social life, and the legal definition of ownership will approximate to the sociological. Although sociologists are accustomed to thinking about ownership sociologically, critics of Marx have often refused to extend to him the same licence. By doing so, I shall try to rescue his theory of property from some of the dilemmas which his own formulations have often provoked.

2 DURKHEIM AND WEBER ON PROPERTY

Marx, Durkheim and Weber all received a legal education, and all three tried to probe beneath the facade of the legal doctrine of private property to its social reality. Marx succeeded in probing deeper than his successors, but their attempts are worth briefly reviewing.

Durkheim's approach to property in *The Division of Labour* was a promising one. He set out to use property law (as he had used penal law) as an *index* of something more fundamental: the shared assumptions and sentiments concerning ownership which were actually current in social practice, and of which the law was assumed to be a more or less abstract codification or crystallised expression. For, however much they may be influenced by what is said and done by lawyers and administrators in the various contexts of lawmaking and legal practice, it is nevertheless these everyday assumptions and sentiments which determine how things actually enter into the general processes of social life and how they function there.

Like Marx, Durkheim appeared also to be aware of the importance of things in human society:

> Things, to be sure, form part of society, just as persons, and they play a specific role in it. Thus it is necessary that their relations with the social organism be determined. We may then say that there is a solidarity of things whose nature is quite special and translates itself outside through juridical consequences of a very particular character.[2]

Since I have defined 'solidarity' in terms of mutual attraction between persons, it is not a suitable term to use for the sentiments linking people with things. Nevertheless, Durkheim used it to make an important point, although his treatment of this theme was, on the whole, disappointing. He went on to argue that 'the most complete relation which can exist between a thing and a person is that which makes the former entirely dependent on the latter.' This is 'real solidarity', so called because it corresponds to the legal category of 'real rights', rights *in rebus*. But he introduced the idea only in order to dismiss it:

> Thus we see what this real solidarity consists of; it directly links things to

persons, but not persons among themselves. In a strict sense, one can exercise a real right by thinking one is alone in the world, without reference to other men. Consequently, since it is only through the medium of persons that things are integrated in society, the solidarity resulting from this integration is wholly negative. It does not lead wills to move toward common ends, but merely makes things gravitate around wills in orderly fashion. Because real rights are thus limited, they do not cause conflicts; hostility is precluded, but there is no active coming together, no consensus.[3]

Marx's treatment allows us to see that Durkheim, in arguing from the legal definition of property rights to their social significance and function, fell victim to a typical 'juridical illusion'. As Marx put it in *The German Ideology*:

> The *jus utendi et abutendi*, the right to dispose of a thing at will, itself asserts . . . the illusion that private property itself is based solely on the private will, the arbitrary disposal of the thing. In practice, the *abuti* has very definite economic limitations for the owner of private property, if he does not wish to see his property and hence his *jus abutendi* pass into other hands, since actually the thing, considered merely with reference to his will, is not a thing at all, but only becomes a thing, true property, in intercourse, and independently of the law.[4]

When we take account of the ways in which ownership functions in men's social metabolism with nature, it is by no means true that it precludes hostility; nor, on the other hand, that it 'contributes nothing to the unity of the social body.'[5]

In *Economy and Society*, Max Weber used the concept of 'appropriation' to develop a sociological analysis of property that Parsons, with perhaps undue neglect of Marx and Durkheim, has called 'unique in the literature'.[6] He treated appropriation, which he did not define, as an aspect of the 'closure' of a relationship against outsiders, by which the 'participation of certain persons is excluded, limited or subjected to conditions.' Closure is usually associated, Weber claimed, with monopolisation of certain advantages for the members, and appropriation is one of the ways in which the monopolised advantages may be made available to the members. They may be left open for competitive struggle by members, or distributed by regulation or rationing, or 'appropriated by individuals or subgroups on a permanent basis . . . The last is a case of closure within, as well as against outsiders.' The following definitions emerge:

> Appropriated advantages will be called 'rights' . . . A party to a closed social relationship will be called a 'member' (*Rechtsgenosse*); if his participation is regulated in such a way as to guarantee him appropriated advantages, a 'privileged' member. Appropriated rights which

are enjoyed by individuals through inheritance or by hereditary groups, whether communal or associative, will be called the 'property' of the individual or the groups in question; and, in so far as they are alienable 'free' property.[7]

The question of the heritability of property which Weber raises here is obviously important for the relationship between property and class structure in sociological theory, and will be dealt with in due course. There seems to be no advantage, however, in tying 'property' to heritability by definition, and making this the distinction between property rights and other rights. It led Weber into making a distinction between 'acquisition classes' and 'property classes', for example, that divides entrepreneurial from rentier status in a somewhat rigid manner. Moreover, while Marx and Weber agreed on the importance of the criterion of alienability, Marx's 'bourgeois property' — which was heritable and alienable — was both narrower and wider than Weber's 'free property' — i.e. *inherited* alienable property. For transmission of bourgeois property by inheritance depended on continuous acquisition through exploitation.

Because he sought to adapt his sociology to subjectivist economics, Weber perhaps underrated the importance of things in social life. He referred to them only under abstract and subjectivistic designations such as 'utilities', 'advantages', etc., without exploring many of the sociological implications of these as distinct social roles occupied by things, and by things of different kinds. But his basic idea, that property arises as social relationships develop into groups and as participants close their boundaries against outsiders, institutionalising the relations to things that are implicit in the initial situation, contains the germ of a more penetrating treatment of property than Durkheim's. In what follows I shall try to develop this germ into a theory that draws on the notions worked out in Chapter 5, beginning with the most elementary of possessory bonds, possession itself.

3 POSSESSION

Marx's notes on James Mill provide a convenient starting-point for our inquiry:

> Economics, as does the actual process, starts from the relationship of man to man as that of private proprietor to private proprietor . . . man as private proprietor [*Privateigentümer*] is presupposed, i.e. man as an exclusive possessor [*exklusiver Besitzer*] who by means of this exclusive possession maintains his personality and distinguishes himself from other men . . .[8]

Here Marx straightaway tried to reduce the spurious universality of 'private property' by classifying it as one (historically specific) form of the wider category of 'possession'. It is the form which possession takes when its object is the attribute by which a social unit ('man') differentiates itself from other units and excludes them from the social space occupied by its personality.

This definition allows 'possession' and 'property' to be related to the previous analysis of solidarity and estrangement. That discussion began from the assumption that differing situations would induce selective perception of the environment, so that persons would be seen as bearers or representatives of situationally dependent attributes. Perception would be not only selective, but abstract and holistic, in the sense that all save the situationally salient aspects of a person would be ignored, while person-plus-salient-attributes would appear as bound up together in a single *Gestalt*, a structured but unanalysed whole. Social attraction would depend on the perceiver's ability to recognise himself as mirrored in the same *Gestalt* and to identify with it; solidarity would require such recognition to be mutual. In all this discussion it was taken for granted that the attributes in question were personal qualities and performances, and experimental findings have mostly related to these also. However, they can just as easily be objects altogether external to the person: in fact, it would probably be exceptional for a *Gestalt* relating to personal qualities or performances not to include relevant external objects as well. The very idea of *situationally* dependent perceptual complexes rather supposes that they will normally be included. Thus, persons and things are seen, with situationally determined saliency, as 'bound up together' into given wholes, and such perceptions of others are also taken as models by which we interpret our own relationships to the things about us. It is no disparagement of the experimentalists' discoveries, relating mutual attraction and hostility in small groups to personal traits and actions, to agree with Marx that most institutional social settings give salience to similitudes and differences established through relationships to *things*, which thus determine the main groupings and divisions in society at large. And in these same phenomena also, it would seem, must be sought the processual sources of possession and property.

In its most elementary form, therefore, possession is simply an aspect of the processes by which collective and hence also individual identities arise. Let us assume that the common attribute in terms of which two persons recognise each other as representatives of their own selfhood — and which becomes a primary similitude from which solidarity and collective personality may develop, as well as a new individual identity on both sides — includes a relationship to some thing or things. This relationship needs to be specified a little further, for it may be either positive or negative in the sense that the attribute may require either the *presence* or the *absence* of the thing. *Use* is the commonest case of the first, *need* of the second. There are clearly other examples of both, but let us take these as paradigms. The primary similitude will then include either the presence or absence of certain things as a necessary condition for the qualities and performances that constitute use or need, and the things in question form part of the same similitude. Possession and its opposite, non-possession, consist simply in the interpersonal or social confirmation of this fact as a special aspect of the situation.

To see how this comes about it is only necessary to remember that with the further development of interaction on the basis of a shared attribute, the attribute tends to become a group norm. Just as a shared quality or performance tends to become a standardised expectation, so too does the presence or absence of the things they entail. It is these shared expectations which are expressed in the everyday use of possessive locutions, when without any implication of rightful, permanent or legal ownership, we speak of having or not having things, of their belonging to people, or call them 'mine', 'his', 'ours', etc. There is no difference between possessing detachable things, at this level, and possessing undetachable attributes or 'properties' of ourselves: physical traits, moral qualities, and so forth are equally 'ours', and are spoken about as 'things' that we have or lack. To simplify the discussion, non-possession is left aside at this point, while possession is analysed further.

There are two interrelated dimensions along which the perception of person-thing relationships may vary. First, the primary similitude between persons may involve either similar relationships to one and the same thing, or similar relationships to separate things. Similar relationships to separate parts of the same thing is an intermediate position. The result will be either joint or individual possession, or some combination of the two. Secondly, the relationship between person and thing, within the perceived whole which they compose, may vary depending on which of them (in Marx's phrase) is its 'predominating moment'.[9] In other words, does the thing appear to be more an attribute of the person, or the person of the thing? Most cases of use approximate to the first, where the thing is an instrument or consumable object, clearly dependent for its motion on the causality of the person. But things which are more often preconditions than objects of use may so exceed the human individual in permanence, size, or causal efficacy that the person appears to pertain to them, rather than the reverse – the land which supports a tribe of hunters, the city which provides the environment of its inhabitants, the river that carries a fisherman in his boat, or a big ship that contains its crew, are examples. This is recognised in common parlance, in that we say the person 'belongs to' the land, the city, the ship, etc., rather than the reverse.

In everyday instances, there is some congruence between these two dimensions of variation. Things which are clearly person-dependent tend also to be objects of separate individual relationship and hence personal possession; while things to which persons seem to belong are more often things to which many persons have a common relationship. Thus while there are obviously cases of unambiguous joint possession – e.g. we would treat three men in a boat as its joint possessors unless or until we knew that one of them was its owner – it is nevertheless characteristic of joint possession that the persons often feel that they belong to the thing just as much as the thing to them, and are also seen and spoken about in this way. This is one of the sources for the institutional differentiation between political sovereignty and property. But it also plays an important role within Marx's theory of property, in that things to which many people 'belong' as appendages – land, ships, machinery – may also become dependent, as property, on the wills of other individuals.

So far, 'possession' has been deduced as a purely cognitive relationship from the model of mutual recognition and identification, but the possessive attitude includes characteristic sentiments also. Possession is usually accompanied by some degree of affection for the thing possessed, by protective care, and a sense of assurance and freedom in its use – all of this varying, of course, with its value in terms of usefulness, scarcity, symbolic association, etc. These sentiments possibly originate from the interpersonal attraction generated in the relationship in which the possessions have their place. To the extent that primary similitudes breed solidarity, this is likely to produce trust and confidence in the relationship and a shared positive evaluation of it. Possessory sentiments, in both joint and individual cases, would seem to be the extension of these effects of solidarity to its material conditions.

But every development in the direction of creating a new collective personality is simultaneously a modification of the individual personalities of the participants: accordingly, social sentiments arising in the social milieu also contribute something to the individual's self-feeling. This is particularly true of possessory sentiments, especially of course where they concern individual possessions. The main reason for this would seem to be that the individual can be alone with his possessions, and interact with them outside the direct interpersonal situation which gives them the meaning of 'his' things. Since they also exist outside his immediate bodily person, they can act as mirrors for his self-identity, substitutes for the other persons who are the real source of that identity. But as merely passive substitutes, they are flattering mirrors, which allow him a greater latitude of self-interpretation than the real others would. All possessions thus have a tendency to become infused with a self-indulgent self-love. 'Sentimental value' is a form of this; so is the collector's love of his specimens, and the suburbanite's cherishing of his status-symbols. But so also is avarice, the love of wealth that goes along with – and facilitates – a purely instrumental attitude to the commodities which are the means of getting it, and which Marx and Veblen saw as a hallmark of the 'pecuniary culture'.

4 OWNERSHIP

Starting from Marx's definition of property as exclusive possession, I have tried to derive 'possession' from the model of mutual identification through primary similitude. The aim of the argument, obviously, is to relate property (as 'exclusive possession') to tertiary similitude; but meanwhile, what of the secondary similitude implied by this? I propose to exploit the fact that the English language has the two words 'ownership' and 'property' where German has only *Eigentum*, and call 'ownership' the relation to things that is established through the secondary similitude of possessors. The principal justification for doing so will appear later, in the context of Marx's discussion of property in pre-capitalist societies, but the point of the distinction must be shown here.

The relation to things which has been called 'possession' is not given – or so it has been argued – in isolation from other attributes, but only in so far as other attributes require the expected presence or continuing availability of certain things. It is true that possession can be singled out and treated as though it were itself a special attribute, as when we apply to somebody the maxim that 'possession is nine parts of the law'. But in that case, the evidence for possession will still be the thing's observed and expected availability for use, etc. Possession may also develop into possessiveness, which may be immediately recognisable as an attribute of persons. But this is, again, merely a type of relation to things which requires their expected presence as its necessary condition: it presupposes possession, but does not establish it in isolation from any other relation or attribute. I stress these points because they imply that the secondary solidarity of possessors always involves, or presupposes, secondary similitude based on some primary similitude *other* than mere possession. The most important application of this is to the apparent historical divorce between ownership and labour. As Marx pointed out, the full significance of this ostensibly independent and self-contained category of ownership was inseparable from its special character as necessary and sufficient condition for *exemption* from labour, and a basis for leisure. As such, it implies ownership of a special kind, namely of means of exploitation, enabling their owners to be supported by the labour of others.

Secondary similitudes only become salient to the extent that the logical category of membership in the group of those sharing a primary similitude develops into a social role. Possession, under these circumstances, becomes the availability of things to persons in their capacity as members of the social group whose shared identity requires this availability. This is what I propose to call ownership, which may be either joint or several, depending on whether the initial relationship is to one and the same thing or to separate things. It will be remembered that social control was shown to arise on the basis of secondary similitude, in so far as it engendered secondary solidarity. For with the introduction of diversity amongst primary similitudes, and the possibility of separating secondary from primary solidarity, the group norm is converted into a common value, the expectation of uniformity becomes an obligation to conform, while reciprocal monitoring becomes mutual surveillance and normative constraint. Under these conditions, possession too acquires moral status. It becomes the availability of things on which the person, *qua* member of such-and-such a group, *ought* to be able to count.[10] Ownership therefore finds cultural expression as 'rights' — rights in what is owned jointly, and rights over what is owned in severalty. The universality inherent in group membership implies equality of rights in what is jointly owned, and equal rights of the several owners *vis-à-vis* one another; although both functional and status-evaluative criteria decree ranked priorities of access and use if (as is always partially the case) the group is inwardly differentiated in these ways.

This several ownership cannot imply absolute freedom to use or dispose of the thing as the owner sees fit. For it is a right founded on the indispensability of the thing for a quality or performance required for group membership, and therefore is likely to be recognised only if activated in conformity with substantive group standards. In other words, the exercise of rights of ownership is circumscribed by the duties inherent in the role that ownership subserves. For the same reason, several ownership differs from legal 'private property' in so far as the latter is a form that can be indifferently satisfied by any and every content. It follows, too, that the extent to which a thing is alienable varies with the conditions of ownership.

An object of joint ownership may sometimes be alienated by common consent, even if it means dissolving the group, as in the winding up of a trust. In other cases, however, as with tribal land perhaps, the community of owners may be taken to include the dead and the unborn, rendering it inalienable. Between joint ownership and several ownership lies a wide range of possible distributions of rights of members in things attached to the group, and such distributions of varying rights in and over the same objects may often make alienation a virtual impossibility. Even the case of individual ownership, where rights in one thing are concentrated in one member, does not imply alienability. In transient groups the loss, destruction or alienation of the things that qualify for membership simply involves loss of membership for the individual. If the thing passes to another, he becomes eligible for membership. In permanent groups, certain things, or kinds of things, requisite for role-performance may become inalienable objects of several ownership; although there is usually a distinction between more and less essential conditions, or different classes of membership for those differently qualified by their possessions.

The recognition of separate ownership by individual members of a solidary group is not a difference that necessarily provokes estrangement, any more than mere human discreteness is. It is true, tritely enough, that simply because things are detachable from persons and interchangeably serviceable to them, individuals from the nursery upwards may be tempted to covet or steal others' possessions, and disputes about ownership – and hence estrangements – arise often enough from simple mistakes. Thus, while Hobbesian behaviour is always deviant and occasional in any settled social context, it still happens often enough, and social contexts are often enough unsettled, for a certain degree of exclusivism, envy and suspicion to surround most individual ownership simply because of what it is, and however solidary the group in which it occurs. This factor may be reinforced by the marginal differentiation that results from tension between the individual personality's drive towards consistency and the collective personality's demand for conformity. In so far as the individual 'presents' his personality as an aspect of his various role-performances, this differentiation isolates him in a circle of estrangement that constitutes his 'private space'. This circle will inevitably contain possessions – his clothing, so far as it is distinctive, and all the intimate 'props' and furnishings with which he tries to stage his uniqueness, his personal style. Thus, through individuated consumption styles, or through occupational specialisations that connect personal attributes with specific instruments or products (as skills, craftmanship, etc.) or that endow the person with distinctive trappings and appurtenances, several ownership may become associated with individuality in ways that provoke estrangement.

This will be the more salient the more competitive the situation, and is pretty much ubiquitous within all solidary groups inasmuch as personal individuation, expressed through possessions, is linked with status-rivalry. However, since esteem is accorded in terms of shared values, the effect of this possessory emulation is not to weaken cohesion, though it may change the content of solidarity through progressive idealisation of primary similitudes. The impact of all these factors is very much enhanced where the solidary group in question is segmented, and the segments are represented by individual heads. An extreme development in this direction is the potlatch, where competitive giving or destruction of family goods by chieftains is the means of winning prestige and discrediting the recipients. Clearly, there is a limit to the amount of estrangement, emanating from such contests, that can be tolerated by a society that depends on solidarity for its cohesion.

Despite all these ways in which individual or subgroup ownership may provide occasions for estrangement within solidary groups, the recognition of separate ownership nevertheless remains distinct from the exclusion of outsiders, where estrangement predominates. Thus, within a family each member is recognised as the owner of certain things, and each thing is familiar as belonging to some particular other person and has its place in family life as part of his or her belongings. No mutual repulsion is involved. Even in a larger solidary group where there is more estrangement, such as a village, it is still generally known to whom most things belong and this bond is seldom questioned.[11] Familiarity and mutual trust underlie both frequency of borrowing and the bitterness of such disputes about ownership as do arise. A rather different example is that of two chess-players, who within the conventions of the game recognise one another as undisputed temporary owners of the pieces of either side, as different parts of a single whole. Regardless of whose 'property' the set may be, the solidarity of playing the game (which combines with the estrangement generated by competition to produce the characteristic tension of games of rivalry) requires each to recognise the other's ownership of 'his' pieces as a necessary condition of his role-performance. In all these examples the sense of non-ownership is not readily distinguishable from acknowledging ownership by known others, and approximates to recognising separate shares in a common stock.

This is in striking contrast with the general assumption of non-ownership of our surroundings that accompanies all activity outside the confines of such solidary groups. This assumption (and sentiment) has as its corollary the supposition that everything belongs to somebody else, unknown and possibly hostile, and a feeling of unease if one appears to be risking an accusation of trespassing on another's preserve. Respect for other people's property, in this situation, is an ingrained repulsion from most of the environment, of which avoidance, and hence abstention from what is not one's own, are mere consequences, without moral significance. This is the counterpart, with respect to things, of the all-round estrangement characteristic of modern urban life and of bourgeois society generally. Its basis is simply the exclusion of any single individual from the sphere of ownership of all but a very few of the myriad mutually estranged groups of which the society is composed.

5 PROPERTY

Mutual attraction and collective identity on the basis of possession carries with it, of course, joint repulsion from non-possessors of the things or thing in question. This secondary difference can become a source of estrangement and of tertiary solidarity on the part of the ownership group. In Marx's words, each member becomes 'an exclusive possessor who by means of this exclusive possession maintains his personality and distinguishes himself from other men.' And although caution is necessary to avoid confusion at this point, it seems not unreasonable to reserve 'property' for this aspect of possessory relations, their quality as *exclusive* ownership. This is consistent with the conclusion which Durkheim reached in *Professional Ethics and Civic Morals*, that 'The right of property can be far better defined negatively than in terms of positive content, by the exclusion it involves rather than the prerogatives it confers.'[12]

The distinction drawn here between ownership and property corresponds to that made earlier between positive and negative solidarity.

Ownership refers to the interior aspect of a collectivity's possessory relations, as spelt out in the sentiments, rights and duties of members regarding the things necessary for the reproduction and maintenance of the whole. Of this, Durkheim might correctly have asserted that it can be activated by imagining that the collectivity is alone in the world. Property, on the other hand, refers to the exterior aspect of possession, deriving from the collectivity's action in establishing its boundaries, distances and immunities against others. And just as the emphasis of a group's solidarity may be either primarily positive or primarily negative, so its possessory relationships may involve either mainly ownership or mainly proprietorship. Thus business firms, trade unions and other secondary associations which operate as mutually estranged units in bourgeois society, so far as they are internally solidary are mainly actuated by collective jealousy and acquisitiveness regarding their property – the negative solidarity of economic conflict-groups. The mention of trade unions in this connection illustrates the terminological point that, while individual 'ownership' – in the shape of entitlement to a certain kind of employment and rate of pay – is a normal part of union membership, to call this 'property' is to refer to the external struggle of the union to protect all its members' earnings and conditions. Wages are here property only *vis-à-vis* capital. But if we wished to talk about competition between individual wage-earners, we should have to refer to wages as the property of the worker's family or household.

It would be a mistake to follow the young Marx and equate property in the sense of exclusive possession with 'private property'. Indeed, private property does not really fit at all into the terminology as so far developed. On the one hand, it corresponds, apparently, to a 'pure type' of property, where the meaning of possession is solely determined by the negative solidarity involved in excluding others from control or influence over an object. But in addition to this, it seems to contain two other conditions which contradict the first. First, it is vested only in individuals; second, these individuals comprise a legal community, mutually recognising each other's rights. These are contradictory because, in our model, if individuals hold property against others, it is always as the representatives of some collectivity which is estranged from others; and because this mutual estrangement is not easily compatible with the solidarity implied by mutual recognition of rights in a *Rechtsgenossenschaft*.

At one level, Marx interpreted private property as an ideological abstraction of those aspects of market relationships which entered the purview of legal practice. Pure property rights in isolation from all duties or stipulations as to the nature or treatment of things owned, and free alienability as a consequence of untrammelled freedom of use – these correspond to formal requirements for entering market transactions. Membership in a market can be obtained with any thing whatever, and it will count as an object of ownership just so long as it has market value. But whether or not it has can only be demonstrated by successful exchange. Thus although at any given time only certain things and not others are actually functioning as commodities in society, the market criterion of ownership is formally open to any and every innovation:anything can be alienated for an equivalent.

The obligations of ownership which *in fact* correspond to the legal abstraction of private property in capitalist society take· the form of economic 'morality' – especially, the dutiful acquisitive assiduity that Weber called 'the spirit of capitalism' – and are not legally formulated. Hence they appear to belong to a 'private' sphere where conscience and not law prevails. In fact, however, what prevails are the norms and values of social classes, and within productive units, the discipline of the capitalist enterprise. For the 'individuals' operating as buyers and sellers in the market are there as representatives of competing and mutually estranged collectivities – firms, families, etc. – and, through them, of the social classes in which these are embedded. Market competition requires a limited solidarity at the point of contact of these estranged units, allowing mutual recognition of property rights to take place. It is not this, however, which brings or holds them together: it merely makes possible the antagonistic satisfaction of their need for one another's wares. The idea of a community of rights is a jurists' abstraction from the fact that the courts must adjudicate, in terms of rights, disputes arising from the very limited character of this solidarity. Its very fragility is evinced in the fact that its norms do not remain at the level of social morality, as class norms do, but must be proclaimed and enforced by means of law, i.e. as a by-product of processes aimed at verifying and punishing breaches of trust.

In addition to these requirements for operating in markets, the legal concept of 'private property' contains two other elements which have grown up in historical conjunction with them. The first is the idea of private property as excluded from, and excluding public ownership, or public property. The basis for this was seemingly the differentiation between two strata of private property within feudalism – that of the monarch, which became increasingly tied to the office rather than the person and family of the ruler – and that of subjects, which became increasingly tied to the person and family of the owner, and divorced from his role as vassal. With the development of a bureaucracy living off the state through fiscal exploitation, this kingly or 'Crown' property was ideologically reinterpreted as 'public property', by analogy with the *ager publicus* of antiquity. Since the bureaucracy found itself increasingly involved in taxing, regulating and sitting in judgment on the property of subjects involved in market transactions, held and expressed as money values, a sharp distinction came to be drawn between state and society, corresponding to public and private spheres, *imperium* and *dominium*, mutually exclusive domains of ownership governed by public and private interest respectively. Different political constitutions and ideologies varied in the degree of primacy accorded to the one over the other, corresponding to the power struggles of elite groups. Historically, this aspect of private property was most significant while the nation-state was still the principal arena for the power and activity of capitalist classes, during the eighteenth and nineteenth centuries. With the rise to predominance of international capital in the twentieth, and its struggle with international socialism, national economic policies came to embrace and largely efface the internal political difference between public and private property, both sides in the struggle contributing to this result.

The second element contained in the idea of 'private property' is more important, sociologically, since it has corresponded closely with a prevalent aspect of social practice and social structure. This is the idea of private property as a right to something which, once acquired, and if not alienated by consent, can cease only with the death of the proprietor. The criterion of consent related primarily to the need for free alienability in a market society, already referred to. The identification of the property right with the biological duration of the individual life, however, in abstraction from any substantive social role or capacity, was an extraneous idea. Its basis was not the society of biological atoms which it appeared to envisage, but a society in which class structure hinged on the succession of property in families and in which the representative function of head, proprietor, and market operator had come to be vested in the male parent as an attribute of his genealogical status in the family. Before the 'public', therefore, the family appeared as a 'private individual', to whose actual person its property pertained. Thus there appeared to be no way, other than through his consent or death, that it could cease to pertain to him.

Thus the ideological conception of the independent individual as the unit of private proprietorship arose out of the historical conjunction and functional convergence of two modes of alienation, each corresponding to a distinct social milieu. On the one hand, market society required that individuals acting as buyers and sellers recognise each other as independent owners of freely alienable commodities; on the other, a class system based on family inheritance required that sons should succeed fathers as genealogical incarnations of the family name and property. Hence property, unless alienated by consent, was deemed to pertain to named individuals throughout their biological lifetime, or until this succession occurred – as it were, by alienation in the course of nature. Underlying all these ideological conceptions arising from contract law and the law of succession, however, are real social processes and formal constraints, which will be examined in the next chapter.

First, however, the utility of the concepts developed in this chapter, for elucidating Marx's treatment of possessory relations, will be put to the proof in a brief examination of primitive communalism, as presented in the *Grundrisse*.

6 POSSESSORY RELATIONS IN TRIBAL SOCIETY

Marx approached the analysis of precapitalist formations by constructing a model that would be the logical antithesis to 'the formula of capital.' In the latter,

> living labour relates to the raw material as well as to the instrument and to the means of subsistence required during labour, as negatives, as not-property . . .[13]

The opposite would be 'the relation of the working (producing or self-reproducing) subject to the conditions of his production or reproduction as *his own*'.[14] Let us call the first (capitalist) model the negative model, and the second the positive model, of the worker's possessory relation to the conditions of production. Marx then supposed that some version of the positive model must correspond to the primordial historical condition of human society. In this case, the conditions of production would themselves be natural, not produced. And since human society emerged from animal existence through natural evolution, it would be absurd to take any other starting point than a 'natural unity of labour with its material pre-suppositions':[15]

> It is not the *unity* of living, active humanity with the natural, inorganic conditions of their metabolic exchange with nature, and hence their appropriation of nature, which requires explanation or is the result of a historic process, but rather the *separation* between these inorganic conditions of human existence and this active existence, a separation which is completely posited only in the relation of wage labour and capital.[16]

The situation corresponding to the negative model, 'the positing of the individual as a *worker*, in this nakedness' – 'as a free worker, as objectless, purely subjective labour capacity confronting the objective conditions of production as his *not-property*, as *alien property*' – could only be 'itself a product of history'.[17] Hence, the historical presence of the free worker, as the basic condition for capitalist production, logically implies that the positive model cannot apply. And on the assumption that it originally did so, this entails, as historical condition for capitalism, dissolution of all social formations to which it once did apply – a process which capitalism itself completes.

Marx then asked what the meaning of the possessory relation would be in the positive model, and his answer, translated into the terminology of this chapter, was that *ownership* predominated. Thus, a situation where the workers are separated from the conditions of production, which belong to non-workers, is necessarily a situation of general estrangement in which *property* — i.e. relations of mutual exclusion — governs economic life. But the union of the worker with the conditions of production, so that 'the individual relates to himself as owner [*Eigentümer*], as master of the conditions of his reality', was also a situation of positive solidarity, where economic life was organised in terms of ownership. 'The individuals relate not as workers but as owners — and as members of a community, who at the same time work.'[18] In what follows I shall take the liberty of translating *Eigentum* by 'ownership' rather than 'property' in cited passages, where appropriate, although the argument turns, of course, not on terminology but on the substance of what Marx said.

The conditions of production were categorised as land and raw materials; instruments of production; and means of subsistence during labour. If an individual producer is to relate to all of these as 'master', the mode of production must be a simple one. In fact, the basic relationship is satisfied only by a possessory relation to the land, the earth: for 'the earth is the great workshop, the arsenal which furnished both means and material of labour' — it includes the other conditions. So the 'natural unity of labour with its material presuppositions' can be fully present only in hunting and food gathering, pastoral, and perhaps agrarian societies.

Marx distinguished two aspects of this possessory relation. First:

> The individual relates simply to the objective conditions of labour as being his; [relates] to them as the inorganic nature of his subjectivity, in which the latter realizes itself . . . a presupposition of his activity just like his skin, his sense organs . . .
> *Ownership* thus originally means no more than a human being's relation to his natural conditions of production as belonging to him, as his, as presupposed along with his own being; relations to them as natural presuppositions of his self, which only form, so to speak, his extended body.[19]

The earth and its natural products are treated as attributes by the individual, as one who reproduces his existence by his own work. They are taken to be parts of a situation defined by reference to *his* labour as its centre. As was stressed in discussing possession, earlier, possessory relations arise from singling out those situationally determined attributes of persons which, unlike their skin and sense organs, are detached from their body. But the sense in which attributes are 'his', whether detached or attached, is the same in both cases.

The second aspect is that

> this relation to land and soil, to the earth, as owned by the labouring individual . . . is instantly mediated by the naturally evolved, spontaneous, or more or less historically developed and modified presence of

the individual as *member of a commune* – his naturally evolved presence as member of a tribe, etc. An isolated individual could no more own land and soil than he could speak . . . If the objective conditions of his labour are presupposed as belonging to him, then he himself is subjectively presupposed as member of a commune, through which his relation to the objective conditions of labour is mediated.[20]

Here Marx ran together three distinct ideas. The first is that the earth, in so far as it is an attribute of the working individual, is so by virtue of also being a primary similitude that links him with others. 'The' working individual here refers not just to one specimen, but to any one of a population of similar units. Only by recognising himself in others is he able to treat the land as 'his' and possess it. For the same reason, his attitude to the land is the correlative and product of his solidarity with his fellows.

Secondly, his relationship to the land goes beyond mere possession, and is one of ownership, rightful possession, because his solidarity with his fellows extends to their secondary similitude as members of the same group, occupying a single territory and working it together or side by side.

Thirdly, his character as labouring individual is, from the first, treated (by himself and his fellows) as part of a larger, more inclusive role: he is a self-reproducing individual. Hence the group which these individuals form is likewise a self-reproducing collectivity: as 'members' and parts of this whole they are defined as reproducers of themselves and of their interrelationship. Thus labour and the relation to the earth, which is an essential component of this role, is nevertheless subordinate to biological reproduction and the particular ideological conceptions through which this is secured. For 'this naturally evolved clan community . . . is the first presupposition – the communality of blood, language, customs – for the appropriation of the objective conditions of their life.'[21] What was in Marx's mind here was that the rights and duties of work and ownership were largely incapsulated within age, sex and kinship roles. No doubt his reasoning already anticipated the point made later by Engels:

The social institutions under which men of a definite historical epoch and of a definite country live are conditioned by both kinds of production: by the stage of development of labour, on the one hand, and of the family, on the other. The less the development of labour, and the more limited its volume of production and, therefore, the wealth of society, the more preponderatingly does the social order appear to be dominated by ties of sex.[22]

The merit of this general idea is clearly independent of its particular applications by Marx and Engels on the basis of inadequate ethnographical data. In the present context, it yielded an interpretation of the positive model as applied to a primordial society where all members work, and share a relation of ownership to their territory and its natural products, by virtue of membership roles in a community primarily organised in terms of genealogical categories. Common descent, language, customs, territory and mode of production provide the basis for a 'mechanical' positive solidarity.

We can follow Marx and call this 'communal' ownership (*Gemeindeeigentum*). However, Marx treated this as synonymous with *common* ownership, and here it is best not to follow him. Ethnography encourages us to recognise that communal ownership (i.e. ownership by virtue of membership in a commune, or tribal settlement, etc.) may take the form either of 'joint' ownership or of 'several' ownership; and our theory certainly permits this. Furthermore, Marx's own treatment of the more developed forms of the primitive community, where several ownership is conspicuous, positively requires this amendment. Marx lacked a concept intermediate between 'possession' and 'property', but 'ownership', as defined in this chapter, fills a gap whose existence is betrayed by confusions and difficulties in his terminology.

In the more primitive conditions of foodgathering, hunting and pastoral economies there is 'communal appropriation (temporary) and utilization of the land' and this is also joint ownership of the land.

> . . . mankind first seizes hold of the ready-made fruits of the earth, among whom belong, e.g. animals, and for him especially the ones that can be tamed. Nevertheless even this situation – hunting, fishing, herding, gathering fruits from trees, etc. – always presupposes appropriation of the earth, whether for a fixed residence, or for roaming, or for animal pasture.[23]

However, not all labour is collective; therefore, individuals must also be enabled to exercise their joint ownership separately. Where this is done in recognised ways, according to Marx, it establishes 'individual possession' within the overall common ownership. Thus there exists both

> the relation to land and soil mediated by the community as its own, as communal land ownership, [and] at the same time individual possession for the individual, or in such a way that only the fruits are divided, but the land itself and the labour remain common.
> . . . wherever ownership exists *only* as communal ownership, there the individual member is as such only *possessor* of a particular part, hereditary or not, since any fraction of the property belongs to no member for himself, but to him only as immediate member of the commune, i.e. as in direct unity with it, not in distinction to it. This individual is thus only a possessor . . . The mode of this possession may

be historically, locally, etc. modified in quite different ways depending on whether labour itself is performed by the private possessor in isolation, or is in turn determined by the commune . . .[24]

'Individual possession' here is consistent with the generic sense of 'possession' introduced earlier. Wherever individuals exercised their rights of joint ownership in tribal land by their own solitary or family labour, those parts of the common whole that pertained to this particular labouring role would appear to others as 'theirs' – as their possessions – and they would be treated accordingly, as legitimate occupiers or users. Yet while not incompatible, these two senses of 'possession' are not the same, for one is presupposed by ownership, while the other presupposes it. We shall have occasion to analyse this second sense later, but for the present may simply define it as the effect of individuals appropriating the use of what is jointly owned. In practice, transitions between appropriating the use and appropriating the thing itself must be frequent, so that possession might even be regarded as the individual's means of converting what is originally given as a natural product of jointly owned land into a movable object of several ownership.

This communal ownership is also, when looked at from the standpoint of the commune's external relations, communal property. It is important to observe that when the commune is protecting its communal property from invasion, it is defending both joint and several ownership. So if we speak of the individual's 'property' here, the reference is to the exclusion from what is severally owned, not of fellow-members of the commune, but of non-members. Whether and how far several ownership develops into exclusive property internally is a separate question, depending on the intrusion of factors such as status rivalry or economic competition, and the fragmentation of the commune into estranged segments or strata.

The premise of joint landownership has to be modified when one turns from pastoral to agricultural societies. With cultivation, the land itself becomes an instrument of production which one man or a family can work in such a way as to appear as the permanent possessor of his plot. Hence several ownership of land becomes possible, and the more probable the more intensive the agriculture. Marx analysed three derivative forms of the primordial tribal model, Asiatic, Ancient and Germanic, which exhibited various forms of this development. I shall not follow his very condensed discussion in detail, but merely touch on the major aspects of their possessory relations.

The Asiatic form is the most archaic, and its basis – village economy – the least dynamic and most persistent. It consists, in fact, of an indefinitely large segmental juxtaposition of communes, which have multiplied and aggregated by colonisation, confederation or conquest from above. 'The state is then the supreme lord. Sovereignty here consists in the ownership of land concentrated on a national scale'[25] – especially where the state actually creates and sustains cultivable land through irrigation works, etc. Hence

> the comprehensive unity standing above all these little communities appears as the higher owner or as the sole owner; the real communities hence only as hereditary possessors.

For the individual, ownership

> appears mediated for him through a cession by the total unity – a unity realized in the form of the despot, the father of the many communities – to the individual, through the mediation of the particular commune . . . A part of his surplus-labour belongs to the higher community, which exists ultimately as a *person*, and this surplus labour takes the form of tribute, etc., as well as common labour for the exaltation of the unity, partly of the real despot, partly of the imagined clan-being, the god.[26]

It is perhaps as well to stress that, in Marx's theory, the oriental despot differed fundamentally from the ruler of a socialist state, in that he represented the unity of his subjects and was supreme landowner not by virtue of his office alone, but in his person.[27] Thus amassing treasure and spending luxuriously, criminal in a socialist dictator, could be political virtue in the despot. However, although Marx says that the combination of despotic ownership and possession by villages is 'not in the least a contradiction', he also points out that

> On the other hand, since in this form the individual never becomes an owner but only a possessor, he is at bottom himself the property, the slave of him in whom the unity of the commune exists.[28]

What is involved here, it may be suggested, is that the multiplication of communes and consequent vertical estrangement between them and the living symbol of their unity develops a contradiction that is latent within the primitive commune itself. This is hinted at by Marx when he says of tribal ownership:

> This relation as owner – not as a result but as a presupposition of labour, i.e. of production – presupposes the individual defined as member of a clan or community (whose property the individual himself is, up to a point.)[29]

The land, in other words 'belongs to' the community, but only on condition that the community can dispose of at least part of the labour of its members. Not only do the occupation and defense of the land have to be undertaken as a group: so also do many primitive hunting and grazing activities. As a link in the chain of human reproduction, moreover, the individual is not only a biological part of the community, he 'belongs to' it in that the disposal of his sexual and reproductive powers is governed by its rules. His co-ownership of communal land, although the condition for his being able to possess and own individual movable goods, nonetheless relates him to an entity which exceeds the scale of his own powers and to which he therefore appears and feels as though *he* 'belongs', rather than the reverse. For him, therefore, common ownership means, on the one hand, belonging to the communal land, and on the other being able to possess it for himself.

Marx suggests that this contradiction results in an ideological relationship of the individual to the totality of land and tribe. '. . . the labour process happens under these presuppositions (i.e. the presence of land and community, and the individual's connection with them as owner-member) which are not themselves the product of labour, but appear as its natural or *divine* presuppositions.' Because of their collective material dependence on the land, individuals are unable to think their double relationship to it as owners and possessors. They see themselves as enjoying possession guaranteed to them by the community personified as a divine being or ancestral spirit, in whom the land is vested and whose creatures they are. (It is in fact *this* relationship to which Marx says the relation of despot and subjects is 'not in the least a contradiction' – both being instances of the *same* contradiction.) If tribal society becomes segmented into lineages and villages this *numen* undergoes fetishisation: tribal solidarity is only mediated to the estranged segments through their common cult. From this point, transition to kingship may occur through appropriation of the cult by a chiefly lineage. Since ownership of all tribal land, in the form of the right of eminent domain, is dependent on the cult, the ruler becomes sole proprietor and hence sovereign. To the extent that this ideological attribute is converted into a monopoly of legislative and judicial functions, and of the means of violence necessary to enforce them, kingship develops into a form of state. This is what Weber called 'patrimonial' rule inasmuch as the monarch administers the realm as a personal estate and extension of his household.

Developments of this nature seem to be presupposed by Marx's concept of the theocratic sovereign landlord, whether in the Asiatic mode or elsewhere. The ideological hypertrophy typical of such despotic regimes can perhaps be explained by the deepening of the primitive contradiction, once the function of representing the unity of the whole has become concentrated in a dynasty estranged from the subordinated segments and sustained by a warrior bureaucracy. Political cohesion and fiscal exploitation necessitate more coercion and ideological pressure. The despot's territorial sovereignty seems to include all his subjects as adjuncts to the land and creatures of his will; yet as hereditary possessors of its parts, they are in fact exercising rights of occupation and use notionally deriving from their role as co-owners with him.

The Ancient type originates in conquest, later by colonisation. The military and therefore also economic and political presence of the fortified city remains a precondition of agrarian occupation, quite apart from the extent to which it also permits evolution of urban crafts, trade, etc. Hence

> in this case, the land is occupied by the commune, Roman land; a part remains to the commune as such as distinct from the commune members, *ager publicus* in its various forms; the other part is divided up and each parcel of land is Roman by virtue of being the private property, the domain of a Roman . . . but also, he is a Roman only in so far as he possesses this sovereign right over a part of the Roman earth.[30]

Here several ownership of land appears alongside joint ownership. Citizens have two relations to the national territory, and these are concretised in spatial terms. To the *ager publicus* they relate as members to a single thing, and to their individual farmland they relate as members to separate parts of a single thing. In that this several ownership is contingent on membership in the political body, and the object of ownership is only a subdivided attribute of the collectivity, this is still ownership within a solidary group, not the private proprietorship of estranged units.

However, three factors tend to modify this initial definition, and to justify Marx's use of the term 'private property' in this context. First, the original collectivity is by no means a primitive or homogeneous tribal unit, but historically developed, and probably a military confederation of diverse groups. Its solidarity from the first tends to be negative:

> . . . the more the purely naturally arisen, spontaneous character of the clan has been broken by historic movement, migration; the more, further, the clan removes itself from its original seat and occupies *alien* ground, hence enters into essentially new conditions of labour, and develops the energy of the individual more – its common character, necessarily, appearing more as a negative unity towards the outside – the more, therefore, are the conditions given under which the individual can become a *private proprietor* of land and soil – of a particular plot – whose particular cultivation belongs to him and his family. The commune – as state – is, on one side, the relation of these free and equal private proprietors to one another, their bond against the outside, and is at the same time their safeguard.[31]

To the extent that negative predominates over positive solidarity in the cohesion of the group, the conditions and obligations of ownership will be limited to those necessary for its external maintenance:

Ownership of one's own labour is mediated by ownership of the condition of labour – the hide of land, guaranteed in its turn by the existence of the commune, and that in turn by surplus labour in the form of military service, etc. by the commune members. It is not cooperation in wealth-producing labour by means of which the commune member reproduces himself, but rather cooperation in labour for the communal interests (imaginary and real), for the upholding of the association inwardly and outwardly.[32]

Strictly speaking, therefore, citizens are several owners of their homesteads only for public and external purposes – for assessment of military duty, tax, etc. For all domestic purposes their mode of union in the *polis* establishes only the mutually exclusive proprietorship of family units. Ideologically, too, the mutually exclusive household cults remained quite external to the civic cults of the political arena. This combination of militarism with family agriculture led to an exaltation of the male family head and an emphasis on family inheritance which maximised the power and independence of the paterfamilias as 'individual' proprietor.

Secondly, the functional differentiation between political and economic activity requires a corresponding division of rights in jointly and severally owned land. Thus the *ager publicus* appears

. . . as the particular economic presence of the state as against the private proprietors, so that these latter are actually *private* proprietors as such, in so far as they are *excluded*, deprived, like the plebeians, from using the *ager publicus*.[33]

Thus 'the form of state property in land and that of private property in land are antithetical.' The first is only accessible to the individual 'as representative of the state', as public functionary, for the commune has a specialised presence 'in the existence of the city itself and of the officials presiding over it'. Thus the customary or legal distinction between public and private corresponds to an avocational differentiation, and therefore provides the basis for an estrangement between rulers and ruled.

The third factor, however, in combination with the second, is what ensures that the antithetical relation of public and private property is also one of social exclusion and estrangement. This is the coincidence of functional with status differentiation. Originally, 'The clan system in itself leads to higher and lower ancestral lineages, a distinction which is still further developed through intermixture with subjugated clans, etc.'[34] Social inequality therefore afflicts the original military constitution of the *polis*. On the one hand were 'the Roman plebs as a totality of agriculturists', available for war: several owners, excluded from the *ager publicus*. On the other, 'The right of using the communal land through *possession* originally appertained to the patricians, who then granted it to their clients.' Thus the patrician, since he 'represents the community in a higher degree' is not only 'the possessor of the *ager publicus* and uses it through his clients, etc.' but 'also appropriates it little by little.'[35] A nobility of office and wealth replaces the older clan nobility.

These three conditions ensured levels of estrangement, within the solidarity of the ancient city state, which justify treating the internal distribution of ownership as 'property'.

Unlike the Asiatic type, the Ancient type contained numerous internal sources of dynamism and dissolution, which Marx discussed briefly and Engels later elaborated: slavery, originating from conquest, but continuing on other foundations; growth of population, hence need for territorial expansion; trade and empire; indebtedness of free peasantry, etc., etc. Though he did not deal with the historical connection between legal private property and the extension of Roman rule over alien peoples, which was central to Hegel's treatment, his analysis of the more archaic situation, where the individual form of communal ownership grew into a type of private property, is compatible with Hegel's interpretation. Marx, however, did also emphasise elsewhere the importance of commodity trade as a factor in the premature appearance of 'bourgeois property' in imperial Rome.

In the Germanic type, the counterpart to dispersed settlement by self-sufficient economic units is the predominance of several ownership of land by households. Marx expressed this by saying that 'individual ownership does not appear mediated by the commune; rather, the existence of the commune and of communal ownership appear as mediated by, i.e. as a relation of, the independent subjects to one another.' The 'relation' in question 'on the one hand, is presupposed in itself prior to the individual owners as a communality of language, blood, etc., but it exists as a presence, on the other hand, only in its real assembly for communal purposes.' Thus several ownership is 'guaranteed by the bond with other such family residences of the same tribe, and by their occasional coming-together to pledge each others' allegiance in war, religion, adjudication, etc.'[36]

The basic point is that the solidarity which is translated into ownership here is (so far as its economic component is concerned) not based on similar relationships to an identical territory, but on similar relationships to separate but neighbouring estates. In so far as the commune is more than this and 'has a particular economic existence in the hunting and grazing lands for communal use, it is so used by each individual owner as such, not as representative of the state (as in Rome)'. Thus 'Among the Germanic tribes, the *ager publicus* appears rather merely as a complement to individual ownership and figures as property only to the extent that it is defended militarily as the common property of one tribe against a hostile tribe.' Thus although common land is genuinely jointly owned, the predominance of several landownership means that it only functions either as an accessory *possession* of individual landowners, or as joint *property* to be protected by the tribe as a whole.

This discussion has not exhausted the richness of Marx's analysis of precapitalist formations. It has ignored the treatment of communities such as guilds and castes which are based on the worker's ownership of instruments of production and non-ownership of land, and also slavery, serfdom and precapitalist modes of exploitation generally. But the aim has not been comprehensiveness; still less has it been empirical application or historical critique. Rather, I have tried to exhibit the major features of Marx's theoretical approach, both its structure and its elements; and at the same time to elucidate it with the aid of the terminology and ideas contained in the foregoing parts of this chapter. It is hoped that the result has tended towards a vindication and clarification of both.

7 CONCLUSION

This chapter has presented a classification and analysis of possessory bonds. These were treated as shared attitudes towards things – assumptions, stipulations, sentiments – which concerned the expected or prescribed availability of particular things for particular persons, and their non-availability for others. As such, they structure human interaction – which necessarily occurs through and amongst a universe of things – into patterned paths of contact and avoidance.

The 'availability' in question is not, of course, availability in general: crying for the moon will not lead to possession, except for the two nations to whom the moon is already available. Possessory bonds relate only those things which are in society, or accessible to it, to society's members. From this point of view, possessory relations are no more than the person-centred (or group-centred) manifestation of what Marx called the 'distribution relations' of society. However, as 'bonds', they are also what allows us to say that a given distribution of things to persons 'exists'.

Strictly speaking, as we shall see, social systems contain two distributions: distributions both of persons and of things to 'situations' (or 'milieus'), through which they enter social processes of perception and interaction as bound up together in abstract wholes of meaning. By the recurrence and standardisation of typical situations and milieus, the qualities and performances appropriate to them crystallise out as roles – elements composing stable structures of social perception and social action – and particular persons and things are distributed to these roles as specimens of the kinds of persons or things that satisfy their requirements. The function of possessory bonds is to link together the objects of these two distributions as opposite poles of a series of person-thing relationships, mediated by the roles to which both are attached and through which their material social being is realised.

The mediation is possible wherever roles imply membership in a social category or collectivity, and hence a distinct mode of solidarisation with other members. The positive social sentiments engendered also embrace the things which enter into the social relationship, and become to some degree, and in the most various ways, specialised as possessory sentiments. In the 'ownership' aspect, these sentiments combine with other motivations in a more or less elaborated array of rights and duties relating to the owner's treatment of the object. In the 'property' aspect, the negative social sentiments towards outsiders, which are also engendered by the relationship, are concentrated upon excluding others from access to the object, and may become codified as rights *against* others. Here the focus is not on the cultural content of the bond between person and thing, but on its social particularity: it is the connection between *this* person (or group) and *these* things which has to be protected from interference.

This terminology has been developed in abstraction from determinate areas of cultural meaning and determinate levels of social organisation. In that sense, it is an exercise in 'formal sociology'. In fact, obviously, the principal interest of possessory relations does not lie in their application to family chattels, games of chess and other special enclaves, but to the structuring of economic culture and the social organisation of economic life, and thus in their effects as aspects and expressions of the basic economic structures of different types of social system. The final section of the chapter sought to show, in a preliminary way, how the proposed terminology, together with the theory linking possessory relations to solidarity and estrangement, could elucidate parts of Marx's treatment of precapitalist formations.

This was bound to be only a partial elucidation, for possession, ownership and property make up only one part of the stratum of social meanings which link things to persons. They are terms for describing the static, fixed aspect of those meanings, or the resting phase of things in their movement between persons of the same and successive generations. To deal with the dynamic aspect, the actual social movements of things, other terms are needed, and these will be introduced in the next chapter.

In examining the institutionalised possessory relations of three archaic types of socio-economic formation, we were in fact examining three sets of what Marx, in the letter to Schweitzer quoted at the outset, called 'property relations', giving 'ancient', 'feudal' and 'bourgeois' property relations as examples. The ancient and feudal categories mentioned here are not identical with the ancient and Germanic categories that have been discussed above. For by the former, Marx referred to the fully developed exploitative systems, based on slavery and serfdom, which are comparable with bourgeois society as major historical types of antagonistic social structure. By the latter, as we have seen, he intended to designate, in the

Grundrisse, no more than the original set of property relations corresponding to the archaic forms of ancient and Germanic society, before they
developed slave- and serf-based economies through conquest and other
means. (These initial conditions also, of course, made slavery and serfdom
possible, partly determining the forms that exploitation took; but were
likewise themselves changed by the consequent emergence of class
domination.[37]) The fact that Marx was here concentrating on the stable,
fixed norms of ownership, within which exploitation only arose later, made
this a suitable text on which to test the proposed terminology of possessory
bonds. Had he been dealing with precapitalist exploitation itself, it would
have been necessary to wait until the concepts of alienation, expropriation,
etc. – which describe the social movements of things, and thus of surplus
products – were available. For it is necessary to remember that the
complete specification of any set of property relations (and not just
exploitative ones, either) must include both its static and dynamic aspects
and the relations between them. Hence, further discussion of property
relations, as institutionalised systems corresponding to historic modes of
production, will be postponed until Chapter 9, when we shall be in a
position to take this more complete view.

7 Alienation and Appropriation

I REAL APPROPRIATION

Possession, ownership and property are categories that enable a given distribution of things to persons and groups in a society to be identified at any particular moment. In a sense, the totality of such bonds existing in a society simply *is* that distribution – or better, what the observer or social scientist describes as the distribution is an abstract 'map' to which corresponds, 'on the ground', the aggregate of possessory relations. In addition, since what is described is a set of prescriptive assumptions of varying force and precision, such a description would imply a prediction, of varying reliability and exactitude over time, of what the distribution would be in the future. It would therefore define the relations to persons within which new objects would enter society through production, from nature. However, the social distribution of things is also always changing because they are continually passing from hand to hand. Many of these movements are merely interchanges of equivalents that would leave the overall pattern of distribution unchanged. Others are regular one-way movements that communicate directional flows to objects passing through society, even though at any moment the distributive map remains much the same. This may be because property is continually flowing from one generation to another as society renews itself by the replacement of its human parts; or because an inflow of things – say, subsistence items – is balanced by its outflow through consumption; or because accumulation is evenly spread, so that only the material volume of society expands. Other movements however produce alterations, whether temporary or permanent, cumulative or sudden, in the social locations of things, corresponding to the rise and fall of families, social classes, tribes, regions, and so forth.

To describe this giving and taking between social units was the chief use to which Marx put the terms 'alienation' and 'appropriation', especially in his later works. Alienation occurs when the possessory bond between a person (or group) and a thing is dissolved while the thing continues in existence; appropriation is the creation of such a bond. As such, the terms do not apply solely to transfers between one person (or group) and another. There is appropriation when a new thing comes into· existence as somebody's possession (e.g. through production) and also when a thing belonging to nobody comes to be possessed for the first time. Similarly, a thing that is alienated is not necessarily appropriated by anyone else. But for the present I shall ignore these cases, and concentrate on transactions where one person's alienation is matched by another's appropriation, or *vice versa*.

Marx also used the phrase 'real appropriation', which has prompted a certain amount of discussion. The difference between this and the uses just considered is that whereas they focus on the particularity of possession, referring to processes by which things become or cease to be the property of A or B, 'real appropriation' abstracts from A and B and refers to the process by which something becomes property *tout court*. To be sure, to be property a thing must be A's or B's; yet it can also be considered simply as something owned, irrespective of who its owner may be – i.e. as a thing playing this distinct social role of being owned. In this sense Marx often spoke of 'real appropriation through labour' – labour being the main avenue by which things in nature enter society as property, whether or not it is the 'direct producer' who actually owns the product of his labour.

But Marx also used the phrase about instruments of production. For example, in relation to the guild system:

> It is clear that wherever ownership of the instrument is the relation to the conditions of production as owned, there, in the real labour process, the instrument appears only as a means of individual labour; the art of *really appropriating* the instrument, of handling it as an instrument of labour, appears as the worker's particular skill, which posits him as the owner of the instrument.[1]

The point of this passage was to contrast handicrafts, where the tool appears as an appendage of the worker, and hence as belonging to him, with industry, where the worker appears as appendage of the machine and hence as belonging to it. This aspect of the contrast will be considered later. It is at once apparent, however, that 'real appropriation' here refers to the particular mode of mastery or control of the object by virtue of which it is seen as a possession and ratified as object of ownership. The focus has shifted from the question of what is involved in *becoming* property to the conditions for *continuing to be* property, given a new cultural definition of the thing: it has ceased to be just a product, has become a certain sort of product, an instrument. Balibar, with this type of example in mind, has defined 'real appropriation' as 'the ability to set to work the means of social production'.[2] This fits the case under discussion, because with means of production it is indeed the ability to set them to work which constitutes the relevant type of functional mastery that is the main condition of ownership. But as a general definition it is too narrow. Real appropriation of the product as a commodity would be, presumably, its circulation through exchange; and real appropriation by consumption is its use or destruction to satisfy needs. Thus, by 'real appropriation' Marx referred to all and any of the various modes of functional dependence of things on persons by virtue of which they begin and continue to play their social role as objects of possession and ownership.[3] Although there would be little use for it, one could also define 'real alienation' as the various modes by which things lose their functional dependence on persons and hence cease to be property, while continuing in existence. Since most human products are designed to be used up in consumption, real alienation would chiefly involve (besides losing things) the disposal of waste – as Marx put it, returning unwanted things 'to the elemental forces of nature'.[4] (Though they lose their social existence as property, waste products may of course return to plague society in other forms, as we know to our cost. Hence the attempts of governments to enlarge the obligations, and prolong the reach, of ownership of waste pollutants, etc.)

It may well be objected to this definition of real appropriation, and indeed to the foregoing discussion of possession and ownership on which it draws, that the 'separation of ownership and control' in large-scale capitalism requires us to recognise, and be able to analyse, situations where ownership involves no functional dependence at all. This objection cannot be answered at this point, other than to note that the vocabulary developed so far would in due course allow the terms of the problem to be rephrased as a separation between ownership of a legal title, and other rights of ownership.

2 FREE ALIENATION AND EXPROPRIATION

Alienation and appropriation designate 'unit acts'. By combining them in various ways, and with a small number of qualifying terms, a range of more complex and detailed concepts or formulae can be constructed, referring to the many varieties of interchange of possession that occur in society. All these phenomena fall into the general class which I have called 'social practices' or (following Simmel) 'techniques of interaction'. Alienation and appropriation are items in the repertoires of social practices which all cultures contain and transmit in a great variety of forms, combinations and contexts. As culturally transmitted capabilities, they may either take the form of individual social skills of general application, or of collectively sanctioned institutions of varying magnitude and complexity. At one extreme we find such spontaneous and commonplace practices as casual giving, lending or swopping, at the other such elaborate institutions as the *kula* ring, commodity markets, or blood donation.[5] We shall call them all 'transmissive practices'.

In the analysis that follows not much attention will be paid to this dimension of variation, i.e. the degree of institutionalisation. The discussion will be conducted largely in terms of the simple components of elementary social practices, but its purpose is, of course, to aid the understanding of complex institutions. The justification for ignoring the degree of institutionalisation is twofold. First, every action of which an institutionalised process such as commodity exchange consists takes the form of a certain prescribed or permitted combination of unit acts – here, an exchange of equivalents between two parties. It thereby concretises and instantiates the basic unit of practice, of whose elaborated repetition and involution the total institution is composed. Secondly, the in-stitutionalisation of a practice consists, partly, in the fact that some of the *logical* requirements of a model specifying its minimal conditions are expressed as social norms and observed or enforced as such. Thus, in studying the logic of an abstract model of a social practice, such as alienation or appropriation, one is simultaneously elucidating factors that take effect in real life through the operation of more or less institutionalised social norms.

Sociologists have perhaps tended to neglect these transactions, along with other social relationships primarily concerned with things, but ethnographers and social anthropologists investigating marriage systems and economic systems different from our own have attested the need for a formal instrumentarium to conceptualise the various structures of giving, taking and exchanging. What follows is to be seen as a contribution towards an analytical classification of this kind.

In their elementary forms, giving and taking are obviously practices that can be spontaneously performed, circumstances permitting, and are not therefore dependent on institutionalised settings. But there is an asym-metry between them, in that giving always involves some interpersonal understandings and social skills – recognising that the object is henceforth another's and, on the other side, acceptance, and the communication of these understandings. Underlying these actions, furthermore, is a shared belief that the object is indeed alienable – 'mine to give' – and hence can rightfully and safely be appropriated. (This is true even where the donor and recipient remain unknown to one another, as with giving and receiving blood, where these understandings and skills are operated through intermediaries.[6]) Taking, on the other hand, can be accomplished without recognising the original possessor as human at all, by mere forcible removal and subsequent control of the object. Thus, giving requires the recognition of some similarity – some minimal common humanity: hence its occurrence implies the likelihood of some prior solidarity between the parties.[7] Taking, however, can occur where there is total estrangement, and for reasons already discussed will only take violent forms where this prevails.

But the significance of this asymmetry goes beyond its implications for the pre-existing socio-emotional matrix. Giving causes gratitude – that is, a new solidarity – while taking causes resentment and jealousy – new estrangements. In both these cases the pattern is, at one level, the same: the two parties' relations with a single thing are salient features of their situation, and their salient attributes in it. But there the resemblance ends. For looked at from one point of view, these relations are similar, even identical: each has the same possessory relation to one and the same thing. But looked at from a different angle, they stand in opposed and mutually excluding relations, for each possesses the thing only on condition that the other does not. The difference in viewpoint, which determines whether identity or opposition is salient, depends on the function of *time* as a defining element in the situation. For the situation as a whole contains two phases. The first defines the recipient or taker as one who *does not yet* possess the thing (and therefore may want, expect, beg, envy or covet it)·and the second defines the giver or loser as one who *did once* possess it (and therefore as one who has been generous, or fulfilled a duty, or expects a return, or regrets a loss, or seeks retribution.) If a favourable set of possibilities is realised in each phase, the two together define the transaction as a gift, in which generosity and gratitude, or mutual recognition of a duty done, solidarise donor and recipient. If an unfavourable set is realised, the transaction is defined as taking, and the desire for acquisition and retaliation estrange the depredator and his victim. But which of these sets of possibilities is realised depends on whether the situation as a whole is defined so that the temporal continuity of the similar relation predominates over the temporal disjunction in its incidence, or vice-versa. Thus giving must involve a shared intention that the thing shall pass from one to the other, for this creates a specious present in which the actual transmission takes place, as it were, timelessly. Taking, on the other hand, involves contrary interpretations of time in relation to the common object. The possessor projects a future that prolongs his present, in which the thing remains his own; while his enemy defines the present from the standpoint of a future in which the thing will belong to *him* – as a space filled with desire and hostile opportunities. This clash of expectations inevitably highlights the moment of transmission as a conflictual discontinuity, where estrangement must result from the struggle between these contradictory destinations of the object.

So giving involves a 'community of intent', and within this, as may happen in any kind of membership group, a special possessory bond develops. But it is also a special *kind* of possessory bond, for the dyad of donor and recipient is not based on just any primary similitude, but on a shared intention as to their possessory relation to a particular object. It is not therefore a matter of membership giving rise to a permanent bond of ownership between person and thing and an exclusive relation of property towards outsiders, as in the standard case analysed in the last chapter. For here the dualism of ownership and property is being deliberately manipulated by the parties to achieve their common goal. The possessory bond that they create is a second-order bond which presupposes a world already organised as ownership and property. For each must recognise the other's claim as excluding his own before and after some point of time agreed or assumed between them. The things which are typically given and received in a society thereby acquire a special type of possessory status, setting them apart from objects of more permanent ownership; and the same is true of other modes of transmission such as exchange. The possessory bonds that result from these practices we may call, then, ownership or property by alienation.

Because of the asymmetry between giving and taking, the historical significance of taking is most conspicuous in non-institutionalised relations between estranged social units – theft, raiding, conquest, etc. – while that of giving is most conspicuous as a more or less institutionalised practice within solidary groups. However, when we examine the matter more closely, it turns out not to be as simple as that. For one thing, taking, in the form of exploitation, has provided the institutionalised basis of the entire development of civilisation. Though exploiting and exploited classes have always lived in relationships of estrangement, their interdependence has never been wholly devoid of solidarity. Conversely, while casual and spontaneous giving flourishes where solidarity is greatest, as long as the capacity for separate possession is also present, institutionalised giving is most conspicuous where there is in fact some estrangement. This is because solidarity is usually greatest where there is common ownership, and hence sharing, which precludes giving altogether. (It is not, as we say, a 'real gift' when a husband presents his wife with some article of common and promiscuous household use on her birthday.) Where solidarity is combined with separate ownership it is also, for reasons noted, likely to be diluted with estrangement. However, in practice, of course, sharing often looks like giving, especially if it is a matter of one person 'sharing out' things on behalf of a group, and there is probably no clear demarcation, in most cultures, between many marginal cases of sharing and giving. But *typical* cases of giving, and therefore those that achieve institutional prominence, will usually occur where some estrangement exists between units that are, nevertheless, predominantly solidary

Furthermore, because giving implies some separation between giver and recipient, it also requires taking, acceptance, as a condition of its completion. Thus there is a difference between the alienation involved in simply abandoning an object, and that involved in offering to give it away. In the first case, the alienation may or may not be followed by appropriation by another, but in the second, appropriation by a designated other is a condition of the alienation being complete. The intended recipient also has a recognised choice of acceptance or refusal.

For taking to be successful, all that is needed is that others generally should recognise what has been taken as belonging to its new owner. As between mutually estranged groups, this does not require acquiescence by the dispossessed. Should he challenge the usurpation, the usurper's fellows will support the claim of their own man, and the outcome is decided by a trial of strength of some kind. But within a community, or any institutionalised setting, acquiescence by the dispossessed is one of the commonest conditions on which others will be prepared to recognise the taker's claim. Taking, within a social context, therefore requires alienation by the dispossessed as a condition of its completion much as giving required appropriation by the recipient as a condition of completion. Wherever estrangement is the prevailing socioemotional tone in society, and some have the power to take from others, forms of taking tend to become institutionalised, reinforcing but stabilising estrangement. However, these forms have a distinctive character, unlike simple acts of dispossession between estranged units. For what is, in reality, taking has to have an appearance of giving. If the taker and his victim are members of a single society, they share an interest in having their property protected: unless the taker could count on this, his taking might be of little use to him. In fact, a good criterion for deciding what constitutes 'a single society' may be that, within a certain population, alienation and appropriation occur against a particular background of presupposed and institutionalised possessory bonds. In that case, the two elements of presupposed fixity and consequent movement compose together a single system of 'property relations'. And in such a system, he who takes also subscribes to the general rule that things should not be taken without their owner's consent. If he nevertheless intends to take things which others would not freely yield, and to do so without blame or reprisal, he must secure the consent of his victim. Institutionalised taking therefore always has the appearance of free alienation.

These preliminary considerations allow a first main distinction to be drawn, between what I shall call 'free alienation' and 'expropriation'. For an act to be 'free alienation', appropriation of the object by another can only follow, and must await, the initiating of alienation by the possessor. For it to be 'expropriation', alienation follows the initiation of appropriation by the non-possessor, to whom the object passes as a more or less compulsory or inevitable consequence. The expropriator, therefore, must be able to constrain another's capacity for free alienation, so that he is able to count in advance on the other's acquiescence in his own dispossession. Admittedly, this is not an easy criterion to apply: things can be asked for in such a way that one has little option but to give, unwilling though one might be. Yet one does, for example, make a practical distinction between a beggar who could be freely ignored and one who blocks the pavement and demands alms as a toll. The fact that one might more often give to the former than the latter merely signifies that the latter's attempted expropriation has failed, not that the former has constrained one's capacity for free alienation by exciting compassion.

To this major dichotomy further distinctions must now be added if a comprehensive typology of transmissive practices is to be built up.

3 A TYPOLOGY OF TRANSMISSIVE PRACTICES

An analytical classification of transmissive practices, adequate for a sociological treatment of the social movements of things, can be constructed using four principal sets of criteria. One of these we have just encountered: the question of whether appropriation occurs as a consequence of free alienation, or alienation as a result of expropriation. This actually yields three categories: modes of giving, where free alienation predominates; modes of taking, where expropriation predominates; and modes of give-and-take where free alienation and expropriation counterbalance each other.

The second set of criteria relates to whether the movement of things is unilateral or bilateral. If unilateral, the unit act is asymmetrical, one movement from A to B. If bilateral, it is symmetrical, incomplete until the movement from A to B has been complemented by a counter-movement from B to A. The latter need not, however, be direct, but may pass through intermediaries. Giving and taking are both, in their simplest forms, unilateral, but the simple acts can obviously be combined by repetition into bilateral or symmetrical units. This can be achieved in two distinct ways. Either the agents in the polar roles change places, so that the giver becomes the recipient, or the taker surrenders in turn to his former victim; or else the giving or taking continues around a ring of agents until the original giver or taker reappears as recipient or victim. These may be called 'reciprocal' and 'rotary' giving and taking respectively.[8]

The dichotomy unilateral-bilateral bears on the trichotomisation of categories under the first set of criteria. Unilateral movements only achieve a balance of giving and taking by chance. The situation where both parties initiate free alienation and expropriation simultaneously, so that the transaction is no more and no less giving than it is taking, seems to be inherently unlikely and unstable. It can be stabilised, however, if both parties simultaneously initiate expropriation, but each also has an object which the other wants and whose alienation he can make conditional on appropriation of the other's. As condition and means of achieving his expropriation of the other, each must freely alienate his own object. But this simultaneous and mutually conditional alienation and appropriation is the general formula for exchange. For though the criterion of simultaneity is usually satisfied by a promise or contract, rather than by actual simultaneous handing over by both sides, simultaneity is crucial in silent barter, which is presumably the most elementary form of exchange. We have already seen that giving involves a community of intent defining the point within a specious present at which property changes hands, and the simultaneity of exchange involves synchronising the two such points in a bilateral interchange. Exchange is thus *irreducibly* bilateral: the first movement is incomplete unless and until the second is also accomplished. Very probably this is the sole effective way of equilibrating give and take.

By combining the first two sets of criteria, therefore, we obtain Figure 4.

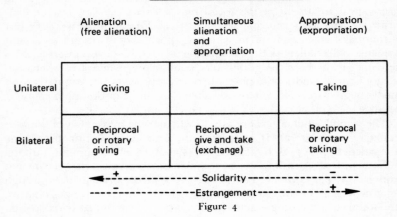

Figure 4

The third set of criteria concerns the relative positions in time of the participant units. This may be synchronic or diachronic. Schutz's terms may be adapted to distinguish between alienation amongst contemporaneous units, and alienation from predecessor units to their successors. Alienation between contemporaries may be either unilateral or bilateral, but alienation from predecessors to successors excludes bilateral movements, so that there can only be free alienation or expropriation – handing over (devolution) or taking over (usurpation) – and no exchange. In the first case, the possessions – which may include the personnel, or some saved remnant of them – are freely alienated by one or more units, on condition of its (or their) dissolution, to one or more others, which are constituted by the same event. In the second case, the same effect is brought about by more or less violent appropriation on the part of the intending successor or successors.

The fourth and final set of criteria, which discriminates amongst both alienations to contemporaries and alienations to successors, concerns the quantitative proportionality of units taking part. At the risk of oversimplification, three main categories can be proposed: one to one; many to one; one to many. This to some extent conceals another distinction which may sometimes prove important – whether the units are separate or form parts of a single whole. Generally, this will tend to correlate with tendencies towards estrangement and solidarity, and hence with free alienation and expropriation, so that it adds little to those dimensions. However, there are sometimes important differences between alienation from the parts to a whole, and vice versa, and alienation from all the parts but one to that part – yet these are conflated in the phrase 'many-to-one'.

The justification for not complicating the typology further by introducing this distinction must be that a 'whole', if it is to alienate and appropriate, must be represented, and the representative tends to act as one part among others. Nevertheless, the difference between giving to a centre (e.g. tribute) and giving to peripheral recipients (e.g. alms) is often very marked, and it is necessary to remain alert to its hidden presence.

These four sets of criteria can now be combined into an analytical classificatory table. The remainder of this chapter is really a commentary on this typology. However, there are several general points which can conveniently be made here first.

UNILATERAL MOVEMENTS

Locus of Initiation of Transmission

To successors

	Free alienation	Expropriation
One to one	Devolution	Usurpation
Many to one	Free merger	Forced merger
One to many	Free partition	Forced partition

To contemporaries

	Free alienation	Expropriation
One to one	Free gift	Seizure
Many to one	Free contribution	Forced contribution
One to many	Free distribution	Forced distribution

BILATERAL MOVEMENTS

To contemporaries

	Free alienation	Simultaneous alienation and appropriation	Expropriation
One to one and vice versa	Reciprocal or rotary gifts	Exchange	Reciprocal or rotary seizures
Many to one and vice versa	Free contribution – distribution Rotary gifts	Synallagmatic contribution – distribution	Forced contribution – distribution
One to many and vice versa	Free distribution – contribution	Synallagmatic distribution – contribution	Forced distribution – contribution

◄ + – – – – – – – –Solidarity– – – – – – – – – – –
– – – – – – – – –Estrangement– – – – – – + ►

Figure 5 Types of Transmissive Practice

Unilateral and bilateral transmission tend to have different effects. As historical events, therefore, they have different consequences, and as institutional patterns they serve different functions. Mere repetition of unilateral transmission, without reciprocation, makes things flow steadily in one direction. The various modes of devolution adapt this effect to resolve the ever-present problem of peacefully canalising society's wealth through the lock-gates of successive generations. Since the direction of flow here is simply that of social structure through time, the result is to reproduce and perpetuate the structure, whatever its outline.

Between contemporaries, however, unilateral transmission tends either to make equals unequal, or unequals equal. Both effects may become institutionalised. Capitalist exploitation is based on forced contribution — 'the theft of alien labour-time' — producing and reproducing inequality. Egalitarian social policies, in so far as they can be effected through socialist legislation within a capitalist system, represent an institutionalised forced distribution. Not only capitalist exploitation, but earlier forms also, have the general form of forced contribution, but based on varying primary transactions. For example, in the same sense that the forced contribution of capitalism is based on commodity exchange (sale of labour-power), that of oriental despotism was based on free contribution (tribute). Other types will be analysed in due course. The great historical confiscations that, in Marx's account, stand at the beginning and end of the capitalist epoch — primary accumulation and proletarian revolution — are, in our terms, mixtures of expropriation from predecessors and from contemporaries. Primitive accumulation created a new inequality by both seizure and surpation of land, by forced contributions through direct taxes, and by other methods of expropriation. Proletarian revolution destroys existing inequality by forced partition and forced distribution. By contrast with these mostly expropriative unilateral movements, bilateralism has most commonly been adapted as a vehicle for the social circulation of equivalents. If it causes things to flow in one constant direction, it is only as a consequence of an equivalent flow of things in the contrary direction.

Karl Polanyi has drawn a threefold distinction between reciprocity, redistribution and exchange as empirically discoverable forms of integration of an economy. They are ways, often combined, in which 'the economy acquires unity and stability, that is, the interdependence and recurrence of its parts.'

> Reciprocity denotes movements between correlative points of symmetrical groupings; redistribution designates appropriational movements toward a centre and out of it again; exchange refers to vice-versa movements taking place as between 'hands' under a market system.[9]

Each form of integration therefore corresponds to, and requires, structural support in the shape of symmetry, centricity, and market respectively.

This trichotomy — or rather, the argumentative weight that Polanyi has made it bear – has been rightly criticised as dealing only with distributive mechanisms; however, that is what we are dealing with here too. But there is also a further limitation: it includes only those aspects of distribution which involve the circulation of equivalents. Thus, it excludes distribution in so far as it is 'the form in which unpaid surplus-labour is pumped out of direct producers'[10] by unilateral appropriation. It is, of course, arguable – since each form of exploitation presupposes and coexists with a particular mode of bilateralism and circulation of equivalents – that the latter is what gives unity and stability to the economy. The entire thrust of Marx's analyses, however, was against such a view. On the contrary, commodity circulation only achieved general preponderance in step with, and in consequence of, the rise and spread of capitalist production on the basis of a commodity market in labour-power. It is the 'laws' of capitalist production, not commodity production, that explain both the unity and the disunity, the stability and instabilities, of the modern world economy. Thus, wherever there is exploitation, the integration of the economy is ultimately to be explained by the reproduction of the corresponding class structure, and the interests which that implies. Polanyi's view is nevertheless tenable wherever exploitation is absent, and not surprisingly has aroused most interest amongst anthropologists puzzled by the economic processes of simple egalitarian societies. Here, indisputably, reciprocity between symmetrical kinship groups, moieties and tribes, or redistribution through a chief as centre, function as major integrating mechanisms. But they do so only because the mode of production in these cases prescribes as the goal for the performance of surplus labour distributive purposes which have egalitarian effects, and which therefore involve a circulation of equivalents and bilateral practices.

Our typology of transmissive practices clarifies the formal basis of what was an inductive conclusion for Polanyi. The most important modes of bilateralism involve either free alienation or simultaneous alienation and appropriation. (Bilateral expropriation requires equality of power to expropriate, and where this obtains there seems to be a general tendency to prefer the compromise of some kind of exchange to the hazards of mutual raiding and vendetta.) Thus the symmetry required by Polanyi's reciprocity is present in the 'one-to-one' condition for reciprocal or rotary giving. It is present in exchange also, but with the added 'vice-versa' of simultaneity, entailing irreducible bilateralism. His 'redistribution' appears in the two forms of free and synallagmatic contribution-distribution, which can be regarded as applications of reciprocal giving and exchange, respectively, to the situation where one 'side' represents a centre and the other represents the segments surrounding it. Empirically, they typically correspond to the reciprocating flows of tribute and largesse through a chieftain's kraal; and to the budgetary balancing of state expenditure on collective goods against fiscal revenue, in traditional ideologies of public finance.

Though Polanyi laid little stress on it, he noted the correlation between his three types and differences in solidarity and estrangement. Reciprocity, since it depends on alienation being returned, with only the sanction of moral obligation and social honour, can only flourish between units linked by some solidarity. 'The closer the members of the encompassing community feel drawn to one another, the more general will be the tendency among them to develop reciprocative attitudes.'[11] Redistribution was, he stressed, most typical of the internal economy of small solidary groups – hunting bands, tribal villages, households, etc. – although the most spectacular examples, as in ancient Egypt, Sumeria or Peru, had different socioemotional correlates. Exchange – especially where prices fluctuate in response to haggling –

> aims at a gain that can be attained only by an attitude involving a distinctive antagonistic relationship between the partners . . . No community intent on protecting the fount of solidarity between its members can allow latent hostility to develop around a matter as vital to animal existence and, therefore, capable of arousing as tense anxieties as food. Hence the universal banning of transactions of a gainful nature in regard to food and foodstuffs in primitive and archaic society.[12]

Although this last point must be treated with caution, Polanyi's analysis is congruent with that advanced in this volume. These correlations between socio-emotional matrices and modes of transmission will reappear in more detailed discussion below.

One final point may be made here. Polanyi overlooked the form of bilateralism where distribution precedes contribution, yet its structural importance is evident. In conjuction with conquest and collective seizure of land, as in both ancient and feudal society, it was an important structural principle. Land or land-use could be distributed amongst the victors in anticipation of future contributions of military service. Within this basic pattern, there was scope for much variation.[13]

Further considerations of a formal kind will need to be added to this typology later. First, however, the main themes that emerge from it will be discussed in the order: modes of devolution and usurpation; modes of free alienation between contemporaries; modes of exchange.

4 MODES OF DEVOLUTION AND USURPATION

We are concerned here with situations where the dissolution of a social unit is the occasion of its possessions being transferred to another which takes its place, and which is to varying degrees constituted by this same act. The act may be either giving or taking, and will be called 'devolution' (or 'free merger', 'free partition') or 'usurpation' (or 'forced merger', 'forced partition') accordingly. Two different sorts of such occasion can be discriminated. First, the devolving unit may be an individual or group whose entire identity and function as a social agent is terminating, so that its possessions have to be handed on to others. With individuals, this cessation of social agency usually coincides with physical dissolution, but there are other forms of social death such as enslavement, exile, monastic vows or insanity which are comparable in their effects. With groups, the occasion is more often a social death such as a divorce, the liquidation of a company, the disbanding of an army, the abolition of an administrative unit, or the subjugation of an independent people; but it may of course involve physical extinction by suicide pact, epidemic or massacre. The second sort of occasion is where the devolving unit is an embodied status, and its dissolution is simply the departure of one occupant prior to the arrival of another. Possessions pass on with the status and must be taken over by the new incumbent. Here again, the occupant may be a collectivity, as when one party succeeds another in government. On these occasions there is no question of a social agent ceasing to exist, but only of the dissolution of its link with a particular status. But the distinction between the two sorts of occasion is not an absolute one, for societies appear to endow their units with the general capacity for social agency by virtue of their occupying some special status, such as member of a lineage or a state, 'sanity', etc.

Where take-overs from predecessors occur by expropriation, the single term 'usurpation' suffices for both sorts of occasion. But where free handovers are concerned, I propose to divide the general class of devolutions into two categories, according to the two sorts of occasion just mentioned. 'Devolution' remains the best generic term, for its dictionary meaning – 'the handing of anything on to a successor' – is applicable to both. Devolution at the termination of social agency I shall call 'inheritance'[14] – 'receiving property as the heir of a former possessor at his decease' – and devolution at a change of status occupancy I shall call 'succession' – 'the process by which one person succeeds another in the occupation of an estate or the like.' For simplicity I shall limit my discussion to cases where the social agents, in either event, are individuals; arguably, these have greater structural importance that those involving groups.

Obviously, societies need to institutionalise both inheritance and succession. For, on the one hand, individuals are recognised as units of social agency in all societies, even if they are not always the most important, so that there is always a problem of transmitting their possessions from one generation to the next. And on the other hand, all societies contain institutions where individuals follow one another in the occupancy of statuses to which possessions are attached, or which require or allow the use of possessions belonging to a larger institutional group.

The purest case of inheritance is, perhaps, where it takes the form of a free parting gift from a dying man to his survivors. Some articles of merely personal possession are treated in this way in most societies. Where testamentary freedom is curtailed by law, the evasion of restrictions by assimilating bequests to gifts *inter vivos* occurs with possessions that are more than 'merely personal'. The subterfuges for avoiding tax on inherited wealth are familiar enough. Similarly, the English law of entail grew up around gifts, not wills, because of the feudal rule that 'a lord could not divert the normal succession of his land, by a will or *devise* taking effect after his death.'[15] Nevertheless, posthumous giving by bequest is a more widespread institution than the parting gift, for who can foretell the hour of his death? Yet this involves a slight paradox, for giving, as was seen, requires a persisting community of intent and is incomplete until the offer has been accepted and the gift received. But by then the posthumous donor is no longer around. This hiatus in the logical requirements of the transmissive practice probably explains the institution of the 'will', which fictively prolongs the testator's presence in a community of intent with his heirs, and allows for his being impersonated by executors until the transmission is settled.

The unavoidable inattendance of the dead at the completion of their last act of alienation partially explains the close match between law and social practice in matters of inheritance. Professional agents have always been needed, and lawyers have always been ready, to step into dead men's shoes on these occasions. Despite this, 'inheritance' here is a sociological, not a legal category, it refers to this devolutionary practice in both its legally defined and its legally undefined aspects. If it ever coincides exactly with a legal definition, this is a contingent though important fact about how the society in question deals with intergenerational transmission of property – by comprehensive legal prescription – but it does not alter the theoretical status of the concept. We may note at this point that the paradox of the absent donor cannot arise at all in cases of usurpation, because the victim's presence is unnecessary for taking to be completed. There is not community but contrariety of intent. Indeed, the victim's absence, by death or otherwise, only facilitates seizure; should his presence be incorporeally prolonged, like that of Hamlet's father, he will seek only executors of his vengeance.

If the purest case of inheritance is where the testator is free to nominate his heir, the purest case of succession is where the successor to the departing status-occupant is designated by fixed institutional rules. In fact, both of these pure types are rare. Inheritance is most commonly assimilated to succession by treating the individual *qua* social agent as member of a family and descent-group, and hence as occupant of family and kinship statuses. On his or her decease, possession normally passes to whoever fills the family status afterwards, or else to the occupant of another kinship status standing in some definite relation to that vacated: thus to firstborn son, sister's son, all offspring equally, or 'next of kin', etc. Inheritance by family succession is therefore a function of the deceased's family status, and of rules governing succession to the rights and duties of that status among his kin and affines. And inheritance by family succession tends to be the general practice even where testamentary freedom prevails, being an essential mechanism of class reproduction.

Family succession naturally tends to be a one-many situation, and the social functions of different sorts of family property have led to this tendency being either institutionally thwarted or buttressed. Primogeniture, like the less civilised custom whereby princes fought to the death in order that the survivor might inherit the crown, sought to impose a one-one pattern on dynastic succession. Primogeniture and entail, also, were used to prevent the dismemberment of big landed estates, especially in England. Peasant-based European societies, however, have tended to recognise the one-many pattern in the *legitim*, the right of children and other close relatives to inherit a share of their father's possessions, including land. Some such partition is usual also amongst urban classes wherever family succession prevails, regardless of how the law varies from one country to another. All these provisions and customs are alternative or supplementary to the will as a method of overcoming the paradox of the absent donor. Possession is treated as inhering in a larger unit whose continuance bridges the gap between giving and receiving. The community of intent is identified with a less ephemeral community to which both legator and legatee belong.[16]

Inheritance by family succession, as a mechanism of class societies, presupposes the isolation of single lines of descent as 'natural' paths of ownership. The problem of intergenerational transmission has come to be focussed on the biological demise of the family 'head', conceived genealogically as the male progenitor. Where common ownership by clans or other communal groupings has prevailed, this was not the case. Property partook of the immortality of the clan. Intergenerational transmission of ownership was not a matter of inheritance but of succession adjusted to the continuous turnover in the composition of the group sharing its use, burdens and exclusive enjoyment. Here the maturation of the younger generation and the senescence of its elders were more important transitions than the deaths of parents. Hence the division of society into age-sets was usually prominent, and initiation into a senior set brought possessory privileges.

A well-marked mode of succession that is structurally intermediate between the clan and the western conjugal family is that found in the joint family. In this very widespread system, married sons continue to live patrilocally, sharing corporate ownership and administration of the family property and usually forming a self-sufficient workforce. At some point, varying in different societies, the family splits up and divides its possessions, usually equally, by free partition. An exceptionally well documented example is that found in Greek mountain pastoral villages. Here families endure for about forty years, partly to ensure that daughters are all married and dowered. At the division of the flock and other goods, an extra portion goes to the youngest son for the support of the parents in their remaining years. Each new household is the nucleus of a new joint family. Thus free partition here enables the social structure to be reproduced intergenerationally by canalising its material basis equally through the male branchings of family trees.[17]

A similar canalisation occurs through the female branches in the form of dowries, which represent an advance of the bride's portion of the common wealth and seldom fall much below parity with the husband's share in his own paternal household. This is a reminder that, just as devolution is not the only way of transmitting property between generations, so there are well-established modes of alienation which necessarily have a *partial* aspect of devolution. The foundation of a new elementary family by marriage is one of these. In so far as it modifies the families of origin which alienate the spouses and some property to the new family, it resembles a devolution, but it is an alienation between contemporaries in that the two families of origin continue in existence alongside one another. Naturally, in the joint family system this element is uppermost, as it is also in clan systems where brides are exchanged between permanent descent-groups. In bourgeois society, however, where descent is cognatic, dowries negligible, and each new family is an independent earning unit, marriage is perhaps best seen as a free merger where two unrelated units sink their identity in a new tripartite structure consisting of the two depleted families of 'in-laws' and the new conjugal family, which is also the sub-unit that is focal for the cohesion of the whole. Alongside and within this transition, however, the three households continue to be separate units with their own interests and contacts, frequently highly mobile, so that the tripartite grouping – which is in any case only a focal sector in a continuous network – is notoriously loose and undemanding.

Clan succession differs from family inheritance in being a genuine case of succession, where possession is attached to statuses through which roll a series of persons within a continuing collectivity. Succession is also the principal mode of intergenerational transmission in socialist societies, and is increasingly important in advanced capitalism. Society's biggest property holdings are vested in specialised formal organisations which continuously recruit young members and retire old ones. Rights to control and benefit from the use of organisational resources are exercised by the bureaucracy which runs the organisation, being unequally distributed and concentrated in top posts. Unlike clan succession, which is based almost wholly on ascriptive criteria, bureaucratic succession is ascriptive only to the degree that it is based on seniority and 'experience'.[18] Otherwise it is governed by 'achievement' inasmuch as initial recruitment is by credentialism – educational or ideological qualification at the start of adult life – and thereafter promotion or inter-organisational mobility is by 'merit' measured by performance against standard career-patterns. But the rules are seldom rigid or unequivocal, and just as free bequest is usually converted into customary family succession in practice, so bureaucratic appointment and promotion is usually tempered by political or personal patronage.[19] Those who control access to bureaucratic posts and their possessory privileges can thereby exercise discretionary free alienation, but within a restricted range of candidates. Where top posts are elective, such as the American presidency, this power of free alienation is vested in the electorate collectively. In principle, it is subject to no restrictions beyond those inherent in the method of election and certain legal qualifications for candidates. In practice, however, party bureaucracies limit the range of candidates in much the same way as with the patronage of appointive posts.

Family succession and bureaucratic succession have been made the distinguishing marks of 'classes of reproduction' and 'classes of nomination'. If feudal stratification epitomises the first, socialist societies are stratified by the second; capitalism moves from predominance of the first towards predominance of the second. A class of nomination recruits its population of potential successors – the bureaucratic personnel – by cultural credentials irrespective of genealogical qualification. In capitalist society, however, and to some extent under socialism too, transmission of 'cultural capital' by means of educational privileges remains an important mode of family succession.[20]

Turning from hand-overs to take-overs, the most conspicuous kind of expropriation of predecessors is by conquest. Conquests may vary from simple seizures of booty to usurpations of fiscal powers or lands, or forced mergers where a new unit arises from the subjection of one community by another and their intermingling. If we think of family succession as mostly private, small-scale, institutional and orderly, and of conquest as public, large-scale, historic and violent, we can nevertheless find examples where the logical affinity between them, which our typology reveals, stands out in reality. Wherever family succession turns on vast and momentous prizes that are also above the law, inheritance and conquest become interchangeable methods of transmission. Royal succession, in European feudalism, and still more in Asiatic despotism, evinces the fact.

Kingship, in general, is the institution that most closely unites family and political devolution. The most characteristic type of one-one take-over is perhaps that of the Frazerian claimant who slays the king and usurps his throne. One-many hand-overs are represented by the partition of a realm among a dead king's sons – a custom present among the Saxons, Visigoths and other barbarian peoples, gradually abandoned for primogeniture or, among the Franks, for a sort of election by notables. Free partition of a state may also, of course, come about non-dynastically by treaty, although such cases shade off into one-many take-overs where separatist movements secede and form successor states.

The expropriation of predecessors, unlike free alienation to successors, appears to be a field of historical vicissitude of little structural interest.

However, there have always been advocates of the conquest theory of history, who have regarded the subjugation of one group by another as a primordial determinant of inequality, progress, and all the grandeurs and servitudes of civilisation. Though Engels argued at length against Dühring's view that force was prior to ownership, and political structure prior to economic processes, it has often resurfaced since. A broad school of critics of Marx, arguing at least the irreducibility of force and politics, seems to descend from Gumplowicz, who influenced separately Mosca, Schumpeter and Oppenheimer, the last of whom influenced Weber; Mosca and Weber were godparents to Wright Mills' proposal to recognise military and administrative determinism as separate factors alongside economic determinism.

This is not the place to deal with all the issues that this raises. However, with reference to forced mergers by conquest and forced partitions by revolution, Marx effectively answered the *crux* in his *Introduction* of 1857. What was confusedly treated as the possible priority of force or politics was, in reality, the question of the relative autonomy of distribution relations *vis-à-vis* production relations. For 'force' is not structurally specific. If it is used to wrest raw materials from nature, it is a force of production; if it is used to make others labour, then it may be a means of exploitation as well. But if it is used to expropriate possessions, it can only be a means of distribution. Marx's argument ran as follows:

> As regards whole societies, distribution seems to precede production and to determine it in yet another respect, almost as if it were a pre-economic fact. A conquering people divides the land among the conquerors, thus imposing a certain distribution and form of property in land, and thus determines production. Or it enslaves the conquered and so makes slave labour the foundation of production. Or a people rises in revolution and smashes the great landed estates into small parcels, and hence, by this new distribution, gives production a new character . . . In all these cases, and they are all historical, it seems that distribution is not structured and determined by production, but rather the opposite, production by distribution . . .
>
> The questions raised above reduce themselves in the last instance to the role played by general-historical relations in production, and their relation to the movement of history generally. The question evidently belongs within the treatment and investigation of production itself.
>
> Still, in the trivial form in which they are raised above, they can be dealt with equally briefly. In all cases of conquest, three things are possible. The conquering people subjugates the conquered under its own mode of production (e.g. the English in Ireland this century, and partly in India); or it leaves the old mode intact and contents itself with a tribute (e.g. Turks and Romans); or a reciprocal interaction takes place whereby something new, a synthesis, arises (the Germanic conquests, in

part). In all cases, the mode of production, whether that of the conquering people, that of the conquered, or that emerging from the fusion of both, is decisive for the new distribution which arises. Although the latter appears as a presupposition of the new period of production, it is thus itself in turn a product of production, not only of historical production generally, but of specific historic modes of production.[21]

The distributive categories which have been isolated and defined, in fact, such as forced merger or forced partition, stand for formal possibilities of expropriative interaction, present wherever there is estrangement and unequal power. Precisely *how* they will be applied – if they are – and with what economic content, depends on the constellation of production relations and productive forces on both sides. Marx went on to comment:

It is a received opinion that in certain periods people lived from pillage alone. But, for pillage to be possible, there must be something to be pillaged, hence production. And the mode of pillage is itself in turn determined by the mode of production. A stockjobbing nation, for example, cannot be pillaged in the same manner as a nation of cow-herds.[22]

Pillage is more a matter of seizure than usurpation, and further consideration of this type of interaction will be left until expropriation between contemporaries is treated. First, however, let us turn our attention to free alienation between contemporaries.

5 MODES OF FREE ALIENATION BETWEEN CONTEMPORARIES (1)

If we may visualise men with the simplest mode of production as living in small, scattered, self-sufficient hunting bands, then there would be little scope or use for giving under such circumstances. Practically all they owned would be shared, and individual possession would be a transitory reservation of use. Hostile to outsiders, they would no doubt prefer to avoid than to fight them, and would have little to go to war about. Shortage of women and the need for exogamy might be the first stimulus to traffic with others.

From this situation, itself possibly imaginary, we can picture the practice of giving developing from opposite extremes. First, if production advanced and communities became larger, there could be room for separate ownership by sub-units, and a need for gifts to pass between them. At the same time, the collecting, pooling and redistribution which necessarily occurs in an economy of sharing would more and more acquire the character of free contribution from the segments, and free distribution from the centre: an economy of tribute and largesse. How far, and in what way, these practices of internal giving developed would of course depend on what the mode of production allowed and required in the way of circulation.

From the opposite extreme, increasing contact with a larger variety of outsiders, if it did not lead to war, could awaken the desire and need for peaceful and regular interchange of goods and services. Gifts from either side would help to establish intercourse, reduce estrangement, and stimulate a taste for foreign products. Where regular interchanges became established, especially of women and consumption goods, we might suppose that the initial distinction between internal and external would become softened; larger, polysegmental systems could arise through partial or total synthesis. The primordial simplicity of inward solidarity and outward estrangement would give way to a complex socioemotional matrix of structured ambivalences. These would be expressed and reproduced by a multiplicity of forms of institutionalised free alienation, each suited to its context, and performing functions either instrumental or symbolic or both.[23]

We should be wise not to take such constructions too seriously. However, one inevitably has such imagery in mind when one reads of primitive social systems of great extension and complexity, whose cohesion seems to consist in ramifying and intricate webs of giving and taking. Malinowski's account of such a system in Melanesia, more particularly in the Trobriand Islands which he studied in depth, is a classic instance. And seen from the standpoint of our typology, Malinowski's account reveals traces of a dual tendency that is, at the least, suggestive of the imagery I have described.

For in their internal system, the Trobrianders tended to practise giving in ways that were not markedly bilateral, and were sometimes intermediate between unilateral and bilateral alienation. For example, chiefs were the recipients of an endless stream of gifts and tribute, but they also dispensed food, valuables and services incessantly. In sum, this approximated to a bilateral flow of tribute and largesse. But it was not designed as such, and the resulting circulation was brought about by a multitude of unilateral actions aimed at securing other ends. An even more notable example was the custom of *urigubu*, which Malinowski classified under the heading 'Customary payments, repaid irregularly, and without strict equivalence'. He wrote:

> The most important of these are the annual payments received at harvest time by a man from his wife's brothers. These regular and unfailing gifts are so substantial, that they form the bulk of the man's income in food. Sociologically, they are perhaps the strongest strand in the fabric of the Trobriands' tribal constitution. They entail a lifelong obligation of every man to work for his kinswomen and their families. When a boy begins to garden, he does it for his mother. When his sisters grow up and marry, he works for them . . .

The reciprocity in these gifts never amounts to their full value, but the recipient is supposed to give a valuable or a pig to his wife's brother from time to time. Again if he summons his wife's kinsmen to do communal work for him . . . he pays them in food. In this case also the payments are not the full equivalent of the services rendered. Thus we see that the relationship between a man and his wife's kinsmen is full of mutual gifts and services, in which repayment, however, by the husband, is not equivalent and regular, but spasmodic and smaller than his own share; and even if for some reason or other it ever fails, this does not relieve the others from their obligations.[24]

The aggregate result of these prestations was indirectly bilateral: a circulation of equivalents among exogamous clans by rotary giving. Yet this was no more than the unintended effect (and hence the functionally adaptive consequence) of what appears to be a type of unilateral dowry.

In striking contrast to these internal reciprocations, those in the external system were self-consciously bilateral, requiring careful attention to the interchange of equivalents. Amongst the various external transactions that occurred, two were especially noteworthy, and closely linked. One was the famous *kula* ring, in which two sorts of *vaygu'a*, or valuables — arm-shells and shell necklaces — circulated against each other in opposite directions around a ring of partners, whose ceremonious interchanges of gifts linked together an entire archipelago inhabited by various tribes. The other, most intensively carried on in conjunction with *kula* expeditions, was the bartering of a variety of subsistence items and consumer durables — a practice known as *gimwali*. *Kula* was a form of reciprocal giving, and *gimwali* a type of exchange. The distinction between the two modes of interaction was strictly maintained by the participants, who would only engage in *kula*, or else in free giving, with their *kula* partners, while bartering only with others — who would, of course, be their colleagues' *kula* partners. This segregation of role-sets was matched by contrasted norms. Haggling, essential to *gimwali*, was forbidden in *kula* interchanges, which had their own dignified code of behaviour that would have been absurdly inappropriate to *gimwali*. But though sharply distinct, both sorts of transaction were strongly bilateral. The interchange of *kula* gifts was not a mere alternation: it consisted of discrete bilateral acts in which 'opening gift' and 'counter-gift' were carefully discriminated, and each had its characteristic ceremonies. Each bilateral act was a free initiation, involving a choice amongst the various partners of the man concerned — a choice dictated by their reputation for prompt and fair dealing, as well as by knowledge of what might be acquired in return — for many of the *vaygu'a* were legendary treasures with their own proper names.

Whatever the origins of this system, it seems clear that *kula* and *gimwali* were functionally interdependent, the first serving to unite groups of strangers who thus enjoyed the material advantages of the second. The character of *kula*, both as gift and as reciprocity, appears to be connected with this function – and very probably with its origin, too – as a bridge-head of solidarity between potential foes. But how are we to explain this significance of giving? And why do we seem to see greater emphasis on bilateralism where giving has this significance, than where it is more of an economic arrangement within a solidary group?

The answer may lie in the recipient's freedom to choose between acceptance and refusal. Acceptance places him in a similar relationship to the thing as that just vacated by the donor. If he is a stranger, he thus creates a new similitude at the most salient point in a tense situation, thereby joining the donor in a community of intent and indicating his willingness to enter a new solidarity. Likewise, if he refuses the offer he not only ratifies the pre-existing state of estrangement, but brings it into high salience by a conflict of wills, which inevitably has a symbolic quality. More is at stake than the gift.[25] If the gift of an engagement ring illustrates this principle at work in our own society, then the return of the ring if an engagement is broken off is equally a token of finality.

This problematic nature of giving, and the risk involved in making an offer, is the more prominent where estrangement is greater. Mauss emphasised this in *The Gift*. Primitive groups are mechanically solidary within, mutually estranged. Yet the course of civilisation has depended on the development of peaceful intercourse between them. 'In order to trade, man must first lay down his spear . . . When two groups of men meet they may move away or in case of mistrust or defiance they may resort to arms; or else they can come to terms.' Universally, offering what one has in the hope of acceptance, is the elementary overture of friendship.

> In these primitive archaic societies there is no middle path. There is either complete trust or mistrust. One lays down one's arms, renounces magic and gives everything away, from casual hospitality to one's daughter or one's property. It is in such conditions that men, despite themselves, learnt to renounce what was theirs and made contracts to give and repay.[26]

In Mauss's opinion, 'total prestation' was the primordial form of mutual giving between clans or tribes, where all participated in collective donations. The alternative, if mutual avoidance was impossible, was war. Similar ideas probably underlay the universal duty of unreserved hospitality to strangers, who might always be decoys.

The risk of offering a gift is all the greater because, in taking the initiative, the donor inevitably exercises power.[27] For his action necessitates a response from the other, and this cannot be evaded: whatever occurs will *be* his response. Furthermore, this necessity – which is insepar-able from all initiating of intercourse between strangers, and leads to all sorts of reticences, overstatements and resentments – is compounded by the fact that if the initiative takes the form of offering a gift, the other can only respond on the donor's own terms. He must accept or refuse *this* offer. Inevitably, the offer will be read as a sign of what the donor thinks of the intended recipient: there is a danger that it will be seen as too mean, implying that he is worth little or can be contented with trifles; or else that it is too lavish, showing a desire to impress and overwhelm by ostentation and patronage.

It is in these considerations, I believe (and not in gratitude for instance, as adduced by Simmel, or self-interest, as Blau maintains[28]), that we should see the cause of the universal tendency towards reciprocity of giving between strangers. If the community of intent involved in giving is to be both an expression and a vehicle of enduring solidarity, then like all solidarity it must enjoin equality of status and rights between members of the solidary group, in their membership capacity. The functional asymmetry of giving and receiving creates a dangerous inequality of power and status which can, however, easily be rectified by reversing roles.

This leaves open the question of whether the content of reciprocal giving is to be competitive, each seeking to outdo the other in the value of his gifts, or aims at equivalence. Likewise, it leaves open the question of whether reciprocal giving terminates with the counter-gift, or continues to alternate.

The greater the emphasis on bilateralism, the more it will take the form of a series of discrete interchanges of equivalents, as in *kula*. Possibly, also, the need for bilateralism will be greater where the institution has to surmount more estrangement. A striking example of alternating reciprocal giving, which was also competitive, is the potlatch as practised among the later N.W. Coast Indians. Originally this appears to have alternated within relatively small social spheres compared with *kula*, and to have been much less competitive than it became later under the influence of European contact.[29] Though Mauss confounded important differences between *kula* and potlatch, and between these and other institutions, by an indiscriminate use of the term 'gift exchange', he was fundamentally right about their common features. Thus he stressed that three obligations – which are also logical preconditions – underlay the successful and regular operation of all these practices: gifts must be offered, gifts offered must be received, and counter-gifts must be offered in return for gifts received.

This explanation of bilateral giving receives some support from an examination of the most marked example of unilateral giving: alms. By soliciting alms, a beggar guarantees the receipt of the gift in advance. He relieves the benefactor of any risk that his offer might be refused as unwanted condescension or as slightingly insufficient. By accepting that the initiative – both as to the giving and the nature of gift – lies with the benefactor, the beggar signifies his acceptance of this unequal power as appropriate to the relationship between them. By begging, he precludes making any return save in expression of gratitude, and thus renounces any claim to equality. Furthermore, it is understood that alms represent the overflow of the benefactor's superfluity, relieving the beggar's extreme need: the underlying distribution is unquestioned. Thus the tenuous solidarity that is established between beggar and benefactor is based on their similar relationship to the alms as a small, dependent, and expendable part of a larger whole, the benefactor's wealth. This shared meaning of the gift implies a parallel assessment of their personal status. Alms therefore appear to be only an extreme form of a type of unilateral giving that is scarcely less universal than the bilateral type. If the latter involved a general tendency towards role-reversal and reciprocity, the former implies incommutability of roles and perpetual asymmetry. The first is premised on the similarity of the parties as equals, the latter on their relation to unequal parts of a common identity.

Reciprocal giving and almsgiving are both therefore means of bridging or mitigating estrangement, but they correspond to different situations. The first corresponds to horizontal estrangement between similiar units, the second to vertical estrangement between unequal strata. Almsgiving is, in fact, an adaptation of free distribution – an internal technique – to the growth of internal estrangement between rich and poor. Obviously, reciprocal giving is a more potent antidote to estrangement than almsgiving, because the unequal power inseparable from the latter immediately renews the estrangement and prevents any deep emotional bond from forming. The benefactor gladly forgets the beggar, and the beggar only remembers the benefactor egoistically, not with affection. Christianity, with its vows of monastic poverty and its advice to the rich to sell up and give to the poor, recognised that mere mendicancy and alms could not solidarise a hierarchical, estranged society. But nor could Christianity's arbitrary levelling down of saintly individuals and groups. Only when classes could treat each other as independent antagonists, on the field of political democracy, could redistributive social policies begin to be based on some degree of reciprocity. Even so, however, forced distribution has in general proved more effective, whether reformist or revolutionary in method.

Ethnographic evidence assembled by Mauss, and adduced by many writers since, has long familiarised sociologists with reciprocal giving as a means of sustaining solidarity between more or less independent and potentially hostile segmental groupings. I shall not recite more of this than is necessary to suggest the characteristic ambivalence of such institutions, where many shades of intermixture of solidarity and estrangement are invariably found. In the Andamans, Radcliffe-Brown reported that reciprocal gifts 'put a seal to marriage, forming a friendly relationship between the two sets of relatives.'

They give the two sides an identity which is revealed in the taboo which from then on prevents them from visiting or addressing each other, and in the obligation upon them thereafter to make perpetual gift-exchange. The taboo expresses both the intimacy and the fear which arise from this reciprocal creditor-debtor relationship. This is clearly the principle involved, since the same taboo, implying simultaneous intimacy and distance, exists between young people of both sexes who have passed through the turtle and pig-eating ceremonies together, and who are likewise obliged to exchange presents for the rest of their lives.[30]

Similarly, amongst the ancient Germans the institution of *wadium* – the giving of a pledge by which one's honour was staked against the fulfilment of a contract or repayment of a debt – presupposed a fragile solidarity. 'The whole ritual takes the form of challenge and distrust, and is an expression of them. In English, "to throw down the gage" (*wadium*) is the equivalent of "to throw down the gauntlet". The fact is that the pledge as a thing given spells danger for the two parties concerned.'[31] Even more conspicuous estrangement prevailed among the potlatching Indians of the Canadian northwest, where 'the agonistic character of the prestation is pronounced. Essentially usurious and extravagant, it is a struggle among nobles to determine their position in the hierarchy to the ultimate benefit, if they are successful, of their own clans . . . everything is conceived as if it were a war of wealth.'[32]

In their detailed forms, these and other types of reciprocating prestation in preliterate societies show a considerable variety. In principle, this variety should be reducible to a limited number of logical conditions added to the basic three enumerated by Mauss. In general, the multiplication and rigour of conditions is usually a way of modifying and institutionalising free alienation to suit situations of diminished solidarity. When this is the case, the obligation to give may come to weigh heavily on donors, who are not so much initiating a free alienation as responding to a stimulus from outside, backed up by the sanction of losing prestige if they do not conform to social expectation. Recipients can then not only count their gains in advance, but also count on them accruing as a result of their own actions. Reciprocal giving may therefore become mutually expropriative. So long as equality prevails between the participants, they have the remedy to a common evil in their own hands, and this sets a limit to how far its character of free alienation can be compromised. When inequality and vertical estrangement encroach, however, transitions to expropriative and exploitative forms may be hard to resist.

6 MODES OF FREE ALIENATION BETWEEN CONTEMPORARIES (II)

The discussion so far has hinged more on the different functions of unilateral and bilateral giving than on differences of function between the varieties of bilateralism. The latter can only be analysed by, first, grasping as a whole any system of circulation that is established through certain kinds of repetition of the unit acts; and secondly, placing this system in its broader socio-economic context. Let us see how reciprocation, alternation and rotation can combine acts of free alienation into various functional patterns.

The typology in Section 3 included a category of many-to-one and one-to-many rotary gifts in order to accommodate two patterns distinguished by a recent writer under the name of 'net generalized exchange'.[33] 'Individual-focused' net generalised exchange is where each member of a group is benefited in turn by the rest acting collectively. The Nigerian *esusu*, a form of mutual aid, is given as an example. Peasants in various parts of the world help each other at harvest time in this way; similarly, friends may club together to give each other birthday parties, and so forth. 'Group-focused' net generalised exchange is the obverse: the members in turn benefit the rest collectively, as with the custom of 'standing rounds' of drinks, and, to some extent, potlatching. The term 'net generalized exchange' is intended to assimilate these practices to Lévi-Strauss's 'generalized exchange', which was applied to the rotary giving of brides in Australian and other tribal societies. However, they are not really very much alike, and whereas these types of rotary giving seem well adapted to spreading the burdens of recurrent collective tasks or festivities, the functions of Lévi-Strauss's patterns were quite different.

Lévi-Strauss's dichotomy of 'restricted exchange' and 'generalized exchange' corresponds to the distinction between reciprocal and rotary giving.[34] In restricted exchange, brides are given alternatively back and forth between two lineages; in generalised exchange they are given progressively around a circle of lineages. 'Exchange' seems to be doubly inappropriate as a name for these patterns. First, because whereas simultaneous initiation is of the essence of exchange, here the unit acts are free alienations in successive generations, linked only by the expectation that for a bride given or taken in one generation, another bride may be taken in the next. Secondly, while reciprocation concludes an act of exchange, both alternating reciprocation and rotation are, in these cases, without any terminal point. Lévi-Strauss used the notion of debits and credits to conceptualise the intergenerational relationships of lineages resulting from these systems. While unexceptionable as a device borrowed from accountancy, which converts discontinuous concrete transactions into continuous, abstract, symbolic series, this would be misleading if it suggested an actual analogy with making and repaying a loan. For a loan is like an exchange, half of which is postponed under a contract that records the original simultaneous initiative. The transaction is complete when the loan is repaid, whereas with the interchange of wives the repayment itself creates a new 'debt' in the former 'creditor'. In this respect, *kula* was a genuine gift-exchange, while these, like potlatching, are patterns of alternating and rotating prestation.

In general, as Lévi-Strauss has emphasised, these patterns of bride prestation can be interpreted in Maussian terms, as devices by which solidarity is maintained between otherwise alien groups, and the range of effective sociation thereby enlarged, or guarded against shrinkage and fragmentation. But it would be surprising if their formal peculiarities were wholly unrelated to their distributive functions. Lévi-Strauss's models and Marx's treatment of commodity circulation have been compared by several writers.[35] Without embarking on an extensive comparison, it may perhaps be suggested that some of the formal contrasts between commodity exchange and bride prestation are explicable by the different problems which the institutions resolve.

For commodity circulation, the problem is: given continuous production of many kinds of goods, and synchronous demand and supply, to find and apply the values in terms of which different kinds of goods can be equated and redistributed in quantities that satisfy existing needs. For bride circulation, the problem is: given discontinuous production of single goods of one kind and fixed, equal value, each of which can satisfy a need, to synchronise supply and demand so that goods are available to change hands when needed. In large societies where supply and demand for brides is continuous this is no problem, and marriage approximates to a free contract. Here, there is room for the *relative* values of brides and bridegrooms, in terms of beauty, accomplishments, status, etc., as objects of one another's personal consumption, to have full play in the establishment of equivalences in a 'marriage market'. But in small societies, where the failure of one family stock is a notable depletion of the whole, the single and more or less identical value of brides as means of human reproduction predominates over others. Simply because it is small, such a society is likely to be chronically threatened with scarcity of brides – i.e. of marriageable girls available when needed by marriageable men – because of discontinuous and slow production. Alternating and rotating prestation between designated lineages overcome this by linking supply and demand to the periodicity of the production cycle from birth to marriageability, through devices by which alienating a sister or appropriating a wife in one generation creates the expectation of being able to appropriate a wife in the *next* generation. Like a loan and repayment, this arranges for an equivalent object to change hands at different times, to meet asynchronous needs, but it differs in being designed to meet indefinitely recurrent but predictable needs of the same sort.[36]

Alternation or rotation of bride-prestation between lineages can be interpreted, then, perhaps, as a way of harnessing biological time to the social structure. In the *kula* ring, rotation was combined with reciprocation to achieve a spatial circulation, and this we might expect to have a different function. The *kula* ring consisted actually of a double rotation:

The sum total of exchanges will not result in an aimless shifting of the two classes of article, in a fortuitous come and go of the arm-shells and necklaces. Two continuous streams will constantly flow on, the one of necklaces following the hands of a clock, and the other, composed of arm-shells, in the opposite direction. We see thus that it is quite correct to speak of the *circular* exchange of the Kula, of a ring or circuit of moving articles. On this ring, all the villages are placed in a definitely fixed position with regard to one another, so that one is always on either the arm-shell or the necklace side of the other.[37]

The 'clock', with and against which the articles circulate, had therefore a specific geographical location, embracing many islands and broad tracts of ocean. The circular flow was articulated with reciprocal giving by the fact that *vaygu'a* were not received in order to be hoarded (though some accumulation occurred) but to be passed on. So each bilateral transaction was initiated in the expectation of participating in another, in the opposite direction, afterwards.

The most obvious function of the ring itself was to create and perpetuate a bounded community within which *vaygu'a* would be prized and circulated: to give meaning to the game and define the players. If we think of it as a board-game, we can see that the double rotation also set the terms on which the 'counters' could move: arm-shells in one direction, necklaces in the other. This also defined their purchasing power as 'gift-exchange-values': a man accumulating arm-shells but not necklaces would be rich in one direction, poor in the other. To some extent, this flow and counter-flow of two different kinds of embodiment of *kula* wealth resembled the flow and counter-flow of commodities and · money, as two different kinds of embodiment of value, in Marx's analysis of the commodity market. But while the complementarity was spatialised in the *kula* ring, it existed only relative to the assumption of roles of buyer and seller in the commodity market. A more important difference was that commodities only embodied exchange-value *qua* use-values, and as such caused money – pure exchange-value – to circulate, while both sorts of *vagu'a* were pure exchange-values. This is the main reason why, though real shell money was used in other parts of Melanesia, *kula* valuables cannot really be treated as currency.

Nevertheless, it is helpful to press the analogy with Marx's market models further. For although *gimwali* was barter trade, and hence involved no circulation of commodities against money, there is a sort of parallel between the *kula-gimwali* contrast, in Malinowski, and the contrast between the C-M-C and M-C-M circuits, in Marx. The money capitalist's intervention in the commodity market consists in buying commodities in order to sell them, moving from money through commodities back to money. So for him, money and commodities *are* both merely different embodiments of value: neither has use-value, so far as he is concerned. By contrast, the producer-consumer who sells commodities he does not need only in order to buy others that he does, is, like the *gimwali* trader, only interested in exchange-value as a means of securing use-values. The words in which Marx set off the rationality of this circuit against the apparent irrationality of the other could be applied, *mutatis mutandis*, to the contrast between *gimwali* and *kula*:

> In the simple circulation of commodities, the two extremes of the circuit have the same economic form. They are both commodities, and commodities of equal value. But they are also use-values differing in their qualities, as, for example, corn and clothes. The exchange of products, of the different materials in which the labour of society is embodied, forms here the basis of the movement. It is otherwise in the circulation M-C-M, which at first sight appears purposeless, because tautological. Both extremes have the same economic form. They are both money, and therefore are not qualitatively different use-values; for money is but the converted form of commodities, in which their particular use-values vanish. To exchange £100 for cotton, and then this same cotton again for £100, is merely a roundabout way of exchanging money for money, the same for the same, and appears to be an operation just as purposeless as it is absurd.[38]

Of course, as Marx argued in full, the rationale of the circulation of money capital depended precisely on the fact that at some point equivalents were *not* exchanged, so that quantitative gains were made. The merchant could exploit a monopoly of some part of the circulation process, or the undeveloped conditions of production in different markets, to make a 'profit on alienation' by unequal trade. Or else the commercial capitalist, converting the commodity output of industrial capital into money, shared in the general expropriation of surplus-value that the free movement of capital spreads throughout all branches of a developed economy. This type of disguised rationality, however, was not present in *kula*, where any individual 'profit on alienation' was only incidental, and supplied neither the purpose of participants nor the function of the institution.

Here, then, was a circulation resembling that of money capital, in that it was not oriented to exchange of use-values, though it helped to promote it; which provided participants with their main symbols of wealth, and the prestige that went with it; yet which appeared to lack the one characteristic that provided the entire motivation of the money capitalist, the competitive pursuit of profit. Granted that the function of *kula* was to extend and secure *gimwali* 'markets', what was the incentive, and what was it in the system which allowed the incentive to operate?

The incentive was, in fact, the competitive pursuit of gain; but its connection with circulation was not the same as that of the money capitalist's profit. To be richer than another Trobriander was not to accumulate marginal gains on each transaction, which could become the expanding basis for new transactions; wealth was measured, apparently, by the *volume of transactions*. Gains were not made by overreaching partners, but by acquiring and keeping them; and wealth was shown not by the accumulation of assets, but by quantity and quality of turnover. This, clearly, was partly a function of the indivisibility of the medium. But what caused this sort of medium, and the kind of incentive that went with it, to suffice? And what gave it its appeal as a vast, institutionalised game of status-seeking?

The answer must be sought outside the sphere of circulation, in the mode of production which formed its real context. To recapitulate the terms of the problem: *kula* and *gimwali* were functionally interdependent practices, possibly the result of a functional covergence of two distinct sorts of transaction: ceremonial interchange of gifts, and direct, competitive exchange of use-values. (The former, perhaps, was a partial democratisation of chiefly prerogatives.) Whatever their origin, the practices had converged upon a socio-geographical synthesis. By the structure of the ring, *kula* afforded the principal occasions of annihilating spatial distance and the means of maintaining solidarity with foreigners, while *gimwali* allowed exploitation of ecological and industrial diversity.

A solution suggests itself when we recall that the productive·function which to some extent always accompanies exchange is that of transportation, and that the historical origins of the trader are bound up with means of transportation which he owned and often operated himself – from the foot-pedlar to the master of fleets and caravans. At the basis of the heterogeneity of *kula* and gimwali, perhaps, lay the contrast between canoes and the products they carried. Chiefs were always the principal owners of canoes, having organised the labour for their building, and they 'received always by far the greatest proportion of *kula* valuables'.[39] Their cargoes, produce of *gimwali* trade, consisted typically of items for personal consumption or tribal distribution, partly as wages for communal labour in canoe-building and other works. Canoes were these people's biggest technical triumph, and their most important instrument of production. Their history was of canoe-borne migration and conquest; their subsistence depended on sea-fishing. Above all, canoes could be used interchangeably for raiding or barter: in an archipelago, canoe ownership and entrepreneurship was the means of appropriating the surplus produce of alien communities, by fair means or foul. The former was much more productive, but it meant carrying trade goods instead of weapons and, above all, having bridgeheads of solidarity abroad.

As we have seen, the offer of a gift is universally a proffer of solidarity – a gage of friendship, which may become a challenge to combat if refused; and its acceptance is a conditional pledge of safety. Such ceremonial overtures must therefore have formed an essential part of realising the function and worth of a trading canoe. Or this function, we might say, consisted in the annihilation of space, both geographical *and* social, because the one was useless without the other if trade was the object. A possible interpretation of *kula* would be, therefore, that by compelling return visits and counter-gifts, it allowed the owners and co-owners of canoes, according to their status, to 'capitalise' on their means of transportation by the prestige of *vaygu'a* wealth, which arose directly out of the diplomacy of the transportation function itself; while *gimwali* items were exchanged more or less at their labour values, for consumption. Naturally, this simple relationship would have become much elaborated over the generations. As *kula* grew into a big institution linking alien peoples, whose extent transcended the vision of any individual or village, *vaygu'a* would have become imbued with a fetishised moral force, like money or capital, surrounded with magical ideology and encrusted with legend. Thus, we have here, perhaps, a primitive form of merchant 'capital', monopolised by high-status menfolk, allowing them to 'profit' and become 'wealthy' out of a skilled, somewhat risky service which they carried on on behalf of the community.

This interpretation differs from that of Mauss, while accepting his basic contention that the function of reciprocal giving is the partial solidar-isation of aliens. For Mauss assimilated *kula* to potlatch and interpreted both as systems of competitive renunciation of wealth in which status was acquired through conspicuous spending, and maintained through the obligation laid on others to spend in return. 'We may truly say that the Trobriand or Tsimshian chief behaves somewhat like the capitalist who knows how to spend his money at the right time only to build his capital up again.'[40] But the cases were different. The Tsimshian chief behaved more like a capitalist in that the potlatch might involve usury, and is therefore an investment, whereas *kula* was a mere exchange of equivalents with deferred payment but little notion of interest. But the Trobriand chief was more like a capitalist in another way, in that he was a versatile entrepreneur in the shipbuilding and carrying industries, by which he acquired a prestigious network of partnerships through which wealth was always flowing.

But this difference only becomes apparent if we place *kula*, together with *gimwali*, back into the total socio-economic context from which native ideology tends to cut it off. Mauss erred by accepting this native abstraction of *kula*, and then interpreting it as an instance of a more comprehensive class of facts, including Tsimshian potlatching and other modes of reciprocal giving. His error was like that of economists who see in market circulation the central economic reality, claiming that the same economic model is applicable wherever there are markets, and that this explains all such economies. Against this, Marx held that the mode of circulation is more superficial than the mode of production. Its 'laws' have the relative autonomy of its social milieus, but its place in the economy as a whole cannot be understood in isolation, for its aggregate results are determined by the underlying process of social production.

If this approach is 'dialectical' in the sense that it views facts within the complex totality of their interconnections, it nevertheless differs from Mauss's insistence on the interpretation of 'total social phenomena'. This meant analysing social facts from primitive societies from the standpoint that 'these phenomena are at once legal, economic, religious, aesthetic, morphological and so on.' While a useful corrective to misplaced abstraction – especially to the tendency often referred to as 'economic formalism' – this is unfortunate if it merely perpetuates confusions in native thought which have definite ideological functions and social causes. Thus Mauss leant towards a Lévy-Bruhlian view of *kula* as expressing a confusion of 'objects, values, contracts and men', which takes us further away from, rather than closer to, an understanding of the system as a whole.[41]

Even Mauss's partially correct idea that social evolution is accompanied by a gradual disentanglement of things and persons from an indeterminate conglomeration of both in the *conscience collective* should be treated with caution. For it combats the false rigour of the ideological distinction between persons and things in continental law with an equally indiscriminate unity of the two. Whereas the probable fact is that men must always have distinguished themselves as persons from *certain* things which were crucial to their existence, however indistinct the boundaries of personal identity in other directions.[42] For all societies, the important matter is to ascertain in *what* respects men (and women and children) were treated as persons, and in what respects as things. Thus capitalist society treats employees as things, as material containers of labour-power that has been purchased; but as wage earners, and as purchasers of subsistence commodities, it treats the same men and women as persons able to conclude contracts. And this discrepancy is fundamental to the logic of the system.

7 MODES OF EXPROPRIATION BETWEEN CONTEMPORARIES

For expropriation to occur, one party must be in a position to constrain another's capacity for free alienation, so that he can count in advance on the other's acquiescence in his own dispossession. There would seem to be three main ways of expropriating another: his capacity for free alienation may be deceived, or coerced, or it may already itself be partially appropriated by the expropriator, who can therefore alter its scope to the other's disadvantage.

Deception is the simplest case. It is obviously a method of expropriation that is peculiarly suited to societal settings. For here appropriation necessarily appears to follow and depend on prior alienation, although this is in fact merely a postponement by the expropriator, who counts on it as a consequence of his own initiative in supplying false information that he knows will induce it. Because it exploits, and hence subverts, the mutual trust of solidaries, fraudulent expropriation seems to be universally reprehended, especially in market society where solidarity is reduced to a necessary minimum anyway. Despite this, it is commonplace wherever estrangement prevails. It enters as an element into every situation where ideological persuasion accompanies appropriation – the trading of promises, based on allegations of fact not known to be true, against contributions, support or payment, whether by priests, politicians, advertisers, witch-doctors or doctors of medicine, of sociology, and so forth. How far such transactions involve conscious deception, self-deception or credulity on the part of the appropriator – and therefore, how far expropriation enters into them – is certainly exceedingly variable, and often hard to determine. This is a familiar aspect of the Marxian theory of ideology and will not be expatiated on further here. Both Marx and Engels, however, stressed that the attempt to deceive was endemic in market relations. This is especially so in the form of concealing relevant knowledge – not only about the faults or harmful effects of commodities, but also about their value. The practice of buying cheap and selling dear, and thus the entire history of unequal trade, would be impossible without some deception of this kind.

Coercion, like deception, may of course be used with other ends in view than expropriation. But here, as in general, it takes two main forms, as Marx already suggested in his notes on Mill:

> Violence excepted, how would I come to alienate my private property in favour of another man? Economics correctly answers: out of necessity, out of need.[43]

Violence is more effective as threat than as deed, and a man can only be coerced through his needs if he is given some kind of promise: thus, coercion works through men's fears and hopes. Its two forms reduce to the conditional withholding, either of pain it is in my power to inflict, or of pleasure it is in my power to confer. Instruments of coercion accordingly fall into two classes: things which can be wielded to cause injury or damage to another, and things whose supply can be controlled to prevent others from satisfying their needs. Both classes are obviously exceedingly various. The first are necessarily adapted to whatever is susceptible of injury, while the second are as diverse as the objects of human need whose supply can in some way be controlled.

Anything wielded with the (understood) intention of threatening injury can be called a 'weapon', for the meaning of this word depends on the role a thing plays in this particular technique of social interaction, and its reference varies accordingly. (The blackmailer's weapon, for example, is information which, communicated to others, would injure the victim's reputation.) That certain sorts of tools and machines have been specially developed as instruments of physical violence ('arms', etc.) merely reflects the facts that the human body is vulnerable, and that most people respond to threats of physical pain.

There is no need to underline further the historical and structural importance of violent expropriation. A major factor shaping human history has been the periodic eruption, from demographic causes, of hordes of pastoral nomads from the steppes and deserts of the world, in vast expeditions of conquest and rapine – Medes, Scythians, Huns, Arabs, Turks, Mongols and many more. The more regular pillaging of the surplus product of other peoples, as booty, has supported many a tribe and nation that lived off a war economy. It has also thereby provided the social framework of a conquering military aristocracy, out of which even more regular, non-violent modes of exploitation have developed, as was seen in Chapter 4. In the forms of reciprocal cattle-raiding, for instance, or robbery combined with trade, violent expropriation may also become semi-regularised as a means of trafficking goods. In Evans-Pritchard's view, the fact that animals, unlike crops and dwellings, can be captured and taken home 'has given pastoral peoples a bias in favour of the arts of war rather than the arts of peace',[44] thereby no doubt influencing them also in the direction of male dominance and patriarchal family-systems. Reciprocal seizure or 'theft-exchange' perhaps needs to be recognised as a practice of some structural significance. Certainly, it is often institutionalised in symbolic forms, for instance in the widespread custom whereby lineages that exchange wives in alternate generations engage in mock battles where the bridegroom wrests the bride from her kin. Rotary seizure – though perhaps more familiar as a motif in jokes and games than in real life – nevertheless enters into a number of primitive systems containing rotary giving.

Hence also the historical and structural importance of those weapons which have general applicability and are themselves easily appropriated, such as arms. As Weber insisted, political expropriation, including the fiscal systems of modern states, rests on a monopoly of the legitimate use of the means of physical violence. Indeed, it is perhaps permissible, for ease of reference, to call coercion by threat of injury 'political coercion', and coercion by promise of satisfaction, 'economic coercion', so long as this is not taken to imply that the use of either method is restricted to the 'polity' or the 'economy' respectively.

Expropriation by deception and political coercion are relatively simple forms, in which one party is made to 'give up' what he would rather keep as a result of external pressures which do not themselves involve any kind of alienation. Economic coercion, however, is more complex, for here seizure is itself dependent on alienation by the expropriator. The purest case is where A has something which he wants to keep, which B covets; B has another object, worthless to him, but which A needs even more than his original object. A is then induced to part with his object in return for B's. The word that best corresponds to 'weapon' as a general term for instruments of economic coercion is probably 'inducement'. This is also consistent with its everyday meaning of a bribe, since bribery involves just this one-sided initiative and pressure.[45]

The formula for economic coercion is, then, a combination of expropriation and free alienation on one side, and the appearance of free alienation on the other. As in the case of deception, this appearance means that economic coercion is well adapted to societal settings. Nor is it generally reprehended, as deception is, for both parties seem to end up better off than they began. The only difference is that B has made a sheer gain, while A's marginal gain leaves him still wanting what he has given up: they are unequally better off. Although it seems possible to speak of this transaction in terms of marginal utilities, it is also misleading to do so. For the language of marginalism was invented to describe market transactions, where it is assumed that all the items circulating are willingly alienated by their owners, who bring them to market with that intention. Comparisons are between the relative satisfactions foregone if money is exchanged for one commodity rather than another, but the money is assumed to be expendable, because the purchaser has come to market to spend it. Economic coercion, however, creates a situation where B compels A, who had no intention of parting with anything, to decide which of two dissatisfactions is the less tolerable. In practice, there is seldom a sharp division between willing and unwilling alienation, however, and inequalities of economic power are a pervasive feature of market society. Indeed, the very existence of market society, according to Marx, was precondition and result of the economic coercion of one class by another. Capitalists offer subsistence, which they do not need, in exchange for labour-power, which the wage-earner would rather not alienate but cannot afford to keep off the market, since he lacks the means of production to earn life for himself. Marx neither denied that the labour market involved an exchange of equivalents, nor allowed that this kind of exchange would occur at all but for the economic power of one class over another.

Formally, the importance of seizure by economic coercion is that it affords a transition from unilateral alienation to exchange. For as well as a repetition of the first movement by one of the agents, simultaneous bilateral alienation also requires an opposite movement by the initiator. In order to take he must also give. As will appear when we examine exchange, the formal possibility of all exchange arises from this type of conditional alienation. It also draws attention to the incompleteness of the typology in Section 3. For simplicity, bilateral alienations where movement and counter-movement are both initiated from the same side were omitted. This was partly, also, because the meaning of actions that involve both a giving and taking are very variable and consequently do not lend themselves readily to institutionalisation, or correspond with settled states of solidarity and estrangement. Very often they imply some change of motive or miscarriage of intention. But they do include this important class of actions which are unified by the intention of exploiting inequalities of economic power, and consist of giving *in order to* take.

The third method of expropriation, beside deception and coercion, is where one person has pre-empted another's capacity for free alienation, and can subsequently exercise it to the disadvantage of the original possessor. It is where a person or group's capacity for alienation becomes divided against itself, and a hostile other opposes and constricts the original possessor, as the representative of his own alienated powers of alienation and appropriation. We recognise here the echo of Marx's *Manuscripts* of 1844, and this is indeed the distributive formula for capitalist and most other types of exploitation. It involves greater difficulties, and is of more interest, than the simple modes of expropriation discussed so far. Further consideration will be postponed until the subject of exploitation is dealt with as a whole. In the meantime, one final aspect of simple expropriation must be mentioned – its bearing on the practice of *restitution*.

One of the most noteworthy examples of reciprocal seizure is the blood-feud or vendetta. It might be thought that 'expropriation' scarcely extends to such acts of injury and revenge against the persons, rather than the possessions, of the 'vengeance-groups' concerned. However, two pieces of evidence suggest that this is a modern scruple, influenced by legalistic distinctions between 'person' and 'thing'. One is that wherever the blood-feud exists, the usual way of preventing or concluding it is by an offer of compensation to the injured group, in money ('blood-money') or kind, and especially in livestock. The other is the prevalence of what is often called 'passive solidarity' – a murdered man's kinsman is not necessarily required to avenge his death upon his murderer; it is enough to take the life of any member of the murderer's kindred. These two facts, taken together, suggest that societies practising the blood-feud think of homicide and vengeance as literally the 'taking of a life' from one group by another: robbing it of one of its most valuable possessions, a unit of living labour. The Anglo-Saxon *wergild*, by which lives were valued on a scale corresponding to their status, was a consistent elaboration of the same idea – lives having a social use-value according to their rank.

In a juridical view, restitution through private vengeance is at an opposite extreme from restitution effected through a civil action in a court of law. And certainly legend has preserved many famous feuds with protracted bloodletting, especially from the Homeric age and the European Middle Ages. However, research on African and Mediter-ranean societies suggests that such cases functioned more as warnings than as exemplars. The dire consequences of vendetta – whether in segmental societies or between the 'families' of American gangsterism – usually impel those whom they implicate in a killing to reach a settlement. It has been shown how, in Africa, the mobilisation of cross-cutting solidarities, based on locality and marital alliance, is the usual means of conciliation.[46] Arbitration by a chief or magician is often customary, too. Thus the inexorable logic of alternating reciprocal seizure, in a society where segmental solidarity is very strong and all men are willing and able to kill, tends to *prevent* inter-segmental estrangement from escalating into civil war whenever a death offers a *casus belli*. Durkheim saw the growth of restitutive law in modern society as indicative of increasing organic solidarity. However, it may show only that with the universal estrangement of market society and the monopolisation of legitimate violence by the state, society contains the resources neither of solidarity nor of force needed to make the implications of reciprocal vengeance a real deterrent. The state therefore pre-empts the duty to avenge the first victim by declaring homicide a crime, and in civil disputes lends its force to one side or the other, which it declares to be in the right.

Restitution does not only take the form of reciprocal seizure, as in the blood-feud and many cases of civil wrong. It may take the form of reciprocal giving, where a conditional gift is voluntarily returned by one who finds himself unable to meet the conditions. More likely, it is a matter of gift followed by seizure, or seizure followed by gift. The first may occur wherever a gift is made in the expectation of some sort of return, which is then unforthcoming. For example, in the *kula*, a man may not take back a gift from his partner. But if the latter is too slow with his counter-gift, his creditor may seize a *vaygu'a* from him by stealth or by force. The second case covers all types of voluntary reparation, such as the payment of conscience money. Like seizure by economic coercion, these last two sorts of restitutive alienation were omitted from the typology in Section 3. They fall into the category where both movement and counter-movement are initiated from the same side; but unlike economic coercion, these instances signal either a breakdown of reciprocating bilateralism or the attempt to cancel a unilateral seizure – i.e. miscarriages or changes of intention. These four types of restitution could be classified according to the locus of initiation in the two movements, as follows:

1. Misalienation and free restitution (reciprocal giving);
2. Misappropriation and forced restitution (reciprocal taking);
3. Misalienation and forced restitution (giving and taking back);
4. Misappropriation and free restitution (taking and giving back).

8 MODES OF EXCHANGE

We have seen that all economic coercion has the form of an exchange, and Marx also argued that exchange of commodities involved mutual economic coercion. Commodities are a species of inducement, produced as such, and their exchange a trial of strength between two antagonists, each controlling 'purchasing power' to the extent that he can withhold what the other needs:

> When I produce more of an object than I myself directly require, my over-production is calculated and refined according to your need. It is only in appearance that I produce more of this object. In reality I produce *another* object, the object of your production that I count on exchanging for my surplus, an exchange that I have already completed in my thought. The social relationship in which I stand to you, my work for your need, is also a mere appearance for which mutual plundering serves as a basis . . . Thus, our mutual product is therefore the means, the mediation, the instrument, the recognized power of our mutual need of each other.[47]

Economic coercion occurs when somebody is induced to give up something he wants to keep, in return for something which has no value to its owner save as an inducement. In commodity exchange, however, both value their commodities only as inducements. They exist for their owners only in order to be alienated, but also only as a means to expropriation. The only reason their owners could have for not wanting to part with them is dissatisfaction with the terms of exchange. On the other hand, each does really want the other's commodity for its use-value, for consumption. In this two-sided asymmetry, so to speak, lies the genesis of the differentiation between use-value and exchange-value, and the quantitative character of the latter. For if the quantities of the two use-values are varied separately, there will always be some ratio at which each would be willing to part with his commodity, as an inducement to the other to do the same. The possibility of their concluding an exchange then becomes a matter of bargaining in order to reach a compromise between these ratios.

The terms of the equivalence at which commodities change hands express the exchange-value of each as a function of the use-value of the other. In Marx's words, they give expression to the 'elementary form of value'.[48] However, as Marx's lengthy analysis of the commodity was intended to demonstrate, we must beware of trying to explain economic value itself from circumstances or motives attending the act of exchange. Exchange brings about differentiation into use-value and exchange-value, but only because every commodity has a potential economic value in so far as it is a *social product*. Circulation only makes manifest the latent social character of products, and is thus the specific locus of value. Economic value begins to exist – to appear socially, as a meaning implicit in things – when products are brought together with a view to exchange; it is realised when, through exchange, the relation between their utilities is made to express the proportions in which their production has engrossed the total labour-time of the social unit corresponding to the extent of their market. But this is scarcely ever a meaning that is evident upon the surface of social life, where prices are the immediate focus of attention. These symbolise (still only indirectly) the independent material and social forms that value takes as commodities and money, as exchange-values. In so far as everyday social curiosity probes behind prices to ask about their formation, it comes upon the fact that objects – products – acquire exchange-value only by acting as inducements in situations of competitive expropriation. Economics has therefore usually explained price-formation by abstracting the assumptions governing these attempts at mutual expropriation: demand and supply, maximising gains and minimising losses. For attempted mutual economic coercion does necessarily reduce to a matter of calculations at the margin. Marx, of course, held that this approach could explain very little about relative prices, and certainly could not provide a law of value that would explain the allocation of resources in the economy generally. Prices are always given on markets as historic prices, and bargaining, if it occurs, is around the given price and therefore cannot explain how given relativities of prices arise and persist. For Marx, then, the circumstances of exchange were merely the proximate causes that transformed value into the actual power that particular inducements wielded in the milieu of circulation.

When commodity exchange is regarded as a mass process, individual victories and defeats in the struggle to expropriate one another cancel out, and are without aggregate effects. 'Who defeats whom is an accident as far as the totality of the relationship is concerned. The ideal intended victory is with both sides, i.e. each has, in his own judgment, defeated the other.'[49] This is because, though each exchange is necessarily a separate dyadic social event, it is also an evanescent moment in the general process of circulation, whose results are determined by the properties of the total system to which it belongs. Commodity circulation is merely the reintegration of a social production process that occurs through an unplanned division of labour. Thus the actual power of different producers is not the result of individual anticipations of others' needs, but of social and historical factors which condition on the one hand a particular social totality and distribution of needs, and on the other a particular distribution of the means of satisfying them.

Thus, while Marx certainly held that everyday market exchanges involved competitive struggle, he also condemned as superficial the liberal view of the economy which saw this Hobbesian war as basic, and which attributed to a providential hand the beneficent result by which private vices were converted into public virtues.

The economists express this as follows: Each pursues his private interest and only his private interest, and thereby serves the private interests of all, the general interest, without willing or knowing it. The real point is not that each individual's pursuit of his private interest promotes the totality of private interests, the general interest. One could just as well deduce from this abstract phrase that each individual reciprocally blocks the assertion of the others' interests, so that, instead of general affirmation, this war of all against all produces a general negation. The point is rather that private interest is itself already a socially determined interest, which can be achieved only within the conditions laid down by society and with the means provided by society; hence, it is bound to the reproduction of these conditions and means. It is the interest of private persons; but its content, as well as the form and means of its realization, is given by social conditions independent of all.[50]

Consequently, sociologically and historically important cases of economic coercion – the imbalance of power in the labour market, or the expropriation of whole occupational classes by capital – only emerge as aggregate results of impersonal forces.[51]

The distinction between form and content in the passage cited from the *Grundrisse* above, reappeared when Marx dealt with exchange in *Capital*, and in a way that enables us to clarify the sense in which exchange involves bilateral free alienation, and to reconcile this with the element of economic coercion:

> . . . If these things are to enter into relation one with another as commodities, the guardians of the commodities must enter into relation one with another as persons whose wills reside in these objects, and must behave in such a way that neither appropriates the commodity of the other, nor alienates his own, except by means of an act performed with mutual consent. They must, therefore, reciprocally recognize one another as private owners. This juridical relation, whose form is that of a contract (whether legally formulated or not) is a voluntary relation, in which the economic relation is reflected. The content of this juridical or voluntary relation is determined by the economic relation. In the case we are considering, the persons exist for one another only as the representatives of commodities, and hence as possessors of commodities.[52]

The *content* of the exchange, clearly, is determined by the structure and movement of the economy as a whole, specifically by the law of value as applied to the items in question. It is this that causes mass effects, such as those mentioned above. On the question of 'form' Marx was not altogether clear. On the one hand, the economic relation is said to determine the content 'of this juridical or voluntary relation', implying that this is a form; but we are also told that the juridical relation 'whose form is that of contract . . .' is a voluntary relation. This suggests that contract is a juridical form whose content is the voluntary relation, and leaves unclear whether the voluntary relation is a juridical relation by reason of its contractual form, or for some other reason.

The most straightforward solution to this puzzle is to regard contract as the legal form of a voluntary relation – a voluntary relation which would also count as a juridical relation in so far as it could, in principle (or in court), be shown to fit the form of a contract; and that the voluntary relation provides the form through which the economic relationship between the commodities is realised. This latter 'form' refers to the social practice of exchange, a specific technique of interaction whose norms are agreed between the parties and which they operate jointly. The formula for this is that appropriation of the other's commodity is conditional on his prior alienation of it, and that alienation is conditional on both subsequent appropriation by the other, and simultaneous alienation by the other of an equivalent. This involves a 'voluntary relation' (*Willensverhältnis*), to be sure, but more accurately it involves a relationship of wills through which voluntary relationships are established. For there is, first, a consensus or joint act of will (*gemeinsames Willensakt*) to cooperate to the extent needed to carry through the interaction involved. This is the community of intent already mentioned in connection with giving. Here, it must enable the two movements to be synchronised, for example by a simultaneous signing and exchanging of contracts, or by less formal synallagmatic understandings. Secondly, as a result of this consensus, each recognises the other's freedom to decide whether and on what terms to relinquish his commodity. Their agreement is motivated by egoism, for each conceives it to be to his advantage to create a situation where his own commodity can be used for its intended purpose: as an inducement to coerce another into parting with what he needs.

It was pointed out in Chapter 5 that a minimum of solidarity was required to achieve this consensus, within the overall estrangement of market competition. Its basis, according to Marx, is not a sense of reciprocity, but the primary similitude that both share the same instrumental view of reciprocity, which is consistent with the fact that businessmen may be mutually attracted by frank cynicism as a way of doing business. For

. . . it is present in the consciousness of the exchanging subjects that each is only his own proper object in the transaction; that each is only a means for the other; finally, that the reciprocity through which each is simultaneously means and end, and indeed only achieves his own end in so far as he becomes means for the other, and only becomes means in so far as he achieves his end – that this reciprocity is a necessary fact, presupposed as a natural condition of exchange, but that as such it is indifferent to each of the two subjects of exchange and only interests either in so far as it is in *his* interest. That is, the common interest which appears as the content of the joint act of exchanging, is indeed in the consciousness of both sides as a fact, but as such it is not the motive, but exists (so to speak) only behind the back of the separate interests reflected in it . . . Each of the subjects returns out of the act of exchange itself, into himself as final goal of the whole process, as totalizing subject (*übergreifendes Subjekt*).[53]

It is now clear how the various sociological elements of commodity exchange fit together. Mutual economic coercion, corresponding to all-round estrangement, can only occur through the establishment of a common technique of interaction, which the mutuality of the coercive intention provides sufficient solidarity to permit; by this common technique, the appearance of free alienation of equivalents on both sides is instituted, as means to intended mutual expropriation. Yet this mutual expropriation is itself, in the end, an illusion. For it is the economic relationship between the use-values concerned which decides the relative power of inducements, and hence the outcome of the struggle. And this is determined by their place and function in the total system of social production and reproduction of which each exchange – and circulation as a whole – is only a mediating moment.

The discussion so far as has been limited to commodity exchange, the application *par excellence* of the exchange form. This includes, as elementary versions, the various types of barter. A word should be added, however, on the centralised forms of exchange, especially synallagmatic contribution-distribution. An element of this is no doubt present in collective life wherever centralised administration is at all developed. Members will be prepared to pool their efforts or belongings, under central command, but on condition of some benefit to themselves. However, we have seen that primitive societies can also operate redistribution economies through informal and customary practices of giving, and that tribute and largesse can result in a rough circulation of equivalents through a centre, without any contractual stipulations being evident. Conversely, despotism rests on forced contributions. In this sphere, reciprocal undertakings originated, no doubt, with the growth of parliaments, wherever nobles could challenge incipient despotism. The attempt to define contractual obligations strictly, however, became most conspicuous with the rise of modern public finance, in societies newly dominated by market relationships and influenced by the political ideology of social contract. Fiscal contributions were supposed to be appropriated to specific, approved public purposes. In fact, the struggle between monarchical bureaucracies and parliaments of landown-ers and merchants revolved to a large extent around the relative scope which the contractual model, or traditional systems of forced contribution, should have in raising public revenues. In seventeenth-century Britain a typical class compromise came out of it. Trade and manufacture were largely untaxed; direct taxes, mainly on land, were supposed to be contractually raised and funded; indirect taxes, falling mainly on articles of mass consumption, remained as a species of 'imperceptible' forced contribution, though subject to nominal parliamentary control. The latter were mainly appropriated to servicing the public debts which provided the basis of military expenditure and of executive power generally. The heyday· of the bourgeois state, in the nineteenth century, saw contractual principles extended as free traders abolished most indirect taxes, and public finance came to centre on a balanced annual budget. In the twentieth century, imperialism, militarism, and the retreat of the bourgeoisie behind the bureaucratic state in domestic class politics, together with the consolidation of international capital as a force seeking to exploit the system of national states to its own advantage, has made the issue largely irrelevant.

9 CONCLUSION: SOCIAL EXCHANGE, RECIPROCITY AND BENEFICENCE

It is pertinent to end this chapter with some remarks on its bearings upon cognate analyses in recent American sociology. One of these is 'social exchange theory'. It has already been pointed out that the major difference between the approach of this book and that of Homans and Blau is the rejection of psychological reductionism. In consequence, I have tried to show how the various modes of alienation and appropriation might correlate with varying socio-emotional matrices, defined in terms of solidarity and estrangement, rather than how they are used by individuals to maximise their psychic 'profits' in interacting with others. It is not implied that the latter is an illegitimate topic, only that it presupposes the former. Hence, the attempt to found upon it a general theory of social structure and social process – and *a fortiori*, theories of societal macrosystems – bypass a necessary level. This, I have claimed, is also the basic level of sociological analysis. Despite this, there are obvious points of contact between the two approaches, for two reasons. The first is that the actual social practices, or techniques of interaction, which are deployed in the various modes of alienation and appropriation, can be treated in much the same way by both, although they occupy different theoretical positions. This difference has led me to multiply typological discriminations in order to discover possible correlates, while it led Blau to lump together and simplify all modes of social reciprocity to the point where they could be assimilated to the model of market exchange and analysed with the concepts of economics. Despite this difference, a Simmelian interest in the practices themselves, as forms of sociation, remains common ground. The second reason for contact is that my 'sociologism' does not exclude the possibility that individuals can take initiatives to construct new parts for their social universe. They can use their cultural repertory of social practices to produce new solidarities and new estrangements. Therefore, in so far as social exchange theory implies a voluntaristic relation of the individual to his social reality (i.e. in so far as it forgets its behaviourist *alter ego*) there is some common ground here too.

But it would be a mistake to exaggerate men's freedom to apply social forms in new ways to new situations. Like all other productive activity, and even more fundamentally, the production of society must be a cooperative undertaking. The participants already find themselves in 'relations of production', predetermined by the existing socio-emotional matrix in which they come into contact. Their available repertory of social practices, too, is a culturally transmitted instrumentarium, whose contents will vary from one culture to another. Thus pioneer settlers in new territory will create different relationships amongst themselves, or between themselves and the natives, depending on whether they hail from closed, solidary societies or open, estranged societies; and on whether they are accustomed to systems of transmission in which free gift, seizure and reciprocal giving are normal, or in which exchange predominates. Thus, it is difficult to resist the impression that the immediate plausibility which social exchange theory seems to have in the eyes of its disseminators is connected with the specific American culture of interpersonal social practice. The universal estrangement and 'equality' of American society creates a strong bias towards bilateralism, and the commercial ethos causes this to be widely interpreted in synallagmatic terms, as an exchange of favours in which, self-evidently, 'An individual who supplies rewarding services to another obligates him.'

This bias, if it is one, is less apparent in the essays in which Alvin Gouldner has defended the view that the norms of beneficence and reciprocity are transcultural basic components of all moral codes.[55] As a development of the insights of Malinowski and Mauss, Gouldner's position is not far removed from that adopted here; but there remain significant differences in approach and conclusions.

The first point is that, where Homans and Blau approach reciprocity from the standpoint of the individual's calculations of costs and benefits, Gouldner's treatment is informed by the more orthodox view that sociology is mainly a study of norms. That has not been the approach followed, for the most part, in this chapter, which has tried to develop a terminology for describing social practices as sets of logically interconnected constituent acts. For it would seem that there are distinct codes or 'moods' into which a unit of social practice may be transcribed. The formulas for different kinds of alienation and appropriation in this chapter have roughly approximated to what might be called the 'logical indicative' (e.g. 'A's doing x_1 is a sufficient condition of B's doing y_1, and A's doing x_2 is a necessary condition of B's doing y_2'). This seems to be the most suitable code for a scientific description in analytic terms, for it might be said to express the orientation of the disinterested observer, concerned only with the accurate identification of facts and their classification in a timeless present, the abstract present of theory. In contrast, the 'normative' code contains idealisation, and implies the existential absence of what is referred to (e.g. 'B ought to do y_1 if A does x_1, but ought not to do y_2 unless A does x_2'). This mood expresses the orientation of the moralising observer, either before or after the fact, enjoining or reproving the choice of one course of action rather than another; hence it may also express the same orientation internalised as the moral will or conscience of the agent. The view of sociology as a study of norms seems to presuppose that the units of social activity are transcribed into this code. Even though such transcriptions can certainly be studied as objective facts, an approach which relies on them is apt to betray leanings towards a concern with ethical distinctions, on the one hand, which corresponds to the pre-occupation of the moralising observer, and on the other towards a concern with motives, corresponding to that of the individual conscience. Socio-logically, it seems to induce explanations of social structure as an effect of 'moral facts' — *conscience collective* or normative order, or else internalised norms and values. Some of the divergences between Gouldner's treatment and my own stem from this difference.

Gouldner stresses the heterogeneity of the norms of beneficence and reciprocity, principally on grounds of motivation. He accuses Mauss of failing to give sufficient emphasis to the distinction. Mauss's triad of obligations regulating gift-exchange — to give, to receive gifts, and to give in return for gifts received — is said to have merged the norm of beneficence (the first and second obligations) into the norm of reciprocity (the third). Further, Gouldner suggests that, besides the functional interdependence of the two, there is also a historical dialectic by which 'the norm of beneficence crystallizes and develops historically in polemical reaction against the norm of reciprocity.'[56] Thus he echoes the charge of Lao-tse against Confucius, of Paul against Moses, and of the young Marx against Locke and Adam Smith: that justice is a primitive and niggardly virtue, which charity will one day supersede. Since Gouldner's 'norm of reciprocity' does not distinguish between reciprocal giving and exchange, it seems likely that this alleged dialectic reflects the historical prestige of these ethical rebellions, which were aimed against social orders dominated more by contractual obligations and exchange than by simple reciprocity, and hence against the high levels of estrangement permitted and encouraged by contractual institutions. Quite possibly, this prestige may blind us to the extent to which the exaltation of a more contractual ideal by Confucius, Moses, or Locke may itself also have reflected an ethical innovation, liberating men from older moralities in which obligations of giving and receiving had become institutionalised as burdensome systems of dependence, tribute and arbitrary favour.

Be that as it may, it seems sensible to distinguish not only between reciprocal giving and exchange, but also between different modalities of the norm of beneficence. There is, very likely, an 'indefinite' norm of beneficence — a duty to give to those who need — in most societies. But it does not normally apply to all situations and relationships. In modern society, it would not apply to political foes (except possibly to prisoners) or to commercial rivals or even professional colleagues (except by way of hospitality). In the individual's relation to the state, or a child's relation to its parents, its place is pre-empted by the norm of obedience. In these and other areas, giving would either be inappropriate or supererogatory; in any case, not obligatory. The limits of the indefinite norm of beneficence, in fact, in conventional morality, are set by the incidence and prevalence of estrangement: there is a general duty to give only where solidarity obtains or is desired, and is not converted into authority.

The indefinite norm of beneficence is supplemented and given precision by 'definite' norms of beneficence. These are the prescriptions corresponding to the particular forms of institutionalised giving in the society. Most instances of norms of reciprocity might well fall into this category. These enjoin duties to give in repayment – and in expectation – of gifts received, usually in connection with a specific institutionalised mode of reciprocal giving. Whether there is a general 'norm of reciprocity' over and above such special rules, and if so, how universal it is, seems to me to be an open empirical question. Very probably there is. But norms of reciprocity do not abrogate, they merely elaborate, the indefinite norm of beneficence. Being particularly bound to give on certain defined occasions, and to certain defined persons, does not absolve me from an indefinite obligation to give. At times Gouldner appears to include the norm of retaliation within the norm of reciprocity. But this is to formulate the norm of reciprocity at a level of abstraction that is scarcely warranted by theory or evidence. To repay kindness with kindness and render evil for evil do not necessarily appear together, as principles governing a single sphere of social relationships. Rather do we find that positive norms of reciprocity are often complemented by other definite norms of beneficence in solidary relationships, including the duty of forbearance, while the *lex talionis*, and a general exemption from the norm of beneficence, tend to prevail together wherever estrangement is dominant.

The principle of repaying evil with evil and good with good is possibly only compatible with exchange relations, where each only gives in so far as he takes, and takes in so far as he gives. In exchange, furthermore, the norm of reciprocity becomes an absolute: give *only* to those from whom you (simultaneously) receive. It is surely in reaction against the encroachments of exchange relations that the norm of beneficence receives what Gouldner calls its 'polemical' formulation at the hands of prophets. The 'strict' norm of beneficence – give to those in need *without* expectation of a return, and without exception – is the ethical reformer's attempt to elevate the indefinite norm of beneficence into an absolute, to transcend the absolute conditionality of exchange. It has no truck with the limitations of conventional morality, but demands an unconditional pursuit of universal solidarity. Unlike the indefinite and definite norms of beneficence, which are merely normative transcriptions of average conduct, the strict norm is an ideological prescription, part of a general religious or metaphysical theory, and in perpetual tension with the social reality of a commercial scoiety, which provokes it and sustains its appeal.

If reciprocity is, from one point of view, no more than a restrictive special application of beneficence, from another, beneficence is an extended application of reciprocity. For a situation where there is a general duty to give to those in need is also one where today's giver may be tomorrow's recipient, a world of swings and roundabouts. Although there is no exact reciprocity, those who cast their bread upon the waters 'shall find it after many days.' From this standpoint one might suggest that the indefinite norm of beneficence is a survival, and the strict norm of beneficence an attempt to revitalise, the ethics of sharing that predominate under primitive communism. The first lingers on in societies that retain a basically communal structure and an assumption of solidarity, while the second arises when this is radically challenged by the advent of market society.

To see these general duties of beneficence as more closely related to sharing than to giving helps to explain a difference between beneficence and reciprocity that puzzles Gouldner. This is that reciprocation tends to be owed directly to another person, and can usually be claimed as a right, while beneficence tends to be owed as a duty to the gods, not to its beneficiary, who can only claim it in the name of the gods, or curse in their name whoever withholds it. The duty to share is precisely a duty to society collectively, and can only be sanctioned by the collectivity, or the fetishised symbol of its unity. Hence it is in the first place *religious* reformers – ideological specialists in the elaboration of that primordial imagery – from whom this ethical challenge emanates; and it is religious ethics, the nostalgia for lost solidarity, which champions the virtue of charity in the most uncompromising manner.

Part IV

Estrangement and Alienation in Historical Materialism: Towards a Sociological Reconstruction

8 Exploitation

In this chapter the concepts developed earlier will be used to elucidate the phenomenon of exploitation of labour. Though Marx often compared and contrasted capitalist exploitation with other forms, he was, as ever, reluctant to theorise about the general features that they shared. He analysed capitalist exploitation in detail, and asserted that some of its basic mechanisms were the same as those underlying the Asiatic state, slavery ancient and modern, and various forms of feudalism.[1] But when he did so he was apt to slip into figurative language, speaking for example of 'the specific economic form, in which unpaid surplus-labour is pumped out of direct producers.'[2] Despite its importance in his thought, the concept of exploitation was not given a clear sociological definition. Partly for this reason, it has been vulnerable to attacks on Marx's theory of surplus-value by economists, as well as to more philosophical allegations of bias. So sociology has largely absorbed Marx's theory of classes, but not, on the whole, the theory of exploitation of labour on which it was based, which has contributed not a little to the confusion besetting class theory in sociology.[3]

I THE MEANING OF EXPLOITATION

Marx did not use 'exploitation' evaluatively.[4] True, it signified a self-interested utilisation of resources. But in his more scientific works Marx did not imply that such selfishness was morally reprehensible, whatever his abhorrence of the societies whose practices he analysed with the aid of the concept. Nor did he write of *people* being exploited, in the vague, humanistic sense that has become commonplace since, meaning any kind of manipulative oppression. Consider the following passage from Marx's discussion of the role of money-capital in the reproduction of the aggregate social capital. (He is arguing that the scale of production is not limited by the amount of capital functioning as money in the process, but this is immaterial for our purposes.)

> Incorporated in capital are elements of production whose expansion wit. in certain limits is independent of the magnitude of the advanced money-capital. Though payment of labour-power be the same, it can be exploited more or less extensively or intensively . . .

The productively exploited nature-given materials – the soil, the seas, ores, forests, etc. – which do not constitute elements of capital-value, are more intensively or extensively exploited with a greater exertion of the same amount of labour-power, without an increased advance of money-capital.[5]

From the second paragraph one may infer that to exploit something is to turn to advantage, and to one's own account, its inherent properties. To exploit natural resources 'productively' is to utilise their natural properties to create objects of human use. Labour, the exertion or expenditure of labour-power, is the means of such productive exploitation.

What, then, is the meaning of 'exploiting labour-power' in the first paragraph? Again, it is a matter of turning something's inherent properties to advantage. The natural property of labour-power, we may say, is to exploit natural resources through production, for human advantage. But human labour always has a specific social form. It is an expenditure of human working time by individuals who are necessarily associated or dissociated in some way or another. For 'it is always a certain social body, a social subject, which is active in a greater or sparser totality of branches of production.'[6] Thus, whereas the properties of natural resources are 'nature-given', the natural property of human labour is 'society-given', in the sense that it appears as the natural property of a totality of social labour. As such, it is the property of creating *value*, a cosmos of economic relativities, whether in the form of directly compared and qualitatively diverse use-values (as, in general, in pre-capitalist modes of production) or as use-values indirectly ranked in a quantitative scale governed by the pursuit of absolute exchange-value (as under capitalism.) It is this property of labour-power that is the object of exploitation in the first paragraph quoted above, as throughout Marx's work. The sense of 'exploitation' is the same, however, whether it is 'nature-given materials' or society-given capacities whose properties are being turned to account.

This social object of exploitation still needs further delimitation. By the exploitation of labour we must always understand Marx to mean the exploitation of *others'* labour-power (*fremde Arbeitskraft*). Exploitation is not just practised *on* a social object, but is also a social relationship *between* distinct persons or classes of persons. In their capacity as exploiters, the subjects of this relationship stand necessarily outside the totality of social labour whose bearers, in their capacity of exploited labour-power, are its objects. In principle, the same concrete individuals could figure in both capacities; Marx, however, limited his analyses of exploitation to the more usual cases where these roles are concretely distributed to separate individuals. Exploitation therefore is a relationship between a set of agents defined as the bearers of social labour-power, or living labour, who are its objects; and another set, its subjects, defined by the negation of the first, as non-workers. These sets are logical classes that are presumed, for purposes of analysis, to exist as social entities – that is, as 'classes' in the sense which gives us models of 'class society' and 'classless society'.

In these contexts, consequently, *'fremde'* must be understood in a strong sense. When writing rapidly in polyglot, Marx rendered this in English not by 'other people's' but by 'foreign', as in the following passage from 'Revenue and its Sources'. (The argument, irrelevant for present purposes, is that J. S. Mill was mistaken in treating part of profit as the entrepreneur's wages.)

> It is incomprehensible how economists like J. S. Mill . . . suddenly convert industrial profit into the individual [*'eigne'*] labour of the capitalist instead of into the surplus labour of the worker, unless the function of exploitation of other people's ['foreign'] labour is called labour by them; the result of this is indeed that the wages of this labour are exactly equal to the amount of other people's ['foreign'] labour appropriated, in other words, they depend directly on the degree of exploitation . . .[7]

It would seem that the sense of *fremd* that Marx wanted to convey here was a term of art – or of dialectic – which included the idea of *alien* otherness. These were others who were no more than others, because no salient similitude or collective personality, no bonds of solidarity or mutual obligation, were shared with them. Rather the contrary, in fact, for the out-group whose labour is exploited is not just casually 'other', but the opposite and mutually exclusive category from that of the exploiters. Thus a condition of estrangement is also a socially given property of the object of exploitation – its socially given *social* property, as distinct from its socially given natural property. This allows living labour – that is, something by nature human and active – to be treated as passive and non-human, and hence to be exploited like a natural resource.

But what is the connection between exploitation and possession? First, since to exploit others' labour-power is to turn to one's own account its capacity to produce value, and since values are realisable only through appropriation in use or exchange, exploitation logically implies the appropriation of some part of the product of social labour by non-workers. Beyond this, three factual connections enter in. First, since estrangement prevails between exploiting and exploited classes, this appropriation will take the form of expropriation. Secondly, if exploitation is to be continuous, there is an upper limit to the share of social labour that can be expropriated by non-workers, since it is the only means whereby living labour can reproduce itself as an object of exploitation. Thus we may follow Marx, and regard exploitation as involving expropriation of the *surplus* product, the line between necessary and surplus labour being drawn historically, within the various modes of production. Thirdly, successful exploitation would seem to require possession of the means of production by the exploiters. For although some things which cannot be possessed — such as a situation, or good weather, or a trusting disposition — may be exploited by anyone who has the requisite opportunity, skill, ruthlessness, etc., things which can be owned, such as the elements of social production, surely need to be owned by those who count on exploiting the labour process that consumes them. Taking all these considerations together, a general definition of the concept of exploitation in historical materialism may be offered, as follows: *the expropriation of the surplus labour of a class of workers by an antagonistic class of non-working owners of means of production*. Since 'surplus labour' cannot be identified apart from the way in which the distinction between necessary and surplus labour can be drawn for some particular mode of production,[8] this definition can only be applied in the context of antagonistic modes of production; but it describes their characteristic process.

Recent studies have suggested that it is mistaken to seek a general theory of modes of production, although the arguments against doing so are perhaps not yet conclusive.[9] The present discussion does not have that ambition, although if successful it must certainly contribute to defining the general features shared by antagonistic modes of production. The following pages attempt to determine the conditions which a mode of production must satisfy if it is to be a vehicle of class exploitation; to enumerate some of the transmissive practices through which these conditions have been realised in the main historical antagonistic modes; and finally, to isolate the distinctive features of exploitation itself, as a complex transmissive practice operating on a large scale.

2 FIVE CONDITIONS OF EXPLOITATION

The conditions that a mode of production must satisfy if it is to be a vehicle of class exploitation can be lumped under five headings. The first two of these refer to *pre*conditions: a state of affairs that must hold outside the production process if what goes on within it is to result in exploitation. Here, Marx emphasised that exploitation can occur only when the worker — the 'direct producer' — is separated from the conditions of production, which confront him as the property of another, alien centre of social agency. We have seen that his concept of the primitive community was constructed as the antithesis to the 'negative model' of the worker's possessory relation to the conditions of production, which was the formula for capital. In the latter,

> living labour relates to the raw material as well as to the instrument and to the means of subsistence required during labour, as negatives, as not-property . . .[10]

Capitalist society provides these exploitative preconditions in their purity – the result of all conditions of production having become human products and hence monopolisable – but earlier forms of exploitation approximated to them more or less closely and in different ways. We may generalise that the potentiality for exploitation is present wherever proprietors of means of production also own, or can control access to, means of subsistence needed by others who lack both but are able to work. This is a double precondition, relating both to the mode of proprietorship in means of production, and the mode of exclusion from means of subsistence; and both sides may be satisfied in variety of ways.

But for this potentiality of exploitation to be realised as a regular aspect and outcome of a continuous process of social production, three further conditions must also be satisfied. From the standpoint of a particular production cycle, these correspond to successive stages or 'functional forms'. They are generalised from the three stages that Marx discerned in the circular movement of capital.[11] In the first of these, 'The capitalist appears as a buyer on the commodity- and the labour-market.' As a consequence, he assembles raw materials and labour-power alongside his means of production, and living labour receives a conditional promise of means of subsistence. The second stage is 'Productive consumption of the purchased commodities by the capitalist. He acts as a capitalist producer of commodities . . . The result is a commodity of more value than that of the elements entering into its production.' He appropriates a surplus produced through a process accomplished under his control but without his direct participation. The third stage is where 'The capitalist returns to the market as a seller; his commodities are turned into money' and in consequence the surplus distributed between accumulation and the revenues of the exploiting agencies. The upshot is the reproduction, outside the production process, of the separation from which it set out. By combining the two preconditions (or results) with the three processual conditions, we obtain five conditions of exploitation, as follows:

1. *Monopoly of means of production and subsistence by a socially cohesive class of proprietors.*The situation in which living labour confronts the conditions of production as not-property must be general, not exceptional or local in incidence. Or, if it is exceptional or local, living labour must be under exceptional or localised constraints which prevent it 'escaping'. If the need for subsistence is to provide an enduring motive for continuously renewed submission, a class of proprietors must effectively monopolise access to society's available means of production and subsistence. Otherwise non-proprietors will migrate to virgin land, obtain credit to produce on their own account, or extort subsistence by political coercion or by appealing to ideological agencies. The cohesiveness of the propertied class, in terms of cultural similitudes, interaction, and extra-economic soli-

darity would appear to be at least a correlative, if not a condition, of effective monopoly.

2. *Plentiful supply of living labour excluded from property in means of production and subsistence, with low social cohesion.* The corollary of the above, but the propertylessness of labour is not a mere obverse of the proprietors' monopoly: it involves a distinct, underprivileged status for the labourer. The ratio of workers to non-workers varies with the productivity of labour, but to the extent that the former are in a large majority their low social cohesion is a condition of successful exploitation by the minority. The status of the excluded individuals is usually conducive to such fragmentation of the working class.

3. *Modes of providing means of production with labour-power, and living labour with subsistence.* Social mechanisms must exist, or be brought into being, by which labour-power is made available for combination with means of production in the production process; and by which subsistence is made conditionally available to living labour.

4. *Control of production and appropriation of surplus product.* The production process must be such, and proprietors must be able to control it in such a way, that it yields not only subsistence for the workers and the surplus requisite for collective purposes, but also a surplus sufficient to maintain the proprietors and their dependent unproductive consumers, without their having to participate in the process except as required for this control. Also, the appropriation of this surplus by the proprietors must occur as a regular unchallenged transaction.

5. *Distribution and consumption of surplus product.* Exploitation is not complete unless the appropriated surplus can be distributed to its final beneficiaries, without reducing the dependence of living labour on proprietors of means of production, and consumed by them in a form that reproduces their social existence as a class of non-workers.

The ways in which these five conditions are fulfilled in the main historic forms of exploitation will now be examined, with special attention to the part played by both static and dynamic possessory relations, as analysed in Chapters 6 and 7. The main historic forms of exploitation are taken to be the combination of *corvée* labour and fiscal rent due to a patrimonial sovereign; servile labour and rent due to a feudal lord; slave labour performed for a slave-owner; and wage-labour for a capitalist.

This selection needs a few words of justification. First, it is not intended to be exhaustive. Other forms of exploitation have existed, such as helotry or peonage, that fall outside these categories.[12] Secondly, these forms of the labour relation can exist in more or less non-exploitative ways outside the particular exploitative property relations specified. Thus *corvée* may exist as a communal obligation; patriarchal slavery may be scarcely at all exploitative, and privileged slaves in exploitative slave-systems may not be exploited;[13] personal dependency approximating to serfdom may be combined with an exchange of services which falls short of exploitation; and wages may be paid for personal labour services, or in an artisan's workshop, or a socialist economy, under more or less non-exploitative circumstances. Thirdly, I shall follow Marx's theoretical assumption that these four forms of exploitation were dominant in the four modes of production to which Marxist tradition has given the names 'Asiatic', 'Ancient', 'feudal' and 'capitalist'. I am well aware of the many weighty objections to doing so, but since the present aim is not to analyse or criticise modes of production, but only the phenomenon of exploitation which appears in antagonistic modes of production, I retain the traditional classifications for simplicity. Fourthly, it is altogether possible and even probable that exploitative forms approximating to these four will be present as subordinate elements within (or alongside) modes of production in which they are not the dominant form. Thus *corvée* labour and serfdom have often coexisted, as have serfdom and wage labour; all three other forms coexisted with slavery in the ancient world, as slavery and *corvée* coexisted with bourgeois capitalism. These qualifications alone give our inquiry a highly abstract and conceptual character, and the use of factual material is inevitably mainly illustrative.

3. CLASS MONOPOLY OF MEANS OF PRODUCTION AND SUBSISTENCE

It might be objected that the first of the four conditions listed above is too strong. Is not a situation where living labour confronts the conditions of production as the monopoly of another class already a situation of class exploitation? And if so, the 'condition' is a mere tautology.

The stipulation is not equivalent to saying that class exploitation exists, however, so long as it refers to the situation existing outside, and in abstraction from, production itself. As such, it merely isolates the moment in which individuals 'stand' over against one another, defined by their respective possessory relations to separate elements of the production process — labour-power on one side, conditions of production on the other. And since this situation is being considered as a condition, not as a result, the combination of these separate elements into a single active process must be conceived as lying in the future. Indeed, the very terms on which this combination will be effected may yet have to be specified. The agents simply 'face' one another, with their possessions, needs and interests, in mutual estrangement. A variety of social situations fits this abstract description, but all are situations external to production, and even to that phase of circulation in which factors of production are assembled. Amongst this variety, a broad distinction can be drawn between two sorts of situation.

The first sort might be envisaged as occurring in a fully developed class society, before the start of a production cycle or else as an antagonistic interruption of one. Under capitalism, examples might be the mutual orientations of employers seeking to hire labour and of workers looking for jobs – say, in a new town; or of representatives of management and labour before a round of collective bargaining; or of managers and workers in a wildcat strike or a factory occupation. Under feudalism, examples might be the relationship of a peasant seeking to 'commend' himself to a lord; or of serfs meeting with their lord's bailiff to negotiate their tenure and services; or even of insurrectionary peasants confronting their masters. Since these are all relationships of estrangement, emphasis is on the bargaining power and the potential for exploitation or resistance inherent in the situation. These potentialities are present in the form of property: primarily, as shared assumptions about the exclusive distribution of things and capacities to persons; secondarily, as the chances of successful exclusion by legal action, political enforcement or political insurgency.

Obviously, in situations of this sort the fact that living labour confronts the conditions of production as the monopoly of a propertied class is itself the result of past exploitation. Thus, once a particular exploitative mode of production is established, exploitation itself becomes the cause of the preconditions for further exploitation being fulfilled. Exploitation, once institutionalised as a dominant mode of production, reproduces both its own material preconditions – living labour-power and means of production – as well as their social distribution and the relationship of estrangement and mutual exclusion between their bearers. When a major form of exploitation is established, therefore, the fulfilment of the last three conditions ensures the fulfilment of the first. This conceptual circularity, which is not logically vicious, simply reflects the cyclical temporal structure of instituted processes of social production.

The second sort of situation to which the first condition could apply is one that is *historically* prior to the development and full elaboration of the exploitative mode of production which is, in fact, to grow out of it. In this sense, living labour confronts the conditions of production as others' property at the *threshold* of feudalism or capitalism. In the first case, peasants deprived of all security of livelihood confront warlords who alone can command access to the land and guarantee subsistence; in the second, 'free' workers – propertyless and communityless men ejected from the dissolving structures of feudalism – confront 'free' capital – money and means of production available for employment outside the restrictions of gilds and the traditional routines of handicrafts, in the hands of 'new men', innovating entrepreneurs. Here, the first condition applies to the period of genesis of a mode of production. The mechanisms that will bring the elements together for production, allowing exploitation to occur, are still uninstitutionalised, in an 'experimental' stage, unstable and bearing marks of the past.

Marx elucidated the sense in which means of production in the hands of others constitute a precondition for exploitation, in the case of capitalism, in the draft entitled 'Revenue and its Sources', from which parts of the third volume of *Capital* were worked up:

> What is capital regarded not as the result of, but as the prerequisite for, the process of production? What makes it capital before it enters the process so that the latter merely develops its immanent character? The social framework in which it exists. The fact that living labour is confronted by past labour, activity is confronted by the product, man is confronted by things, labour is confronted by its own material-ised conditions as alien, independent, self-contained subjects, personifications, in short, as *someone else's property* and, in this form, as 'employers' and 'commanders' of labour itself . . . Capital, as the prerequisite of production, capital, not in the form in which it emerges from the production process, but as it is before it enters it, is the contradiction in which it is confronted by labour as the labour of other people and in which capital itself, as the property of other people, confronts labour. It is the contradictory social framework which is expressed in it, and which, separated from the production process itself, expresses itself in *capitalist property as such.*[14]

And a little later, he distinguished the two senses in which this property could be a 'prerequisite' of exploitation – within, and anterior to, the developed mode of production:

> Labour as wage-labour and the conditions of labour as capital (that is, consequently, as the property of the capitalist . . .) are expressions of the same relationship, only seen from opposite poles. This condition of capitalist production is its invariable result. It is its *antecedent* posited by itself. Capitalist production is antecedent to itself and is therefore posited with its conditions as soon as it has evolved and functions in conditions appropriate to it. However, the *capitalist production process* is not just a production process pure and simple. The contradictory, socially determined feature of its elements evolves, becomes reality only in the process itself, and this feature is the predominant characteristic of the process, which it turns precisely into that socially determined mode of production, the *capitalist production process.*
> The *formation process* of capital – when capital, i.e. not any particular capital, but capital in general, first evolves – is the *dissolution process*, the *parting product* of the social mode of production preceding it. It is thus a *historical process*, a process which belongs to a definite historical period. This is the period of its *historical genesis.* . . . The process of capital becoming capital or its development *before* the capitalist production process exists, and its realization in the capitalist process of production itself belong to two historically different periods. In the second, capital is

taken for granted, and its existence and automatic functioning is presupposed. In the first period, capital is the sediment resulting from the dissolution of a different social formation.[15]

In these two different sorts of situation the first condition is fulfilled in different ways. In a fully developed mode of production it is fulfilled to the extent that the class difference between non-workers and workers, created by exploitation, has achieved general recognition as an unassailable set of habitual assumptions about static possessory relations. It must have become a fixed, unquestioned part of everyday social consciousness that plantations do not belong to slaves, manors to serfs, or factories to wage-labourers. These like all other assumptions about the fixed, permanent aspects of the distribution of possessions in society must, furthermore, have become codified in custom or law which can, if necessary, be enforced by coercive sanctions. As a mode of production enters its phase of dissolution and crisis this taken-for-granted character of its framework breaks down. As basic assumptions are brought into the arena of class struggle, the consensual fulfilment of the first condition cannot be maintained and it has to be upheld more and more by force.

In the genesis of a new mode of production the qualification added to the first condition becomes relevant – i.e. if the situation is exceptional or local, living labour must somehow be restrictively contained within it for exploitation to occur. In precapitalist forms this is already inherent in slavery, and in the patrimonial or feudal forms of personal dependence, through which exploitation develops. In the origins of capitalism, poverty has itself been an important agent of containment. So have apprenticeship, indenture, and restrictions on unemployment and mobility such as measures to prohibit vagrancy or travelling, or forcible transplantation of populations to new areas of colonisation or industrial growth. For similar reasons, Marx emphasised the crucial intervention of political compulsion in the establishment of every new mode of production. A new mode of production can only grow in the interstices of a social formation based on other modes, and the pre-existing property relations will themselves have a containing effect. Thus the persistence of feudal landed property alongside nascent capital prevented resettlement of the land by free landless labourers and thus circumscribed their capacity to escape confrontation with the new conditions of production. Conversely, where a bourgeois political revolution allows peasants to appropriate feudal estates as smallholdings this may have a retarding effect on the development of capitalism.[16] Wherever land is plentiful and freely available – in nineteenth-century America or Australia, for example – capitalism can only develop if special restrictions are laid on labour, slavery in the American south being an extreme case.[17] Otherwise, its conditions are only likely to be satisfied in fully settled areas, and if a continuous inflow of poor immigrants can be maintained.

Thus living labour may, at first, confront the conditions of production as property of *various* kinds, held by various classes. These may not always be exploiting classes: a free peasantry and artisan labour may be no less effective an obstacle to propertyless men establishing themselves as independent producers than landlordism. Furthermore, the development of both slavery and capitalism into dominant modes of exploitation requires a certain volume of commodity production and circulation to have appeared. Hence the situations in which slave-labour and wage-labour emerge must include possessory bonds established through commodity circulation – 'property by exchange' – as well as forms of landed property, etc. derived from pre-existing modes of production. Indeed, the form in which the conditions of production confront living labour as the property of others may not be a *class* form at all. Thus Marx described how non-exploitative *corvée* obligations of a communal kind were transformed into a system of feudal exploitation in Wallachia.[18] Here it was sufficient that part of the conditions of production confronted the peasants as common land, from which they were excluded from making merely individual use, for expropriation by others to be possible. In Asiatic states, exploitative *corvée* labour must have developed against a similar background. Slavery in antiquity developed in the context of initially non-exploitative relations of public and private property established by the Ancient mode of production. In this case the first condition was fulfilled through exclusion from civic status – either because living labour was conquered or captured in the shape of aliens, or because civic rights had been forfeited through debt or other causes.

For pre-existing forms of property to be consolidated as a monopoly over against living labour, whether of a community or of classes, established modes of transmission from one generation to the next are also a prerequisite. Otherwise, propertyless men could appropriate dead men's possessions and become independent. Hence the first condition includes the requirement that modes of devolution appropriate to the pre-existing forms of property should be generally practised and upheld. Likewise, as a new mode of production and form of exploitation become established, it requires modes of devolution to develop that allow the class monopoly of the new means of production to be preserved and transmitted. For if exploitation and circulation are the transmissive processes through which the continually reproduced stock of social matter is distributed to persons in a fixed pattern of class relationships, devolution is the means whereby successive generations of individuals are distributed to the existing pattern of distribution of social matter. And as has already been remarked, devolution of access to property through certain lines, whether of descent or organisational succession, is simultaneously the taken-for-granted denial of access to those who succeed to positions outside these lines.

Modes of devolution are closely connected with the extra-economic sources of solidarity of the propertied class. Where family succession prevails, this tends to emphasise the cohesion of the propertied class or classes by virtue of their being consanguine groups bound by resulting ties of intermarriage and kinship intercourse. Also, for example, rules governing female inheritance of various sorts of assets may encourage either class endogamy (e.g. to preserve landed property) or class exogamy (e.g. to merge landed and industrial wealth). Where organisational succession to collective or corporate property prevails, the dominant class will emphasise its ideological bonding as a status elite of privileged and loyal servants of gods, kings, corporations or 'the people'. The privileged castes of India and elsewhere exemplify a combination of family and organisational succession, the solidarity of common caste membership being founded mainly on this combination and its ideological reflection.

The question of class cohesion has to be examined under the same two aspects as proprietorship of means of production: as preceding a new mode of production, and as accompanying it once established. Extra-economic factors will be important in both cases, but in different ways. At the outset, the solidarity of a class of potential exploiters must be compatible with, and adequate for, the process of imposing itself upon living labour, whether this process be political or economic in character. In most precapitalist forms conquest has been a frequent cause of exploitative social formations arising, and one that Marx's theoretical models recognised. Here the bonds of culture, descent, political interest and military hazard which divided victors and victims fostered both internal cohesion and an instrumental attitude to the latter. These were reinforced by the negative solidarity engendered by conflict and defeat. In the case of capitalism, the class solidarities of nobility, gentry and bourgeoisie were established social facts that the nascent proletariat confronted along with the latter's monopoly of capital. We have seen also how Marx saw the corporate cohesion of the bourgeoisie in mediaeval towns as facilitating the relegation of immigrant serfs and peasants to an exploitable status.[19]

But as an exploitative mode of production becomes established, the solidarity of the propertied class undergoes a change. At first, it will have been a resultant of the historical development of a social formation based on a previous mode of production. The new mode however will initiate a quite different historical development and new type of social formation. Just as exploitation creates the conditions for further exploitation, so that the class monopoly of means of production becomes a self-reproducing condition, so it also creates the hegemony of a new class as the agents who realise that condition. The new mode of production thus comes increasingly to determine the extra-economic solidarity of the dominant class. Marx alluded to this in relation to exploitation originating through conquest:

If human beings themselves are conquered along with the land and soil as its organic accessories, then they are equally conquered as one of the conditions of production, and in this way arises slavery and serfdom, which soon corrupts and modifies the original forms of all communities, and then itself becomes their basis. The simple construction is thereby negatively determined.[20]

At first, 'Antiquity unanimously esteemed agriculture as the proper occupation of the free man, the soldier's school.'[21] But with the growth of slavery, all manual work was stigmatised. Furthermore,

> The citizens hold power over their labouring slaves only in their community, and on this account alone, therefore, they are bound to the form of communal ownership. It is the communal private property which compels the active citizens to remain in this spontaneously derived form of association over against their slaves. For this reason the whole structure of society based on this communal ownership, and with it the power of the people, decays in the same measure as, in particular, immovable private property evolves.[22]

Under feudalism, too, there occurred 'the development of landed proprietorship out of purely military relations of subordination.'[23] Similar ideas appeared in Marx's discussions of how the rising bourgeoisie absorbed aristocratic and gentry strata, and the 'ideological classes' that had previously been dependent on their patronage.

A principal factor in this transformation and assimilation would seem to be the rising class's identity as a consumer class, or 'leisure class'. It shares this with its predecessors, and can therefore affiliate itself with a tradition of status-validating culture. The more that the new form of exploitation defines what is to count as 'productive labour', the more does the common experience of the exploiting class as an unproductive stratum devoting its revenues to the pursuit of status provide the situations and similitudes on which its solidarity is based. The direct experience of power arising from the actual practice of exploitation, being occupationally specific and much less widespread, remains enveloped within the more general identity defined by such terms as 'twice-born' or 'gentleman'.[24]

The satisfaction of the first condition, because it is only a necessary starting-point for the process that realises exploitative opportunities, can mostly be specified in static terms. Excluding and excluded classes confront each other as proprietors and non-proprietors, in static possessory relations. Dynamic relations such as commodity circulation or devolution, in so far as they have also been treated as prerequisites, have concerned us only in their static results: the existence of property by exchange or by succession as parts of a stable order. To go beyond this state-description and show how the two sides move towards each other involves further dynamic relations, the transmissive practices that will be described as part of the fulfilment of the third condition. First, however, the other side of the first condition must be examined: the status of living labour as a class excluded from the conditions of production.

4. CLASS EXCLUSION FROM SUBSISTENCE AND MEANS OF PRODUCTION

The way in which living labour relates to subsistence and means of production as not-property depends in part on the terms in which the bearers of labour-power are confined to their role and excluded from proprietorship. Marx formalised these with the abstractions current in nineteenth-century social science. Vinogradoff, introducing his study of English villeinage, contrasted these broad abstractions with the multi-fariousness of historical fact; nevertheless, he allowed the validity of the general concepts for comparative study:

> There is no doubt that great landmarks in the course of social development are set by the three modes hitherto employed of organizing human labour: using the working man (1) as a chattel at will, (2) as a subordinate whose duties are fixed by custom, (3) as a free agent bound by contract. These landmarks probably indicate molecular changes in the structure of society . . . And still we must not forget, in drawing such definitions, that we reach them only by looking at things from such a height that all lesser inequalities and accidental features of the soil are no longer sensible to the eyesight.[25]

My present point of vantage, of necessity as well as by theoretical aim, remains at this altitude.

We may say, then, that there are three ways in which labourers may be excluded from the conditions of production. First, they may be treated as capable of proprietorship, but be unable to acquire any means over which to exercise it. Secondly, they may be treated as incapable of exercising any proprietorship even if by chance they were able to get hold of means for their own use. Or thirdly, they may be regarded as not incapable of proprietorship in general, but as disqualified from exercising it over the particular means they are compelled to confront – and also be unable to acquire other means over which to exercise it. The first of these is the situation of the free, propertyless proletarian; the second, of the slave; and the third corresponds to the position of the personal dependent of a feudal lord, or the personal subject of a patrimonial sovereign, who is disqualified from owning the means of livelihood to which he is tied and confined by his dependency or subjection.

These different states of propertylessness result from interpreting the worker's exclusion from means of production in the light of his own relation to his body and its labour-power – or in other words as an extension of the status by which he is defined and treated as a bearer of living labour. For the worker's primary relation to the social production process, within a given mode of production, is to its labour component, just as the non-working proprietor's primary relation is to its non-human components. Hence the class relation in which non-owning worker and non-working owner confront each other directly, outside the production process, is conditioned by the primary relation of each to the process itself. The free proletarian's capacity for proprietorship in general is the result of the fact that his relation to the capitalist production process is mediated through his proprietorship of his body. It is inalienable, though he may and indeed must alienate its labour-power. The slave's general *in*capacity for proprietorship is likewise the result of his relation to the slave production process being mediated through his non-proprietorship of his body. It may belong to anybody who is not himself a slave and may be freely alienated, together with its labour-power, by its owner. (Thus it may even be alienated, by manumission, to the non-slave that the manumitted slave will be.) The subject of the patrimonial sovereign differs from the slave in that his body and labour-power can belong only to the ruler. It is inalienable and irredeemable; the subject is not necessarily incapable of all forms of proprietorship, but the question of a possible independent status is unlikely ever to arise. The dependent of a feudal lord is in a similar position, except that his body may be alienated to another lord, along with the land to which it is bound, and can also under certain conditions be reclaimed by himself. He may be capable of owning some means of production – animals and other instruments of production, for example – but usually under political constraints and disabilities. In both these cases of personal subjection or dependency, the worker's disqualification from owning the means of livelihood to which he is tied results from his relation to the production process being mediated through the ownership of his body by a landlord whose political jurisdiction confines it to his own territory.[26]

The status of labour also has to be regarded from two points of view: as an original and as a subsequent, reproduced precondition of the operation of a particular mode of production. In both cases it is the static result of dynamic processes and practices, but of different kinds. In the second context, it is the continually reproduced result of the transmissive practices through which the means of production are furnished with labour-power, and living labour with subsistence, and through which the product is appropriated, distributed and consumed. In other words, it is the result of the ways in which the third, fourth and fifth conditions of exploitation are fulfilled, just as it is also their prerequisite. As such, it also conditions the ways in which new entrants are recruited into the labouring class, the potential labour-force. In the first context, however, the latter is the main cause of the new status of labour being what it is. It results from the ways in which the new type of labour-force is initially recruited from a population still practising a former mode of production – and thus from the ways in which the breakdown of that mode of production has made living labour available for new forms of subjection to the property of others. Since the ways in which the third, fourth and fifth conditions of exploitation are satisfied will concern us anon, here I shall only review some of the practices through which labour is recruited, both initially and in the ongoing process of a mode of production.

(a) *Capitalism*

The original creation of a capitalistic labour-force need not be dwelt on. The story has been told by historians before and after Marx; the very words in which Marx made the essential points have become familiar, but bear repetition for the sake of their theoretical condensity.

The economic structure of capitalistic society has grown out of the economic structure of feudal society. The dissolution of the latter set free the elements of the former.

The immediate producer, the labourer, could only dispose of his own person after he had ceased to be the slave, serf, or bondman of another. To become a free seller of labour-power, who carries his commodity wherever he finds a market, he must further have escaped from the regime of the guilds, their rules for apprentices and journeymen, and the impediments of their labour regulations. Hence, the historical movement which changes the producers into wage-workers, appears, on the one hand, as their emancipation from serfdom and from the fetters of the guilds, and this side alone exists for our bourgeois historians. But, on the other hand, these new freedmen became sellers of themselves only after they had been robbed of all their own means of production, and of all the guarantees of existence afforded by the old feudal arrangements. And the history of this, their expropriation, is written in the annals of mankind in letters of blood and fire.[27]

Given an early decline of serfdom in certain countries, from causes partly inherent in the structure of feudalism, living labour lost its status of personal dependency carrying access to subsistence. The creation of a proletariat of free but destitute individuals was one possible direct outcome of this, and since wage-labour had existed as a subordinate adjunct to feudal exploitation, this expanded and cheapened the pre-existing labour market to the point where it became a major institution. But two other possible direct outcomes were the conversion of serfs and guildsmen into free commodity producers, owning their means of production;[28] or the emancipation of the village commune as a co-operative enterprise, at least to the extent of common pasture. Marx's chapters on 'the so-called primitive accumulation' recount how these outcomes, to the degree that they occurred in England, were cut off or circumvented by various modes of seizure and usurpation practised by landed and moneyed capitalists.

Scarcely less well known are Marx's words on 'simple reproduction', describing how capital, once instituted, produces and reproduces the proletarian form of living labour that its structure requires:

> But that which at first was but a starting-point, becomes, by the mere continuity of the process, by simple reproduction, the peculiar result, constantly renewed and perpetuated, of capitalist production. On the one hand, the process of production incessantly converts material wealth into capital, into means of creating more wealth and means of enjoyment for the capitalist. On the other hand, the labourer, on quitting the process, is what he was on entering it, a source of wealth, but devoid of all means of making that wealth his own. Since, before entering on the process, his own labour has already been alienated from himself by the sale of his labour-power, has been appropriated by the capitalist and incorporated with capital, it must, during the process, be realized in a product that does not belong to him. . . . The labourer therefore constantly produces material, objective wealth, but in the form of capital, of an alien power that dominates and exploits him; and the capitalist as constantly produces labour-power, but in the form of a subjective source of wealth, separated from the objects in and by which it can alone be realized; in short, he produces the labourer, but as a wage-labourer. This incessant reproduction, this perpetuation of the labourer, is the sine qua non of capitalist production.[29]

This simple reproduction accounts for the fact that, capitalism once established, there is no need of any special status of slavery or dependence to maintain a permanent supply of living labour dependent on capital for employment and subsistence. 'The Roman slave was held by fetters: the wage-labourer is bound to his owner by invisible threads. The appearance of independence is kept up by means of a constant change of employers, and by the *fictio juris* of a contract.'[30] It does not by itself explain the self-recruitment of the working-class, although it requires only a small extension to do so. So long as average wages equal the average cost of a working-class family's subsistence, divided by the average number of wage-earners per family, the incomes of the entire class can, on this model, be held at a level which precludes saving.[31] In the heyday of capitalism, with high unemployment and bourgeois control of the state, simple family succession to proprietorship and non-proprietorship of means of production therefore sufficed to perpetuate the working class. With the emergence of democracy, trade unions, full employment and free education, an increasing role in this perpetuation is played by these very agencies – the 'ideological state apparatuses' of Althusser.[32] Each new right which the working-class political struggle succeeds in attaching to the proletarian's basic status of citizenship is perverted into a means of control by the bourgeoisie in its ceaseless efforts to maintain its social superiority.

But there is no need here to retail what has become a major theme of sociological researches goaded by social democracy's apparent inability to alter the structure of capitalism by mollifying its effects.[33]

(b) *Slavery*
Enslavement is the most openly expropriative way of recruiting labour. Universally, the slave — if he is not born or bought as a slave — is a captive, one who is *taken*, whether raided from his homeland, a prisoner of war, or the subjugated inhabitant of a conquered land. In a world based on the assumptions of tribalism, an individual plucked from his native soil and community has even fewer human rights and attributes than a displaced or stateless person in a world of nations — for at least the latter can often find a job, thanks to the transnational character of capitalism. (On the other hand, when capitalist nations, expanding into unpoliced territories, needed slave labour, they did not hesitate to find tribal victims against whom they could turn tribal assumptions.) Because the essential human attributes of the slave are treated as the adventitious qualities of an object of ownership, there are seldom any qualitative restrictions on the uses to which they may be put. Slaves may be set to work, or prostituted, or made into concubines or eunuchs, gladiators or soldiers; for the same reason, they may occasionally become important officials or wealthy merchants without losing their slave status.

Marx said that the 'slave economy . . . passes through a metamorphosis from the patriarchal system, mainly for home uses, to the plantation system for the world market.'[34] This transition should be seen as analogous to that from simple commodity production to capitalist production. For patriarchal slavery, like simple commodity production, never exists as a distinct and independent mode of production, but only as a subordinate adjunct to another mode. Yet it is a precondition for the historical emergence of plantation slavery — the real 'slave economy' — much as simple commodity production necessarily preceded capitalism. For it seems unlikely that a tribal people would impose general slavery on conquered subjects unless the slave status already existed in the one society or the other. Even colonial slavery in north and south America developed against a background that included the Graeco-Roman model, indigenous West African patriarchal slavery, and the Arab slave trade.[35]

In patriarchal slavery the slave was usually a captive or other alien who had lost his tribal status and become incorporated into the family and tribe of his owner, but at the lowest level and without effective rights. Such slaves did not necessarily transmit their stigma to their descendants, who might become full members of the community. Their labour was not exploited, because no distinct mode of production defined a surplus pruduct of which they were dispossessed. Their yoke was often light, but their hold on life precarious. For example, Maori slaves were liable to be killed at a moment's notice to provide a feast for distinguished guests, though in general they were well treated. Indeed, this brings into relief another aspect of primitive slavery – for a Maori chief's wife might suffer the same fate too. Both cases are probably to be seen as conspicuous consumption. Possessions of the greatest value were recklessly sacrificed, rather than have the chief and his tribe shamed by meagre hospitality. The mildness of patriarchal slavery as well as this liability to instant sacrifice both expressed the same fact: that under primitive conditions a slave could be a very valuable means of production. Because of this, he could count on free subsistence and was even privileged in certain ways. Thus a degree of *quid pro quo* was involved, which tended to become contractual over time. Under primitive conditions, it is true, slaves could only be afforded by chiefs; at the same time their productiveness depended very much on whether they could be trusted, which affected the way they were treated.[36] Only when slavery developed into a large-scale institution geared to the market, with regular sources of supply, did individual slaves become relatively expendable. Then the fact that they were worked to death or killed for sport was indeed a reflection of their economic powerlessness, and of the fact that as commodities they had a definite and discountable value. Even in Rome, America, and other plantation slave societies, however, there were usually some legal restraints on their use and abuse.

Just as much of the ideology of capitalism, especially in Marx's time, invoked an imaginary past of simple commodity production unsullied by the exploitation of man by man, so the ideology of slave economies recalled their patriarchal origins. The Greeks emphasised the natural inferiority of alien barbarians, as preordaining them to enslavement and the service of their superiors. The Romans derived slavery 'from a supposed agreement between the victor and the vanquished, in which the first stipulated for the perpetual services of his foe, and the other gained in consideration the life which he had legitimately forfeited.'[37] These ideas bore little relation to the reality of recruitment of slave labour in the developed slave economies of antiquity, where slaves were as likely to have been sold by parents or creditors as captured, and were not necessarily aliens. It is true, of course, that breeding is a slow and expensive way of reproducing a slave labour-force, and slave economies always rely partly on external seizure. As Marx pointed out,

> The slave market maintains its supply of the commodity labour-power by war, piracy, etc., and this regime is not promoted by the process of circulation, but by the actual appropriation of the labour-power of others by direct physical compulsion. Even in the United States after the conversion of the buffer territory between the wage-labour states of the North and the slavery states in the South into a slave breeding region for the South . . . this did not suffice for a long time, so that the African slave trade was continued as long as possible to satisfy the market.[38]

But despite this, the status of the slave in a developed slave economy owed nothing to the method of recruitment, let alone its historical origins. It was the continually reproduced result of the mode of production itself. Thus it was true of Rome as of America that

> . . . the slave-holder considers a Negro, whom he has purchased, as his property, not because the institution of slavery as such entitles him to that Negro, but because he has acquired him like any other commodity, through sale and purchase. But the title itself is simply transferred, and not created by the sale. The title must exist before it can be sold, and a series of sales can no more create this title through continuous repetition than a single sale can. What created it in the first place were the production relations.[39]

(c) *Patrimonialism*

Earlier chapters have already suggested that Marx's model of the primitive community enables us to treat several developmental outcomes as intelligible consequences of its structural assumptions and socio-emotional matrix – that is, given sufficient causation to bring them into being. Thus externally, mutual estrangement between tribal peoples and the possibility of appropriating the inhabitants of conquered regions as spoils of war or accessories to the land allow slavery and serfdom to be understood as effects of the invasion of settled areas by mobile communities in search of new land. Internally, long settlement and expansion by colonisation may cause segmentation as the community is enlarged, especially if there is 'a combination of manufactures and agriculture within the small commune, which thus becomes altogether self-sustaining.'[40] The concomitant enlargement of the authority and tributary catchment of chiefs will probably increase the wealth, power and prestige of their lineages; enhanced military and ideological functions may stimulate the development of privileged castes. Stratification may therefore accompany segmentation, each reinforcing the other and provoking vertical and horizontal estrangement.

Processes of this nature are presupposed by the status of labour in Marx's 'Asiatic mode of production'. Rather than discuss all the difficulties which have vexed that concept, however, I shall simply assume that there is – or in principle could be – a form of exploitation corresponding to the relation of a patrimonial ruler to his subjects. The concept of patrimonialism is borrowed from Max Weber, but not in the abstractly political form that Weber gave it. For it seems both legitimate and necessary to retain Marx's assumption that 'Sovereignty here consists in the ownerhsip of land concentrated on a national scale.' Such sovereignty is typically wielded by a sacred king, but this sort of theocratic domination did not have to be Asiatic to show the tendencies that, in parts of Asia, culminated in various forms of 'oriental despotism'. Marx noted them also in Etruria and pre-colombian America, and they are now recognised as widely diffused. Sacred kingship has been as common in Africa, and even formerly in pagan Europe, as in Asia.[41] 'By virtue of that divine sovereignty,' writes an ethnographer, of Ruanda, 'the king could require tribute. Because everything and everybody was his, he could confiscate any cattle or agricultural produce, and take the labour or even the life of everybody.'[42] Whether this 'could' was more than hypothetical depended, of course, on the effective threats which the king could use. Thus wherever tribal kingship has developed into patrimonial exploitation it has been accompanied by the consolidation of an executive staff as a ruling class, more or less dependent on the ruler whose personal servants they are, and supported by fiscal exactions and forced labour on the basis of centralised proprietorship of land and labour-power.

Marx expressed the status of labour in this instance as follows: 'Since in this form the individual never becomes a proprietor but only a possessor, he is at bottom himself the property, the slave of him in whom the unity of the commune exists.'[43] It has already been argued, in Chapter 6, that patrimonial domination results from a contradiction within the status of the individual as member and yet also as a subordinate part of the primitive community – 'whose property the individual himself is, up to a point.'[44] We can now trace the formal steps through which the contradiction develops, but first it is necessary to elucidate the distinction between 'proprietor' and 'possessor' on which the dependent status of the subject turns.

This is the same distinction as we have already met, between communal ownership (or proprietorship) and individual possession, in the primitive community, where 'possession' was provisionally defined as the effect of individuals appropriating the *use* of what is jointly owned. Marx borrowed the distinction from legal terminology, and this sense of 'possession' is found quite frequently in his works, contrasted with the 'property', 'mere ownership' or 'title' held by a collectivity or another individual who does not have the use of the thing but retains some reversionary claim upon it.[45] I shall not follow this use of 'possession' and this contrast between 'property' (or 'ownership') and 'possession', because I have already defined and used 'possession' as a generic and comprehensive term for all possessory relations, and 'ownership' and 'property' for their institutionalised inclusive and exclusive aspects. But the distinction that Marx made in this way is an important one, and I shall mark it by the pair 'title' and 'tenure', the subjects of these relations being the 'title-holder' and the 'holder' respectively. This overcomes a second difficulty in Marx's use of 'possession', which arises from the way in which he sometimes contrasted the pre-capitalist land-holder, who paid a labour rent for the use of another's land as means of production, and the capitalist land-holder, who paid a money rent for the use of another's land as a means of exploiting labour. In doing so, he called the former a 'possessor' and the latter a 'tenant'.[46] But the present discussion is being conducted at a level of generality and abstraction that requires a single term to cover both these relationships of a thing — in this case, land — to a landlord who holds the title to it, and to a holder in whose tenure it is for purposes of use. 'Title', 'tenure' and 'holder' already have a sufficiently wide range of applicability in ordinary usage for this to be a natural extension of it — for example, they refer equally to feudal and capitalistic land tenure. They also readily suggest what seems to be the underlying symbolism of this relationship: one party has not quite let go of something which another has taken and holds in his hand. In practice, since the recipient must be free to use the thing, the donor can only keep hold of it figuratively, by keeping back a piece of it, or a simulacrum, which — like 'strings attached' to it — has the power of restoring it, or some of its fruits, to his own possession.

What then *is* the double relationship of the thing which I have designated in this way? It is simply the static relation, or possessory bond, corresponding to the dynamic relation, or transmissive practice, of alienating and appropriating the *use* of a thing, rather than the thing itself. Title and tenure stand in the same relation to this practice as 'property by alienation' or 'property by exchange' or 'property by devolution' stand to the practices that create them. Title and tenure are in fact a particular sort of property by alienation, only whereas simple alienation necessitates two similar but successive relations, altering the thing's point of social ligature but not the nature of the ligament, alienation of use converts a single relation into two different but simultaneous relations, dividing the original bond into two unequal strands. One of these must include the recipient's use of the thing, while the other defines the original owner's claim upon it.

These practices of alienating and appropriating the use of something were not explicitly noticed in the table of transmissive practices in Chapter 7, where it was assumed that the object of alienation was a 'thing' that simply passed over from one subject to another. But alienation and appropriation of use are no less important in social life. Furthermore, since sharing things is simply having their use in common, then — if sharing is a more primitive practice than giving — alienation of use is probably no less ancient a component of human culture than alienation of the thing itself. In fact, of course, the two are not sharply distinct. For if alienating a thing is to alienate the whole use of it, to alienate the use is to alienate the thing, while reserving for oneself a reversionary claim which in practice may become attenuated or merely nominal.

A vast range of social practices comes into view at this point, the exploration of which would prolong this digression indefinitely. I shall do no more than note some main dimensions within which alienation of use may vary, and some formal characteristics of the practice which help us to understand its typical applications in economic life. First, the qualitative limits of use may be defined restrictively or unrestrictively — e.g. land may be granted or leased for agricultural or residential use only, or for any sort of occupation. Secondly, the quantitative – that is, temporal – limits of use may be unspecified and indefinite, or else specified impersonally or personally. The return of something hired or lent may fall due on a predetermined date, or on the occurrence of some event specified in advance; or it may be left to the convenience of either party, or to be arranged by agreement, etc. Thirdly, the object whose use is alienated may be returnable, or, if its use necessitates consumption or alienation by the user, the original owner's claim may be only to the return of an equivalent, as with money and subsistence goods.

All these stipulations deal, of course, with what in a commercial loan would be the principal, i.e. the thing itself whose use is alienated. They are the conditions which allow the transaction to be mere alienation of use, rather than of the thing itself. Since alienations of use have a time-limit, they have the *form* of reciprocal giving. Indeed, they can be construed as an adaptation of this form for a different purpose. A particular mode of conditional bilateral giving, where the transaction is completed when the original thing or its equivalent is given 'back', is being used as a vehicle for unilateral alienation of the use of the thing. A gives B the use by giving the thing, on condition B gives it back to A after using it.[47] This may, of course, be more of a taking than a giving, as with the exercise of *jus primae noctis*. Or it may have the form of simultaneous give-and-take, when things change hands temporarily, by double reciprocal giving, as a way of exchanging their uses – e.g. in a temporary exchange of homes. However, for exchange to be applied to the alienation of use, it is obviously not necessary that it should be an exchange of *uses*. Use may be exchanged for a thing directly. To the form of conditional bilateral giving (of the principal) is added the form of a conditional periodic unilateral gift (of the interest) in order that the use foregone by the lender may be compensated, as well as the object returned. Interest, rent and wages all represent particular applications of this general form under capitalism, depending on whether money, land or the labour-power of the worker's body are the objects whose uses are alienated. In these cases the practice of commodity exchange, already instituted in the market place, is extended to provide a framework in which these quite different kinds of exchanges can be made through special markets. Wherever commodity production and circulation develop, whatever the mode of production, subsidiary markets in the use of money, land and labour-power are likely to make an appearance; under capitalism, however, these are central and indispensable functional components of the mode of production itself. Further discussion of these and other types of alienation of use can be deferred until they arise again in the context of the third condition of exploitation.

Let us return to the question of how patrimonial exploitation may be conceived as originating through changes that develop the contradictory status of the individual in the primitive community. It is now clear that segmentation and growth of estrangement between cellular units are to be explained through the appropriation of the use of means of production and of labour-power once jointly owned and used. Appropriation of land-use by villages or families is likely to accompany the evolution of a sedentary agriculture, by which the unit transforms its territory into an instrument of production that is, as such, largely its own artefact and no longer just a part of 'the original unity between a particular form of community and the corresponding property in nature'.[48] The units become holders, probably hereditary holders, of the land, while the superior collectivity retains the title to it. Consequently, 'the relation of the individual to the natural conditions of labour and of reproduction as belonging to him . . . appears mediated for him through a cession by the total unity . . . to the individual, through the mediation of the particular commune.'[49] This title, or eminent domain, may be effectuated in various ways: by common rights of use for certain purposes, rights to reclaim in full for the collectivity, by periodic reallocations, or penal expropriation, or by contributions of produce for common funds, etc. Secondly, this appropriation of land-use implies also appropriation of use of the inhabitants' own bodies, as the labour-power needed to work it, by the units. The superior collectivity again retains the title, as representing the original unity to which the individuals 'belonged' as members and subordinate parts. In practice, this title means that the collectivity can make claims on the surplus labour of the individuals, for military or administrative services, for labour on public lands or installations, for participation in ceremonies, or, again, for contributions from their own produce to common funds or stores.

The second element in the emergence of patrimonial rule is that the collective title to the community's land and labour may now itself become an object of appropriation.[50] This may, of course, happen through conquest by a neighbouring ruler or the leader of a warrior horde, but it is unlikely that such an alien authority could be imposed without some form of enslavement or enserfment of the population, unless the subjects were already accustomed to the personal appropriation of the collective title – or unless there is a very great disparity in material culture, e.g. as between tribal peoples and capitalist imperial powers. The 'normal' emergence of patrimonial rule is probably through the growth of internal stratification. Whether it occurs through the unchallenged ascent of a single chief's lineage, or a struggle between rival lineages, or through the seizure of temporal power by a priesthood, or of peacetime power by a war-leader, or by the federation of tribal kings under a 'great king' or suzerain, the effect is that the collective title becomes the personal attribute and property of an individual – and of his dynasty or caste – who thereby establishes himself as the representative of the community and as its sovereign.

Patrimonial sovereignty is unlimited: this is both presupposition and consequence of centralised political authority operating directly as a form of exploitation. Of course, the sovereignty of tribal kings may be unlimited yet not enable them to exploit their subjects. For this, the further conditions for exploitation, which have yet to be discussed, must also be fulfilled. But it is relevant here to point out that this sovereignty must actually give the ruler power to exclude any particular productive and fiscal unit from its lands by massacre, destruction or banishment; otherwise the subjects no longer confront the land as their not-property, which they occupy only by the sovereign's grace and favour. This implies command of sufficient loyal and organised force to crush the opposition that such action would arouse. Only then is the status of living labour under patrimonial rule that of a subject whose body is ultimately the property of a sovereign to whose territorial ascendancy he is bound by ineluctable ties of communal membership, land tenure and material dependence. Its reproduction is a matter of the reproduction of a very simple type of economic cellular unit, which contains very little potential for change, and of family succession, for this is a form of society in which all functions tend to become hereditary.[51]

(d) *Feudalism*
These last two points apply equally to feudalism. Indeed, regarded simply from the standpoint of the relation of living labour to the exploiter, and of the reproduction of that status, feudalism resembles a decentralised, multiple and miniature patrimonialism. The land and its inhabitants are the property of a class of mounted warriors or lords, amongst whom it is parcelled out in the form of manorial estates, which are also units of political jurisdiction.[52] The major differences, from this standpoint, lie in the character of the political superstructure and in the typical processes by which this becomes the framework of a form of exploitation. Scholars from Marx to Bloch have emphasised personal dependence as the characteristic feature of feudalism. But whereas the dependence of a vassal on his lord is the basic relationship from which the superstructure of the feudal state was constructed, both Marx and Bloch would agree with Vinogradoff in seeing the serf's dependence on his lord as mediated by a second characteristic feature: 'We may say, that the unfree peasant of English feudalism was legally a personal dependent, but that his personal dependence was enforced through territorial lordship.'[53] In tracing the antecedent processes through which the status of serfdom appeared, therefore, we need to distinguish the transactions through which serf and lord both came to share in a single hierarchy of personal dependence, and those through which an exploitative class dichotomy between landlords and serfs was established.

Patrimonial exploitation and slavery were merely developments of tribal assumptions. The first could result from expansion of the primitive community to the point where solidarity gave way to internal estrangement, and the second merely elaborated consequences of the external estrangement of opposed communities. Feudal dependence, however, by which in principle every man was 'the man of another man', was an innovation. It involved the adaptation of tribal assumptions to create a new social bond, elastic enough to contain both the solidarity of a ruling class and the estrangement between exploiter and exploited. The stimulus to innovation was the breakdown of social and political order, especially prolonged deficiencies of solidarity which eroded customary expectations of trust and security. The typical seedbeds of feudal tendencies have been long periods of disturbance, usually combined with the dissolution of an ancient agrarian mode of production: production retreats to a primitive self-sufficiency and the protection of person and property becomes an imperative need.[54] Marc Bloch eloquently described such a situation in Merovingian Gaul:

> Neither the state nor the family any longer provided adequate protection. The village community was barely strong enough to maintain order within its own boundaries; the urban community scarcely existed. Everywhere, the weak man felt the need to be sheltered by someone more powerful. The powerful man, in his turn, could not maintain his prestige or his fortune or even ensure his own safety except by securing for himself, by persuasion or coercion, the support of subordinates bound to his service. On the one hand, there was an urgent quest for a protector; on the other, there were usurpations of authority, often by violent means. And as notions of weakness and strength are always relative, in many cases the same man occupied a dual role — as a dependent of a more powerful man and a protector of humbler ones. Thus there began to be built up a vast system of personal relationships whose intersecting threads ran from one level of the social structure to another.
>
> In yielding thus to the necessities of the moment these generations of men had no conscious desire to create new social forms, nor were they aware of doing so. Instinctively, each strove to turn to account the resources provided by the existing social structure and if, unconsciously, something new was eventually created, it was in the process of trying to adapt the old.[55]

Unlike patrimonial dependence, feudal dependence originated in relationships deliberately created *ex nihilo* by individuals in varying degrees of mutual estrangement. Because it was improvised and spontaneous, its origins show little uniformity of practice or of language. Models were provided by reminiscences of Roman clientage, as well as of Celtic or Germanic companionage. But the general result, arising in different ways, was that by acts of imposition or submission individuals unequal in power became linked by virtually indissoluble, diffuse bonds, as inferiors and superiors. The effect was an exchange of services for protection, but the solidarity needed to bring this about contractually, by exchange of promises, was generally lacking. Hence a more drastic transaction was required: a giving or taking of the whole person of the inferior into the superior's possession. This secured for the inferior the protection that the superior would extend to all his belongings, and for the superior the use of the dependent person's services. But the superior did not merely want a slave, to own as 'a living labouring machine',[56] for times were not settled enough for running a slave economy. What he needed was support, political loyalty – even from men who could serve him only as common foot-soldiers. He appropriated the inferior not as an object, but as a subject: it was the socio-emotional orientation and political initiative of his dependents that he wanted to call his own, so an oath of fealty was an essential element in the transaction, whether freely given or forcibly demanded.[57]

This is the point that Marx made when he wrote, of the 'relation of personal servitude' as part of the status of the labourer under feudalism, that

. . . it forms, at bottom, only a mode of existence of the landowner himself, who no longer works, but whose property includes, among the other conditions of production, the workers themselves as bondsmen, étc. Here the *master-servant relation (Herrschaftsverhältnis)* as essential element of appropriation. Basically the appropriation of animals, land, etc. cannot take place in a master-servant relation, although the animal provides service. The presupposition of the master-servant relation is the appropriation of an alien *will*. Whatever has no will, e.g. the animal, may well provide a service, but does not thereby make its owner into a *lord and master.*

And Marx noted that the same relation held between consumers, as well as between consumer and producers, as in

client-relations in the various forms in which *not-proprietors* appear in the retinue of their lord as co-consumers of the surplus product and wear the livery of their master as an equivalent, participate in his feuds, perform personal services, imaginary or real, etc.[58]

Feudal dependence has a distinctive structural logic. If a man may have many dependents but only one lord, as the rule was, there is pressure towards hierarchy.[59] The general quest for protection and support is likely to create strategic centres where lines of dependence converge. Each centre will be surrounded by concentric rings of dependents, each ring more populous than that which it encloses. Since dependency also creates vertical social distance, these rings represent the superimposed sections of hierarchical social cones. Ultimately such centres might become grouped in a single societal system of dependence, extending from the cottage to the palace. Furthermore, those who were masters of none were likely to be more numerous than those who were themselves masters, even though also dependent on higher lords. Thus feudal dependency tended to generate not only hierarchy, but a dichotomised hierarchy whose structure could easily accommodate the solidarity of a class of lords, bound by ties of vassalage, and the subjection of a class of serfs forming its broad base.

Whether this dichotomy appeared as a class cleavage depended on whether an exploitative mode of production was established within the framework of personal dependence. And this in turn was more likely where the growth of feudal tendencies coincided with the conquest of one people by another. Ethnic and cultural closure by the victors and the estrangement between them and the vanquished would reinforce the dualistic tendency of the feudal structure. Ties of dependence would be imposed on the peasantry from above in the form of serfdom, and maintained amongst the conquerors in the form of vassalage by voluntary acts of homage. In Marx's view, the military organisation required for conquest contributed largely to the form taken by vassalage:

> The feudal system was by no means brought complete from Germany, but had its origin, as far as the conquerors were concerned, in the martial organization of the army during the actual conquest, and this only evolved after the conquest into the feudal system proper through the action of the productive forces found in the conquered countries.

Repeated conquests, causing the transplantation of feudalism from one country to another, would tend to perfect the system even more:

> . . . when a form of intercourse which has evolved on another soil is brought over complete to the conquered country: whereas in its home it was still encumbered with interests and relationships left over from earlier periods, here it can and must be established completely and without hindrance, if only to assure the conquerors' lasting power. (England and Naples after the Norman conquest, when they received the most perfect form of feudal organization.)[60]

Once established in this way, 'The hierarchical structure of landownership and the armed bodies of retainers associated with it, gave the nobility power over the serfs.' For 'This feudal organization was, just as much as the ancient communal ownership, an association against a subjected producing class.'[61]

In the case of conquest, feudal dependence was established by threats, a direct expropriation of the conquered by political coercion. But there did not have to be conquest for feudalism to arise in coercive ways. Offers of protection are often indistinguishable from threats, as in the 'protection racket': the expropriator offers to 'protect' the victim from violence that he will otherwise inflict, by witholding it. Protection also affords opportunities for economic coercion, in the sense defined earlier. B, the victim of A's threats, turns to C for protection; C can then take advantage of B's need to extort a high price for his help. This was very probably a common response to the depredations of Saracens and Vikings in Europe, and whenever 'commendation' was widespread. More important than either plain political coercion or plain economic coercion, possibly, was a blend of the two. For in a situation where loosely connected groups of a marauding people gradually overrun a country, each of the native communities may try to cut its losses by seeking the protection of one of the invaders against the rest. If this goes ahead on all sides, a country may become feudalised through a series of separate acts of economic coercion, which nevertheless add up to the expropriation, by political coercion, of one whole people by another.

It is worth briefly comparing the origins of European feudalism with the feudal tendencies found in the East African states of the Interlacustrine Bantu, especially Ankole and Ruanda.[62] For here also a sedentary agricultural population was raided, infiltrated and finally conquered, over a long period, by pastoral immigrant tribes with military organisation. The result was semi-feudal hierarchies of clientage which, as in Europe, incorporated a major cleavage between two ethnically and culturally distinct strata. Amongst the Ruanda, the equivalent of feudal homage was *buhake*, a relationship which the inferior entered by a ceremonial gift which seems to have symbolised the giving of himself and his services, for it was accompanied by the words 'Be my father: I shall be your child'. The *buhake* bond could be formally broken, but only on conditions disadvantageous to the client, and it was usually regarded as hereditary. As with feudal dependence, *buhake* patronage operated both within and between the two major groupings of the society.

The role of hereditary personal dependence in feudal systems is analogous to that of commodity exchange and contractual relations in capitalist society. Both provide a universal form which facilitates, contains and conceals an exploitative process of social production. Both act as vehicles through which the factors of this process are assembled and its products distributed: both at the same time obscure the basic class dichotomy by appearing as the ostensible bond linking all the parts of society into a unified system, whether of personal inequality and dependence or of personal equality and freedom, each implying its own mode of hierarchical or contractual solidarity. The significance of both changes in the same way as between the period in which the new mode of production originates, and that in which it is fully established. At first, the adaptation of the market method to recruiting labour in a large and permanent way was an important innovation, opening up a new autonomy for the individual and creating both a new type of labour-force and a new type of property. Similarly, at first, the adaptation of military companionage and other traditional relationships to the organisation of labour represented a greater freedom for the individual than slavery, and provided for real security and some solidarity in times when both were lacking. But as capitalism and feudalism developed, both labour contract and servile homage became little more than a *fictio juris*, part of the ideology of class societies held together and reproduced by exploitation. Thus it can be said of feudal dependence as Marx said of the exchange of labour-power for wages, that when regarded in isolation 'as it appears on the surface, as in *independent* system, then it is a mere *illusion*, but a *necessary illusion*.'[63] Much the same can be said of the status of living labour under slavery and patrimonial rule. The notion of the alien whose life becomes forfeit and therefore can belong to an owner who feeds and keeps him became, as we have seen, increasingly inapposite to a developed slave economy. The equal dependence of subjects on a patrimonial ruler who is 'father of his people' becomes merely the means and mask by which a class or caste of beneficed officials exploits the cultivators.

But what sort of means? Or, more generally, if the specific status of living labour *vis-à-vis* property in the means of production becomes an illusion, in what sense is it still 'necessary'? Marx's answer is that it is a necessary condition for the 'formal subjection' of labour-power to the means of production as property.[64] Precisely because they designate units of *property*, the social meanings corresponding to categories such as 'capital', 'the slave estate', 'the patrimonial kingdom' or 'the manor' do not function in reality in these general and abstract forms. To occupy *any* status over against the means of production as property, living labour must be susceptible of being employed by some particular named capital, or enslaved to the named owner of a particular villa or plantation or must be the subject of the ruler of a particular realm (and part of a particular fiscal unit) or the serf of the lord of a particular manor. And this enrolment of labour under some determinate portion of the ruling class's total means of exploitation necessitates transactions in which the labourer's status, more or less crystallised in custom and law, whether as owner of his person or as object of ownership or as personal dependent, is an indispensable part of the definition of the situation.

This formal subjection of labour to the means of production is in turn a necessary condition for the 'real subjection' or 'material subjection' through the labour-process itself. This will be discussed in connection with the fourth and fifth conditions for exploitation. More relevant to the present stage of the argument, it is also a necessary condition for the enforcement, if necessary, of living labour's exclusion from means of production and subsistence. It is as a free citizen and legal subject that the wage-labourer is subject to the law of private property and its penalties, that exclude him from all resources to which he has no contractual right. It is as private property that a refractory slave can be punished by his owner, or returned to him if found escaping; and a serf is subject to the same liabilities by his personal dependence on the lord of the manor to which he is attached. Similarly, it is as his subjects that defaulting taxpayers can be, if necessary, killed, expelled or sold into slavery by a patrimonial ruler.

The question of enforcement shows up a difference in the status of living labour as between capitalism and slavery, on the one hand, and patrimonialism and feudalism on the other. The statuses in which capitalist and wage-labourer, or slave-owner and slave, confront each other are economic, while those in which rulers and lords confront their subjects or serfs are also political. Capitalist and wage-labourer meet only as commodity proprietors, slave-owner and slave only as owner and object of ownership; but ruler and subject, lord and serf are related not only as owner and owned but also by ties of sovereignty or feudal jurisdiction. Consequently the ways of enforcing the propertylessness of labour differ. In the case of capitalism, it is only indirectly enforceable by the state acting on behalf of the class whose collective position is protected by laws. The same is true of slavery, except that the slave-owner can enforce it directly by virtue of legal rights granted and underwritten by the state. In the cases of patrimonialism and feudalism, however, it is directly enforceable by the ruler or lord, upon his own authority, or by the state acting on his personal behalf. Thus also in the first cases we find a separation between state and economy, public and private statuses, which is absent in the second. Here, both are fused in single systems of personal dependency. Hence, the survival of the status of labour as a 'necessary illusion' in the developed exploitative mode of production occurs at different superstructural levels. Under capitalism and slavery it takes the form of a *legal* status, specifically relating to private law, and stimulates a corresponding ideology. Under patrimonialism and feudalism it survives as a religio-political or political status (as exclusion from a privileged caste or estate, etc.) and stimulates ideologies of religious or political paternalism. We shall see in the next section how Marx explained these differences.

We are now at last in a position to complete the discussion of the extra-economic solidarity of the ruling class which was left unfinished in the last section. Extra-economic class solidarity can only arise from three sources. First, from similitudes pertaining to the various spheres of unproductive consumption, outside the processes of production, distribution and exchange that make up an 'economy'. (These spheres of unproductive consumption include the superstructures of political and ideological institutions and activities.) Or, secondly, from similitudes pertaining to sex, kinship and the organisation of human reproduction. And thirdly, from similitudes arising out of the spatial (or for that matter, temporal) localisation of any of these activities. Because of the exclusively economic status of living labour *vis-à-vis* capital, as a marketed commodity, the extra-economic solidarity of the bourgeoisie is bifurcated, or bifocal. On one hand are solidarities arising from intercourse on the basis of kinship, family life, and the formal or informal occupational, associational and localised pursuit of the values of bourgeois ideology. On the other hand are solidarities arising out of political association and action, whether forming part of the exercise of public authority or merely oriented to it. From the standpoint of the political superstructure this bifurcation corresponds to the duality of private and public spheres.[65]

Patrimonial and feudal systems lacked this bifocal solidarity of the ruling class, although feudal systems especially have tended towards institutional separation of political and religious superstructures. Ignoring this last complication, we may say that ruling class solidarity arose in both cases from similitudes in which kinship, locality and political organisation were fused. But what characteristics distinguish the political superstructure of patrimonialism, with its corresponding class solidarity, from that of feudalism?

The main points have already emerged. Under patrimonialism, the title to all land and to the persons of the ruling class itself was vested in the sovereign *ab initio*; and despite the tendency for benefices to be appropriated and become hereditary, they remained linked to offices in a centralised and more or less bureaucratic fiscal administration. The efficiency of fiscal administration remained the *sine qua non* of exploitation. Furthermore, there was no sense in which the privileged beneficiary was a 'free man' compared with the cultivators whom he exploited, however superior his status. Under feudalism, however, decentralisation was basic. Central monarchies developed through confederation of separate hierarchies of personal dependence, each having its own legitimacy. It was true, as Marx said, that

> The grouping of larger territories into feudal kingdoms was a necessity for the landed nobility as for the towns. The organization of the ruling class, the nobility, had, therefore, everywhere a monarch at its head.[66]

But landowners would surrender their territorial rights to a more powerful superior only on the understanding that they would be returned as a virtually permanent and heritable grant, reinforced with stronger jurisdiction, and subject only to duties of political allegiance and military assistance. Though vassals, they remained free men over against their serfs. In this accretion of feudal territories a large part was played by marital alliances, inheritances and dowries. Likewise by conquests by armies of freely allied knights, hungry for land and glory, whose *dux* might declare himself a *rex*, but could seldom rule as more than *primus inter pares* among the barons who were his tenants-in-chief.

The decentralised character of feudalism rested on the localised combination of landed property and political jurisdiction in the manor – 'the constitutive cell of English mediaeval society', in

Vinogradoff's words.[67] Although it would be an exaggeration to regard the manor as a sovereign unit, a large fief containing many manors and dependent knights could function as an independent political bloc. This gave feudal territorial sovereignty a fundamentally pluralistic character. Personal dependence and vassalage was therefore a necessary bond for the political superstructure, even if it became only a necessary illusion for the economic base. For while 'the possession of a manor carries the possession of cultivators with it',[68] the lord of the manor and his own overlord were both free to give or take fealty elsewhere at the death or disloyalty of the other party. Hence the unity of feudal states tended to be the hard-won and precarious outcome of unifying struggles. By contrast, the unity of patrimonial states was not in dispute, however precarious and fluctuating their frontiers and extent.

It has generally been held that the character of the manor, as the cellular unit of this system, was determined by three factors. First, it constituted a unit of land adequate to the agricultural production of a village community in an agrarian system based on the heavy plough and simple crop rotation, in which the land itself was therefore the principal means of production. Secondly, it constituted a 'knight's fee' whose surplus product could keep a mounted and armoured knight available for war and furnish his escort of men-at-arms. Thirdly, the lord's territorial authority enabled him to extract the surplus product by giving him virtually absolute power over the cultivators who depended exclusively on him for protection.[69] So wherever we find feudal tendencies which remain undeveloped within tribal kingdoms, as in Africa or Celtic Ireland, it seems to be because, on the one hand, more pastoral economies, without dietary dependence on staple crops and hence with more shifting or subsidiary cultivation, gave less predominance to land as the major means of production; and on the other, because the armoured knight, requiring a larger surplus product for his maintenance, had not become the principal means of warfare. Under these circumstances the manor failed to develop. Patrons would grant cattle, not land, to their dependents, for by monopolising cattle a dominant group could extract some surplus product from herdsmen-cultivators through systems approximating to *métayage*. But it could not reduce them to serfs bound to an estate over which the patron had political jurisdiction. And so long as the organisation of military force remained subject to the ruler through some more or less professionalised form of tribal levy, with infantry as the major means of warfare, the protection that the patron could offer his clients was limited to support in lawsuits or against fiscal extortion. In these instances, therefore, although feudal dependence provided a framework for the solidarity of a ruling group and also, combined with a monopoly of certain means of production, for the exploitation of a dependent group, it failed to absorb the main military, political and administrative functions of the state. And this was because the mode of production did not require the combination of personal dependence with a class monopoly of *land*. This would have dissolved the territorial sovereignty of the patrimonial or tribal ruler into manorial pluralism, divided the population into free and unfree according to their relation to the land, and made possible advances in military technology that would, literally, have put the lord of the manor into the saddle and hence reinforced the decentralisation of state functions.[70]

This section cannot be concluded without reference to the condition for effective exploitation, that the cohesion of the exploited class be relatively weak. All the modes of formally subjecting labour to the means of production as property of others have the added effect of dividing labour against itself. Capitalism has not only created the proletariat and the conditions for its unification and class-consciousness: it has also created formidable obstacles to that process. Individual competition for jobs, divergent interests of employed and unemployed, distinct and often opposed interests of employees of different firms, or in different occupations or industries, or at different skill levels, and so forth – all these are so many potential causes of estrangement. Working-class poverty also prolongs, at least to the age of the mass media, the narrow localism that has been the principal divisive factor in earlier forms of exploitation based on attachment to the land. When to this localism is added direct dependence on the will and power of a superior, whether owner or lord or sovereign, the obstacles that precapitalist forms of exploitation placed in the way of solidarisation by the exploited class are seen to be overwhelming. Hence the precapitalist world was enveloped by ideologies of resignation which banished the hope of release from suffering to another, imaginary life.

5 SUPPLY OF LABOUR-POWER TO MEANS OF PRODUCTION AND OF SUBSISTENCE TO LIVING LABOUR

The first two conditions for exploitation specified how living labour must confront the conditions of production as the property of estranged others, outside the production process and therefore at its outset. This established a unique set of static preconditions for each form of exploitation. For exploitation to begin, the elements of this initial situation must be set in motion. Labour-power has to be made available for use in combination with means of production, and means of subsistence for consumption by living labour. For each mode of production, specific transmissive practices bring these elements into dynamic relationship. These practices are largely implicit in the static preconditions already discussed, just as the preconditions are themselves, once a given mode of production is established, largely the result of the dynamic relations.

There is no need for detailed description of these transactions in the case of capitalism. The sale of labour-power to a capitalist, the assembling of a labour-force as variable capital, the periodic subsequent payment of wages, and their expenditure on subsistence goods produced by other capitalists – all this is familiar enough. The appropriation of labour-power and the alienation of means of subsistence by capital takes the particular form of an exchange because living labour confronts it in a wholly independent form, outside the sphere of ownership of the proprietor of means of production. Its exclusion from means of livelihood is a result of destitution, not of political coercion by an owner, ruler or lord who holds a monopoly of force. It therefore takes the form of need for subsistence, a situation which invites economic coercion by proprietors of means of production in need of labour-power. And economic coercion, as we have seen, customarily takes the form of exchange if the institutional framework for its exists – in this case, if commodity markets are sufficiently developed. This economic coercion – the deliberate depressing of wages to their lowest – is clearly one element in capitalist exploitation, but by no means the only condition for realising surplus-value.

Presupposing the independence of the worker, capitalism therefore also reproduces this status on an ever-expanding scale. Marx described its double aspect of self-proprietorship and destitution in the following paragraphs:

> But in order that our owner of money may be able to find labour-power offered for sale as a commodity, various conditions must first be fulfilled. The exchange of commodities of itself implies no other relations of dependence than those which result from its own nature. On this assumption, labour-power can appear upon the market as a commodity, only if, and so far as, its possessor, the individual whose labour-power it is, offers it for sale, or sells it, as a commodity. In order that he may be able to do this, he must have it at his disposal, must be the untrammelled owner of his capacity for labour, i.e. of his person. He and the owner of money meet in the market, and deal with each other as on the basis of equal rights . . . The continuance of this relation demands that the owner of the labour-power should sell it only for a definite period, for if he were to sell it rump and stump, once for all, he would be selling himself, converting himself from a free man into a slave, from an owner of a commodity into a commodity. He must constantly look upon his labour-power as his own property, his own commodity, and this he can only do by placing it at the disposal of the buyer temporarily, for a definite period of time. By this means alone can he avoid renouncing his rights of ownership over it.
>
> The second essential condition to the owner of money finding labour-power in the market as a commodity is this – that the labourer instead of being in a position to sell commodities in which his labour-power is incorporated, must be obliged to offer for sale as a commodity that very labour-power, which exists only as his living self.[71]

Although the purchaser of labour-power advances money, in the sense that he must pay wages when due, this is of course in the expectation that their value will be replaced by the labour bought.

> The purchase of labour-power for a fixed period is the prelude to the process of production; and this prelude is constantly repeated when the stipulated term comes to an end, when a definite period of production, such as a week or a month, has elapsed. But the labourer is not paid until after he has expended his labour-power and . . . produced, before it flows back to him in the shape of wages, the fund out of which he himself is paid, the variable capital; and his employment lasts only so long as he continues to reproduce this fund . . . The illusion begotten by the intervention of money vanishes immediately, if, instead of taking a single capitalist and a single labourer, we take the class of capitalists and the class of labourers as a whole. The capitalist class is constantly giving to the labouring class order-notes, in the form of money, on a portion of the commodities produced by the latter and appropriated by the former. The labourers give these order-notes back just as constantly to the capitalist class, and in this way get their share of their own product. The transaction is veiled by the commodity-form of the product and the money-form of the commodity.
>
> Variable capital is therefore only a particular historical form of appearance of the fund for providing the necessaries of life, or the labour-fund which the labourer requires for the maintenance of himself and his family, and which, whatever be the system of social production, he must himself produce and reproduce.[72]

By following up this path of analysis, Marx shows both how the wage-earner's labour's relation to his subsistence resembles that of the slave's, and also how they differ:

> The capital given in exchange for labour-power is converted into necessaries, by the consumption of which the muscles, nerves, bones and brains of existing labourers are reproduced, and new labourers are begotten. Within the limits of what is strictly necessary, the individual consumption of the working class is therefore the reconversion of the means of subsistence given by capital in exchange for labour-power, into fresh labour-power at the disposal of capital for exploitation . . . The fact that the labourer consumes his means of subsistence for his own purposes, and not to please the capitalist, has no bearing on the matter. The consumption of food by a beast of burden is none the less a necessary factor in the process of production, because the beast enjoys what it eats. The maintenance and reproduction of the working class is, and must ever be, a necessary condition to the reproduction of capital. But the

capitalist may safely leave its fulfilment to the labourer's instincts of self-preservation and of propogation.[73]

The form taken by these transactions under slavery needs even less comment than the capitalist version. The precondition here is that means of production and living labour already belong to the one owner, by whatever means. Supplying labour-power to the means of production is therefore a matter of the discipline of the slave establishment. It involves coercive authority of the same type as the capitalist exercises in the factory, only here it must regiment the whole life of the worker. Similarly, supplying subsistence is like feeding, sheltering and breeding draught-animals, in that only a rudimentary transmissive practice is involved – for domestic animals, too, can acquire some personality in human society and can, in a minimal way, possess things. Supply of subsistence is therefore included in the total productive activity and costs of the single enterprise, instead of being left to individual appropriation on a class basis, outside the enterprise. The slave-owner must therefore himself obtain means of subsistence, either by producing or purchasing them, which limits the flexibility of a slave economy.

Under patrimonialism and feudalism these transactions assume more complex forms. The result is to make exploitation less complete than under slavery or capitalism, but also more naked than under capitalism, since the veils of the commodity and money forms do not intervene, yet less stark than slavery because the religious or political integument is more opaque than the chattel status of the slave. The precondition in both patrimonialism and feudalism is that means of production (above all, land) and living labour belong to one proprietor, who is also the direct political superior of the labourer. Unlike slavery, however, where this proprietorship is undivided, here it functions partly as a title, tenure of both land and labour-power being conditionally vested, in part, in the workers. Hence, though no specific transactions beyond this conditional alienation are needed to supply living labour with means of subsistence, they are needed to supply labour-power to means of production retained as property by the sovereign or lord, and likewise to supply subsistence to any living labour that is retained as property. After this general introduction, it is probably more convenient to set out the differences in the transactions, as between the two modes of production, in a schematic form.

(a) *Patrimonialism*

I MEANS OF PRODUCTION

1.1. Use of most of the land is conditionally distributed to families or villages of subjects, which occupy it as hereditary corporate holders, individuals being more or less tied, politically, to their locality.

1.2. The sovereign realises his hereditary title to the land by periodic forced contributions from the holders of a fiscal rent in kind or money.

1.3. The sovereign retains full ownership of some means of production, comprising the royal partimony, including (*a*) royal estates; (*b*) estates whose use can be distributed as (usually, non-heritable) benefices to personal retainers who constitute his executive staff, and who live off them, and off rents accruing from them; (*c*) technological, military or ideological installations such as irrigation works, granaries, communications, fortifications, temples, tombs, etc. that are real or imagined conditions of the continued occupation, use and productiveness of the land for the subjects.

2 LABOUR-POWER

2.1. Labour-power is distributed to its bearers, the subjects, who have tenure of their bodies for the purposes of (*a*) producing their own subsistence and the surplus necessary for family and village contingencies, support of unproductive consumers, etc. and (*b*) producing the surplus that constitutes the sovereign's fiscal revenue.

2.2. The sovereign realises his hereditary title to his subjects' bodies by periodic forced contributions of labour-power for the construction and maintenance of installations both 'public' and 'private'. Subsistence for *corvée* labour-forces is provided out of the fiscal rents.

2.3. The sovereign retains full ownership of some labour-power, comprising his 'household', which is used for personal, military or administrative services. This labour-power may be more or less distributed, and more or less hereditarily so, amongst its bearers in so far as they are retainers holding executive offices which they may, in practice, largely appropriate together with their benefices. Some of the sovereign's entitlement to the labour of his subjects may be distributed amongst his retainers also. Although this model has been constructed in terms of a political or 'royal' sovereign, it is applicable *mutatis mutandis* to religious castes and orders exercising monopolistic domination over land and men, whether as a political theocracy or as a church whose temporal power is recognised or incorporated by lay authorities.

(b) *Feudalism*

A model dealing with this aspect of feudalism is a decentralised version of the above. But the factor of decentralisation is basic, for it enters at the level of the assumed precondition. This is that means of production (and more particularly land) and labour-power are the property of a class of mounted war-lords, amongst whom the land and its inhabitants are divided up into manorial estates, which are also units of political jurisdiction. The provision of subsistence and appropriation of labour-power occur at the level of the manor, not of society as a whole. The model therefore relates to that level, and resembles a miniature patrimonial sovereignty except that each lord's proprietorship and jurisdiction is conditioned by his place in a hierarchy of vassalage that constitutes the politico-military organisation of the feudal class as a state.

1 MEANS OF PRODUCTION

1.1. The use of part of the manorial land is distributed to individual families of serfs, generally forming one or more village communities, which occupy it as more or less hereditary holders under conditions corporately determined by manorial and village custom.

1.2. The lord realises his hereditary title to the land by periodic forced contributions from the holders in the form of rent and other incidents of tenure, usually in money.

1.3. The lord retains full ownership of some means of production, comprising the demesne, including (*a*) land that is worked directly for him; (*b*) technological and military installations such as mills, weirs, studs, bridges, castles, etc. which are to some degree preconditions for the continued occupation and use of the land by its inhabitants.

2 LABOUR-POWER

2.1. Labour-power is distributed to its bearers, the serfs, who have tenure of their bodies for the purposes of (*a*) producing their own subsistence and the surplus necessary for the support of unproductive consumers in their families, and (*b*) producing the surplus that constitutes the lord's rent revenue.

2.2. The lord realises his hereditary title to his serfs' bodies by periodic forced contributions of labour-power (*a*) to work his demesne land, and (*b*) as needed, to discharge his obligation as a vassal to field a stipulated military force.

2.3. The lord retains full ownership of some labour-power, comprising his 'household' of personal retainers and servants.

These models are not 'ideal types'. Rather, they are intended to specify the set of logically possible transactions for combining labour-power with means of production, and subsistence with living labour, on the basis of the assumed preconditions, given simple agrarian technology and the appropriation of the surplus product by the proprietor of the means of production. In particular, the proprietor's double monopoly, of both a bounded territory and the living labour attached to it, had as its consequence the characteristic dual organisation of both patrimonial and feudal economies. For, on the one hand, the use of land can be distributed to raise a rent from the title; and on the other, direct labour can be employed co-operatively to produce for the proprietor. But the first possibility requires some of the labour-power to be distributed to complement the distributed land-use, while the second can only be realised if some land is retained to be worked by forced labour. The dual organisation of patrimonial and subject territory, or of demesne and open fields, resolved these dilemmas while simultaneously making available subsistence for the proprietor's compulsory labour-force. Hence the double emphasis in Marx's discussions of Asia, on both self-supporting village communes and centralised public works built and maintained by *corvée* labour, which has bedevilled later arguments about the 'Asiatic mode of production'. And hence also, as Professor Postan has noted, the 'bilateral composition of the manor and of its revenues was the true hallmark of the typical manor.'[74] Yet, as Postan also stresses, medieval manors showed great variation in the extent to which their structure emphasised one side or the other of this duality, and consequently in the ways in which their elements were combined. Doubtless even greater variety is to be found amongst the very numerous and culturally diverse instances of patrimonial rule.

The transactions described in this section only begin the process of exploitation. They ensure the maintenance of the workers during production, and the reproduction of the workforce. They fence off the place of work under the name of the owner, and cause workers to be driven into it by one compulsion or another. But for exploitation to be effective, the lion's share of the product must be carried out through another door and into the keeping of the owner. To see how this is possible we must pass in with the workers to see what goes on in the arena of production itself. Or, as Marx put it in the case of capitalism, playing Virgil to the reader's Dante:

> The consumption of labour-power is completed, as in the case of every other commodity, outside the limits of the market or of the sphere of circulation. Accompanied by Mr Moneybags and by the possessor of labour-power, we therefore take leave for a time of this noisy sphere, where everything takes place on the surface and in view of all men, and follow them both into the hidden abode of production, on whose threshold there stares us in the face "No admittance except on business." Here we shall see, not only how capital produces, but how capital is produced. We shall at last force the secret of profit-making.[75]

6 CONTROL OF PRODUCTION AND APPROPRIATION OF SURPLUS PRODUCT

Marx defined the degree of exploitation by the ratio of surplus-labour to necessary labour expended in the process of social production. Necessary labour was that needed to reproduce the 'labour-fund' – the subsistence of the labour-force while working – and to reproduce the labour-force itself (or to produce the value in wages of these costs of production). Surplus-labour was the remaining labour performed, over and above necessary labour plus that needed to reproduce the means of production used up in the process, or to transmit their value to the product. Marx made it clear that this was not a definition applicable only to capitalism, although the capitalist mode of production was uniquely aimed at absorbing surplus-labour, in the form of surplus-value, on an ever-expanding scale.

> Capital has not invented surplus-labour. Wherever a part of society possesses the monopoly of the means of production, the labourer, free or not free, must add to the working-time necessary for his own mainten-ance an extra working-time in order to produce the means of subsistence for the owners of the means of production, whether this proprietor be an Athenian devotee of the Good and the Beautiful, an Etruscan theocrat, a Roman citizen, a Norman baron, an American slave-owner, a Wal-lachian boyar, a modern landlord or a capitalist. It is, however, clear that in any given economic formation of society, where not the exchange-value but the use-value of the product predominates, surplus-labour will be limited by a given set of wants which may be greater or less, and that here no boundless thirst for surplus-labour arises from the nature of the production itself.[76]

Marx followed this passage with a comparison between the different ways in which production cycles are divisible into separate periods in British capitalist industry and in Rumanian feudal agriculture. In the first case the division is only visible under analysis: it 'is not evident on the surface. Surplus-labour and necessary labour glide into one another.' But 'It is otherwise with the *corvée*. The necessary labour which the Wallachian peasant does for his own maintenance is distinctly marked off from his surplus-labour on behalf of the boyar. The one he does on his own field, the other on the seignorial estate.' Despite this difference, exploitation appears in both cases in the fact that industrialist and boyar increase, by any and every available means, the ratio of surplus to necessary labour. In Wallachia, 'The legal day's work for some kinds of agricultural labour is interpretable in such a way that the day begins in May and ends in October.'[77] Marx's chapters on 'absolute' and 'relative' surplus-value analyse the greater variety of methods by which the same result can be achieved in capitalist industry.

The ratio of surplus-labour to necessary labour provides merely an operational definition of the degree of exploitation. Calling it 'exploita-tion' implies more than the mere existence or variance of such a ratio. For

> Surplus-labour in general, as labour performed over and above the given requirements, must always remain. In the capitalist as well as in the slave system, etc., it merely assumes an antagonistic form and is supplemented by complete idleness of a stratum of society. A definite

quantity of surplus-labour is required as insurance against accidents, and by the necessary and progressive expansion of the process of reproduction in keeping with the development of the needs and the growth of population, which is called accumulation from the viewpoint of the capitalist.[78]

Thus there is exploitation when the performance of surplus-labour takes an antagonistic form — i.e. when it is performed by non-owning workers under the coercion of non-working owners — and to the degree that the ratio of surplus-labour to necessary labour is enlarged through the unilateral action of the owner. This definition is neutral as between different motives for, or consequences of, extracting surplus-labour: whether private spending or accumulation, or social benefit, be the intended or unintended result is immaterial. All that is requisite is (1) that the owner should, as a result of appropriating surplus-labour, be in a position where he need not work for his subsistence beyond what is required by this task of appropriation itself, and (2) that the workers should not participate in decisions that enlarge the ratio of surplus to necessary labour, except to combat them. Furthermore, this definition implies no condemnation of the instrumentalism it presupposes. For its owner, labour-power in his possession has only one use: to produce a surplus for him to appropriate over and above what is needed to keep it in existence. He therefore 'exploits' this useful capacity just as he would any other advantage offered by something at his disposal. Though Marx abominated social systems that allowed human beings to be exploited like chattels, he did not attach his censure to the meaning of 'exploitation', any more than to the other words he used to analyse them.

What does the task of appropriating surplus-labour involve? Different things, obviously, in different modes of production, but always more than the 'complete idleness' in the passage just cited. To be sure, an exploiting class may be able to live in idleness, but only by delegating to others the work of exploitation itself. For exploitation involves antagonism: hence appropriation of the product has to be an active and continual *taking*, not just a passive recipiency. But does this taking have a general form, invariant as between the different antagonistic modes of production?

The preparatory or ancillary transactions that have been examined up to now all involved unilateral expropriation between individuals having unequal power in a stratified situation or system. Political or economic coercion was used to force or induce those lacking secure means of subsistence to surrender some or all of their labour-power to owners of means of production. We may add that this was always a many-to-one movement, hence 'forced contribution'. For, depending on the historic level of productivity, it has always taken the surplus-labour of a number of workers to provide the entire subsistence of a non-working family, over and above their own necessary labour. But once labour-power has been surrendered, does the extraction of surplus labour from its expenditure, and the appropriation of that surplus, involve yet more coercion?

In part, the answer is obviously affirmative. Capitalist management continually uses threats and inducements to make workers work harder, just as slavedrivers whipped on their slaves and patrimonial rulers or feudal lords used their superior power to make extortionate demands from their dependents. But we should not expect major forms of exploitation, such as have provided a basis for the continuous reproduction of entire social systems with their accompanying civilisations, to depend simply and wholly on this coercion. Marx recognised perfectly the importance of institutionalisation:

> . . . the constant reproduction of the basis of the existing order and its fundamental relations assumes a regulated and orderly form in the course of time. And such regulation and order are themselves indispensable elements of any mode of production, if it is to assume social stability and independence from mere chance and arbitrariness.[79]

For similar reasons, it has already been pointed out that taking, in societal contexts, tends to be disguised. And we have seen that the preparatory transactions already investigated tended to disguise the taking of labour-power. The proletarian's surrender of his labour-power was disguised by the market as a free exchange; the slave's captivity was disguised, thinly enough, as preordained by heredity or natural justice; subjection to a patrimonial ruler was disguised as a free or obligatory offering of oneself to the ideological representative of a sacred polity; dependence on a feudal lord was disguised as originating in an act of fealty given in return for protection. The second stage of exploitation, the taking of surplus labour, was equally disguised, though in a different way.

When detailing the types of expropriation between contemporaries, in Chapter Seven, logical room was found for a third method, beside coercion and deception. This was where one person has pre-empted another's capacity for free alienation, and hence for appropriation, and can subsequently exercise it to the disadvantage of the original possessor. This, it was asserted, was the usual method of taking where exploitation was concerned. This assertion must now be made good by showing that this is, in fact, how surplus-labour is expropriated in the major forms that are being considered. If so, then two conditions must hold. First, as a result of appropriating labour-power, the owner of means of production must also have pre-empted the workers' capacity to appropriate the product of their labour, so that some or all of it falls within his sphere of ownership. And secondly, the owner must be able to control the labour-process in such a way that he can unilaterally determine the surplus which thus accrues to himself. Marx examined the first of these, with regard to capitalism, under the heading of 'the law of appropriation', and we shall do the same.

(a) *The Law of Appropriation*

The phrase and the idea were taken from an early nineteenth-century Swiss economist, A. E. Cherbuliez. It referred to the natural law principle, proclaimed by the jurists and economists of the seventeenth and eighteenth centuries 'as the fundamental presupposition of civil society', that 'the worker has an exclusive right to the value resulting from his labour.'

A disciple of Sismondi, Cherbuliez was critical of capitalism but feared democracy, because capitalism would degrade the masses whom democracy brings to power. Typical spokesman of a traditional petty-bourgeois economy, disoriented by the spectacle of the revolutions of his time, he veered from a socialistic utilitarian radicalism to extreme conservatism. He himself derived the law of appropriation from a psychological basis in human nature, somewhat in the manner of Hume, and was ambivalent towards it. In his book *Riche ou Pauvre?*, which marks the climax of his radicalism, he argued that when a worker's labour was sold to a capitalist, the latter therewith acquired the worker's right to the whole resulting value, and thus to any return above its cost price. Thus the property of the capitalist in the product of the labour of others was 'a strict consequence of the law of appropriation whose basic principle was, on the contrary, the exclusive title of every worker to the product of his own labour.'

The importance of this seeming paradox is that it might explain the fact that, under capitalism, the existence of surplus-value, and the capitalist's right to it, are never spontaneously challenged by the workers. They resist only its continuous expansion at the expense of the share of new value returning to labour. Capitalism has grown up, historically, on a terrain of small commodity production, where peasants and artisans owned the products they made and sold. Such an economy might possibly breed the assumption that the product belongs to the producer, because it embodies his labour. If, instead of working himself, the owner of means of production bought the labour of others, he would therewith be assumed to have bought the right to the product of that labour. Thus, by acquiring their labour-power, the capitalist would pre-empt the workers' capacity to appropriate its products. If he also controlled their capacity to produce, he could tap this like a force of nature to yield a stream of products, all falling within his sphere of ownership. So long as the cost of labour-power – i.e. the value of the workers' subsistence – was always below the new value added by the use he made of their combined labour-powers, he could appropriate and accumulate a surplus, to which his claim would never be questioned. The workers will struggle only to maintain customary conditions of work and living standards.

This view is consistent with the way in which European law adjusted to capitalism. It is consistent also with the fact that when socialist intellectuals first challenged capital, they appealed to the traditional natural law principle. The workers collectively were urged to reclaim the whole value of their product. Cherbuliez's own writings were a part of this movement. But the fact that the challenge could be raised in this form also betrayed the ambiguity of the alleged principle. If the labour bought by the capitalist did not coincide with that expended by the workers, then it could be claimed that the capitalist was cheating them by appropriating a surplus. But this ambiguity had been present from the outset, so that the principle could always have been applied to justify either side. Therefore it seems unlikely that it reflected a basic assumption which actually *did* allow capitalists to pre-empt the workers' capacity for appropriation.

This was certainly Marx's view, for his socialism did not depend on any kind of ethical premiss that the worker was entitled to the product of his labour. The so-called 'law of appropriation', he considered, was itself merely part of the ideology of capitalism. It was not characteristic of small commodity production, where the individual producer's right to his product was based on some form of socially or communally mediated individual ownership of means of production, i.e. land or craft tools; and, as property, on the logical prerequisites of the exchange relationship itself. The idea that labour alone might raise a title to ownership of the product could not have emerged, historically, before labour, abstracted and isolated from all other contexts of meaning, had become an object in society in its own right, i.e. as a commodity.

This fundamental law is pure fiction. It arises out of an apparent feature of the circulation of commodities. Commodities exchange in relation to their value, that is to say, the labour they contain. Individuals confront each other solely as owners of commodities and can therefore only take possession of the commodities of others through the alienation of their own. Hence it *appears* as though they have only their own labour to give in exchange, since the exchange of commodities which contain *alien* labour (unless they have themselves been obtained in exchange for commodities of one's own) presupposes other relationships between men than those of commodity owners or buyers and sellers. In capitalist production, this appearance – which is that of the surface of capitalist production itself – vanishes. What does not vanish, however, is the illusion that originally men confront each other only as commodity owners, and hence that each is only a proprietor in so far as he also labours. This 'originally' is, as I have said, a delusion arising from the superficial appearances of capitalist production, which has never existed historically. Everywhere man appears in the role of proprietor, whether in isolation or collectively, before he appears in that of worker. . . . As soon as his original animal state comes to an end, property in nature is always already mediated through his existence as member of a community, family, tribe, etc., through a relation to other men which conditions his relation to nature. The 'propertyless worker' as 'fundamental principle' is, rather, a creature of civilisation and appears at the historical stage of capitalist production.[80]

The 'law of appropriation' was therefore a reflection, in the theorizing language of juridical ideology, of the commonsense illusion of bourgeois society that Marx christened 'commodity fetishism'. To all those outside the role of dependent producer, capitalism appeared under the guise of market society, where the production and circulation of commodities, not capital, prevailed. The higher the development of capitalism, the more completely commercialised become all social spheres and the more perfect the illusion. The 'individual' of natural law, claiming to own that with which he 'mixes his labour', was a 'product on one side of the dissolution of feudal forms of society, on the other side of the new forces of production developed since the sixteenth century.' To ideologists, he appeared 'as an ideal' whose existence they project into the past. Not as a historic result but as history's point of departure.'[81] Professor Macpherson has well shown how this abstraction was necessitated by the desire to justify capitalist accumulation within a traditional framework of ethical ideas. In Cherbuliez, as with the utopian socialists, it has no better credentials.

In what was originally intended as part of the second chapter of *A Contribution to the Critique of Political Economy*, to be entitled 'The Appearance of the Law of Appropriation in Simple Circulation', Marx had already tried to show how labour's right to property in its product, together with the *bourgeois* versions of liberty, equality and utility, arose as abstractions from the experienced structure of market relationships. But whereas the contract of employment – in one sense, as we have seen, a *fictio juris* pertaining to the same bounded social horizon of the sphere of circulation – was nevertheless real in its social consequences, enabling labour to be formally subsumed under capital, the 'law of appropriation' was, on the whole, merely an ideologists' elaboration of the same set of ideas. The only valid assumption that could be made about the genesis of the property presupposed in the model of market society was that it lay outside the terms of the model:

> In circulation itself, the exchange-process as it stands out on the surface of bourgeois society, everyone gives only in so far as he takes, and takes only in so far as he gives. In order to do either the one or the other, he must *have*. The procedure by which he has reached the position of having does not form one of the analytic elements [*Momente*] of circulation itself. Only as private proprietors of exchange-value, whether in the form of commodities or money, are the agents subjects of circulation.

A world-view that misdefined social reality in the categories and perspectives of commodity circulation had to forge its own missing links, and did so in ways that created a coherent cosmos in which both reason and capital could feel at home. So if society, conceived as a market, could establish no priority between the labour-power and the products that appeared within it as property, and as givens, ideology's recourse was to declare one to be the natural progenitor of the other.

The ambiguity which had vitiated the so-called principle. as traditionally stated, disappeared once Marx had distinguished between the purchase of labour-power and the consumption of labour, and between exchange-value and use-value. But with it went any prospect of justifying socialism by the workers' right to the product, or attacking capitalism on the grounds that property is theft. As Marx explained:

> The value of the new product further includes: the equivalent of the value of the labour-power together with a surplus-value. This is so because the value of the labour-power – sold for a definite length of time, say a day, a week, etc. – is less than the value created by its use during that time. But the worker has received payment for the exchange-value of his labour-power and by doing so has alienated its use-value – this being the case in every sale and purchase.
>
> The fact that this particular commodity, labour-power, possesses the peculiar use-value of supplying labour, and therefore of creating value, cannot affect the general law of commodity production. If, therefore, the magnitude of value advanced in wages is not merely found again in the product, but is found there augmented by a surplus-value, this is not because the seller has been defrauded, for he has really received the value of his commodity. It is due solely to the fact that this commodity has been used up by the buyer.
>
> The law of exchange requires equality only between the exchange-values of the commodities given in exchange for one another. From the very outset it presupposes a difference between their use-values, and it has nothing whatever to do with their consumption, which only begins after the deal is closed and executed.
>
> Thus the original conversion of money into capital is achieved in the most exact accordance with the economic laws of commodity production and with the right of property derived from them. Nevertheless, its result is:
>
> (1) that the product belongs to the capitalist and not to the worker;
> (2) that the value of this product includes, beside the value of the capital advanced, a surplus-value which costs the worker labour but the capitalist nothing, and which none the less becomes the legitimate property of the capitalist;
> (3) that the worker has retained his labour-power and can sell it anew if he can find a buyer.[82]

Clearly, this 'result' is not also a logical consequence, but merely a paradoxical factual outcome. Marx referred to it as the 'inversion' and 'dialectical reversal' of the law of appropriation as analysis proceeds from the sphere of circulation to that of production. For since scientific analysis is simultaneously a rational critique of the irrationalities in a society's own self-interpretation, so it can expose contradictions between ideology and practice.

The general conclusion to which this points is that the methods by which labour-power is surrendered to owners of means of production cannot necessarily be taken to involve any pre-empting of the workers' capacity to appropriate the product of labour. But can Marx's argument against Cherbuliez be applied to precapitalist modes of exploitation too? Here too labour-power was taken or given, more or less freely, and it might seem that the workers' capacity to appropriate the product was appropriated or alienated at the same time. The more so, perhaps, since these transactions seemed to establish civil statuses in which property could not be owned, or was effectively reduced to conditional tenure. But closely examined, there do not appear to be any firmer foundations for institutionalised exploitation here than in the sale of labour-power for wages. The slave's status was defined by agreement among the owners; wherever it was possible for slaves to acquire possessions by labour they were keen to do so, and to defend them, despite the fact that all their labour theoretically belonged to another. *Corvée* done for a despot was, theoretically, done for the public good: the workers as his subjects also had a claim to the benefits resulting from their labour. As for serfs, they were so far from having lost their capacity to appropriate the product of their labour that manorial histories, if fully told, would probably reveal a continuous struggle, by subterfuge, wrangling and bullying, over the division of the product: a struggle which tended towards the commutation of labour service into money rents and the transformation of the serf into a free tenant.

Although these indications are not conclusive, they suggest that the civil statuses by which precapitalist workers were denied some of the attributes of men, including all or some of their capacity to appropriate, were more effect than cause of the dehumanised instrumentalism with which they were treated in the processes of production. Though these unfree statuses reinforced the institutionalisation of exploitation, most obviously in the case of slavery, it is not at all certain that they were its foundation. When discussing these statuses above, it was indicated that as states of propertylessness they resulted from interpreting the worker's exclusion from means of production as an extension of his own relation to his body and its labour-power. The same is true if they are treated as interpretations of the worker's exclusion from the product of his labour. But it by no means follows that these were *logical* extensions of the status by which the worker was treated as a bearer of living labour, nor yet again that they were extensions that carried practical moral force, whether logically or not, in the social formations in question. In so far as they were ideologically current in those formations, it may have been only in the same way as the 'law of appropriation' was current in bourgeois society – as a theorists' justification of established practices derived from a mythical primordial condition by the light of a delusive view of social reality.

If so, we seem driven towards the conclusion that owners of means of production, in the major forms of exploitation, were not able to pre-empt workers' capacity to appropriate the product of their labour simply by having appropriated their labour-power. If this means abandoning the attempt to explain the institutionalisation of exploitation, except perhaps by deception, then we should have to accept a Macchiavellian view of all historical inequalities, as effects of coercion and fraud. However, Marx provides the clue to an alternative solution in the very passage quoted above, where he expounded his corrected version of Cherbuliez's paradox. 'The exchange of commodities,' he asserted, 'has nothing whatever to do with their consumption.' If the appropriative capacity of workers is pre-empted as a result of the owner's acquisition of their labour-power, it may be in consequence not of the method of acquisition, but of the method of use. Put differently, it may result not from the procedures by which labour-power is formally subjected to means of production as the property of others, but from its *real* subjection. Let us consider the question under that heading.

(b) *The Real Subjection of Labour to Means of Production*
After describing the labour-process in general, Marx itemised the 'two characteristic phenomena' which it exhibits when 'turned into the process by which the capitalist consumes labour-power': 'First, the labourer works under the control of the capitalist to whom his labour belongs.'

> Secondly, the product is the property of the capitalist and not that of the labourer, its immediate producer. Suppose that a capitalist pays for a day's labour-power at its value; then the right to use that power for a day belongs to him, just as much as the right to use any other commodity, such as a horse that he has hired for the day. To the purchaser of a commodity belongs its use, and the seller of labour-power, by giving his labour, does no more, in reality, than part with the use-value he has sold. From the instant he steps into the workshop, the use-value of his labour-power, and therefore also its use, which is labour, belongs to the capitalist. By the purchase of labour-power, the capitalist incorporates labour as a living ferment, with the lifeless constituents of the product . . . The labour-process is a process between things that the capitalist has purchased, this process belongs, therefore, to him, just as much as does the wine which is the product of a process of fermentation completed in his cellar.[83]

From this, two points are clear. First, that the capitalist's right to the product arises from the consumption of labour, not from the exchange of labour power, and thus from the specifically capitalist character of the production process. Secondly, in parting with his labour-power the worker gives up only the use-value he has sold: he does not also concede any capacity to appropriate the product, even though he could never have sold his labour-power unless the capitalist was counting in advance on owning the product. Since all that the capitalist has appropriated from the worker is the use of his labour, his right to the product can only come from the way in which he uses it. And it arises not just because he 'incorporates' it with his means of production, but specifically because he subordinates it to them. As Marx often put it, living labour is subjected to dead labour. For a rule of appropriation is implied here clearly enough: the product belongs to the capitalist because it is the result of 'a process between *things*' that have become his property.[84]

Now, labour-power and labour itself are not spontaneously treated as things. In themselves, they are capacities and activities of the human being. They are not likely to be treated as things unless and until they are placed amongst things and subjected to the material necessity that governs the relations of thing to thing. Labour does not convey a right to the product because it is sold somewhat as though it *were* a thing; rather, it is purchased, by a convenient fiction, as though it were a thing, because it is to be utilised as one thing amongst others. And only in *this* capacity, which it first acquires in the production process, can its expenditure transmit to the owner a right to the product. For this claim to be apparent, labour has to be referred to as a ferment or yeast, as some non-human agent of transformation.[85] It is, in fact, only because labour *no longer appears as labour*, but as a mere natural force, a source of ductile energies, that the capitalist's right to the product appears to be beyond question.

Thus, beneath the capitalist's exploitation there lies, as well as coercion, which it limits and supplements, a rule of appropriation analogous to that of Cherbuliez, but quite different in substance. It is the simple idea which finds legal expression in the *jus fruendi*, that what a thing naturally produces belongs to its owner: fruit to the owner of the fruit-tree; foals to the owner of the mare; oil to the owner of the land above. No hair-splitting analysis is needed to promulgate such a rule. It seems to be rooted in the natural economy, primordial, a part of man's prehistory stretching out its hand over history. Labour can only generate an automatic supply of property for another if it is somehow made over into a mere part and appendage of material means of production owned by the other. Only when the specifically human character of living labour is lost in the objectified substance of dead labour, can its effects appear to be the natural yield of the latter, coming into being within the sphere of its proprietor. Ownership of the product then arises without alienation, as though it were a direct appropriation from nature. Contrasting production from the point of view of creating surplus-value with production from the standpoint of the simple labour-process, Marx wrote:

It is now no longer the labourer that employs the means of production, but the means of production that employ the labourer. Instead of being consumed by him as material elements of his productive activity, they consume him as the ferment necessary to their own life-process, and the life-process of capital consists only in its movement as value constantly expanding, constantly multiplying itself. Furnaces and workshops that stand idle by night, and absorb no living labour, are 'a mere loss' to the capitalist. Hence, furnaces and workshops constitute lawful claims upon the night-labour of the workpeople. The simple transformation of money into the material factors of the process of production, into means of production, transforms the latter into a title and a right to the labour and surplus labour of others.[86]

The solution to the riddle of how exploitation becomes institutionalised is thus a very simple one, stated in these general terms. Furthermore, it explains the prominence given to ownership of material means of production in historical materialism. For this is both the condition on which the worker's capacity to appropriate the product can be pre-empted, and the means of controlling the production-process to maximise the surplus-product. Thus *both* conditions for expropriation through pre-emption of the capacity to alienate and its subsequent exercise to the victim's detriment are given *simultaneously* wherever a mode of production is established which permits the real subjection of living labour to means of production that can be monopolised by a class of non-workers. For the rule of appropriation found to apply in capitalism is by no means peculiar to it and probably underlay every previous form of exploitation too. At any rate, Marx's interpretation of the major precapitalist forms is both consistent with, and illuminated by, this supposition. It may even be permissible to claim that the whole momentous difference between antagonistic, progressive epochs and stationary, vegetative conditions in human history turns on this simple coincidence. Given a universal assumption that a thing's products 'naturally' belong to the thing's owner, it is necessary only to reduce labour to being a subordinate part of an owned thing for the owner to have both the power and an unchallenged right to live off others' surplus labour.

But as a practical task, the subjection of living labour to dead labour is no simple matter. Its feasibility depends on the character of the productive forces. This does not mean that the historical incidence of exploitation is wholly technologically determined, but that there is a specific dependence of exploitation on the productive forces as providing certain indispensable conditions. What these are seems to depend, in turn, on considerations mentioned in Chapter Six. There it was suggested that persons are more likely to appear as attributes of a thing where it much exceeds the human individual in permanence, size or causal efficacy, so long as the person's actions are inextricably bound up with the thing's existence; and that this is the more likely where a number of persons are similarly dependent on a single thing, whose character will then largely determine the nature of the social whole that they comprise. It is true that we are now not only concerned with how things are perceived, but also with how they are. Yet, since the real subjection of labour to means of production can only exist socially as a socially validated relationship between persons and things, social perception and social meaning are an indispensable part of the objective conditions that productive forces must fulfil if they, in turn, are to serve as bases for exploitation. Thus exploitation will only be possible where non-workers can both monopolise and control the operation or availability of relatively large-scale productive forces upon which a particular formally subjected labour-force is materially and collectively dependent for carrying on production.

Marx usually distinguished three aspects of a set of productive forces, all of which are present in every production process and which can only analytically be separated. These are, first, material or technical; secondly, social or organisational; and thirdly, intellectual—which, since both technique and organisation involve knowhow, is really a more or a less specialised component of the first two, which may or may not be separated off in special institutions and artefacts of intellectual production. A distinct mode of subjection of workers to the means of production corresponds to each of these aspects of the productive forces active in the process of production.

The crudest examples of the material subjection of workers to the means of labour are to be found with slavery. The slave was attached—often literally, with fetters—to a particular galley, or mine, or plantation, as part of the human engine that made it productive. A specific means of production determined the entire ecological situation and cultural attainment available to its enslaved labour-force. Overseers and their weapons merely prevented escape or respite from this all-embracing material determinism. By the pace of work they co-determined, with the means of labour, the life-span of the worker. But the very crudity of this material subjection—above all, the fact that it could scarcely have been maintained without auxiliary physical means of confining the slave to his place and instruments of labour—also shows how little it was due to technical exigencies of the process itself. Slave production was not associated with any specific technology and has usually been regarded as incompatible with the use of advanced implements.[87]

The subjection of the patrimonial subject and feudal serf was mediated by attachment to the soil. Formal subjection by means of the political superstructure allocated him and his descendants to a particular commune or manor: within this, his lifetime's energies were articulated with the land and other physical plant in an ever-recurrent cycle of seasonal work, and a primitive yet closely inter-locked and often hereditary system of occupational interdependence. The entire bio-cultural being of the dependent peasant was thus determined by this constricted ambience and the necessity of unremitting labour. But this was only half the story. It has been seen that both patrimonial kingdoms and feudal manors exhibited a dual structure, in which certain means of production were retained in the ruler's or lord's hands to be worked directly by forced labour. But they also retained ownership or effective title to control certain instruments of production essential to the reproduction of the village communities themselves. Exaggerated as Wittfogel's thesis on 'hydraulic civilisations' may be, the emphasis placed by Marx and also Weber on the importance of patrimonial despots' monopolies of irrigation works in arid lands has its place at this point. The subjects are thereby made materially dependent on his ownership of installations which are preconditions for their successful occupation and use of the land. Under some circumstances the provision of military defence – the protection offered by the lord's castle to a village's livestock, for example – may also be a sufficiently basic precondition to function as a means of exploitation. The real foundation of Pharoah's power to tax away his subjects' surplus was – as the story of Joseph's dream and his subsequent policies vividly depicts – their material dependence, in times of famine, on supplies of food and seed from royal granaries.[88] Feudal lords showed equal ingenuity in monopolising the essential resources of small-scale manorial economies. They could control access to pasture, to ploughs or ploughbeasts, stud animals, water, mills, fisheries, harbours, etc. In all these and other ways patrimonial and feudal exploiters could reduce their dependent labour-forces to organic appendages to the land and the installations needed to make it habitable and fruitful.

Marx divided the rise of capitalism into two periods, in the first of which manufacture predominated, and in the second, machine industry. Each subjected the workers to means of production in its own way. Characteristic of manufacture was detail work where once separate handicraft operations were decomposed into a combined process of specialised and divided labour in a workshop. The worker's physique and skill was sacrificed to the requirements of simplified manipulations, continually repeated. 'It is just because handicraft skill continues, in this way, to be the foundation of the process of production, that each workman becomes exclusively assigned to a partial function, and that for the rest of his life, his labour-power is turned into the organ of this detail function.'[89] Thus manufacture 'converts the labourer into a crippled monstrosity, by forcing his detail dexterity at the expense of a world of productive capabilities and instincts. . . . unfitted to make anything independently, the manufacturing labourer develops productive activity as a mere appendage of the capitalist's workshop.'

Not only do the workshop and its tools determine the bio-cultural being of the detail worker: it also begins the separation of mental from manual labour which reaches its climax in automated industry. Material subjection and intellectual subjection advance hand-in-hand:

> It is a result of the division of labour in manufactures, that the labourer is brought face-to-face with the intellectual potencies of the material process of production, as the property of another, and as a ruling power. This separation . . . is completed in modern industry, which makes science a productive force distinct from labour and presses it into the service of capital.[90]

Here, in the factory of the industrial period,

> By means of its conversion into an automaton, the instrument of labour confronts the labourer, during the labour-process, in the shape of capital, of dead labour that dominates, and pumps dry, living labour-power . . . The special skill of each individual insignificant factory operative vanishes as an infinitesimal quantity before the science, the gigantic physical forces, and the mass of labour that are embodied in the factory mechanism and, together with that mechanism, constitute the power of the 'master'.[91]

Although economic coercion governs the formal subjection of labour to capital, capitalism minimises the direct intervention of political compulsion and allows 'free' movement of the labourer between employers and localities. On the other hand, it maximises the material dependence of the workers on the instruments of production, through the scale, complexity and power required to produce anything that can compete as a commodity in capitalist society, and by subjecting the workers directly to the risks, rhythms and potencies of machinery. These very factors can then be used to subject them further. For technical knowledge is here being applied to maximise yield under conditions of estrangement, developing the workers' plasticity in the form of specialised malleability, not of polyvalent competence. Whether 'nature' be conceived in terms of traditional, practical empiricism or of scientific theory, labour is here converted into part of a single 'natural' technical process whose product is, precisely, a 'yield' to its owner.

This material subjection is mediated, and also supplemented, by socio-organisational subjection. Corresponding to every set of material means of production is a specific 'mode of co-operation'.[92] This is determined by the technical exigencies of those means, but also by possibilities and constraints issuing from organisational variables — e.g. the scope and limits for specialisation and interdependence; the need for co-ordination by rules or commands; problems arising from communicational patterns, varying with the size, dispersal, etc. of the work-group; time and motion factors; and so forth. Every mode of co-operation generates a distinct 'collective force' and adds a specific 'social productive power' to that attributable simply to labour with implements and materials. It is 'the special productive power of the combined working day'.[93] The mode of co-operation is a matter of applied organisational technique. In an age of cybernetics and systems theory we are accustomed to the idea of an applied science of organisation in general, which can be used, *mutatis mutandis*, to plan both efficient human interaction and efficient mechanical processes. Such a science has, however, a long and largely unresearched prehistory in mankind's repertories of practical skills. Marx seems to have realised this, and saw also that the development of machine-systems involved, at first, literal 'dehumanization' of what, in manufacture, was an organisation of human interactions: social combination 'solidifying' into mechanical combination.

The importance of organisation as a means of subjection is that it brings into being a new, intangible productive force, whose effect is felt, if not understood, by the workers; and which seems to originate wholly outside their own alienated labour-power, which it dominates. In fact, of course, it is due to their association, and to the efficiency with which 'the new power that arises from the fusion of many forces into one single force' is harnessed.[94] But since it is capital (or the exploiter in general, the 'lord of labour') who first brings the workers together into active combination, and who directs and co-ordinates their efforts, this mysterious force appears to be a gratuitous attribute of his property and authority. It both inspires and oppresses them, and in either case subjects them further to the material means of labour to which the mode of co-operation is adjusted.

An important prerequisite for organisational subjection is that the employer should not only have means capable of occupying a large work-force, but also the means of subsistence to support them. This, rather than impressive technology, is the basis of the subjection of slaves in systems of large-scale simple cooperation. Likewise, it explains the massive exploitation of *corvée* labour by oriental and other despots, to erect colossal monuments: revenues of grain and other produce were extorted on an equally vast scale to feed the workers. The preponderance of social over material subjection in this case is possibly reflected in the exaggerated ideological powers attributed to such rulers. The workers perhaps took the 'collective power' of their own fused energies for the *mana* of their overlords. This was combined with intellectual subjection in so far as the rulers monopolised calendrical, hydraulic and other technologies on which the real and imagined productivity of labour depended. Feudal exploitation, by contrast, tended towards secularism, and separation between the lords temporal and spiritual. And this may have been related to the small-scale social organisation and unspecialised knowledge on which it rested. For the smaller the scope for organisational subjection, the more exploitation must depend on the merely personal dependence of the worker on his lord, and on his direct subjection to the material means – his being tied to the land – rather than on his prostration before the 'sacred' personification of collective force.

Feudalism involved seasonal cooperation by families for ploughing and harvesting, and village cooperation for clearance, reclamation and other work. But it always coexisted with small-scale production by individual craftsmen and peasant households. When capitalism first appears against this background, 'capitalistic co-operation does not manifest itself as a particular historical form of co-operation, but co-operation itself appears to be a historical form peculiar to, and specifically distinguishing, the capitalist process of production.'[95] From the first, capitalism was primarily an *organisational* revolution. The technical revolutions, first of manufacturing and then of industrial capitalism, were born from the impact of organisation on existing technologies. Hence, from the first, 'the social productive power of labour that is developed by co-operation, appears to be the productive power of capital.'[96] This social subjection of the workers to capital wanes as mechanisation absorbs more and more of their interactive roles and isolates them. A similar, though slightly lagged, evolution occurs in the sphere of intellectual labour. Organisation is applied to control and communication in the form of 'bureaucracy', which subjects office workers to the hierarchical constraints and detail labour of processing documents, in a manner that parallels the 'collective worker' of the manufacturing period in manual labour. Mechanisation and automation advance more slowly here. Eventually, however, automation can presumably eliminate human initiative from control and communication as fully as it eliminates human energies from production. Thus workers are extruded more and more from both the logical and mechanical necessities of production processes. In principle, this should improve the capability of the remaining labour-forces to determine and institute their own organisational patterns. That workers' self-management has made slow progress is due, in part, it would seem, to monopolisation of the necessary organisational knowledge and skills by privileged managerial strata in both capitalist and state socialist societies.

It was pointed out earlier that material, social and intellectual aspects of the productive forces, and consequently of the real subjection of the workers to means of production, can only be separated analytically, not in reality. The same is true of formal and real subjection. For in practice, the workers' subjection, both formal and real, occurs as subordination to a composite totality in which the predominant and determining element is something uniquely specific to each mode of production – a capital, a manor, etc. – i.e. its particular production relation, which structures each unit of combined elements whose activity releases a certain quantity of productive force. Fully to elucidate this formulation of the 'dialectic of the concepts productive force (means of production) and production relation' would require an exposition of Marx's theory of reification, which cannot be undertaken here. Nevertheless, the crucial point is that the actual and active subjection of the workers, in the real process, – a subjection that is simultaneously material, social and intellectual – to the means of production operating *as* capital, manorial land, etc. is what establishes the thing-like, dehumanised character of labour's role. The workers are perceived, and experience themselves, as 'belonging to' the firm or the manor or the kingdom – the totality represented by the capitalist, the lord or the ruler in his capacity as owner of the means of production around which it is structured; and to which their labour and its products therefore belong too. This both pre-empts the workers' capacity to appropriate the product, and allows labour-power to be controlled as an auxiliary 'natural' force to produce a surplus. It also reacts back on the procedures and institutions through which formal subjection occurs, causing the status of living labour to be defined in ways that derogate from the society's standard of full humanity. The bearer of living labour is converted, even outside the labour process, in his general social existence, partially or wholly into a social 'thing', whether owned by another or owning his own person as a thing whose use must be sold to others. If the estrangement prevailing between different ethnic groups or different strata, or between conquerors and conquered, is a historical precondition for the instrumental orientation between persons out of which exploitation arises, the dehumanised instrumentalism implicit in every established form of exploitation soon transforms this precondition into the class antagonism characteristic of every exploitative mode of production, and its specific result.

This section began by asking what is involved in the task of appropriating surplus-product. It has sought to show that it involves a kind of institutionalised taking, by pre-empting the workers' capacity for alienation and exercising it to their detriment. Little has been said about the second aspect, but it has been mentioned that Marx likened the ways in which Rumanian boyars manipulated the actual length of the stipulated 'day's work' due on their estates to the ways in which capitalists constantly revolutionised the technical and social arrangement of factory production to increase their share of surplus-value. With slave-labour, since all labour is surplus labour, all measures designed to increase productivity simultaneously turn against the slave his own incapacity for appropriating the product.

There is no need to multiply details; let us pursue the general cardinal points. Control of the production process by (or for) the owner of means of production is indispensable for exploitation to occur. This means control of the particular *combination* of elements comprising the process. Since these include living labour, the combination has the form of a socio-technical system, in which the material organisation of things is blended in various ways with the social organisation of men and women (or, in Engels' Lancashire, children). Control is therefore both indirect, exercised through mechanical technological routines to which the labourers must conform their actions, and direct, exercised through the enforcement of discipline and commands. Broadly speaking, the first of these aspects is 'management' and the second 'supervision'. If all the other prior conditions for exploitation are present, this work of management and supervision is simultaneously a process of expropriation.

Marx dealt at some length with this problem; I quote only the most relevant paragraphs, which state the most general position:

> The labour of supervision and management is naturally required wherever the direct process of production assumes the form of a combined social process, and not of the isolated labour of independent producers. However, it has a double nature.
>
> On the one hand, all labour in which many individuals co-operate necessarily requires a commanding will to co-ordinate and unify the process, and functions which apply not to partial operations but to the total activity of the workshop, much as that of an orchestra conductor. This is a productive job, which must be performed in every combined mode of production.
>
> On the other hand . . . this supervision work necessarily arises in all modes of production based on the antithesis between the labourer, as the direct producer, and the owner of the means of production. The greater this antagonism, the greater the role played by supervision. Hence it reaches its peak in the slave system. But it is indispensable also in the capitalist mode of production, since the production process in it is simultaneously a process by which the capitalist consumes labour-power. Just as in despotic states, supervision and all-round interference by the government involves both the performance of common activities arising out of the nature of all communities, and the specific functions arising from the antithesis between the government and the mass of the people.[97]

There are really two separate points being made here. The first is that in exploitative modes of production the technically 'necessary' superintendence is inseparably interwoven with superintendence made necessary by antagonistic social relations. For it is only analytically that the 'mode of co-operation' can be isolated, as an area of applied organisational technique, from other social aspects of the work milieu. In reality, both are fused into a single concrete situation, the historical result of a series of similar fusions at every instant in the past. The form taken by the division of labour, or by authority, or by any other 'purely organizational' aspect of the combination of labour is, actually, determined also by the prevailing socio-emotional matrix. And in an exploitative system, this is of course antagonistic. Thus

> . . . the labourer looks at the social nature of his labour, at its

combination with the labour of others for a common purpose, as he would at an alien power; the condition for realising this combination is alien property, whose dissipation would be totally indifferent to him if he were not compelled to economise with it. The situation is quite different in factories owned by the labourers themselves, as in Rochdale, for instance.[98]

The second point is that, even apart from the socio-emotional factor, all aspects of control, whether technically necessary or not, are inescapably also levers of expropriation because of the structure of the production relations within which they occur. The real subjection of labour to the means of production as the property of others converts all management and supervision into the activation of *exploitative* control. This facilitates its delegation as a special task:

> The labour of supervision and management, arising as it does out of an antithesis, out of the supremacy of capital over labour, and being therefore common to all modes of production based on class contridictions like the capitalist mode, is directly and inseparably connected also, under the capitalist system, with productive functions which all combined labour assigns to individuals as their special tasks. The wages of an *epitropos* [Greek slave overseer], or *régisseur*, as he was called in feudal France, are entirely divorced from profit and assume the form of wages for skilled labour whenever the business is operated on a sufficiently large scale to warrant paying for such a manager . . . The capitalist mode of production has brought matters to a point where the work of supervision, entirely divorced from the ownership of capital, is always readily obtainable. It has therefore come to be useless for the capitalist to perform it himself.[99]

Precisely because it appears to be no more than a productive function, superintendence can become a specialized occupation for employees, whose inherently exploitative consequences are masked by the absence of the owner from the scene of production.

This functional differentiation, under capitalism, was already implicit, Marx argued, in the internal division of profit into the categories of interest and profit of enterprise. For

> Interest as such expresses precisely the existence of the conditions of labour as capital, in their social antithesis to labour, and in their transformation into personal power vis-à-vis and over labour. It represents the ownership of capital as a means of appropriating the products of the labour of others. But it represents this characterisitic of capital as something which belongs to it outside the production process and by no means as the result of the specifically capitalist attribute of this

production process itself . . . Interest is a relationship between two capitalists, not between capitalist and labourer.

On the other hand, this form of interest lends the other portion of profit the qualitative form of profit of enterprise, and further of wages of superintendence. The specific functions which the capitalist as such has to perform, and which fall to him as distinct from and opposed to the labourer, are presented as mere functions of labour . . . Due to the alienated character of capital, its antithesis to labour, being relegated to a place outside the actual process of exploitation, namely to interest-bearing capital, this process of exploitation itself appears as a simple labour-process in which the functioning capitalist merely performs a different kind of labour than the labourer.[100]

Hence, all the apologetics of industrial harmony between industrialists and workers, and ideological polemics intended to unite them against *rentiers*. But with the socialisation of capital through the credit system comes the 'Transformation of the actually functioning capitalist into a mere manager, administrator of other people's capital' and finally his replacement by professional management. 'Only the functionary remains and the capitalist disappears as superfluous from the production process.'[101] Thus only at a high and late point in the development of a mode of production is surplus labour 'supplemented by complete idleness of a stratum of society'.

This is a dangerous situation for the ruling class, for others may draw the logical conclusion from their superfluity which, put into practice, will relegate their supremacy to history. Marx saw the Co-operative movement doing this in his own lifetime; today, trade unions and the state, in so far as it has been colonised or captured by socialism, have carried the process in some respects further, in others not so far. In an earlier period it was the capitalist tenant, whether farmer or manufacturer, who drew conclusions fatal to feudalism from the plight of absentee landlords fleeced by their bailiffs; or else it was the usurer who gave credit to the would-be capitalist from interest extorted from spendthrift noblemen intent on consuming their inheritances. Or similarly, feudal monarchs usurped patrimonial powers when feudal aristocracies, losing their productive political function to a royal bureaucracy, became courtiers. And conversely, patrimonial retainers had established themselves as feudal lords by absorbing the productive political function of *fainéant* sovereigns, as in Japan, possibly also Tibet and elsewhere.

In conclusion, we may note that the fusion of control with expropriation in exploitative modes of production reflects one of the central historical theses of Marxism: that modes of co-operation do not develop as self-conscious applications, by society, of organisational techniques to its productive problems. Rather, they emerge as practical and self-interested manipulations of social milieus, and social relations, that are themselves merely given, in the form which Marx called 'production relations', and which are thereby unwittingly reproduced along with their contradictions. In that modes of co-operation have developed, it has been through the pressure of exploitation within antagonistic production relations; but the contradictions of these relations have been developed at the same time. Thus the modern science of organisation was born of capitalists' need to economise on constant capital by more efficient manipulation of the social structure of the combined working day.[102] Modern critiques of organisation theory, based on Marxist and related conflict-theory approaches, likewise contain an ideological reflection of the workers' resistence to this manipulation, and of the desire to turn the same science to the ends of industrial democracy.

7 DISTRIBUTION AND CONSUMPTION OF SURPLUS PRODUCT

So we come to the fifth and final condition for effective exploitation: that there must be institutionalised practices for distributing the appropriated surplus product, which do not lessen the workers' dependence on owners of means of production for subsistence; and practices also for its consumption by those who benefit from this distribution.

The first aspect of distribution is the threefold division of the appropriated surplus between reserves and insurance, replacement and accumulation, and revenue for consumption.

Historically, contribution to collective reserves, or means of insurance, has been one of the starting-points for the appropriation of the collective title to the surplus by rulers:

> . . . a certain amount of labour was due for the communal reserves, insurance so to speak, and to meet the expenses of the community as such, i.e. for war, religion, etc.; this is the first occurrence of the lordly *dominium* in the most original sense, e.g. in the Slavonic communes, in the Rumanian, etc. Therein lies the transition to villeinage, etc.[103]

This passage (which is no more than a parenthetical suggestion) assimilates the origins and functions of political and ideological superstructures rather closely to the social need for means of insurance. And though the economic functions performed by these superstructures, in their primitive forms, were somewhat various, it is true that a large part of them can be explained as precautionary. Military protection in case of attack, adjudicative arrangements in case of disputes, police facilities in case of disorder, magical or religious methods of divining, preventing and remedying malice, misfortune or disaster – these are all forms of insurance against harmful contingencies that require some collective provision, no less than the maintaining of granaries or irrigation works or other more directly economic precautions.

We have already seen how proprietorship of essential preconditions for the collective occupation and cultivation of the land entered into patrimonial and feudal exploitation. It is now apparent that in these modes of production, what converts an appropriated title to land and labour into a basis for exploitation is its combination with a monopoly of means of insurance essential to the regular operation of the production process. The nature of these means will naturally vary widely, but apparently must always involve a combination of monopolised political and/or ideological functions with monopolised control over vital economic precautions. Regular contributions of surplus labour must be forthcoming as the condition of continued production – the more extortionately, the more completely cultivation can be rendered dependent on the monopolised preconditions. It was noted, in connection with protection rackets, that what begins as insurance against interruption may become a condition of continued existence. Thus irrigation or grain storage may begin as a precaution against flood or famine but grow into the indispensable infrastructure of an expanded agriculture. Similarly, feudal protection accepted in turbulent times may grow into a system of vassalage and honorific competition that encourages feuding and raiding and thereby perpetuates the peasants' dependence on seignorial protection. Finally, men may seek magical preservation from sickness, catastrophe and malevolence, but 'If man attributes an independent existence, clothed in a religious form, to his relationship to his own nature, to external nature and to other men so that he is dominated by these notions, then he requires priests and their labour' – and the latter will perpetuate the 'spiritual' needs that religion alone can satisfy.[104]

But though the need for social provision against contingencies could become a basis for exploitation, Marx did not regard this as inevitable. In small and primitive communities, as to some extent in the Asiatic village commune, collective control over contributions and reserves for these purposes did not pass out of the hands of the direct producers, where custom dictated its exercise. Similarly, Marx thought, communist society would need to take account of this category of needs in its democratic division of the collectively appropriated surplus product. The transition from exploitative monopolisation of means of insurance in precapitalist societies to collective provision under communism was to occur via capitalism and socialism. With the rise of a form of exploitation based on manufacture and industry, these formerly exploitative functions were subordinated to it. They were either incorporated into the public sphere and compulsorily supported out of the surplus product, as state functions or established religion; or else left to the sphere of professional services, to be bought as commodities out of revenue, as with insurance, medicine, denominational religion, etc. They thus served the ruling class, either indirectly through state and church, or directly by purchase. Consequently, the emergence of socialism within the antagonistic framework of capitalism proceeded, in part, by establishing a 'welfare state'. Provision for the worst contingencies of proletarian life was installed as a public function, partly at the cost of surplus-value, under the control of a state run by socialist parties in the workers' interests, either intermittently or permanently.

Replacement and accumulation are the functions which, under capitalism, take the forms that Marx called simple and extended reproduction of capital. We have already seen that it is by simple reproduction that the initial confrontation between free labour and potential capital, at the outset of capitalist development, is converted into the situation where propertyless living labour confronts, in the persons and power of capitalists, the representatives of dead, materialised labour, the social capital existing as the composite result of past exploitation. The same process converts the primitive into the developed form of the separation and confrontation between living labour and means of production in precapitalist modes. Under feudalism, for example, the confrontation between alien military commanders, able both to expropriate and to protect the cultivators, and a free but defenceless peasantry, is transformed by years of feudal service into a situation where serfs confront their lords as the representatives of manorial lands whose continued reproduction – whether in an improved or exhausted condition, or altered by clearance and reclamation – embodies past surplus labour by the servile class.

Capitalism differs from all precapitalist modes, of course, in the way that it supersedes simple by extended reproduction, and in the fact that this accumulation is channelled exclusively through reinvestment of expropriated surplus product. In the middle ages, for example, accumulation was mainly 'accumulation of capital in the towns where . . . it was principally due to the exploitation of the countryside'[105] by unequal exchange and by fiscal expropriation from rural commodity producers by urban corporations that monopolised market facilities. In general,

> To a certain extent accumulation of wealth takes place in all stages of economic development, that is, partly an expansion of the scale of production and partly, the accumulation of treasure, etc. As long as wages and rents predominate – that is . . . as long as the greater part of the surplus labour and surplus product which does not accrue to the worker himself, goes to the landowner (the state in Asia) and, on the other hand, the worker reproduces his labour fund himself, i.e. he not only produces his own wages himself, but pays them to himself, usually moreover (almost always in that state of society) he is able to appropriate at least a part of his surplus labour and is surplus product – in this state of society, wages and rent are the main sources of accumulation as well . . . Only when the capitalist mode of production has become predominant, when it does not merely exist sporadically, but has subordinated to itself the mode of production of society; when in

fact the capitalist directly appropriates the whole surplus labour and surplus product in the first instance, although he has to hand over portions of it to the landowner, etc. – only then does profit become the principal source of capital, of accumulation, of wealth saved from revenue and used with a view to profit. This at the same time presupposes (as is implicit in the domination of the capitalist mode of production) that "a considerable advance in the power of national industry has actually taken place".[106]

Through capitalist accumulation,

> With the advance in the productivity of social labour, accompanied as it is by the growth of constant capital, a relatively ever increasing part of the annual product of labour will, therefore, fall to the share of capital as such, and thus property in the form of capital (apart from revenue) will be constantly increasing and proportionately that part of value which the individual worker and even the working class creates, will be steadily decreasing, compared with the product of their past labour that confronts them as capital. The alienation and the antagonism between labour-power and the objective conditions of labour which have become independent in the form of capital, thereby grow continuously.[107]

This is, however, only one side of a contradictory development. For the 'accumulation' is such only in terms of value, measured in human labour-time.

> But to the degree that large industry develops, the creation of real wealth comes to depend less on labour time and on the amount of labour employed than on the power of the agencies set in motion during labour time, whose 'powerful effectiveness' is itself in turn out of all proportion to the direct labour time spent on their production, but depends rather on the general state of science and on the progress of tech-nology . . . (What holds for machinery holds likewise for the com-bination of human activities and the development of human intercourse.) . . . [Capital] calls to life all the powers of science and of nature, as of social combination and social intercourse, in order to make the creation of wealth independent (relatively) of the labour time employed on it. On the other side, it wants to use labour time as the measuring rod for the giant social forces thereby created, and to confine them within the limits required to maintain the already created value as value.[108]

The self-conscious pursuit and utilisation of this *real* accumulation – social accumulation of scientific knowledge of nature and society, and of technical and social skills – was reserved, Marx thought, for the society that would discard the 'miserable foundation' – 'the theft of alien labour-time, on which the present wealth is based'.[109]

It is in the division between accumulation and consumption that the difference between capitalism and all previous modes of production is most evident. In pre-capitalist modes, production is primarily for use, hence exploitation takes the form, in general, of direct expropriation of use-values from their producers. Its aim is consumption by the ruling class, and accumulation occurs mainly as personal hoarding. Thus, high rates of exploitation mean only excessive consumption by a few, not rapid economic growth – 'production for luxury as it presents itself in antiquity is a necessary result of the slave relation. Not over-production, but over-consumption and insane consumption . . .'[110] Whereas for the capitalist,

> so far as he is personified capital, it is not values in use and the enjoyment of them, but exchange-value and its augmentation, that spur him to action. Fanatically bent on making value expand itself, he ruthlessly forces the human race to produce for production's sake . . . Moreover, the development of capitalist production makes it constantly necessary to keep increasing the amount of the capital laid out in a given industrial undertaking, and competition makes the immanent laws of capitalist production to be felt by each individual capitalist, as external coercive laws. It compels him to keep constantly extending his capital, in order to preserve it, but extend it he cannot, except by means of progressive accumulation.
>
> So far, therefore, as his actions are a mere function of capital – endowed as capital is, in his person, with consciousness and a will – his own private consumption is a robbery perpetrated on accumulation . . .[111]

But this dedication to his role, Marx claimed, was characteristic only of the primitive capitalist, the Weberian ascetic entrepreneur:

> As capitalist production, accumulation, and wealth become developed, the capitalist ceases to be the mere incarnation of capital. He has a fellow-feeling for his own Adam, and his education gradually enables him to smile at the rage for asceticism, as a mere prejudice of the old-fashioned miser . . .
>
> At the historical dawn of capitalist production – and every capitalist upstart has personally to go through this historical stage – avarice, and desire to get rich, are the ruling passions. But the progress of capitalist production not only creates a world of delights; it lays open, in speculation and the credit system, a thousand sources of sudden enrichment. When a certain stage of development has been reached, a conventional degree of prodigality, which is also an exhibition of wealth and consequently a source of credit, becomes a business necessity to the

'unfortunate' capitalist . . . Although, therefore, the prodigality of the capitalist never possesses the bona fide character of the open-handed feudal lord's prodigality, but, on the contrary, always has lurking behind it the most sordid avarice and the most anxious calculation, yet his expenditure grows with his accumulation, without the one necessarily restricting the other.[112]

Marx used this excursion into the social psychology of the entrepreneur as the basis for a critique of the ideology of 'abstinence' in the economics of his time, which we need not pursue. We may note in passing, however, that modern corporate capitalism has resolved the 'Faustian conflict between the passion for accumulation, and the desire for enjoyment' in the breast of the Victorian capitalist. Undistributed profits provide for both investment and the income – especially the institutional consumption – of the managerial capitalist.

Insurance and reproduction being set aside, there remains the question of how the appropriated surplus is distributed as revenue among the various classes of beneficiary. First, it must take a form in which it is distributable. This may occur in kind, but one of the most primitive functions of money has been to provide a means of payment of tribute, taxes, rent and interest. The need to convert part or all of the surplus product into money likewise requires and stimulates the intervention of commodity markets and commerce. This has been occasional in patrimonial regimes, common under feudalism, usual with slavery, and is indispensable in capitalism.

With regard to the question of *cui bono*, the crux is that the workers should not be able to claw back enough of their alienated surplus labour at a later stage of its distribution to reduce their dependence on the owners of means of production. So long as all the other conditions of exploitation are present, this condition will be satisfied by the following requirement: the direct exploiters should transmit shares of the expropriated surplus only to those having the economic, political or ideological power to extract payment for making available or secure, for the exploiter, certain indispensable preconditions of exploitation. Thus the patrimonial sovereign, whether or not he is himself a sacred figure, will sacrifice part of his fiscal rent to the gods and thereby maintain a priesthood to bolster belief in his fertilising and protective powers. The feudal lord must convert some of his surplus into military labour, and some into money, to contribute to the monarch's personification of his class as a political state; and some again will be tithed by the church which, being itself a feudal landowner, gives ideological support to his supremacy. The capitalist must pay not only taxes, but rent and interest too. In the case of the last two, commodity exchange is not only the means of converting surplus product into a distributable form (i.e. of realising it as surplus-value): it also provides the framework of transmissive practices by which distribution is carried out.

As we have seen, special markets develop in which the use of land or money capital can be purchased. The landowner's or moneylender's title, consisting in a periodical share in the surplus product, is made good in the form of a 'price' paid for the use of his property. The assimilation of this procedure to that of the labour market, in the bourgeois mind, was the source of the specific illusion that Marx christened the 'Trinity formula'. Land, capital and labour are conceived as the three essential factors of production, and rent, interest and wages as the fair returns for the contribution of their uses to the capitalist. In fact, rent and interest represent the institutionalised form of economic coercion exerted by monopolistic social groups, to which the capitalist only submits because it enables him to emerge as the prime beneficiary of jointly exploiting, with them, and by means of the wage-form of subsistence, the bearers of labour-power.

The coercive criterion for distributing the surplus product only preserves the subordinate position of labour if the other conditions of exploitation are already present. Specifically, unless there is a plentiful supply of labour, and the social and political cohesion of the working-class is weak, it cannot be relied on by the exploiter to reproduce the dependence of the workers on his means of production. For if the supply of labour is insufficient or risky, or can be made scarce by combination, its owners can extract a 'price' for its use above the current subsistence norm, which may thus itself become ratcheted higher and higher. While this may force capitalism into familiar crises, it does not *fatally* reduce labour's dependence, however. For as long as labour is content to exert its collective power by pressure on capitalist employers, its capacity to participate in surplus-value remains limited by capital's ability to exploit labour. This situation is less paradoxical than its sounds, since the profitability of any particular capital, and hence its owner's ability to afford high wages, does not depend solely on the rate at which it exploits its own labour-force, but on the relation of that to the average rate. Thus in reality each group of workers is trying to participate in capital's exploitation of others. In an era of international capital, this is a well-known engine of unequal deprivation between the proletariats of developed and undeveloped countries. This augmentation of wages by a 'rent' extorted by workers through collective monopolies of labour-power supply requires the continuation of capitalism, since the basic production relations remain unchanged unless organised labour uses its collective power in the manner advocated by *The Communist Manifesto* – to 'bring the property question to the fore'. But since it also involves a weakening of the conditions for effective exploitation, it undermines the system on which it depends, without replacing it with another.

The completion of this final condition of exploitation is that owners of means of production should be able to consume the expropriated surplus in a way that reproduces their social existence as a class of non-workers, as a leisure class. For 'every kind of consumption . . . in one way or another produces human beings in some particular aspect.'[113] It is this specifically – the distinctive style of life which exploitation makes possible – that fixes the social distance between the stratum of families which include the exploiters and owners of means of production, and that of the workers. The consumption of the latter, being limited to subsistence, can express little more than its members' roles as embodied labour. In La Bruyère's famous words,

> Certain wild animals, male and female, are scattered over the country, dark, livid, and quite tanned by the sun, who are chained, as it were, to the land they are always digging and turning up and down with an unwearied stubbornness; their voice is somewhat articulate, and when they stand erect they discover a human face, and, indeed, are men. At night they retire to their burrows, where they live on black bread, water, and roots; they spare other men the trouble of sowing, tilling the ground, and reaping for their sustenance, and, therefore, deserve not to be in want of that bread they sow themselves.[114]

It is by contrast with this base-line, whether it be low or high in absolute terms, that prestige comes to be attached to the occupations, activities, attributes and symbols that make up the rising tiers of the status hierarchy, and that certain contents of culture acquire their specific halo as 'values', while others are stigmatised. Above all, it is this contrast which maintains estrangement between strata, keeping the dominant class relatively homogeneous and impermeable, and fostering the instrumentalism that is prerequisite and result of exploitation.

Three factors appear to be of importance in connection with consumption of expropriated surplus product. First, the activities involved in controlling the labour process, which, in the earlier phases of a mode of production especially, must be performed by the owner of means of production in person, must be susceptible of some elaboration into a 'noble' life-style, expressing maximum dissociation from the 'base' life of labour. Patrimonial sovereigns have carried this furthest, with the hieratic and ceremonial extremes of sacred and despotic courts. The ruling classes of patrimonial retainers typically converted the trappings of their priestly, bureaucratic or military roles into status-attributes of privileged castes or strata. Feudal lords elevated the knight's calling into the secular culture of chivalry. Unlike these classes, who could easily differentiate the ideological and political functions that secured their exploitative positions from the economic life that maintained them, slave-owners and capitalists have had difficulty in glorifying their role. Hence they have preferred to delegate it where possible, to pursue the arts of secular ideology and civil politics. Marx cited Aristotle: 'Whenever the masters are not compelled to plague themselves with supervision, the manager assumes this honour, while the masters attend to affairs of state or study philosophy.'[115] The bourgeoisie, aware of the dangers of *rentier* status, has hankered after the ideal subtly satirised by Robert Musil in the figure of Arnheim – the intellectual tycoon, equally at home in industry, in high finance, in the corridors of power and the literary salon. The Protestant ethic, whatever its bearing on work and its effects on production and accumulation, was certainly also an attempted transvaluation of the life-style of the middle-class consumer, elevating simple frugality above extravagance and refinement, and converting noble largesse into bourgeois philanthropy. And as though to compensate for the ignoble character of business, capitalism supports within the bourgeoisie a huge intelligentsia of specialised professionals, and constantly promotes education as a criterion of class recruitment and class membership. In consequence, class boundaries are blurred and bourgeois ideology is criticised and discredited: disaffected intellectuals spearhead the socialist challenge.

The second factor is the need for the social organisation of consumption in appropriate units. The family household has always served as such a unit, and is perhaps the basic unit of consumption classes in all modes of production. In ruling classes households have usually been swollen by smaller or larger numbers of unproductive dependents. And household or family consumption has always been supplemented by a variety of forms of institutional consumption – in courts, armies, monasteries, colleges, clubs, corporations and so forth. This social organisation of conspicuous consumption provides the basis for a large part of what sociologists study under the rubric of stratification, and here Veblen's theory of the leisure class is still an important supplementation of Marx's perspective.

The third factor is the demand generated through exploitation for the production of the specific goods which, consumed in the households of the dominant class, will validate its members' status in terms of its cultural values. This raises the whole question of luxury production, its connections with long-distance trade, etc. More importantly, however, it structures the division of labour and location of occupations, in precapitalist modes of production especially. Thus in the patrimonial mode, 'Cities . . . form alongside these villages only at exceptionally good points for external trade; or where the head of the state and his satraps exchange their revenue (surplus product) for labour, spend it as a labour-fund.'[116] Marx was much impressed with Bernier's comparison of the oriental city with an overgrown military encampment, and Richard Jones' account of how all but the simplest types of manufacture developed as occupations dependent on the needs of the households and armies of sovereigns and satraps, clustered around these urbanised camps.[117] Feudalism, based on a class of lords dispersed over the countryside on relatively small agricultural estates, and inheriting – at least in Europe – urban centres of trade and ideological power, evolved a different but equally dualistic system. Instead of the contrast between village and capital city, here the contrast, and conflict, between town and country was dominant. Handicrafts and commerce had to organise themselves as independent urban communes to resist the violence of the nobility, and could then profitably equip the nobility with the consumption goods their households required, in unequal exchange for agricultural produce. Under capitalism, the importance of consumer durables – above all, the motor car – as symbols of middle-class status has had repercussions of the greatest magnitude upon the persistence of capitalism; likewise the vast expansion of the tertiary sector, much of it providing services in exchange for revenue, has apparently counteracted the concentration of capital in manufacturing industry.[118] These remarks are intended as no more than indications of the important reactions upon a mode of production that may flow from the condition that expropriated surplus product can be consumed as befits a class of non-workers – and, under capitalism, from the fact that a second-class version of the same privilege may even be extended to the workers themselves.

7. CONCLUSION: EXPROPRIATION AND CLASS EXPLOITATION

It has been argued that exploitation operates through four main phases. The first consists of the two preconditions: (1) monopoly of the means of production by a class of owners, from which (2) workers are excluded. The second consists of two sets of transactions – which we may call 'primary transactions' – effecting (1) appropriation, by owners of means of production, of 'alien labour-power' – the use of the labour of others, with whom they stand in a relationship of estrangement; (2) the provision of guaranteed security of means of subsistence, or of means to obtain them, for the workers by the owners. These transactions may have the appearance of free alienation on both sides, or of exchange, but are likely in fact to be more or less coercively brought about by the owner. Alternatively, the appropriation of labour-power may be openly expropriative. As a result of this phase, a labour-force is assembled and formally subsumed under the name of the owner, within a system of roles which subordinate the workers to the means of production. The third phase consists of (1) the actual subjection of the workers to these means in the process of production itself, by their treatment as insentient adjuncts to the material, social and intellectual productive forces mobilised on behalf of the owner; and thus also of pre-empting, for the owner, of their capacity to appropriate the products of labour; (2) the running and adapting of the productive process in such a way as to provide a surplus, over and above what is needed for the workers' subsistence, which falls 'naturally' to the owner. This may be achieved in a variety of different ways, but is likely to involve further coercion, especially in precapitalist modes of production. The overall result of the third phase is to leave the owner of means of production with a surplus product, expropriated by pre-empting the workers' capacity for appropriation. The fourth phase consists in the realisation of this surplus through two further sets of procedures, or 'concluding transactions', for (1) dividing it between insurance, reproduction, and various consumption revenues; and (2) conserving or consuming the divided and distributed surplus in ways that maintain and reproduce – perhaps on an extended scale – the original separation between owners and workers. The process thereby returns to its point of renewal. This is the general pattern of the forms of exploitation.

There remains a final apparent difficulty. The taking that becomes institutionalised in forms of exploitation is – it has been argued – the method of expropriation in which a person's capacity for alienation is pre-empted by another, and then exercised to his disadvantage. But expropriation itself was defined earlier as taking something from another in such a way that alienation is a consequence rather than a prerequisite of appropriation. Can we really, therefore, regard as a type of expropriation a transfer that only occurs after the capacity to alienate has itself been lost, and is by definition absent? By the time the transfer occurs, its source has lost the social meaning of an independent human agent who could keep or give or take anything, and has become a simple factor of production whose yield reverts to its owner. The most we seem entitled to say is that the primary transaction which placed the worker in this dependent position might, or might not, have been expropriative – that is, coercive or deceptive – and that any subsequent benefit to his employer deriving from his employment is a consequence of it. This problem is not just an artefact of terminology that I myself have introduced into the discussion. Marx himself frequently has difficulty in explaining just how it is, if the worker exchanges his labour-power at its value, that the capitalist can be said to have taken something further, 'without equivalent' in return.[119] It would be simple enough, of course, to have recourse to an ideological premise of natural justice or human essence, such as Cherbuliez's 'law of appropriation'; but Marx had already barred that path. The subject of the involuntary alienation that occurs within the production process, through expropriation of the surplus, must be identifiable within the model of the mode of production in question, as a possible social construct.

Marx answered this question by altering the perspective. So long as one remains at the standpoint of the individual worker, any expropriation suffered can certainly be attributed only to coercive or deceptive induction into the employer's service. This is the standpoint of the primary transactions, for these all establish separate relationships of individual dependence: only later are the workers collected into social labour-processes. But the result of the primary and productive phases combined, in the ongoing processes of social reproduction, is to divide society into two permanent classes of exploiters and exploited, and thus to convert the original more or less fortuitous estrangement of unequals into the structured hostility of an antagonistic class system.

It is from this standpoint, so Marx claimed, that the appropriation of surplus-product, through pre-emption of the capacity to alienate and by control of production, can be regarded as the expropriation of one class by another. Having pointed out that labour-powers are bought at their value in the market, Marx continued:

> To be sure, the matter looks quite different if we consider capitalist production in the uninterrupted flow of its renewal, and if, in place of the individual capitalist and the individual worker, we view them in their totality, the capitalist class and the working-class confronting each other. But in so doing we should be applying standards entirely foreign to commodity production.[120]

By these standards, or from this perspective,

> This exchange of equivalents proceeds; but it is only the surface layer of a production which rests on the appropriation of alien labour *without exchange*, but with the *semblance of exchange*.[121]

In reality, as we have seen,

> . . . the result of the process of production and realization is, above all, the reproduction and new production of the *relation of capital and labour itself*, of *capitalist and worker*. This social relation, production relation, appears in fact as an even more important result of the process than its material results.[122]

By reproducing the production relation itself, the mode of exploitation simultaneously reproduced and solidified two unequal social groupings. These classes are not defined by the sum of individual workers and of individual capitalists, as they confront each other in the production relation of wage-labour and capital; nor even by the same individuals organised into antagonistic blocs in the production process. Rather, we have to define them as the categories amongst which the annual social product is divided for purposes of consumption. For this is the standpoint of reproduction, and hence of the *persistence* of classes as a social structure, and as a social fate for the individuals of their successive cohorts. But 'consumption' must be taken in the widest sense, not as contrasted with production or investment. For it must include not just consumption by households, but also of raw materials and of means of production by capital – i.e. the 'productive consumption' of privately owned production units. This is the standpoint from which Marx broached the question of how aggregate social capital is reproduced:

If we study the annual function of social capital . . . and its results, i.e. if we study the commodity-product furnished by society during the year, then it must become apparent how the process of reproduction of the social capital takes place . . . The annual product includes those portions of the social product which replace capital, namely social reproduction, as well as those which go to the consumption-fund, those which are consumed by labourers and capitalists, hence both productive and individual consumption. It comprises also the reproduction (i.e. maintenance) of the capitalist class and the working class, and thus the reproduction of the capitalist character of the entire process of production.[123]

Only if the exploiting class is defined in a way that includes household consumption can it be grasped as a self-renewing section of population, and only if productive consumption is included can the definition capture the class inequality involved where rates of exploitation and replacement or accumulation are high, but capitalist revenues are not much higher than those of skilled workers. In precapitalist societies, where exploitation is aimed more at personal use and enjoyment, this consideration is naturally less important. In all cases, however, what is needed is a composite measure of class membership and class inequality that cuts across the conventional distinction between personal and corporate income in order to show the distribution in society of the power to make decisions to consume the social product – whether productively or unproductively. The finding that decisions about productive consumption were concentrated in the hands of individuals who fell into the upper strata of the population, as measured by the consumption power of households, and that unproductive corporate (i.e. extra-household) consumption favoured the same strata, would be an operational way of identifying a class society. To the extent that these inequalities could not be accounted for by general deliberate consent, nor by unequal economic and political power, and hence by coercion in the labour-market, or in circumstances bearing upon it (i.e. by primary transactions), the hypothesis is advanced that it occurs through working individuals losing some of their capacity to appropriate, and individual non-workers benefiting, in consequence, through control of the labour process.

It may be objected that this solution is beset with familiar problems concerning false consciousness. If expropriation cannot be imputed to a social agent that has lost the capacity to alienate, how can it be imputed to one that has not yet acquired it? For class, in this sense, is an analytical category to which, in reality, only a confused medley of social definitions and self-assignments would be found to correspond. At most, the collective victim of exploitation would seem to be a latent group, unless politically mobilised and propagandised with ideas like Marx's own.

This objection is not a very formidable one, however. All that is required, for expropriation to have a victim, is that the proposed subject exists as a structural possibility in the model. Classes, as defined, exist in this way: but the individual worker who has sold his labour-power and been subjected to capital does not. His self-definition is given precisely by this role, which excludes alienation of the product; apart from this role, he has no existence at this point in the model. If in practice somebody acquires the consciousness of an exploited individual, at work, this is of no theoretical significance unless it is part of a collective movement, in which case the model has to take account of how capitalism *changes* under the influence of class conflict – a different problem. Otherwise it remains something subjective and incidental. It is either unexpressed in reality, or if expressed, probably causes the individual to be sacked anyway, and hence to vacate the role. :

Basically, the reason why the worker within the exploitative labour-process cannot be the subject and victim of exploitation is because his role in the model is already too determinate, with regard to alienation. Classes may be taken as subjects just because they are so indeterminate, and their social personality so vague and inchoate. The individual worker can therefore only become a conscious subject of exploitation as a member of his class, and as part of an antagonistic movement extending outside production, in the total social milieu. As an individual or as a member of a company's labour-force, or of a particular occupation, he may suffer and resist the coercion incidental to exploitation, and hence develop 'trade-union consciousness'. But to move to the point where he challenges the capitalist's right to appropriate surplus-product *at all*, involves the emergence of a new, totalistic class-consciousness.

The working class therefore cannot come to see itself as exploited unless the separation of household consumption from production (the 'Mallet effect') is overcome. The privatised and apolitical 'secular' voter and the wages-and-job-oriented trade-unionist whose public horizon is limited to the workshop or plant would have to find a new common identity within a politicised class community conscious of a fundamental estrangement in society, and of the need and possibility of fundamental change. In his earliest revolutionary writings, Marx cast the proletariat for the revolutionary role of 'universal class' because it was 'a class in civil society which is not a class of civil society' – fundamentally estranged from the society in which it lived, 'totally opposed to the assumptions of the German political system', a class of outsiders.[124] But as industry developed and European socialism grew up with it and as Marx's political judgment matured, his emphasis shifted. The revolutionary mission of the working class was now based on the tendency of the capitalist oligarchy itself to become a class of outsiders, functionless parasites whose efforts to shore up their privileged command over the economy were visibly anachronistic and damaging to the common interest. The capitalists, not the workers, were now a class estranged from society. Working-class movements could therefore claim to represent the true heritage of their nations, as well as mankind's hopes for the future, and the workers' perceptible interests in every sphere of life would lead them to demand the vindication of both. As the representatives of the general popular interest, the working class would be backed by the irresistible force of the majority. The resulting upheaval would be no more — and no less — than 'the expropriation of a few usurpers by the mass of the people.'[125]

9 Possession, Production and Society

The last chapter has shown that each of the main historical forms of exploitation, as Marx identified them, can be analysed (though not exhaustively) into a combination of various sorts of transmissive practice. Central to each is the expropriation of surplus labour by a class that monopolises means of production, through pre-emption of the workers' capacity to alienate and appropriate their products, and control of their capacity to produce. Preceding and following this are other institutionalised transmissive practices, more or less expropriative, which prepare for and conclude the central act of exploitation. The precondition and cumulative result of this three-step, cyclical process is the existence of exclusive possessory relations between mutually estranged social groups, effecting a separation between labour-power and other conditions of production. Initially, this separation is given historically and extraneously, as property and not-property by devolution, exchange, expropriation, etc. Once exploitation is established it becomes, we may say, property and not-property by exploitation. Likewise, the primary similitudes and differences that unite the two groups internally and divide them from each other lose their original adventitious character as historical givens, and acquire a class basis, structurally determined by the antagonistic mode of production through which exploitation occurs.

Thus Marx's theory of exploitation can to a large extent be elaborated in terms of the concepts developed in earlier chapters – the transmissive practices, or dynamic possessory relations, tabulated in Chapter 7; the static possessory relations, or bonds, discussed in Chapter 6; and the solidarity-estrangement polarity developed in Chapter 5. This is not an exhaustive elaboration, and hence not a reduction, because no form of exploitation can be described without reference to the mode of production through which it is effected. Therefore the particular productive forces characteristic of that mode must enter into an account of the form of exploitation, and so must the production relations by which those forces are structured. And although, in antagonistic modes of production, the production relations contain or imply the transmissive practices composing the form of exploitation, they also include the moment of reification. We have already seen that such theoretical concepts as 'capital', 'the manor', etc., correspond to practical social meanings through which (and through the actions of those who 'personify' them) things and persons are structured into the productive units in which the real subjection of living labour to dead labour occurs. For

> ... in the real life of capitalist production, as well as in its theory, *materialized labour* appears as a contradiction to itself, to *living labour*. In exactly the same way in religious reasoning, the product of thought not only claims but exercises domination over thought itself.[1]

Reification, as a social process, is mediated by a cognitive-evaluative reaction to estrangements generated by divisions of social structure within a single field of social force. It creates depersonalised, apparently objective, cultural contraints, and thus largely explains the fixation of social practices as intitutional forms. Because it is necessary to speak of one thing at a time, this study has left on one side the concept and theory of reification. For this reason, the discussion of social integration has been left incomplete, for integration through solidarity is only one form, and in its absence the integration of estranged units must occur through reification. Similarly, the discussion of social practices has abstracted from the dimension of institutionalisation, including the institutionalisation of power, for this, again, occurs through reification. Finally, there has been no analysis of the concept of 'personification', which Marx linked closely with property, because this too presupposes reification. So for a complete reduction of forms of exploitation, and *a fortiori* of modes of production, to their constituent elements, the theory of reification would have to be developed. But for that there is insufficient space in the present volume.

Three tasks can however be accomplished in this concluding chapter. First, the relation between static and dynamic aspects of possession must be investigated, so that we have a fairly complete picture of the area where the sociological theories of estrangement and alienation meet – of its theoretical topography, so to speak. These are, as I have reiterated throughout, analytical terms whose definitions and theoretical connections have been framed and charted at the highest possible level of generality and abstraction, on the supposition that they can refer to any and every social process, whatever its extent, duration or content. The aim has been to construct a theoretical schema at the level of general or formal sociology, which can plausibly be seen as implicit in Marx's work as well as relevant to subsequent sociological theory.

This dictates the second task: to indicate, at least in outline, how this general sociology, or theory of social processes in general, connects up with the main body of Marx's theorising. The latter has one rather undeveloped limb, historical materialism, and one well-developed, the theory of capitalist society. The first can be regarded as a set of general theories about the origins, succession, structure, functioning, development and decomposition of the historic social systems of mankind; and the second as a set of special theories about the economic infrastructure of the most recent and extensive of these. Both are, in a wide sense, bodies of sociological theory. So the second task is really to trace the links between (*a*) a theory of social processes in general, (*b*) general theories of social systems, social change and historical sequence, and (*c*) special theories pertaining to a structural region of a particular type of social system. Obviously, this would be a colossal task to undertake in detail, since the outlines of Marx's sociology are by no means firm even in these more familiar and fully elaborated parts, while nearly all the problems involved are still very much in dispute among sociologists. However, it is clear that a strategic position in both historical materialism and in Marx's theory of capitalism is occupied by the concept of 'production relations'. It will therefore be an advance if the foregoing analysis of estrangement and alienation can be related to this concept. To do so means following a thread that runs from social emotions and possessory relations to production relations, by way of two other concepts that we have frequently skirted round in these pages: 'property relations' and 'distribution relations'.

The third task follows on as a natural conclusion. It is to indicate, in brief, how much of Marx's thought has *not* been covered or even illuminated, so far, by the considerations advanced, and to suggest where some of their further implications might fruitfully be drawn out.

I STATICS AND DYNAMICS OF POSSESSORY RELATIONS

Since both the static and dynamic aspects of possessory relations were connected, in different ways, with the predominance of solidarity or estrangement, the simplest way of bringing the two aspects together is with reference to this common correlate. It will be recalled that ownership was defined as referring to the interior aspect of a collectivity's possessory relations, or the availability of things for *members*, and thus depends on their positive solidarity; while property was defined as referring to the exterior aspect, availability in so far as it depends on the exclusion of non-members, where negative solidarity prevails. Where people relate as owners solidarity predominates between them, whereas estrangement predominates between proprietors.

The hypothesis has also been put forward that sharing and giving, on the one hand, and taking, on the other, are social practices associated respectively with the predominance of solidarity and estrangement.

To bring these variables into relation with one another, we need to be able to translate freely between the language of ownership and property and that of alienation and appropriation. The former, we have said, refers to assumptions, expectations and norms about the necessary or rightful availability and unavailability of things, which pattern the interactions of persons, as owners and proprietors. They denote cognitive-evaluative phenomena, collective representations concerning the social bonding and separation between persons and things. Alienation and appropriation, however, were defined as social practices – specifically, transmissive practices – which involve action and the social movement of things. This apparent asymmetry arises from taking as starting-points the concepts most prominent in actual everyday life. It reflects the fact that where the social immobility of an object is concerned, it is mostly obtained by collective *recognition* of its social location as a property of the thing. To the extent that a given pattern of ownership of property is part of the taken-for-granted situation, no very specific social practices are needed to confirm it as a social fact. On the other hand, alienation and appropriation involve deliberate change. It must be effected by a social act that interrupts and rearranges the taken-for-granted pattern of possession, and confirmed by the people concerned behaving differently to one another in respect of the object. Thus change of ownership is identifiable as a distinct social practice, and very often becomes symbolically distinguishable by stereo-typed overt behavioural formulae. 'Changing hands' may be both means and symbol of appropriation.

But the fact that social practices corresponding to ownership and property are rather unspecific and indistinct – comprising all the various activities that might amount to 'keeping' or 'witholding' something – does not mean that they do not exist. And conversely, transmissive social practices presuppose a cognitive-evaluative dimension, that we have referred to with the phrase 'community of intent'. The apparent asymmetry therefore conceals a real symmetry. And this is natural enough, for ownership and transmission of ownership are not different kinds of social fact. Ownership and property would have no social existence if their constitutive meanings lacked behavioural manifestation, and transmissive behaviour is only recognisable as such because of the meaning it bears. We can therefore translate ownership and property out of the mentalistic mode in which they have been grasped hitherto – as assumptions, expectations, norms, etc. and into the practical mode, regarding them as techniques of interaction or social practices. In contrast to transmissive practices, they will be called 'retentive practices'. Retentive and transmissive practices then create and correspond respectively to static and dynamic possessory relations. Figure 6 suggests how they correlate with socio-emotional factors.

A table containing such inexact terms looks rather banal, but it is the best that can be done when beginning to theorise about units of process that have to be identified through meanings current in everyday life. It is intended to show, first, that in interaction among joint owners the distinction between retentive and transmissive practices disappears. Complete effacement of the distinction is actually the limiting case, exemplified when a single thing is jointly owned, used in common, and yields a collective benefit. Forms of social movement allowing for partial or

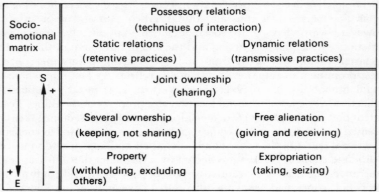

Socio-emotional matrix	Possessory relations (techniques of interaction)	
	Static relations (retentive practices)	Dynamic relations (transmissive practices)
− S + ↑	Joint ownership (sharing)	
	Several ownership (keeping, not sharing)	Free alienation (giving and receiving)
+ ↓ − E	Property (withholding, excluding others)	Expropriation (taking, seizing)

Figure 6 Types of Possessory Relations (I)

temporary possession appear if the thing is used in turn, or in parts, or if there are many things used separately, or if some enjoy privileged access, or greater benefit, and so forth. These practices involve some degree of alienation of use, in severalty, while the collectivity retains the joint title. But discussion of title and tenure must be postponed for the moment.

In this way there is a conceptual transition to the second type of case, where free alienation is the normal way in which things move between owners in severalty. Transmissive practices of giving and receiving, typical where solidarity predominates over estrangement, are matched by retentive practices that involve non-participatory 'keeping'. There is a shared assumption that the capacity to use and dispose of the thing is restricted, not promiscuous, but defensive safekeeping is unnecessary and inappropriate. Rententive practices here may be somewhat competitive — for example, showing off one's acquisitions in the *kula* ring — but this ostentatious possession in a consensual game differs from conspicuous proprietorship of what others lack, which relies on the protective power of praetorians, janissaries, policemen or other henchmen of the ruling class. The socio-emotional correlations indicate the hypothesis that sharing requires a greater preponderance of solidarity over estrangement than several ownership — but not, of course, that positive social emotions must be more intense for sharing to be possible. Also, solidary relationships between both joint and several owners are always liable to irruptions of interpersonal estrangement connected with the coveting, damaging or usurpation of possessions, much as functional disturbances in the body are accompanied by a rise in temperature. Such outbreaks will be met with defensive or retaliatory action and we have already noted some of the ways in which environing solidarities can be mobilised to restore an equilibrium — by expulsion, 'the peace in the feud', or restitution.

The retentive practices of proprietorship, as distinct from several ownership, reflect mistrust and the expectation of seizure as a settled mutual orientation. Locksmiths and bankers, security guards and store detectives are specialised occupational adaptations to this milieu, which makes a necessity of 'the conservative virtues of lock and key'. 'Finders keepers', 'Trespassers will be prosecuted' and 'Guard dog, beware!' are its watchwords.

These correspondences are still very crude. They suggest that where certain patterns of solidarity and estrangement prevail, certain retentive practices will suffice, or be required, to maintain existing possessory bonds – or vice versa – and that any movement of things between persons will occur through corresponding sets of transmissive practices. To refine the discussion somewhat, further distinctions need to be drawn.

Implicit in earlier discussions has been a distinction between two sorts of static possessory relations. Whether joint ownership, several ownership or property, these may be either *sessile*, in the sense that they tend to remain fixed in one social location, or *labile*, in the sense that they are prone to social movement. There has already been occasion to speak of 'ownership by alienation', 'property by exchange' and 'property by exploitation' in cases where the meaning of the bond depends on the transmissive practice that creates it. Certain classes of object derive most of their social importance from their movement, and in these cases the mode of retention will be largely determined by the mode of transmission. To the extent that this is so, the bond will be called labile. An extreme case would be where it was actually dangerous or damaging to keep an article out of circulation at all, as in the game of 'passing the parcel'. In real life, the *kula* ring is slightly like this, for if a participant is 'slow' with his partners he earns opprobrium. The importance of *vaygu'a* depends almost entirely on their dynamic role as circulating treasure. Their static role – the sense in which they are owned during the resting phases of their circulation – is, accordingly, determined by their history, function and future prospects within the *kula* ring:

> 'Ownership', therefore in Kula, is quite a special relation. A man who is in the Kula never keeps any article for longer than, say, a year or two . . . On the other hand, each man has an enormous number of articles passing through his hands during his lifetime, of which he enjoys temporary possession, and which he keeps in trust for a time. This possession hardly ever makes him use the articles, and he remains under the obligation soon again to hand them on to one of his partners. But the temporary ownership allows him to draw a great deal of renown . . .[2]

But the prime example of such cases is, obviously, the commodity. Produced for alienation by exchange, commodities are kept as property only fugitively in the process of circulation. In a passage that has already been analysed, Marx explained how the possessory bond uniting commodities with their 'guardians' acquired its character of exclusive personal property, abrogable only by mutual consent, as a result of assumptions logically required by the act of exchange. Thus the static possessory relations of market society – commodity property – derive their character from the dynamic relations composing the circulation processes through which market society subsists. If 'ownership by alienation' is used to refer to labile bonds created by the variously conjugated forms of giving, 'property by exchange' can refer to labile bonds arising from exchange. And it has been seen that this contributes to the meaning of the legal category of 'private property'.

Labile bonds of this kind will develop only where the determining dynamic relation is institutionalised. Therefore the only significant case of 'property by expropriation' will be the result of exploitation, the major case of institutionalised taking. To classify the expropriated surplus product as labile property is to emphasise its dynamic character, as a one-way flow from production to consumption, which must be continuously renewed to maintain the superior position of the dominant class. If, with Marx, we liken exploitation to a pump which forever raises the products of labour from a lower to a higher social level, property by exploitation is like a cistern whose function is to receive and contain them, in the form of value, before they are piped off into replacement, accumulation, or consumption.

This categorisation of the expropriated surplus therefore bears differently on capitalism and pre-capitalist modes of production. The labile character of pre-capitalist property by exploitation is due to its consisting mainly of use-values destined for consumption. Replacement or accumulation of means of production enter very little into the surplus at this stage. The major means of production, land, stands in contrast with its products. The latter are transient objects of exploitation and circulation, while the former, notwithstanding changes in its use-value through exhaustion or improvement, remains as something given and immovable; and so too, in general, do the possessory bonds which tie people to it. But because capital is a form of exploitative property based on the production of *value*, this contrast disappears under capitalism. Here the labile character of property by exploitation extends, through the ceaseless necessity for replacement and accumulation of capital, to the means of production themselves. True, they do not circulate as use-values any more than land did previously; but they circulate as value, embodied in the commodities they are used to produce. Thus Marx's distinction between fixed and circulating capital is drawn relative to any given moment of production. At that moment, some part of the capital value of means of production is circulating and the remainder is fixed.[3] Eventually, however, all capital circulates, for it 'is a movement, a circuit-describing process going through various stages' and 'can be understood only as motion, not as a thing at rest.'[4] Capitalist production therefore accelerates and generalises the tendency of money to dissolve all sessile property into labile property:

Because money is the general equivalent, the general power of purchasing, everything can be bought, everything may be transformed into money. But it can be transformed into money only by being alienated, by its owner divesting himself of it. Everything is therefore alienable, or indifferent for the individual, external to him. Thus the so-called inalienable, eternal possessions, and the immovable, solid property relations corresponding to them, break down in the face of money.[5]

It may be objected, against this classification of capital as a kind of labile property, that particular capitals—both family and corporate wealth—show marked continuity of possession; and that, in any case, it is the static relation—the fact of owning value as capital—that determines, through the method of outlay in means of production and labour-power and the need to obtain a return from sales, the dynamic relations that the capitalist will enter. These are valid points about individual capitals, but are not valid as objections. For capital is only labile in its aspect as property by exploitation. This, as we have seen, is a relation between classes, so the subject of the possessory bond is the capitalist class as a whole, not its constituent units. This class property, which has no legal recognition as such, exists only as a mass of value circulating continuously between industrial capitalists and workers, through the various metamorphoses of variable capital, labour-power and surplus labour, and expanding with every circuit. It is dead labour whose social vitality, as class property, depends on its absorption of living labour. It is labile by virtue of being composed through and through of alienated labour.

These various classes of object—*vaygu'a*, commodities, capital—can be classified as objects of labile possessory bonds because their specific use-values emphasise the importance of their social movement. Other sorts of things are objects of sessile bonds because their use-value depends on fixity of possession. Consumer durables, for instance, are typically owned for as long as they serve their purpose, and this determines the mode of disposal. Mortgage, hire-purchase, part-exchange, secondhand dealers, auto-wreckers, etc. are institutions reflecting the fact that transmissive practices here are dependent on retentive practices. The same is true, in general, of means of production. This is most obviously so where the producing unit is self-sufficient, so that its life depends on stable possession for as long as the means themselves are usable, and then on their replacement within an equally stable relation. Where the means are virtually inexhaustible, as with good land, the bond may share the longevity of the unit. Thus joint ownership of land by a self-reproducing, sedentary community may represent the extreme case of a sessile bond, where there is perpetual possession and complete inalienability. For the members of such a community 'to exchange their land, their residence, to pawn it to alien communes, would be treason.'[6] Individual peasant property shows the same sessile features on a dwarf scale.

Use-value also decides the classification of individual capitals as sessile property. Here, however, the use-value is not that of the means of production as a source of products, but as means of exploitation. By owning capital, the individual can participate in the exploitation of labour. Since there is no point in owning capital unless it is retained long enough to yield a profit, this retentive limitation determines the corresponding transmissive practices that will be performed. For the industrial capitalist himself, it means that parts of his capital must be laid out as 'property by exchange' in order to purchase instruments, raw materials, and labour-power in certain proportions, and that all his product must likewise be converted into property for exchange. Yet his capital exceeds all these particular metamorphoses, which are the dynamic relations required if the retention of capital is to have the effect of allowing its owner to participate in the ruling class's expropriation of surplus-value. The sessile character of individual capitals, as property, is therefore the counterpart and condition of the labile character of social capital, as a class monopoly. For capital must operate through discrete units of sessile property in the sphere of circulation if it is to function exploitatively, as a totality of labile property in the sphere of social production.

The sessile character of land and capital finds specific reflection in the modes through which they are transmitted, both to contemporaries and to successors. We have seen that the inalienability of jointly owned land tends to dissolve, in practice, through alienation and appropriation of *use*, into some combination of collective title and individual tenure. And this is the characteristic form which transmissive practices take when determined by a sessile bond. The reversionary claim enshrined in the title defines the dynamic relation as, in principle, a reversible movement that only modifies or interrupts the static relation.

> . . . thus landed property is initially held in common, and even where it advances to private property the individual's connection to it appears as posited by his relation to the community. It appears as a mere fief of the community, etc. etc.[7]

When exploitative relations emerge on this basis, they mostly take patrimonial or feudal forms, where the use of land is granted conditionally to personal dependents. When capitalism arises within a social formation dominated by precapitalist landed property, its agents can only appropriate the use of land as tenants, while the landlords convert their titles into claims to a share of surplus-value, as rent. Money capital, existing outside industry, is made available in the same way: its sessile character depends on its use-value as a source of unearned income, from interest.

In discussing devolution in Chapter 7, a distinction was drawn between inheritance and succession as two principal ways of transmitting things to chosen successors. The purest case of the first was said to be a free parting gift from a dying or departing person, and of the second, the accession, by a new occupant selected by fixed rules, to all the attributes of a status just vacated by his predecessor. This distinction reflects that between labile and sessile property in the matter of devolution. Inheritance typically occurs with arbitrary personal bequests, the mode of whose retention is usually determined by the nature of their transmission. Thus they are usually treated as a windfall gain, and spent appropriately. Or else the bequest is charitable, assimilated to alms which are a clear case of property by alienation. (Thus the assets of charitable organisations are based on gifts, and treated accordingly by tax authorities, etc.) Or the bequest may be a personal souvenir, whose meaning for the recipient is inseparable from the memory of the transmittng agent. In all these cases, devolution is closely assimilated to free alienation between contemporaries, and property by inheritance has much the same labile character as property by alienation.

At the other extreme are clan succession and bureaucratic succession, where the continuity of the collective's retention of its means of operation determines who shall succeed to what, when and for how long and for what purpose. In bureaucratic succession especially, transmission from one generation to another is largely assimilated to succession between status-occupants who remain contemporary members of the organisation. Though new recruits replace those retiring, they do not succeed directly to the attributes of their status, if at all. Joint-family and family succession, in that order, synchronise succession more closely with biological turnover in a genealogy, but the basic point is the same: the dynamic relation serves the family's need, as a self-reproducing unit, to reproduce also its static bond with its means of livelihood. This is so, whether the property is a direct source of livelihood, as use-value, or indirectly, as capital. Thus the prevalence of family succession to means of production in all exploitative modes of production reflects the sessile character of such units as villas, manors, capitals, etc. as the basis on which ruling-class families perpetuate their members' ability to participate in the process of exploitation. Where classes of reproduction are weaker, classes of nomination, based on ideological credentials for membership in bureaucracies, churches, corporations or parties, filter inter-generational access to the surplus product through organisational succession. In all these cases, devolution is assimilated to alienation of use. The continuing collectivity that bridges the generations – whether primary or secondary group – is treated as joint title-holder, and the sequence of individuals as successive holders acceding to a more or less circumscribed tenure of things that are held, as it were, in trust for their own successors.

Alienation of use creates two bonds, title and tenure. The first of these represents what Marx would call the determining moment, preserving the

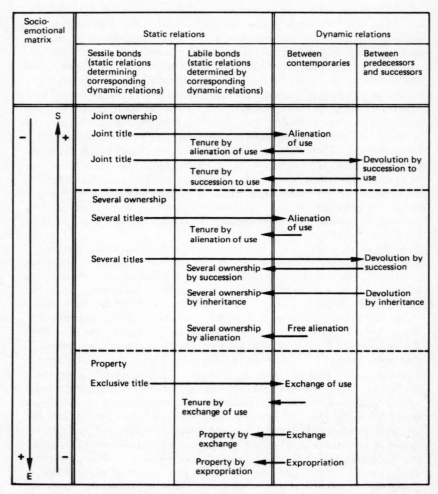

Figure 7 Types of Possessory Relations (II)

sessile character that determines this mode of social movement. Tenure, on the other hand, is a labile bond, determined by the dynamic relation, the alienation of use itself. But as such, it remains subordinated to the sessile bond in which the alienation originates. Circumstances may change this, of course. The strength of the sessile bond may wane, and the social importance of the alienation of use may increase, so that the title becomes a mere formality. Thus there may be a transition from tenure to several ownership or private property, or from succession to inheritance or free alienation – as when bureaucratic offices become properties in the gift of their holders – or to exchange, as when tenancies or offices can be sold freely by their holders. The connections between these various types of possessory relations are summarised in Figure 7, which may be read as a partial elaboration of the simpler categories in Figure 6.

2 POSSESSORY RELATIONS, DISTRIBUTION RELATIONS, PRODUCTION RELATIONS

The main theme of this book has been that the young Marx's conception of 'man's self-alienation' divided, in his later work, into two separate conceptual strands. One led, through 'estrangement', into the socio-emotional dimension of human relationships; the other, through 'alien-ation', into the social movement of things between possessors. (That a third strand led through 'reification' into the social causes and functions of hypostatised meanings has also been several times indicated.) These two leads have been followed further, consistently with Marx's theories, by developing conceptual schemata of the socio-emotional matrix and of static and dynamic possessory relations. The terms in each of these have been hypothetically correlated with each other. The problem now is to situate these concepts within Marx's theorising.

It is clear that they should be referred to that part of Marx's theory which contains the terms 'property relations' and 'distribution relations', and which is bounded 'above' (i.e. from the side of the 'superstructure') by 'legal relations' and below (i.e. on the side of the 'base') by 'production relations'. This can be most directly demonstrated from certain passages in the *Grundrisse*, e.g.:

> In order to express the relations into which capital and wage labour enter as *property relations* or *laws*, we need do no more than express the conduct of both sides in the *realization process* as an *appropriation process*. For example, the fact that surplus labour is posited as surplus value of capital means that the worker does not appropriate the product of his own labour; that it appears to him as *alien property*; inversely, that *alien labour* appears as the property of capital. This second law of bourgeois property, the inversion of the first – which, through laws of inheritance, etc., attains an existence independent of the accidental transitoriness of individual capitalists – is just as well established a law as the first. The first is the identity of labour with property; the second, labour as negated property, or property as the negation of the alien quality of alien labour.[8]

The worker's propertylessness, and the ownership of living labour by objectified labour, or the appropriation of alien labour by capital – both merely expressions of the same relation from opposite poles – are fundamental conditions of the bourgeois mode of production, in no way accidents irrelevant to it. These modes of distribution are the relations of production themselves, but *sub specie distributionis* . . . The 'laws and conditions' of the production of wealth and the laws of the 'distribution of wealth' are the same laws under different forms, and both change, undergo the same historic process . . .[9]

To these should be added a lengthy section where Marx analysed commodity exchange as bilateral conditional alienation and appropriation, involving a threefold contrast.[10] First, the 'economic relation' of equality between the exchange-values reflects the relativity of the quantities of socially necessary labour-time they contain, given a particular development of productive forces (including division of labour). Secondly, 'voluntary relations' arise from the fact that participants express their socially conditioned freedom of occupation and tastes through the use-values, or content, of acts of exchange, and thus through their choice of occasions and partners, as well as in the joint regulation of the act itself.[11] Finally, both of these contrast with the 'juridical relations' of contract law in which they are formalised as ideal procedures.

From these passages we can see that Marx recognised a distinct set of processes and relations, and of 'laws' describing them, which involved property and appropriation—i.e. static and dynamic possessory relations—as relations involving socially constituted subjects and objects. Though socially defined, reproduced and limited, such subjects could nevertheless engage voluntarily in transactions appropriate to their milieu. One kind of transmissive practice, therefore, such as commodity exchange, may contain an element of personal freedom or social latitude—of chance, indeed, from the standpoint of structural laws—while another, like exploitation, may 'forcibly assert itself like an overriding law of nature.'[12]

> To the single individual . . . distribution appears as a social law which determines his position within the system of production. The individual comes into the world possessing neither capital nor land. Social distribution assigns him at birth to wage labour.[13]

Property or not-property thus may determine the subject's limits, what he can and cannot personify in his social intercourse. Moreover, in so far as they are mutually exclusive and opposed, 'positing the self as an end in itself' these subjects are described by Marx as 'alien', estranged; but in so far as they are collective subjects, the implication is that they are socially cohesive, either through solidarity or by the pressure of a reified social bond.[14]

These relations and processes were distinct from 'economic relations', but closely related to them. Exchange 'reflected' the economic relations in which the law of value operated; property relations 'expressed' as an appropriation process the same conduct which economic relations expressed as a process of realising surplus-value. The laws, or modes of distribution are the laws, or relations, of production themselves, but 'under different forms', seen from another aspect. Thus each historic mode of production has its corresponding mode of distribution, which is also one of its 'fundamental conditions'. Marx frequently reiterated this point, reproving Sismondi for 'not realizing that the relations of distribution are only the relations of production seen from a different aspect', or J. S. Mill 'who considers the bourgeois relations of production as eternal, but their forms of distribution as historical, and thereby shows that he understands neither the one nor the other.'[15] But precisely what he thought the relation of distribution relations to production relations was remains to be elucidated.

A demarcation must also be established, from the opposite side, between 'property relations' and legal or juridical relations. Although in the *Preface* of 1859 Marx called property relations a 'legal expression' of production relations, we have already noted that in his letter to Schweitzer a few years later he wrote that a critical analysis of political economy would examine bourgeois *'property relations* as a whole, not in their *legal* expression as *voluntary relations* but in their real form, as *relations of production.'* This suggests that 'property relations as a whole' are not themselves a legal expression of anything, but *have* a legal expression, in which they are construed as voluntary relations, and are themselves 'real' – which could perhaps mean 'causally determined and determining' – in so far as they function in a particular way, in (or as) the form of something else: production relations. Moreover, in analysing exchange it seemed that Marx regarded contract as the juridical or legal form of an exchange of property, in so far as it was a voluntary relation, and the exchange itself as a form whose content was determined by an 'economic relation'. If the economic relation is the law of value, the content of the exchange is the production relation between the exchangers as commodity producers.

This is a bit of a muddle, as one would expect from culling snippets out of several texts, but sense can be made of it without undue stretching. Let us begin by calling law, as it appears in the statute book or the courts, or in documentary instruments such as contracts, a set of juridical or legal relations. These relations are normative, and hold between conceptual entities, idealisations, such as 'the owner', 'the vendor', 'the lessee', 'the premises' 'chattels' etc. These examples come from the law of property and contract, a subset of legal relations, and the only ones that concern us here. Distinct from this subset is the set of all the actual social relations between persons (or other social subjects) and things (or other social objects) existing in a society over a given period that *could*, if regarded from the standpoint of a lawyer, be described as falling with a greater or lesser degree of conformity under this subset of legal relations. I have described this set of actual social relations in these terms for expository reasons, not because it could not equally well be identified independently of a knowledge of the legal relations.[16] In previous pages the case for treating these possessory relations sociologically, as an independently identifiable set of social facts, has already been sufficiently laboured. The point is, though, that *if* construed in legal terms, these actual relations would have to be construed as voluntarily sustained by the agents. This is simply because the law's business is to impute responsibility for failures to conform. Hence, unless there is explict provision or proof to the contrary, the idealised agents in the normative system are assumed to be the free and conscious authors of deeds whose meaning consists solely in their agreement or disagreement with an ideal standard. Thus the set of possessory relations *could* be described in the language of legal relations, and if it was, they would be treated as voluntary relations. If we now equate this set of possessory relations with Marx's 'property relations', or more especially his 'property relations as a whole', we can understand why they might be regarded both as being a legal expression of something else, and as being something that could have a legal expression different from themselves; and why, in either case, the legal expression would treat them as voluntary relations.[17]

This interpretation of Marx's 'property relations' is not yet quite accurate, however. He was not interested in *all* the possessory relations present in a society over a given period, but only in a selected and abstracted subset of these. Selected, in that he used the term to refer to those possessory bonds whose objects were the conditions and elements of the social production process. Abstracted, in that *particular* sets of property relations were defined as 'wholes', or systems (i.e. 'property relations as a whole') by reference to particular theoretical models of the social production process. Thus when Marx wrote to Schweitzer of ancient property relations, feudal property relations and bourgeois property relations he was designating property systems specific to the social formations corresponding to these three modes of production. The latter, in turn, were defined by the structuring of determinate productive forces through the production relations of villa and slave labour, manor and serf labour, capital and wage labour.

If these arguments establish that property relations and distribution relations are distinct from legal relations, on the one hand, and from production relations, on the other, and that they both refer to part of the field covered by my term 'possessory relations', it remains to decide how they are related to each other. In an earlier chapter it was asserted that possessory relations are no more than the person-centered or group-centered manifestation of the distribution relations in a society or social formation, but that as such they are also 'bonds' and 'transmissions' which enable us to say that a given distribution 'exists'. It was suggested that what an observer might describe as a distribution, i.e. as an abstract 'map' or statistical model, would be 'on the ground', an aggregate of concrete possessory relations sustained by appropriate practices.[18] Is this compatible with Marx's actual use of the term 'distribution relations'?

Marx several times distinguished between two sorts of distribution, regarding one as a consequence of the other. The simplest version of this distinction is in *Critique of the Gotha Programme:*

> The distribution of the means of consumption at any time is only a consequence of the distribution of the conditions of production themselves. The latter distribution, however, is a feature of the mode of production itself. The capitalist mode of production, for example, rests on the fact that the material conditions of production are in the hands of non-workers in the form of property in capital and land, while the masses are only owners of the personal conditions of production, *viz*, labour power. If the elements of production are so distributed, then the present-day distribution of the means of consumption results automatically.[19]

In an earlier discussion of the subject, in the 1857 *Introduction*, Marx had made a similar distinction, but added to the distribution of means of production a distribution of individuals. This appears to mean their distribution both in the social division of labour, amongst different occupations and industrial sectors, and under the production relations (i.e. capital and labour) through which these are articulated by the capitalist mode of production:

> . . . before distribution can be the distribution of products, it is: (1) the distribution of the instruments of production, and (2), which is a further specification of the same relation, the distribution of the members of the society among the different kinds of production. (Subsumption of the individuals under specific relations of production.) The distribution of products is evidently only a result of this distribution, which is comprised within the process of production itself and determines the structure of production.[20]

The same text contains the earliest example of Marx's argument that distributive categories, e.g. wages, merely refer from a consumer standpoint to economic quantities that have already featured in the analysis of production – in this case, as labour for capital, or as means of subsistence for labour-power. As such, they are also determined by production:

> The relations and modes of distribution thus appear merely as the obverse of the agents of production. An individual who participates in production in the form of wage labour shares in the products, in the results of production, in the form of wages. The structure of distribution is completely determined by the structure of production. Distribution is itself a product of production, not only in its object, in that only the results of production can be distributed, but also in its form, in that the

specific kind of participation in production determines the specific forms of distribution, i.e. the pattern of participation in distribution.[21]

This last phrase amounts to a definition of 'distribution relations', which reappears in the difficult discussion of the same problems in the penultimate chapter of *Capital*. Here similar points are made, and two sets of 'distribution relations' are distinguished. The first refers to 'the various titles to that portion of the product which goes into individual consumption', while the second, which might be regarded as presupposed by capital, consists of

> the expropriation of the labourer from the conditions of labour, the concentration of these conditions in the hands of a minority of individuals, the exclusive ownership of land by other individuals, in short, all the relations which have been described in the part dealing with primitive accumulation . . . [These distribution relations] are the basis of special social functions performed within the production relations by certain of their agents, as opposed to the direct producers. They imbue the conditions of production themselves and their representatives with a specific social quality. They determine the entire character and the entire movement of production.[22]

The first type of distribution relations are, Marx argued again, 'essentially coincident' with the production relations, and 'their opposite side, so that both share the same historically transitory character.' On the other hand since the production relations are a 'definite social form of the conditions of production', and since it is the second type of distribution relations that 'imbue the conditions of production themselves and their representatives with a specific social quality', it would seem that this second type is fundamental to the mode of production. This obviously raises a major query, in the light of Marx's insistence that production, not distribution, is the prime determinant of society and history. But before trying to resolve this problem, some further clarification of these obscure and incomplete texts is needed.

To avoid the tedium of a detailed textual analysis, I propose to make four bold points. First, Marx seems not to have distinguished between two senses of 'distribution'. The first is that of a distribution in the sense of an abstract 'map' created by the investigator, showing how the items of a given stock are grouped at a certain time, or change their grouping over a period, in relation to the members of some other aggregate, or to some set of positions assumed as fixed. The second is the concrete grouping, or concrete movement, of the real items themselves, as a fact more or less consciously constituted in social reality, and of which the first sense is a more or less theoretical representation for descriptive purposes. If the latter is a distribution of things to possessors, it clearly equates with possessory relations, or property relations, as used hitherto. Since Marx was mainly concerned with the distribution of the social product (rather than, for instance, the distribution of sickness and health, or wives to husbands, etc.) we can treat most of his references to 'distribution' and 'distribution relations' as references either to actual possessory bonds and transmissions or to more or less abstractly described sets or patterns of these. As was remarked earlier, 'possessory relations' refer in a person-centered way to what 'distribution relations' refer to in a non-centered way.

The second point is that Marx, as has just been seen, referred to a distribution both of things to persons, and of persons to productive functions or roles. This is consistent with the position first developed in *The German Ideology* that 'The various stages of development in the division of labour are just so many forms of ownership, i.e. the existing stage in the division of labour determines also the relations of individuals to one another with reference to the material, instrument, and product of labour.'[23] This is also equivalent to the 'subsumption of the individuals under specific relations of production'. This can be illuminated with the aid of the distinction developed above, between labile and sessile possessory bonds. Wherever there are labile bonds, we can speak of things being distributed to persons (or collectivities) through processes of circulation, etc. And wherever there are sessile bonds, we can speak of persons being distributed to things, and hence to roles associated with them. So clan ownership of means of production distributes its members, by sex, age, generation and descent to the objects and localities required for their productive function, both synchronically, by tenure, and diachronically, by succession—both sessile bonds. In exploitative systems, it is by subsumption under the sessile bond represented by the means of production as embodiments of the dominant production relation—the villa, the manor, a capital, etc.—that workers are distributed to the instruments they use, and thereby also to the role that they occupy, in production. Similarly, it is through the sessile bond of family ownership or non-ownership of means of production that individuals are recruited into the exploiting or exploited class by family succession—or, in late capitalist and emergent socialist societies, through the sessile bonds of bureaucratic élites' control of 'cultural capital'. Thus there is no difficulty about expressing the occupational distribution of the division of labour as a 'further specification' of the possessory distribution of means of production. This does not imply the complete dependence of the former on the latter. On the contrary, Marx was unquestionably right in pointing out that the division of labour was an aspect of the structure of the productive forces, and that changes in the division of labour were, in general, cause rather than effect of the type and distribution of property.

The third point is that there is every reason to accept Marx's view that, in every mode of production, there is a category of distribution relations which constitutes 'production-determined distribution'[24]—namely, the distribution of the annual product between insurance, replacement and accumulation, and various revenues for consumption. Here it is broadly true that 'the specific kind of participation in production determines the specific form of distribution, i.e. the pattern of participation in distribution', and this has already emerged in the analysis of the forms of exploitation. There it was seen that 'the various titles to . . . the product' were a result of how living labour was subordinated to dead labour in the production process itself. Initially, it is true, some extraneous cause of ownership of means of production by a class which can exclude non-owners has to be posited:

> If it is said that, since production must begin with a certain distribution of the instruments of production, it follows that distribution at least in this sense precedes and forms the presupposition of production, then the reply must be that production does indeed have its determinants and preconditions, which form its moments. At the very beginning these may appear as spontaneous, natural. But by the process of production itself they are transformed from natural into historic determinants, and if they appear to one epoch as natural presuppositions of production, they were its historic product for another. Within production itself they are constantly being changed.[25]

The very process of replacement thus ensures that the dead labour embodied in the means of production themselves is the result of the past exploitation of living labour, of past surplus production. The only autonomous distributive element that we were able to detect here was a possibly universal 'law of appropriation' — an assumption that the natural products of one's own property are themselves one's own.[26]

These distribution relations, specific to each mode of production, are the principal means by which the system engenders the motivation and agency it requires if its structure is to be reproduced in processes that, in turn, express and evince it. It is the pursuit of wages and profits, rent and interest, that

> . . . appear as preconditions in real production because the capitalist mode of production moves within the forms it has created itself and which are its results . . . As such, they in fact determine the actions of individual capitalists, etc., and provide the motives, which are reflected in their consciousness.[27]

This causal influence of distribution relations as the mediating variable between the mode of production and motivation in the various activities comprising the corresponding social formation extends further than this specific instance of economically motivating the participants in the production process. For consumption is itself dependent on distribution, and so also therefore is the division not only between productive and unproductive consumption, but between individual and social consumption. Productive individual consumption is the same as the reproduction of labour-power, and hence covers the various demographic structures contained in that process. Unproductive individual consumption creates differences of life-style and hence status-structures. Productive social consumption is identical with social production, but unproductive social consumption embraces the whole material basis of the political and ideological superstructures. All these structures of consumption outside the sphere of production itself – demographic, status, and superstructural – are sources of motivation which, together with those arising directly from distribution, operate within the general field of social action – specifically, of class action. Furthermore, just as superstructures display partial autonomy within the limits of infrastructural determinism, so distribution and consumption, as parts of infrastructure subordinate to production, nevertheless may also be expected to display some autonomy vis-à-vis production, and for the same basic reason. Every distributive and consumptive milieu, like every political or ideological milieu, has its own socio-emotional matrix where group formation and fission proceeds on the basis of both the structurally determined (distributive, consumptive, political, etc.) attributes, and of others which may be contingently present in the situation, or which are generated by interaction itself. Every such milieu thus acquires a more or less distinctive social structure, subculture, constellation of interests and history of its own, and defines reality from its own distinctively distorting perspective.[28] Marx and Engels consistently recognised this in allowing for reactive effects of distribution on production, as of superstructure on base.

These distribution relations – and the consequential consumption relations – are explicit categories of action within the social formation and its corresponding social consciousness. For example, it is the distributive sphere of circulation that typically provides the paradigm of an exchange economy through which bourgeois society has misinterpreted to itself its character as a system of capitalist production. We may call these distribution relations 'manifest' or 'secondary', in order to distinguish them from the more fundamental distribution relations which, as Marx says, 'determine the entire character and the entire movement of production.'

My fourth point consists simply in identifying and accounting for these fundamental or primary distribution relations. Unlike the secondary distribution relations, these are not necessarily socially explicit, but may be hidden, visible only to the eye of the analyst. Whereas the secondary, manifest distribution of the capitalist mode of production is a 'bourgeois distribution', the primary distribution is what 'imbues the conditions of production themselves and their representatives with a specific social quality' – in the capitalist case, the very quality of being 'bourgeois production'. As Marx put it:

> The specific features – and therefore also the specific limitation – which set bounds to bourgeois distribution, enter into bourgeois production itself, as a determining factor, which overlaps and dominates (*übergreift*) production. The fact that bourgeois production is compelled by its own immanent laws, on the one hand, to develop the productive forces as if production did not take place on a narrow restricted social foundation, while, on the other hand, it can develop these forces only within these narrow limits, is the deepest and most hidden cause of crises, of the crying contradictions within which bourgeois production is carried on . . .[29]

An older style of Marxist exegesis would have assumed without question that what is referred to here is simply the historical class struggle. A contradictory mode of production and corresponding superstructure, together with the development of crises, etc. would all have been unhesitatingly viewed as consequences of antagonistic class interests. The modernist style in Marxology, which treats the historical class struggle as the social consequence of contradictory modes of production, as itself structurally determined, is an advance on this crude notion of history. In terms of the present discussion, for instance, social classes are congeries of overlapping collectivities formed through negative solidarity on the basis of shared economic attributes that become salient in the course of production, distribution, and consumption, and of superstructural activity, *within* the manifest categories of a contradictory mode of production. We can therefore agree with Giddens' use of the term 'class structuration' [30] The extent to which these various tendencies to group-formation, on the basis of structurally interconnected attributes, actually do coalesce and accumulate to form a single all-embracing division of society into two hostile groups that confront each other in production, society, politics and ideology is a matter of degree and variation, and for investigation in every case.

This structural interpretation receives support from an important passage in 'Revenue and its Sources' which indicates that what causes the production relations of capital and wage-labour to appear as the social forms of the production process, far from being class interests, is *nothing but their continuous reproduction*:

> If no surplus-value were produced, then of course together with surplus-value the part of it which is called interest would also cease to exist, and so would the part which is called rent; the *anticipation* of surplus-value would likewise come to an end, in other words, it would no longer constitute a part of the costs of production in the shape of the *price*

of commodities. The existing value entering into the production process would not emerge from it as *capital* at all, and accordingly, could not enter into the reproduction process as *capital*, nor be lent out as *capital*. It is thus the continuous reproduction of the same relations — the relations which postulate capitalist production — that not only causes them to appear as the social forms and results of this process, but at the same time as its continual *prerequisites*. But they are these only as·prerequisites continually *posited*, created, *produced* by the process itself. This reproduction is therefore not conscious reproduction; on the contrary, it only manifests itself in the continuous existence of these relations as *prerequisites* and as *conditions* dominating the production process . . . The bourgeois sees that the product continually becomes the condition of production. But he does not perceive that the production relations themselves, the social forms in which he produces and which he regards as given, natural relations, are the continuous prerequisite of this specific mode of production.[31]

Now, we have already seen that what remains hidden so long as one observes only the manifest operation of capitalism, as a special form of commodity production obeying the laws of the market, but becomes clear from the standpoint of reproduction — of 'capitalist production in the uninterrupted flow of its renewal' — is precisely the expropriation of those who lack means of production, by owners of these means, through exploitation of their labour. So we arrive at the following: when a process of social production and appropriation of the product, carried on through contradictory production relations and corresponding manifest distribution relations, is considered as a process of social reproduction, it is also found to be a process of social redistribution, operating through the latent distribution relation of expropriation of the workers. This latent distribution relation is a dynamic possessory relation, and there corresponds to it a latent labile bond: that of property and not-property by exploitation, of which the production relation and the ensuing class struggles are, in fact, an unrecognised expression. The subjects of this bond, it was suggested at the end of the last chapter, are *latent* classes defined by the total distribution of power to consume the social product.

This latent bond, and division of a population into two categories, are theoretical conceptions which describe the structure of an unconscious process, which only has real existence in the form of a continuous social movement of objects and the mutual estrangement of subjects. The sense in which the results of this exploitative redistribution constitute 'property' is certainly a marginal one, but it is not incompatible with the definition of property used in this book. For although class property in means of production, and means of life generally, through exploitation, is not established through negative solidarity on the part of the owners — that is, by conscious collective exclusion of the workers — it is nevertheless constituted as the unintended mass consequence of the separate exclusion of the workers – as well as of other owners – from each owner's sphere of property. It thus results from the *pattern* of estrangements existing in bourgeois society, as an authentic feature of the 'deep structure' of its socio-emotional field. For whereas solidarity and practices of inclusion necessarily build closed, self-conscious communities, concomitant estrangements and practices of exclusion produce bounded yet open aggregates which may lack any collective awareness of their negatively defined social identity and structure. The latent classes that are subject and object of exploitation both exist in this negatively defined way, as by-products of other estrangements and exclusions.

For this reason, Marx described property by exploitation as something *independent*, which confronts labour as a hostile force, and also confronts capitalists as an external compulsion with which they must conform if they are to continue as capitalists:

> . . . the objective conditions, that is (considering the process as a whole) the products, confront labour as independent forces, not as the property of labour but as the property of someone else, and thus in the form of *capital*.
>
> Labour as wage-labour and the conditions of labour as capital (that is, consequently, as the property of the capitalist; they are themselves properties personified in the capitalist and whose property in them, *their property in themselves*, they represent as against labour) are expressions of the same relationship, only seen from opposite poles.
>
> The fact that value – whether it exists as money or commodities – and in the further development the conditions of labour confront the worker as the *property of other people*, as independent properties, means simply that they confront him as the property of the non-worker or, at any rate, that, as a capitalist, he confronts them[the conditions of labour] not as a worker but as the *owner* of value, etc., as the subject in which these things possess their own will, belong to themselves and are personified as independent forces.[32]

Thus, corresponding to the latent labile bond of property by exploitation is the reified existence of the means of production as capital, the dominant production relation through which 'man is confronted by things, labour is confronted by its own materialized conditions as alien, independent, self-contained subjects' and the 'economic structure of society' thereby given its distinctive bourgeois form and motive impulse. Because the subject of exploitation is a negatively defined class that exists latently within the processes of society, its activity is socially manifest as that of *capital*, which as a reified totality is itself the '*übergreifendes Subjekt*' of the process of social production. To explain why the cohesion and movement of a society

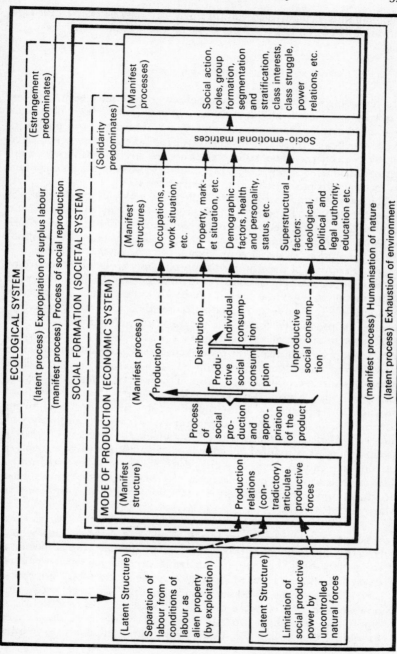

Figure 8 Marx's Theoretical Model of Exploitative Social Systems

predominantly structured by estrangement can only be effected through reification is however beyond the scope of this volume.

3 CONCLUSION: SYSTEM, STRUCTURE AND PROCESS

The preceding argument can be summarised and extended with the aid of a diagram. Figure 8 attempts to set out the general lines of Marx's theoretical model of exploitative social systems. The model resembles a set of Chinese boxes: three systems enclose one another. A system is defined simply as a coherent set of structured processes: structure and process are distinguished in each case as separate analytical aspects. My commentary on the diagram proceeds from the centre outwards.

The core system is what Marx called the 'mode of production', or economic system. It consists of a process of social production and appropriation of the product, which is itself made up of three types of sub-processes—direct production itself, distribution (including circulation) and consumption, as detailed in Marx's 1857 *Introduction*—by reason of universal features of the transformation and appropriation of nature by human populations. This process is structured as a specific, historical mode of production by what Marx called (in the *Preface*) the 'economic structure of society,—a distinctive set of production relations articulating a distinctive set of productive forces. In the case of exploitative modes, the production relations will be 'contradictory', although the precise meaning of this cannot be explored in the present context. The economic system is a subsystem of what Marx called the 'social formation', or the societal system. And it determines the structure of the societal system, as a specific, historical type of social formation, through the output of the social production process. This consists of all the structuring factors—occupation, property, demography, personality, authority, culture, etc.—that are normally taken by sociologists as the bases of role sets, group-formation, stratification, class conflict, political cleavage, ideological division and so forth in society itself.[33] These latter constitute a distinctive set of societal processes for every economically determined set of structural inputs. It was of this aspect of the bourgeois social formation that Marx wrote:

> When we consider bourgeois society in the long view and as a whole, then the final result of the process of social production always appears as the society itself, i.e. the human being itself in its social relations. Everything that has a fixed form, such as the product, etc., appears as merely a moment, a vanishing moment, in this. The direct production process itself here appears only as a moment. The conditions and objectifications of the process are themselves equally moments of it, and its only subjects are the individuals, but individuals in mutual

relationships, which they equally reproduce and produce anew. The constant process of their own movement, in which they renew themselves even as they renew the world of wealth which they create.[34]

This societal process is therefore always a particular institutionalised type of social process. Like social processes in general, it is, theoretically speaking, a region in which individual and collective subjects are socially constituted out of the relations in which men perceive and encounter one another in their milieus of interaction. These relations depend on the situationally determined salience of their attributes, and Marx's economic determinism is a theory specifying the types of attribute that will saliently structure a *societal* system, differentiating it from other possible kinds of social system. Like all social processes, the societal process occurs through the medium of socio-emotional matrices, developing solidarities and estrangements on the basis of these structural attributes. The place of the socio-emotional matrix in the societal process is analogous to that of the differentiation into subprocesses of direct production, distribution and consumption within the process of social production. In both cases there is a universal structuring factor – the method by which human populations appropriate nature; socio-emotional forces – whose precise historical mode of effectivity is overridingly determined, directly or indirectly, by the specific mode of production. It should now be clear in what sense the mode of production is a subsystem of the social formation, for the process of social production occurs only in so far as there is input from the societal system in the shape of social cognitions, emotions and action to bring the economic structure to life. This input appears in the diagram as feedback from the societal process to the mode of production. It occurs as a conscious and purposive infusion of the material and biological basis of production with social action, in so far as solidarity predominates (whether positive or negative) over estrangement, thus creating self-conscious and self-steering social agents able to collaborate, innovate and organise, to economise with time, labour and materials, to appropriate, exchange, compete, bequeath and consume – in fact, equipped to engage in all the practices that go to make up the economic system.

All that has so far been described belongs to the world of manifest and socially constituted meanings: it expresses the social consciousness which reflects it. But it is a model that abstracts process and action from the concrete temporality of historical flow and movement. To separate structure and process as analytical moments or aspects is to make an artificial distinction between a meaning which somehow 'remains' or is 'fixed' and a movement of behaviour through time which 'expresses' it. In fact, however, all reality moves 'forward' together in time. Structure only exists as instantaneous social communication of meaning by behaviour, or in the perceptible traces that this leaves behind, and in the extrapolations 'backward' and 'beyond' made by the human brain, linking the signals it receives with the messages it has stored and the plans it is preparing. Out of the multiform reciprocation of semantically isomorphic behaviours and their enduring evidences, the recording observer and analyst can reconstruct relatively persistent patterns which can then be conceptually isolated as 'fixed' structures, almost as though the corresponding processes could somehow have had an existence without them, or they without the processes which were their reality. If we now abandon this artificiality and think of the social formation as the continuously structured and continuously changing process that it really is, we are in a position to make another distinction, a different artificial slicing-up of the given. This is the distinction between process in so far as it is repetition and persistence of a set of structures, and process in so far as it is variation, innovation and change. The total process will then be a synthesis of two processual aspects: the process of social reproduction, and the process of social change. Since the theory of social change is outside the scope of this book, the diagram shows only the process of social reproduction, as a prolongation or enlargement by repetition of the social formation.

As such, it is a manifest process, the element of conscious continuity in social life. This is not necessarily to be equalled with tradition. The equation is apt where the mode of production permits little accumulation, when continuity is enshrined in the reproduction of a particular way of life in its detailed immediacy. But continuity may take the form of growth and linear progress, e.g. if continual accumulation is a condition of remaining an agent of production, as under capitalism. In that case, the process of social reproduction ensures continuity of social and cultural forms whose content and extension changes. A part of the process of social change is thereby subsumed under social reproduction, and the extension of this subsumption is, of course, one of the aims or hopes of communism. Under capitalism, however, progress remains the haphazard and unplanned result of an unrecognised process of exploitation. Thus what is from one point of view the manifest process of social reproduction is from another a latent process of expropriation of surplus labour.

Social reproduction necessarily involves the humanisation of nature, even though only on a small scale: hunting affects the ecological balance of nature, agriculture changes the landscape, and so forth. Industrialisation turns this into a massive and rapid transformation of the globe. As a manifest process, and as the purposive material aspect of social reproduction, this involves the creation of a civilised and controlled environment. But in its unintended consequences it is also the depletion and exhaustion of mankind's stock of terrestrial resources. Game and forests disappear, soil is over-grazed and eroded, or over-cultivated and impoverished, and minerals, fossil fuels, etc. are used up. Here, as Postan has shown for feudalism, and as capitalism is learning from the contemporary energy crisis, the latent environmental consequences of a mode of production will sooner or later impinge upon and exacerbate the social conflicts and upheavals resulting from its latent distributive consequences.[35]

What I am suggesting is that, developing Marx's hints, we should view as a single processual complex the manifest processes of social reproduction and humanisation of nature, together with the latent processes of expropriation of surplus labour and the exhaustion of the environment; and that these constitute the processual aspect of the human ecological system. The latter is defined as the system of adaptation between a socially organised population and its natural surroundings. As such, its universal features define it – like the economic and societal systems – as a complex of sub-processes, in this case specified by the pairs social/natural, controlled/uncontrolled. Beyond this, it is structured as a specific type of ecological system by historically persisting elements of both sides in the adaptation process, which set limits to its variation and flexibility. As manifest processes, social reproduction and humanisation of nature are structured by the production relations and productive forces of the mode of production through which they occur. But as we have seen, the latent consequence of this reproduction is the continuous reproduction of property and not-property by exploitation, or the separation of labour from its conditions, which confront it as alien property, and this is also what structures the corresponding latent process as one of an expropriative exploitation of labour. Similarly, the limits to the mastery of nature available to any given set of productive forces are set by the uncontrolled forces of nature with which they interact or on whose presence they depend. This determines the latent process of environmental exhaustion that accompanies the manifest process of humanisation of nature.

These latent structures appear on the left of the diagram, and their effects upon the societal system are shown as mediated through the production relations and productive forces, respectively, of the mode of production. For if the production relations of a mode of production arise as a historically given conjuncture, their perpetuation as the structuring framework of social production must occur through the reproduction of their latent distributive consequences. That these are *latent* consequences is determined by the degree to which estrangement predominates in the unintended socio-emotional matrices that result from the societal process. For to the extent that this process contains solidary relationships, these can form the basis of deliberate social action which remains within the manifest sphere. Residual estrangements, however, structure the latent basis of social exclusion, property and exploitation as gaps in social communication and barriers to social consciousness and social control. The resultant reifications impose themselves, through *contradictory* production relations, as fundamental constraints on the freedom with which social action based on solidarities can be effective in the process of social production. In exploitative systems, uncontrolled societal consequences dominate the intentional social control of production.

These considerations allow us to see how the diagram would need to be altered to depict a Marxian model of non-exploitative societies. Non-contradictory production relations would ensure that solidarity could predominate throughout social production, which would therefore function as a planned, or at least consensual and customary, process. Residual estrangements would be minimal, and in any case would not feed back to generate a latent structure which separated labour from its conditions as alien property. The process of social reproduction would not be also a latent process of expropriation of surplus labour, but would include collective appropriation of surplus labour as part of the manifest process, structured by communal or associative production relations. In so far as the ecological system was structured by the persisting elements of social organisation, therefore, these would be either the traditional values of a static society, or the deliberately chosen persisting goals of a rational and dynamic society. Which of these two we are talking about — i.e. primitive or advanced communism — would depend on the level of development of the productive forces. In the primitive case, the manifest process of humanisation of nature would be wholly determined by the structure of uncontrolled natural forces. The low impact of technology on the environment would make exhaustion negligible, and a natural equilibrium, exactly like that of any other animal species, would persist so long as the productive forces remained undeveloped and the society depended on the natural productivity of an uncomprehended environment for satisfaction of its simple wants. In the case of advanced communism, the limitation on social production by uncontrolled natural forces would be negligible. Inexhaustible resources would be developed, terrestrial nature would be completely humanised, and although the ecological system would still be structured by long-term forces, such as the evolution of the solar system, it would mainly be a manifest part of the process of social reproduction. Human society would have effectively internalised its natural environment.

Hopefully, the diagram and accompanying commentary have situated the argument of this book in the context of Marx's own theorising, and also indicated how historical materialism might be reconstructed in a way that maximises its common ground with other types of sociological theory. It also indicates the solution to the problem that was noted as outstanding in the last section: how to reconcile the apparently fundamentalist claims that Marx made both for primary distribution relations and for production. Production remains the 'motor' of all three systems, on account of their Chinese box character. It alone can fulfil this role, because the mode of production, by unleashing productive forces, generates the energies that propel a society forward, as a structured whole, against the otherwise overwhelming pressure of the natural environment which constantly threatens human beings with starvation, the human artefact with decay, and consequently the entire fabric of social meaning with dissolution and extinction. Primary distribution relations are, in a sense, the source of the structure of what production propels, just as secondary distribution relations provide the motivation and agency through which the propulsion occurs; equally, however, structure and agency are available only to the extent that production reproduces their sources. Further investigation of Marx's concepts of productive forces, social forces, and reification would probably show, moreover, that the constraining power which reification communicates to the production relations itself originates from production. It is probably a consequence of conversion of the energies unleased by the productive forces into a distinctive set of social forces, accomplished through the intervention, between human needs and the objects of their satisfaction, of the estrangement contained in primary distribution relations.

These brief remarks on the subject of productive forces and reification, too condensed and incomplete to be convincing, must suffice to indicate that there are large parts of Marx's theorising that the present discussion has scarcely touched. Not only has his treatment of labour and production, time and economy, reification and personification been left unexamined, but even the basic concept of production relations has been only partially explored. A closer approach to a general theory of modes of production, and hence of societal systems, would require these gaps to be filled. Only then, moreover, would one be in a position to tackle the numerous difficult problems that still remain in defining the relationships between mode of production and social formation, base and superstructure, social structure and social consciousness, social consciousness and ideology, contradiction and conflict, reproduction and change – problems still unresolved despite the major advances of recent Marxian scholarship – and to pursue the hope of a critical alignment of these categories of Marxian theory with those of other sociological approaches. It is in the belief that such a work of critical synthesis at the theoretical level is both feasible and worthwhile, that these pages have been written.

Notes

INTRODUCTION

1 Because my own approach to 'the problem of alienation' departs rather fundamentally from the approaches of most other writers on the subject, I have not entered into detailed discussion of their arguments. Nor do I aim to give any sort of complete bibliography on the subject. The works which I have found most helpful and stimulating are the following: S. M. Lukes, 'Alienation and Anomie' in Laslett and Runciman (eds), *Philosophy, Politics and Society*, 3rd series (Oxford, 1967); L. Althusser, *For Marx* (London, 1969); B. Ollman, *Alienation* (Cambridge, 1971); R. Schacht, *Alienation* (London, 1971); I. Mészáros, *Marx's Theory of Alienation* (London, 1972); and J. P. Plamenatz, *Karl Marx's Philosophy of Man* (Oxford, 1975). With the partial exception of Althusser, these authors have mainly stimulated me to disagree, and helped me to formulate positions different from theirs; thus my debt to them is mostly negative, but a negative debt is, after all, the best kind.

2 Unlike 'self-alienation', which may refer to a real social relation to another, 'self-estrangement' always refers to internalised relationships within a divided self. This is simply because 'estrangement' refers directly to a self-other relationship, so that the reflexive form can only refer to an 'other' internal to the self. Hegel has a rather different sense of 'self-estrangement' from this, as we shall see.

3 A classic expression in the O.T. is Job, 19, vi – xxii.

4 See p. 241, below. Similar etymological links exist in other languages. E. g. Welsh *alltud* (stranger, foreigner) originally meant 'member of another *tud* or tribe'.

CHAPTER I

1 See J. W. Gough, *The Social Contract* (Oxford, 1957) Chs. 3, 4, 7 for examples.

2 See Gough, op. cit., Ch. 11; and cf. also pp. 151–3, on the logical difficulties encountered by Thomasius, who had tried to construct a social contract theory without abandoning the scholastic and Aristotelian emphasis on man's natural *socialitas*.

3 Somewhat similarly, economics and statistics emerged as 'political' economy and arithmetic respectively.

4 S. von Pufendorf, *De Officio Hominis et Civis juxta Legem Naturalem*, trans. F. G. Moore (New York, 1927) vol. II, p. 92.

5 J. J. Rousseau, *The Social Contract*, Everyman ed. (London, 1913) p. 15.

6 Ibid., p. 221.

7 Ibid., p. 212.

8 Ibid., p. 237.

9 Ibid., p. 59.

CHAPTER 2

1 All page references in this chapter, unless noted otherwise, are to G. W. F. Hegel, *The Phenomenology of Mind* trans. J. Baillie (London, 1949).
2 p. 459.
3 p. 165.
4 p. 230.
5 p. 231.
6 p. 218.
7 p. 226.
8 p. 239.
9 loc. cit.
10 p. 227.
11 loc. cit.
12 p. 480.
13 p. 504.
14 p. 505−6.
15 p. 504.
16 p. 245 (my italics). Historically, of course, this refers to the Hellenistic era, when the 'soulless community' appeared for the first time.
17 p. 251.
18 p. 252 (my italics).
19 p. 253.
20 p. 256.
21 p. 252.
22 p. 266.
23 p. 265−6.
24 p. 272.
25 G. W. F. Hegel, *The Philosophy of History*, trans. Sibree (New York, 1956) p. 318.
26 p. 510.
27 p. 511.
28 *The Philosophy of History*, pp. 341−3.
29 p. 509.
30 p. 514.
31 p. 515−6.
32 p. 517.
33 p. 533.
34 p. 540.
35 p. 541.
36 p. 546.
37 p. 515.
38 p. 376.
39 H. S. Harris, *Hegel's Development. Towards the Sunlight, 1770−1801.* (Oxford, 1972) pp. 511−12.

CHAPTER 3

1 See D. McLellan, *The Young Hegelians and Karl Marx* (London, 1969) p. 64.
2 L. Feuerbach, *Sämtliche Werke*, ed. W. Bolin and F. Jodl, vol. 2.

3 K. Marx, *Early Texts*, trans. and ed. D. McLellan (Oxford, 1972) p. 116. I have used this translation except in cases where Milligan's more precisely conveys a point that is important for my argument. Occasionally I have given my own translation if it seemed necessary.

4 Ibid., p. 132.

5 The previous efforts of Hess, and even Engels, were not strictly systematic.

6 L. Feuerbach, *The Essence of Christianity*, trans. M. Evans (London, 1881) pp. 31, 136, 248.

7 Ibid., p. 157.

8 Ibid., p. 281.

9 Ibid., p. 157.

10 *Early Texts*, p. 160.

11 K. Marx, *Economic and Philosophical Manuscripts of 1844*, trans. M. Milligan, ed. D. J. Struik (London, 1973) p. 178.

12 'Manifesto of the Communist Party', in K. Marx and F. Engels, *Selected Works* (London, 1968) p. 57.

13 'Theses on Feuerbach', in op. cit., p. 29.

14 *Early Texts*, p. 159.

15 K. Marx and F. Engels, *The German Ideology* (London, 1965) p. 54.

16 Ibid., p. 59.

17 Ibid., p. 84.

18 *Early Texts*, p. 129.

19 *The German Ideology*, p. 54.

20 *Early Texts*, p. 128.

21 *The German Ideology*, p. 38.

22 K. Marx and F. Engels, *The Holy Family*, trans. R. Dixon (Moscow, 1956) p. 78. Cf. pp. 101–2.

23 Ibid., p. 125.

24 *Economic and Philosophical Manuscripts*, p. 140.

25 This position shares with positivistic Marxism (e.g. Otto Neurath, *Empiricism and Sociology* (Dordrecht and Boston, 1973)) the view that Marx out-Comted Comte in breaking with metaphysics, but rejects the corollary that this commits Marxists to behaviourism. Though Marx often used the language of ontological realism in his later writings, implying that scientific knowledge revealed the real essences of phenomena, it seems most unlikely that this was intended in a metaphysical sense. Not only does the sarcastic reference to 'scholasticism' in the second thesis on Feuerbach suggest an Occam's razor approach to redundant entities such as essences, but there are such unequivocal statements as the following: 'when we conceive things thus, as they really are and happened, every profound philosophical problem is resolved . . . quite simply into an empirical fact' (*The German Ideology*, p. 57.). (Cf. also *Randgiossen*, pp. 365ff.) When interpreters such as Mészáros or Ollman attribute an ontology to Marx, they appear to establish only that Marx was committed to certain broad existential generalisations, or to a certain type of existential generalisation. See I. Mészáros, *Marx's Theory of Alienation* (London, 1972) Ch. 6, B. Ollman, *Alienation* (Cambridge, 1971) pp. 15, 35, 62–6.

26 For example in 'Wage Labour and Capital', in *Selected Works*, p. 80.

27 I use this as one possible translation of Marx's difficult phrase 'übergreifendes Subjekt' (e.g. K. Marx, *Grundrisse der Kritik der politischen Ökonomie* (Berlin,

1953) p. 374: cf. also p. 912), but without any commitment to the individualistic metaphysics with which it is associated in Sartre's *Critique de la Raison dialectique*.

28 It gave no warrant, of course, for reconstructing as 'dialectical materialism' the materialist metaphysic that Marx seems definitely to have abandoned after 1844.

29 K. Marx, *Capital*, trans. Moore and Aveling (London, 1970) vol. I, p. 20.

30 *Early Texts*, p. 194.

31 Ibid., p. 177.

32 Ibid., p. 175.

33 *Capital*, I, p. 8. Cf. Marx's rebuttal of the way in which Rodbertus and Wagner understood his theory of value: 'In the first place, I do not proceed from "concepts", and therefore not from a "concept of value" . . . My starting-point is the simplest social form in which the product of labour is presented [*sich darstellt*] in contemporary society, which is the "*commodity*". I analyze this, and to begin with indeed in the form in which it actually appears . . .' (*Randglossen*, p. 369). (The significance of this source was first pointed out to me by Terrell Carver.)

34 'Preface to *A Contribution to the Critique of Political Economy*', in *Selected Works*, p. 182.

35 A third implication of the epistemological argument in the *Theses*, slightly developed in *The German Ideology*, was the much disputed view that epistemology itself, as the seience of a particular kind of praxis, the production of knowledge, must become dependent on the more general science of human activity: men's social being determines their consciousness.

36 *The German Ideology*, p. 38. Even the idea of man's species-being did not entirely disappear when it lost its metaphysical trappings, but retained at least three sorts of relevance to Marx's social science. First, man's biological character and environmental dependence remained a conditioning factor, or set of factors. Secondly, Marx occasionally spoke of social man as a species-being in so far as group formation and role differentiation were based on biological repro-duction. Thirdly, 'history' for Marx was knowledge of human existence on this planet – the science of a single subject-matter, although itself part of 'the history of nature, so-called natural science' (ibid., p. 28).

37 *Early Texts*, p. 159.

38 *The German Ideology*, p. 58.

39 '. . . there exists a materialistic connection of men with one another, which is determined by their needs and their mode of production . . . This connection is ever taking on new forms, and this presents a "history" . . .'(*The German Ideology*, p. 41). This was especially emphasised by Bukharin, *Historical Materialism, A System of Sociology* (London, 1926).

40 Ibid., p. 41.

41 Ibid., pp. 36–7.

42 *Marx-Engels Werke* (Berlin, 1956ff) Ergänzungsband I, p. 451 (my trans.). Cf. *Early Texts*, pp. 193–4.

43 *Early Texts*, p. 149.

44 Ibid., p. 199.

45 Ibid., p. 149.

46 *Werke*, Ergbd. I, pp. 538–9 (my trans.). Cf. *Early Texts*, p. 150.

47 *Early Texts*, p. 155.

48 *Selected Works*, p. 29.
49 K. Marx, *Grundrisse*, trans. M. Nicolaus (London, 1973) p. 83.
50 *The German Ideology*, p. 50.
51 *Early Texts*, p. 117 (my italics).
52 Ibid., p. 121–2.
53 *Werke*, Ergbd. I, p. 467. Cf. *Economic and Philosophical Manuscripts*, p. 63.
54 Loc. cit.
55 *Werke*, Ergbd. I, p. 452. Cf. *Early Texts*, p. 194.
56 *Economic and Philosophical Manuscripts*, p. 57.
57 'It goes without saying that the *proletarian*, i.e. the man who, being without capital and rent, lives purely by labour, and by a one-sided, abstract labour, is considered by political economy only as a *worker*. Political economy can therefore advance the proposition that the proletarian, the same as any horse, must get as much as will enable him to work. It does not consider him when he is not working, as a human being, but leaves such consideration to criminal law, to doctors, to religion, to the statistical tables, to politics and to the poorhouse overseer.' (*Economic and Philosophical Manuscripts*, p. 72.)
58 Loc. cit.
59 Ibid. p. 106.
60 *Economic and Philosophical Manuscripts*, p. 129.
61 Ibid., p. 70.
62 Ibid., p. 107.
63 Loc. cit.
64 *Early Texts*, p. 116.
65 As implied by the arguments against Feuerbach in *The German Ideology*, pp. 59–60.
66 See L. Althusser, *Reading Capital*, trans. B. Brewster (London, 1972) pp. 94ff.
67 *Early Texts*, p. 105.
68 As Marx said of Feuerbach's standpoint (which had also been his own) ' "Man" is really "the German".' (*The German Ideology*, p. 54.)
69 *Early Texts*, p. 100.
70 Ibid., p. 99.
71 Ibid., p. 105.
72 *Selected Works*, p. 29.
73 *Economic and Philosophical Manuscripts*, p. 136.
74 *Werke*, Ergbd. I, p. 519; cf. *Early Texts*, p. 142.
75 *Early Texts*, p. 148.

CHAPTER 4

1 *Economic and Philosophical Manuscripts*, pp. 107, 115.
2 Ibid., p. 110.
3 Ibid., p. 112.
4 Ibid., pp. 114–15.
5 *Capital*, trans. E. and C. Paul, Everyman ed. (London, 1930) p. 29n.
6 *Economic and Philosophical Manuscripts*, p. 115.
7 Ibid., p. 116.
8 *Early Texts*, p. 197.

9 *Economic and Philosophical Manuscripts*, pp. 201–2.
10 *Early Texts*, p. 192.
11 Ibid., p. 194.
12 K. Marx, *Pre-capitalist Economic Formations*, trans. J. Cohen, ed. E. J. Hosbawm (London, 1964) p. 96.
13 *Marx's Grundrisse*, ed. and trans. D. McLellan (London, 1971). (In this and the preceding quotation, and occasionally elsewhere, I have used translations of the *Grundrisse* other than Nicolaus', as being more germane to the point at issue. I have used both translations of *Capital*, I, for the same purpose. In such cases, however, I have not exploited different translators' deviations from the sense conveyed by the original German.)
14 *Capital*, I, pp. 72–3.
15 *Early Texts*, pp. 199–200.
16 Ibid., p. 202.
17 *Grundrisse*, trans. Nicolaus, p. 164.
18 *Pre-Capitalist Economic Formations*, p. 96.
19 *Grundrisse*, trans. McLellan, p. 17.
20 *The Sociology of Georg Simmel*, trans. and ed. K. H. Wolff (Glencoe and London, 1964) p. 403.
21 *Capital*, I, trans, E. and C. Paul, pp. 63–4. As P. Anderson points out in *Passages from Antiquity to Feudalism* (London, 1974) p. 223, Marx was partly right and partly wrong on this point.
22 M. Weber, *General Economic History*, trans. F. Knight (New York, 1961) vol. 1, pp. 50, 151–3. Cf. *Capital*, III, pp. 325–6.
23 E. Mandel, *Marxist Economic Theory*, trans. B. Pearce (London, 1968). For interesting examples of silent barter, see E. W. Bovill, *The Golden Trade of the Moors* (Oxford, 1970) pp. 82, 123–5.
24 *Pre-capitalist Economic Formations*, pp. 89, 91.
25 Ibid., pp. 89, 103.
26 *Capital*, III, pp. 770–4.
27 R. E. Park, 'Human Migration and the Marginal Man', *American Journal of Sociology*, vol. 33 (1928) pp. 888–9.
28 K. Marx, *Ethnological Notebooks*, ed. L. Krader (Assen, 1972) pp. 301–2.
29 *The German Ideology*, p. 66. It is worth noting that Marx here uses the idea which Mosca made the basis of his 'theory of the ruling class': 'the dominion of an organised minority . . ., over the unorganised majority is inevitable.' (G. Mosca, *The Ruling Class*, trans. H. D. Kahn (New York, 1939) p. 51.) See below, p. 153.
30 See, e.g., F. Engels, *The Condition of the Working Class in England*, trans. and ed. W. O. Henderson and W. H. Chaloner (Oxford, 1958) pp. 104–7, 139; *Capital*, I, 663–7; *Selected Correspondence*, pp. 288–9.

CHAPTER 5

1 *Economic and Philosophical Manuscripts*, pp. 154–5.
2 G. Homans, *The Human Group* (London, 1951) p. 112. A similar point is made in J. G. March and H. A. Simon, *Organizations* (New York, 1958), and cited by D. Cartwright and A. Zander, *Group Dynamics* (London, 1960) p. 47.

3 The concept of 'solidarity' is as much a French contribution to sociology as 'estrangement' is a German one. Its source was in the co-proprietorship and hence collective responsibility of the Roman *gens*, especially for debts. (See G. Glotz, *La Solidarité de la famille dans le droit criminel en Grèce* (Paris, 1904).) From Roman Law the term passed into French literary usage: Voltaire wrote of the Jesuits' feeling of solidarity; J. B. Say was perhaps the first to speak of the solidarity of mankind. The *Code Civile* stated flatly, with regard to debts, that 'la solidarité ne se présume point' – a motto, so to speak, for a society based on universal estrangement. More sociological uses appeared in Proudhon (*Contradictions Economiques*, I, p. 32), Bastiat and Comte (in *Discours sur l'Esprit positif*, cited by Gide and Rist, *Histoire des doctrines économiques*, p. 673). Since Marx had demolished Proudhon's book in *The Poverty of Philosophy*, despised Bastiat as the shallowest of the 'harmonizers' (see, e.g., *Grundrisse*, trans. Nicolaus, p. 249) and had 'a very poor opinion' of Comte (K. Marx and F. Engels, *Selected Correspondence 1846–1895* (London, 1936) p. 313) he was unlikely to borrow a concept which they used rather in the sense of Hegel's *Versöhnung*, as a principle of social reconciliation. This ideological implication was developed further by C. Renouvier and the 'solidarist' movement that his works inspired, where the concept was used to promote and justify social reform by means of a type of social contract theory. 'Solidarité' thus had the same ideological function for French radicalism as 'social conscience' had for English liberalism, and as the idea of the *Rechtsstaat* as arbiter of class conflict had for the *Kathedersozialisten* in Germany. Durkheim's *The Division of Labour in Society* just preceded most of the solidarist literature, but despite ideological affinities with it, succeeded in giving the term a scientific status. Its place in the sociological vocabulary has long been secure, but it has suffered from vagueness of definition. Glotz's usage has since influenced a reapplication of the term to modern Greek exemplars of the extended family of antiquity, in J. K. Campbell, *Honour, Family and Patronage* (Oxford, 1964) and J. du Boulay, *Portrait of a Greek Mountain Village* (Oxford, 1974). Glotz's Durkheimian approach (see S. M. Lukes, *Emile Durkheim* (London, 1973) pp. 624–6) led him to regard the solidarity prescribed by law and custom as an indication of an underlying 'real solidarity', and these ethnographic analyses, in the Durkheimian tradition of British social anthropology, use the term not only to describe the norms but also the 'structure of sentiments' within the society to which the norms apply. The only Marxist theoretician to make much use of the concept was Max Adler, who defined two basic types of society, solidary and unsolidary. However he did not use these labels in a way that added anything to the economic explanation of classlessness and class conflict. (M. Adler, *Soziologie des Marxismus* (Vienna and Cologne, (1964) vol. III ('Die solidarische Gesellschaft') p. 9 ff.) See S. Feilbogen, 'Die Solidaritätsphilosophie in Frankreich' in *Festsehrift für W. Jerusalem* (Vienna, 1915) and J. E. S. Hayward, 'Solidarity', *International Review of Social History*, iv (1959) pp. 261–84. and Lukes, op. cit. pp. 350–4.

4 E. Durkheim, *The Division of Labour in Society*, trans. G. Simpson (Glencoe, 1933) pp. 66–7.

5 *Grundrisse*, trans. Nicolaus, pp. 85–6.

6 Loc. cit.

7 For a collectivity, one might say, solidarity is the equivalent of the self-feeling that constitutes the subjective unity of an individual personality.

8 M. Weber, *The Theory of Social and Economic Organization*, trans. and ed. T. Parsons (New York, 1947) p. 137.

9 G. Simmel, *Conflict and the Web of Group Affiliations*, trans. Bendix and Wolff (Glencoe, 1964) p. 20. The same passage reappears in 'The Metropolis and Mental Life' in *The Sociology of Georg Simmel*, pp. 415–16. Cf. Engels' description of London in *The Condition of the Working Class in England*, p. 30–1.

10 By H. Martins, 'Time and Theory in Sociology', in J. Rex (ed.), *Approaches to Sociology* (London and Boston, 1974) p. 252.

11 See especially M. Gluckman, *Custom and Conflict in Africa* (Oxford, 1956).

12 L. A. Coser, *The Functions of Social Conflict* (London, 1956) p. 34.

13 R. Dahrendorf, *Class and Class Conflict in Industrial Society* (London, 1959) p. 164. Dahrendorf has since retracted this suggestion in *Essays in the Theory of Society* (London, 1968).

14 See especially Lévi-Strauss's rejection of explanation by social sentiments, from the standpoint of mind-body dualism, in *Totemism*, trans. R. Needham, (London, 1962) p. 71. Anthropological explanations can only be in terms of 'the intellect', that is to say, of culture.

15 J. L. Moreno, *Who Shall Survive?* (New York, 1953) p. 3.

16 Ibid., p. 72.

17 Ibid., p. 79.

18 Ibid., pp. 255, 363–4.

19 Ibid., p. 315.

20 Ibid., p. 246.

21 Ibid., p. 315.

22 Ibid., p. 73.

23 Ibid., p. 311.

24 Ibid., p. 247.

25 J. L. Moreno *et al.*, *The Sociometry Reader* (Glencoe, 1960) p. 52.

26 D. Cartwright and A. Zander, *Group Dynamics* (London, 1960) p. 105.

27 *Conflict and the Web of Group Affiliations*, p. 107.

28 *Who Shall Survive?*, p. 317.

29 Ibid., p. 697.

30 See *Group Dynamics*, pp. 104ff.

31 In terms of the observation of interaction processes, this means that Moreno's view is closer to the Bion-Thelen approach, where every unit of interpersonal behaviour is treated as containing both a work element and a social-emotional element, than to Bales' approach, where units are classified as *either* 'task behaviour' *or* 'social-emotional behaviour'. See A. P. Hare, *Handbook of Small Group Research* (New York, 1962) pp. 64ff.

32 *The Sociometry Reader*, pp. 53–4.

33 *Capital*, I, p. 8.

34 C. Lévi-Strauss, *Structural Anthropology*, trans. C. Jacobson and B. G. Schoepf, (London, 1968) pp. 48ff.

35 F. Nadel, *The Theory of Social Structure* (London, 1957).

36 *Who Shall Survive?* p. 55.

37 *The Sociometry Reader*, p. 52.

38 Ibid., p. 81.

39 Ibid., p. 52.

40 C. Lévi-Strauss, *The Elementary Structures of Kinship*, trans. Needham *et al.*

(London, 1969) pp. 85–7.
41 *Capital*, I, trans. E. and C. Paul, p. 59.
42 G. C. Homans, *The Human Group* (London, 1951) pp. 111–12.
43 Ibid., p. 247.
44 Ibid., p. 244.
45 Cf. Coser's criticisms in *The Functions of Social Conflict*, pp. 62–3.
46 *Handbook of Small Group Research*, p. 278.
47 This is a more generalised version of an assumption underlying conventional role theory. Cf. 'Obviously the people in any one group have a variety of social identities. In a classroom, for example, there are those identified as "students", but these same people are also identified as men, women, young, mature, and so on. In this classroom situation it is primarily their identity as students that others in the group regard as central and properly salient. It is also the expectations congruent with this salient identity that are most appropriately activated and have the fullest claim to application . . . Social identities have to do with the way in which an individual is in fact *perceived* and classified by others in terms of a system of culturally standardized categories.' (A. W. Gouldner, 'Cosmopolitans and Locals', *Administrative Service Quarterly*, Vol. 2, Dec. 1957 – March 1958, pp. 283–4.) Merton also assumes that 'Differing situations activate different statuses which then and there dominate over the claims of other statuses.' (R. K. Merton, 'Insiders and Outsiders', in *Varieties of Political Expression in Sociology* (Chicago and London, 1972) pp. 24–5.)
48 *Group Dynamics*, p. 416.
49 *The Division of Labour in Society*, p. 62.
50 *Handbook of Small Group Research*, p. 139.
51 Ibid., pp. 139–41, and sources cited. Similar findings, of course, occur repeatedly in non-experimental studies. See, for example, the study of 'value-homophily' by P. F. Lazarsfeld and R. K. Merton, 'Friendship as Social Process' in M. Berger, T. Abel and C. H. Page, *Freedom and Control in Modern Society* (New York) 1954, pp. 18–37; and among innumerable community studies, N. Elias and J. L. Scotson, *The Established and the Outsiders* (London, 1965).
52 *Group Dynamics*, pp. 108–9, 115.
53 *The Division of Labour in Society*, p. 55.
54 *The Theory of Social and Economic Organization*, p. 139.
55 *Conflict and the Web of Group Affiliations*, pp. 43ff.
56 *The Human Group*, p. 113.
57 *Conflict and the Web of Group Affiliations*, p. 48.
58 If a social relationship is to develop into a group it is necessary, first, that *this* relationship is fixed and prescinded from the web of relationships; and secondly, that the parties be distinguished as recognisable on another occasion. So the relationship must get a name. For example, if two people who met on a plane eat together afterwards and continue to interact they become 'we-who-met-on-that-plane' instead of just 'you' and 'I', 'I' and 'you'. This pronominal phrase functions like a proper name and there is only a difference of degree between 'the passengers on the *Titanic*', 'the middle classes' and properly designated groups like Mensa, General Motors, or the U.S.S.R. And at the same time each person acquires a name or other designation as a particular, recognisable member. This may be an office or title, or just 'his' name on a list, a nickname,

or a number, a badge etc. These twin processes, by which relationships become formalised as groups, and persons-in-relationship become individualised as members, must not be confused with another pair of processes which often accompany them. This is the conversion of practices into institutions, and the particularisation of general institutional categories into roles.

59 See T. Newcomb, *Social Psychology* (New York, 1950) pp. 226–7. The arguments advanced above constitute an attempt to ground the study of social structure and social process in the logic and sentiments of collective life, in a way that would, if successful, take explanatory priority over reference group theory. Merton, who wished to give reference group theory the widest possible scope, nevertheless admitted 'the general hypothesis that some similarity in status attributes between the individual and the reference group must be percieved or imagined, in order for the comparison to occur at all. Once this minimal similarity obtains, other similarities and differences pertinent to the situation, will provide the context for shaping evaluations.' And he noted that 'This minimum of status similarity apparently presupposed by reference group behaviour clearly requires systematic study.' It seems likely that along this route a bridge could be found from the theory advanced above to the closely related concerns of reference group theory. (R. K. Merton, *Social Theory and Social Structure* (New York, 1957) p. 242.)

60 Cf. Simmel's treatment of 'inclusiveness and exclusiveness as group principles' the 'The Secret Society', *The Sociology of Georg Simmel*. pp. 368–9. Gramsci noted that 'for the moment, American negroes have a national and racial spirit which is negative rather than positive, one which is a product of the struggle carried on by the whites in order to isolate and depress them'. *Selections from the Prison Notebooks* (Tr. Hoare & Nowell-Smith, London, 1971) p. 21.

61 This is the difference between competition and emulation, which is cooperative rivalry: competition is subordinated to promotion of a common cause. In contests, competition occurs in the framework of a common interest in an identity which defines the *possibility* of winning. The idea that identical goals conduce to solidarity, and opposite goals to estrangement, appears to be controverted by the phenomenon noted by Michels: 'The hatred of the party is directed not in the first place against the opponents of its own view of the world order, but against the dreaded rivals in the political field, *against those who are competing for the same end.*' (Cited by Coser, *Functions of Social Conflict*, p. 70.) But such cases are to be analysed in terms of goal-displacement: causes would have to be shown (electoral systems, potential voters, organisational interests, etc.) for opposition of means becoming more salient than identity or opposition of ends.

62 S. Freud, *Civilization and its Discontents*, trans. J. Rivière (New York, 1958).

63 *Conflict and the Web of Group Affiliations*, pp. 28, 30.

64 'It is when we try to grapple with another man's intimate need that we perceive how incomprehensible, wavering and misty are the beings that share with us the sight of the stars and the warmth of the sun. It is as if loneliness were a hard and absolute condition of existence . . .' Joseph Conrad, *Lord Jim* – literature contains many such examples.

65 Classically depicted by Tolstoy in *The Death of Ivan Ilyich*.

66 *The Essence of Christianity*, p. 158. C. H. Cooley spoke somewhat similarly of the 'looking-glass self', but in a moralistic mode. See *Human Nature and the Social*

Order (New York, 1912) p. 151.

67 *Capital,* I, trans. E. and C. Paul, p. 23n.

68 This Marxian theory of identification differs from that which, together with object-cathexis, formed the basis of Freud's social psychology in *Group Psychology and the Analysis of the Ego.* It is as though the Freudian ego, very sure of itself, looked about and asked 'Who shall I be like? What shall I have?' and found answers in its own appraisal of the persons and things around it; while the Marxian ego asks 'What am I? Who am I? What do I need? What can I do?' and expects answers from its environment. Thus Freud's ego is like a *bon bourgeois,* while Marx's is in the same position as the proletariat, divested of its class identity on the morrow of revolution, and faced with the task of making man, for the first time, in man's own image.

69 *Conflict and the Web of Group Affiliations, p. 141.*

70 D. Riesman, *The Lonely Crowd* (abr. ed., New Haven, 1961) pp. 46–7.

71 R. D. Laing, *Self and Others* (London, 1969) Ch. 2. In this way we can interpret Schopenhauer's image of mankind as a crowd of freezing porcupines, who huddle together for warmth, only to be repelled by one another's quills – 'until they had discovered a mean distance at which they could most tolerably exist.' (Cited by Freud in *Group Psychology and the Analysis of the Ego* (London, 1922) p. 54.
    It would obviously be desirable if all phenomena that have been conceptualised in terms of social space could be also formulated in terms of solidarity and estrangement. 'Attraction' and 'repulsion', together with other spatial terms in group dynamics, present no great difficulty in this regard, being metaphors of convenience. But the oppositions inside-outside, high-low, near-far may well be universally embedded in the basic assumptions on which group identity and the hierarchical or lateral ordering of inter-group relations are premised. Hence the spatiality contained in 'internal solidarity/external estrangement' or 'vertical/horizontal estrangement' may be unavoidable and justified by *consensus gentium.*

72 J. Rawls, *Theory of Justice* (Oxford, 1975) p. 3. Rawls draws over-specific conclusions from an inquiry into the implications of 'membership' in abstraction from values, roles, power, etc.

73 Cf. E. Goffman, *Asylums* (London, 1968) and P. Selznick, *The Organizational Weapon* (New York, 1952).

74 'The internal differentiation of collectivities based on a single status thus provides structural bases for diverse and often conflicting intellectual and moral perspectives within such collectivities. Differences of religion or age or class or occupation work to divide what similarities of race or sex or nationality work to unite. That is why social movements of every variety that strive for unity – whether they are establishmentarian movements whipped up by chauvinistic nationals in the time of war or antiestablishmentarian movements designed to undo institutionalized injustice – press for total commitments in which all loyalties are to be subordinated, on demand, to the dominant one.' (Merton, 'Insiders and Outsiders', op. cit., p. 24.)

75 To speak of A's 'interest' is to refer to an attribute of an action or policy open to A in a given situation: namely, that if pursued it would tend to maintain or increase A's opportunities to get what he wants or needs. This definition is modelled on that of B. M. Barry in *Political Argument* (London, 1965) Ch. X.

76 And, of course, from the historical prominence of specific 'anomic' patterns in French society due to rapid social change.

77 *The Division of Labour in Society*, p. 55.

78 Ibid., p. 56.

79 Hare, *Handbook of Small Group Research*, p. 141.

80 *The Division of Labour in Society*, p. 62.

81 *Conflict and the Web of Group Affiliations*, p. 179ff.

82 Ibid., p. 64.

83 *Early Texts*, p. 199.

84 Ibid., p. 202.

85 *Economic and Philosophical Manuscripts*, p. 165.

85a A challenge to the similarity hypothesis, not involving complementarity, appears in C. Nakane's argument that in Japan solidarity flourishes between seniors and juniors, by age or duration of membership, while equal seniority breeds hostility. An explanation may be that, since Japanese apparently *expect* all relationships to be hierarchical, the ability to relate in terms of this unambiguous ascriptive criterion may give it salience as a *common* basis of conduct, overriding other differences. Inability to do so, however, may make salient other and more ambiguous differences, from which seniority can only be achieved competitively. See C. Nakane, *Japanese Society* (London, 1970) especially p. 75.

86 *The Division of Labour in Society*, p. 108.

87 Trans. by J. A. Jones and A. T. Scull in *Economy and Society*, vol. ii, no. 3 (1973) pp. 285–308. Mead's theory of punishment is superior to Durkheim's, in that it invokes 'the attitude of hostility to the lawbreaker as an enemy to the society to which we belong . . . uniting all members of the community in the emotional solidarity of aggression.' G. H. Mead, 'The Psychology of Punitive Justice', *Am. Jnl. of Sociology* (1918) pp. 585–92, repr. in L. A. Coser and B. Rosenberg (eds.) *Sociological Theory* (New York and London, 4th ed. 1976).

88 H. H. Gerth and C. W. Mills (eds.), *From Max Weber* (London, 1948) p. 189.

89 If these are cases of latent solidarity between estranged groups, a converse appears in the socio-emotional tone of 'joking relationships'. Here joking is an interaction technique introduced to express and resolve tension between overt intergroup solidarity at the level of economic cooperation and mutual aid, and latent estrangement issuing from kinship differences. (A. R. Radcliffe-Brown, *Structure and Function in Primitive Society*, (New York and London 1965) pp. 94–5.) Similarly, Gramsci observed that 'The peasant's attitude towards the intellectual is double and appears contradictory. He respects the social position of the intellectuals and in general that of state employees, but sometimes affects contempt for it, which means that his admiration is mingled with instinctive elements of envy and impassioned anger.' A. Gramsci op. cit. p. 14.

90 *Selected Works*, pp. 170–1. Cf. A. Gramsci, op. cit. p. 181.

CHAPTER 6

1 *Selected Correspondence*, pp. 170–1.

2 *The Division of Labour in Society*, p. 115.

3 Ibid., p. 116.

4   *The German Ideology*, p. 79. Cf. Durkheim, *Professional Ethics and Civic Morals*, trans. C. Brookfield (London, 1957) pp. 125–6.

5   *The Division of Labour in Society*, p. 117.

6   *The Theory of Social and Economic Organization*, p. 40.

7   Ibid., p. 140.

8   *Werke*, Ergbd. I, p. 452 (my trans.).

9   *Ubergreifendes Moment.*

10 Ownership, in this sense, therefore covers two aspects of 'property' which Macpherson has singled out as preceding capitalist property: the right not to be excluded from use or benefit of something set apart for common use; and property as a right to a revenue. (C. B. Macpherson, *Democratic Theory*, (Oxford, 1973) p. 124, 129.

11 See, e.g. Rees' account of borrowing in the economy of Llanfihangel, in R. Frankenberg, *Communities in Britain* (London, 1966) p. 52.

12 *Professional Ethics and Civic Morals*, p. 142.

13 *Grundrisse*, trans. Nicolaus, p. 498.

14 Ibid., p. 495 (*their own*, in the case of common ownership).

15 Ibid., p. 471.

16 Ibid., p. 489.

17 Ibid., pp. 472, 498.

18 Ibid., p. 471.

19 Ibid., pp. 485, 491.

20 Loc. cit.

21 Ibid., p. 472.

22 In 'The Origin of the Family, Private Property and the State', *Selected Works*, pp. 449–50.

23 *Grundrisse*, trans. Nicolaus, pp. 472, 192.

24 Ibid., pp. 492, 477.

25 *Capital*, III, p. 772.

26 *Grundrisse*, trans. Nicolaus, pp. 472–3.

27 B. Hindess and P. Q. Hirst, in *Precapitalist Modes of Production* (London and Boston, 1975) ch. 4, treat the 'Asiatic' ruler as chief functionary of an impersonal state, which partially vitiates their 'proof' that an Asiatic mode of production cannot be specified. For Marx, the ruler represents, in his own person, a lineage that has successfully appropriated the collective (tribal, etc.) title to the land and to the surplus-labour of its inhabitants. He can mobilise against the village communes the same power of exclusion that the feudal landlord can exert against individual tenants. Communes defaulting on their tax rental can be dispossessed by massacre, enslavement or expulsion into the desert. For in both Asiatic and feudal modes of production the social division between non-worker and worker coincides with that between specialised and usually mounted warrior and peasant footsoldier. It is the former's control of military force (a major precondition of occupation of the soil and means of distribution) that renders effective the landed monopoly of a patrimonial or feudal ruling class. In the Ancient mode of production this military specialisation is absent: the commune is a self-governing fortified city of warrior peasants. These points – which are conceptual and not empirical in their bearings – help to elucidate the puzzling articulation of the political and economic 'instances' in all these modes.

28 Loc. cit.
29 Ibid., p. 495.
30 Ibid.; p. 477.
31 Ibid., p. 475.
32 Ibid., p. 476.
33 Ibid., p. 483.
34 Ibid., p. 474.
35 Ibid., pp. 477, 479.
36 Ibid., pp. 484–5.
37 See *Capital*, I, trans. Moore and Aveling, p. 334, n. 3.

CHAPTER 7

1 *Grundrisse*, trans. Nicolaus, p. 499 (my italics).
2 Althusser and Balibar, *Reading Capital*, p. 214.
3 There seems to be no warrant for claiming, as Balibar and other Althusserians do, that Marx intended the terms 'property' and 'real appropriation' to denote a 'double connexion' between the elements of a mode of production, or to distinguish in these terms between 'the *double function* of the capitalist as the exploiter of labour-power ("property") and as the organizer of production ("real appropriation").' (Balibar, loc. cit.) The text on which Balibar mainly leans (*Capital* I, trans. Moore and Aveling, pp. 508ff.) does not support his reading. Balibar's admission that 'Marx constantly confounds them in a single concept' (op. cit., p. 215) suggests the more natural interpretation that Marx in fact used one concept because there was only one type of relation involved. Balibar's assimilation of the alleged distinction between 'property' and 'real appropriation' to the distinction between 'property' and 'possession' – particularly important in precapitalist formations – involves a further confusion, and a misplaced criticism of confusion in Marx, where Marx was relatively clear. For 'property' and 'possession' see below, pp. 259ff. (This is not to belittle the value of some of the further distinctions that Balibar goes on to make with the aid of this ill-chosen dichotomy.)
4 *Early Texts*, p. 195.
5 Though the term 'unit act' is Parsonian, the main inspiration for isolating *practices* as a species of 'cultural atom' (cf. pp. 115–16 above) comes from Wittgenstein's *Philosophical Investigations*. J. L. Austin, in *How to Do Things with Words*, (Oxford, 1962), named the 'illocutionary acts' whose ubiquity in human communication Wittgenstein had perceived, and characterised them as a species of social action susceptible of *logical* analysis. Systematic classification of such acts, and analysis of their logical structure, was first undertaken by J. R. Searle, in *Speech Acts* (Cambridge, 1969). That this is the same type of undertaking as Marx's analysis of commodity exchange in *Capital* has not been noticed, because of the historical 'accident' that a philosopher's concern with problems of the meaning and truth-conditions of propositions led to the isolation of *speech* acts from other kinds of social practice. (The fact that acts which are not, as such, speech acts may nevertheless require the performance of speech acts for their accomplishment is a further complication that needs more attention.) The analysis of alienation and appropriation which follow are not

modelled on Searle's analyses, which presuppose a distinction between 'brute facts' and 'institutional facts' that is slightly unclear to me. One of its effects is to abstract the logical from the temporal structures of the act, although the latter reappears in logical disguise (e.g. 'preparatory rule'). Marx's dialectical logic is perhaps more appropriate to the analysis of practices because it declines to make this abstraction.

The practices or techniques of which human praxis is composed are not necessarily directly social, as communicative and transmissive practices are. Labour, for example, considered in abstraction from cooperation, is not. For an outline of an analysis of another class, see M. Mauss, 'Techniques of the Body', trans. B. Brewster, *Economy and Society*, vol. 2, no. 1 (1973) pp. 70–88.

6 Cf. R. M. Titmuss, *The Gift Relationship* (London, 1970) especially pp. 75ff. Adoption provides another relevant example.

7 Despite appearances to the contrary, one cannot 'give' something to a dog, because it cannot know the difference between giving and lending. However, the custodians of pets or sacred animals may receive gifts on their behalf.

8 This criterion combines two: first, the number of movements; secondly, whether or not they form a closed circuit. Unilateral acts involve one movement, bilateral two or more. Reciprocity is the limiting case of rotation, where the number in the closed circuit is two. Triadic rotation may have special properties. The case of multiple movements forming an open series is treated simply as repetition of unilateral acts, not as a distinct compound act.

9 K. Polanyi, 'The Economy as Instituted Process' in E. E. LeClair and H. K. Schneider (eds) *Economic Anthropology* (New York, 1968) p. 128.

10 *Capital*, III, p. 771.

11 *Economic Anthropology*, p. 130.

12 Ibid., p. 131. A practice that possibly is intended, and functions, to minimise estrangement in exchange situations is the oriental method of 'dumb bargaining', where the dealers haggle by an invisible finger-language inside one another's sleeves.

13 Rationing by means of coupons, successfully used as a model to explain the role of raffia mats in certain African systems of bridewealth payment, is an example of this mode. See Mary Douglas, 'Primitive Rationing: a study in Controlled Exchange' in R. Firth (ed.), *Themes in Economic Anthropology* (London, 1957).

14 Strictly, one might distinguish 'bequest' and 'inheritance' as the two poles (alienation and appropriation) of this transaction. See J. Goody, 'Inheritance, Property and Marriage in Africa and Eurasia', *Sociology*, vol. 3, no.1 (1069) pp. 55–76; and K. Davis, *Human Society*, (New York, 1966) pp. 409–14.

15 A. Harding, *A Social History of English Law* (London, 1966) p. 90.

16 It is only necessary to prove the correct kinship to succeed automatically to whatever share the law reserves for that status. Very often the family as a hereditary *occupational* group has been the persisting community – in India, the Roman empire, and feudal Europe. Thus villein tenements held on condition of pursuing a certain occupation in the manorial economy effectively bound devolution to occupational predestination; the guild system was not dissimilar in its effects.

17 J. K. Campbell, *Honour, Family and Patronage* (Oxford, 1964) pp. 187–9.

18 This difference is partly due, of course, to the fact that intergenerational transmission is not a declared objective of bureaucratic succession, unlike clan

succession, but a consequence of ensuring continuity of operation despite the turnover of bureaucratic cohorts.

19 'Patronage' is a kind of free alienation between contemporaries, where a status (which usually gives access to possessory privileges) is itself treated as a possession 'in the gift' of the patron, and hence as a thing. Sale of offices involves treating offices as things of a different sort: commodities.

20 See F. Parkin, 'Strategies of Social Closure in Class Formation', in *The Social Analysis of Class Structure* (London, 1974) pp. 6–7 especially.

21 *Grundrisse*, trans. Nicolaus, pp. 96–7.

22 Ibid., p. 98.

23 Hindess and Hirst conceptualise the expansionary possibilities of primitive communism in much this manner: *Pre-capitalist Modes of Production*, p. 57.

24 B. Malinowski, *Argonauts of the Western Pacific* (New York, 1961) p. 180.

25 Cf. C. Lévi-Strauss: 'There is no way of refusing the neighbour's offer of his glass of wine without being insulting.' (*The Elementary Structures of Kinship*, p. 59.)

26 M. Mauss, *The Gift*, trans. I. Cunnison (London, 1954) pp. 79–80.

27 Cf. the discussion in P. M. Blau, *Exchange and Power in Social Life* (New York and London, 1967) pp. 97ff.

28 Ibid., p. 92.

29 See. S. Piddocke 'The Potlatch System of the Southern Kwakiutl: a New Perspective', in *Economic Anthropology*, pp. 283–99.

30 Mauss, *The Gift*, pp. 17–18.

31 Ibid., p. 61.

32 Ibid., pp. 4–5, 35.

33 P. Ekeh, *Social Exchange Theory* (London, 1974) pp. 53ff.

34 *The Elementary Structures of Kinship*, pp. 177ff.

35 e.g. M. Godelier, 'Structure and contradiction in *Capital*', in R. Blackburn (ed.), *Ideology in Social Science* (London, 1972) pp. 334–68.

36 Boas, cited with approval by Mauss (*The Gift*, p. 100), noted that potlatch had an insurance function, with regard to the donor's children, which parallels in respect to material wealth the function of insuring the next generation's marriage chances in the systems examined by Lévi-Strauss.

37 *Argonauts of the Western Pacific*, p. 93.

38 *Capital*, I, p. 149.

39 *Argonauts of the Western Pacific*, p. 119. Chiefs also hired out canoes, and were paid in *vaygu'a*.

40 *The Gift*, p. 72.

41 Ibid., pp. 24, 96.

42 See Marx's speculations in *Randglossen*, pp. 362–3.

43 *Early Texts*, p. 195.

44 E. E. Evans-Pritchard, *The Nuer* (Oxford, 1940) p. 50.

45 The cant phrase of gangsterism – 'make him an offer he can't refuse' – underlines the affinity between inducements and weapons, coercive offers and threats. This sense of 'inducement' is not to be equated with that of C. Barnard, *The Functions of the Executive* (Cambridge, Mass., 1962) pp. 93–4. Also the distinction between political and economic coercion here is not identical with Weber's distinction between political and economic action, according to whether 'violent' or 'peaceful' means are used. But it does correspond to Blau's two types of negative sanction as bases for power relations – 'threatening to

deprive others of benefits they currently enjoy' and (conditionally and easily) 'providing needed benefits others cannot easily do without.' It also accords with the assumptions underlying Emerson's power-dependence schema, which Balu uses. However, Emerson and Blau do not sufficently notice that their strategies are premised on mutual estrangement between the parties. Dependence on another's help does not confer power on him if he wants or is obliged to give help (*Exchange and Power in Social Life*, pp. 115–19). I have conceptualised these relationships in terms of coercion rather than power in order to focus on techniques of interaction, not the capacity for successful goal-attainment which an agent may have through employing them.

46 M. Gluckman, *Custom and Conflict in Africa*, Ch. I.

47 *Early Texts*, p. 200.

48 *Capital*, I, trans. Moore and Aveling, p. 60.

49 *Early Texts*, p. 200.

50 *Grundrisse*, trans. Nicolaus, p. 156.

51 Cf. *Capital*, III, p. 807.

52 *Capital*, I, trans. E. and C. Paul, pp. 59–60. Marx explicated this passage further in *Randglossen* (P. 377, my trans.):

> First comes *commerce*, and then a *legal order* develops out of it. I have shown in the analysis of the circulation of commodities that in developed market exchange the negotiators tacitly recognise each other as equal persons and as owners, respectively, of the goods that they exchange. They *do* this already in the acts of offering their goods to each other and concluding their bargains. This *factual* relationship, arising at first in and through exchange itself, later receives *legal form* in contract, etc; but this form creates neither its content, the exchange, nor the actual interrelationship of the persons present within it [*die in ihr vorhandene Beziehung der Personen untereinander*], but rather vice versa.

53 *Grundrisse*, p. 911 (my trans.).

54 Blau, *Exchange and Power in Social Life*, p. 89.

55 A. W. Gouldner, *For Sociology* (London, 1975) Chs. 8 and 9.

56 Ibid., pp. 298–9, 283.

CHAPTER 8

1 *Capital*, I, p. 217.

2 *Capital*, III, p. 772.

3 A Giddens, in *The Class Structures of the Advanced Societies* (London, 1973), has clearly seen the need for a theory of exploitation if Marx's theory of class structure is to be 'rethought'. But the 'Weberian' definition of exploitation that he uses – 'any socially conditioned form of asymmetrical production of life-chances' – amounts to little more than a general formula of social inequality.

4 Though he often made value-judgements about the facts it referred to. (see, e.g., *Grundrisse* (trans. Nicolaus) p. 853.)

5 *Capital*, II, p. 359.

6 *Grundrisse* (trans. Nicolaus) p. 86.

7 K. Marx, *Theories of Surplus Value* (Moscow and London, 1972) Pt III, p. 506. The words in square brackets are taken from the German text in *Werke*.

8 See *Capital*, III, p. 854.

9 Especially Hindess and Hirst, *Pre-capitalist Modes of Production*, introduction.

10 *Grundrisse* (trans. Nicolaus) p. 498. (See p. 312 above.)

11 *Capital*, II, p. 25.

12 For peonage, see *Capital*, I, p. 168n.

13 Also, 'Mere household slaves, whether they perform necessary services or are kept as luxuries for show, are not considered here. They correspond to the modern servant class.' (*Capital*, II, p. 483.)

14 *Theories of Surplus Value*, Pt. III, pp. 475–6.

15 Ibid. p. 491. Cf. *Grundrisse* (trans. Nicolaus) p. 459.

16 Development of smallholdings may of course occur from other causes. See *Capital*, I, p. 716 n.

17 A point Marx noted from Merivale's *Lectures on Colonization*. (*Grundrisse* (trans. Nicolaus) p. 834.) Cf. Hindess and Hirst, op. cit., pp. 158ff.

18 Capital, III, p. 783.

19 The solidarity of the ruling class is discussed further in the next section, below, p. 269ff.

20 *Grundrisse* (trans. Nicolaus) p. 491.

21 Ibid., p. 477.

22 *The German Ideology*, p. 33.

23 *Grundrisse* (trans. Nicolaus) p. 165.

24 'The word *gentleman* originally meant simply a man born in a certain rank. From this it came by degrees to connote all such qualities or adventitious circumstances as were usually found to belong to persons of that rank. This consideration at once explains why in one of its vulgar acceptations it means any one who lives without labour, in another without manual labour, and in its more elevated signification it has in every age signified the conduct, character, habits and outward appearance, in whomsoever found, which, according to the ideas of that age, belonged or were expected to belong to persons born and educated in a high social position.' (J. S. Mill, *System of Logic*, vol. ii, p. 240.) Cf. the discussion of the term *yoki hito* ('good person') in the aristocratic culture of Heian Japan, in I. Morris, *The World of the Shining Prince* (London, 1964), who compares with this the Athenian *Kalokagathoi*.

25 P. Vinogradoff, *Villeinage in England* (Oxford, 1892, repr. 1968) p. 43.

26 For the points in this para, see *Grundrisse* (trans. Nicolaus) pp. 464–5 and 245 n.

27 *Capital*, I, p. 715.

28 *Capital*, III, p. 786.

29 *Capital*, I, pp. 570–1.

30 Ibid., p. 574; cf. p. 737

31 Marx recognised that 'The labour-power withdrawn from the market by wear and tear and death, must be continually replaced, by, at the very least, an equal amount of fresh labour-power. Hence the sum of the means of subsistence necessary for the production of labour-power must include the means necessary for the labourer's substitutes, *i.e.* his children, in order that this race of peculiar commodity-owners may perpetuate its appearance in the market.' (Capital, I, p. 172.) Wages would therefore be at levels sufficient to

cover the costs of reproduction of labour-power.

32 L. Althusser, *Lenin and Philosophy* trans. B. Brewster (London, 1971) pp. 121ff.

33 See, e.g. J. Westergaard & H. Resler, *Class in a Capitalist Society* (London, 1975)

34 *Capital*, III, p. 784. Cf. p. 326.

35 E. Williams, *Capitalism and Slavery* (London 1964).

36 See, e.g., Oberg on slavery in Ankole, in M. Fortes and E. E. Evans-Pritchard, *African Political Systems* (London, 1940) p. 133. Even in the centralised West African states that grew up in connexion with the European slave trade in the eighteenth century, such as Ashanti, the children of slaves were recognised as free subjects.

37 H. Maine, *Ancient Law* (London, 1901) p. 163. Possibly these ideas influenced Hegel's 'dialectic of master and slave'. See, in general, the interesting construction of a 'slave mode of production' in Hindess and Hirst, op. cit., ch. 3, and P. Anderson, *Passages from Antiquity to Feudalism* (London, 1974) ch. 1.

38 *Capital*, II, p. 142.

39 *Capital*, III, p. 757.

40 *Grundrisse* (trans. Nicolaus) p. 473.

41 See 8th International Congress for the History of Religions, 'La Regalità Sacra' (Leyden, 1959).

42 J. Maquet, *The Premise of Inequality in Ruanda* (London, 1961) p. 108.

43 *Grundrisse* (trans. Nicolaus) p. 493.

44 Ibid., p. 495. See p. 321 above.

45 See p. 318 above. See Marx's usage in *Capital*, III, p. 337: loan capital 'passes but temporarily out of the possession of its owner into the possession of a functioning capitalist.' On p. 368 the distinction is between 'the owner of capital and the employer of capital', and in *Theories of Surplus Value*, Pt. III, p. 458, between 'owner' and 'possessor'); while on p. 619 *rentiers* enjoy 'a purely private ownership of Nature by non-producers, a mere title to land'; and on p. 775 rent in kind is paid 'by the direct producer, who is in *possession* of the labour conditions needed for his own reproduction . . . to the *owner* of the land'.

46 *Capital*, III, p. 779.

47 Cf. Marx's analysis of lending, *Capital*, III, pp. 342, 345.

48 *Grundrisse* (trans. Nicolaus) p. 475.

49 Ibid., p. 473.

50 In *Theories of Surplus Value*, Pt. III, p. 495 Marx speaks of a king as 'owner of the kingship' by virtue of which he 'plays the role of commander-in-chief'. For titles becoming objects of appropriation, cf. the discussion of stock capital for public works, etc. (*Capital*, III, pp. 466–7).

51 *Capital*, III, pp. 774–7.

52 Or of fiefs consisting of such estates.

53 Vinogradoff, *Villeinage in England*, p. 58.

54 See *The German Ideology*, p. 35.

55 M. Bloch, *Feudal Society* (London, 1965) vol. 1, p. 148.

56 *Grundrisse* (trans. Nicolaus) p. 465.

57 Thus commendation involved an undertaking of *obedienta et reverentia* on the part of the vassal. That the bond which tied the vassal to his lord was one of negative solidarity is emphasised by the nature of the oath which he swore: 'To shun all that he shunned, to hate all that he hated.' See F. J. West, 'On the

Ruins of Feudalism – Capitalism?', in E. Kamenka and R. S. Neale (eds), *Feudalism, Capitalism and Beyond* (London 1975) p. 54.

58 *Grundrisse* (trans. Nicolaus) pp. 500–2.

59 With the passage of time, the rule ceased to hold. The more that feudal land tenure came to resemble private property, the more likely a landowner was to owe vassal service to various lords, for different manors which he had acquired. In Japan, the *shō*, functionally equivalent to the manor, permitted multiple obligations from the start because of the subdivision of usufructuary rights. Such considerations limit the power of the logical model to explain the hierarchical character of feudal society.

60 *The German Ideology*, pp. 88–9.

61 Ibid., p. 35.

62 As described by Oberg, op. cit. and Maquet, op. cit. See also J. Goody, *Technology, Tradition and the State in Africa* (London, 1971).

63 *Grundrisse* (trans. Nicolaus) p. 509. Cf. Bloch, *Feudal Society*, vol. 2, p. 442. Cf. also Spanish colonial feudalism, through which a surplus extracted from *encomiendo* labourers, tied to the estate, or *encomienda*, was transmitted to Europe. 'The social relationship by which the *encomendero* completely dominated the native was a result of the specific economic situation in which the cultivation of a given area of land required the labour of a certain number of Indians. In exchange for protection, which was only a formality, and dead letter, the Indians paid their masters goods and economic incomes' S. Barraclough, *Agrarian Structure in Latin America* (New York, 1973) p. 7.

64 *Capital*, I, p. 330.

65 Incomplete bifurcation of these solidarities, marking an intermediate stage of structural differentiation, is represented by a political system like that of eighteenth-century England, revolving partly around political opportunities for patronage, exercised on the basis of kinship, locality, and other non-political criteria. American-style patronage represents a further stage, where party careerism is differentiated from other interests. See Chapter 7 n. 19.

66 *The German Ideology*, p. 36.

67 *Villeinage in England*, p. 223. At this level, the capitalist enterprise is the corresponding constitutive unit of bourgeois society. The commodity form, which Marx referred to as the 'economic cell' of bourgeois society, has its feudal counterpart in personal dependence – as Bloch put it: 'to be the "man" of another man'. To change the metaphor, the latter are cultural atoms of which the socio-economic molecules, enterprise and manor, are composed.

68 Ibid. p. 57.

69 See M. M. Postan, *The Mediaeval Economy and Society* (London, 1975) chs. 5 and 6; L. White, Jr., *Mediaeval Technology and Social Change* (Oxford, 1962).

70 See Goody, op. cit., and Marx's comments on Maine's description of feudal tendencies in Celtic Ireland in *Ethnological Notebooks*. In mediaeval Irish texts, 'to accept cattle from' means to 'be dependent on', or 'owe homage to'. For métayage, see *Capital*, III, pp. 782–3.

71 *Capital*, I, pp. 168–9.

72 Ibid., pp. 567–8.

73 Ibid., p. 572.

74 *The Mediaeval Economy and Society*, p. 98.

75 *Capital*, I, pp. 175–6.

364 Estrangement, Alienation and Exploitation

76 Ibid., p. 235.
77 Loc. cit.
78 *Capital*, III, p. 799.
79 Ibid., p. 774.
80 *Theories of Surplus Value*, Pt. III, p. 378. Cf. *Grundrisse* (trans. Nicolaus) p. 514–15.
81 *Grundrisse* (trans. Nicolaus) p. 83. See C. B. Macpherson, *The Political Theory of Possessive Individualism* (Oxford, 1962). In *Democratic Theory* (p. 130) Macpherson shows that this justification of private property was still used by J. S. Mill and T. H. Green.
82 *Capital*, I, pp. 584–5.
83 Ibid., p. 185.
84 Cf. *Grundrisse* (trans. Nicolaus) p. 462.
85 Cf. ibid., p. 298.
86 *Capital*, I., p. 310.
87 Ibid., pp. 196–7n.
88 See Tolstoy's interesting use of this story in *What Then Must We Do?* ch. xx.
89 *Capital*, I, p. 339.
90 Ibid., pp. 360–1.
91 Ibid., p. 423.
92 *The German Ideology*, p. 41.
93 *Capital*, I, p. 329. Though he never admitted it, Marx probably owed this idea to Proudhon's *What is Property?* However, he found earlier sources – see ibid., p. 325, and sources cited; also *Grundrisse* (trans. Nicolaus) p. 584ff.
94 Ibid., p. 326.
95 Ibid., p. 334.
96 Loc. cit. Cf. also p. 624.
97 *Capital*, III, p. 376.
98 Ibid., p. 85.
99 Ibid., p. 379.
100 Ibid., p. 375.
101 Ibid., pp. 427, 380.
102 'Even the continual improvements, which are [i.e. in economising through the 'social nature of labour'] possible and necessary, are due solely to the social experience and observation ensured and made possible by production of aggregate labour combined on a large scale'. (*Capital*, III, p. 79.)
103 *Grundrisse* (trans. Nicolaus) p. 473.
104 *Theories of Surplus Values*, Pt. III, p. 456.
105 Ibid., Pt. II, p. 232 et seq.
106 Ibid. Pt. III, pp. 420–1.
107 Ibid., Pt. III, p. 416. Cf. Pt. III, p. 352.
108 *Grundrisse* (trans. Nicolaus) pp. 705–6.
109 Loc. cit.
110 Ibid., p. 434. Cf. *Theories of Surplus Value*, Pt. II, p. 528.
111 *Capital*, I, p. 592.
112 Ibid., p. 594.
113 *Grundrisse* (trans. Nicolaus) p. 91.
114 *The Characters of Jean de la Bruyère*, trans. H. Van Laun (London, 1929) p. 318.
115 *Capital*, III, p. 377.

116 *Grundrisse* (trans. Nicolaus) p. 474.
117 *Theories of Surplus Value*, Pt. III, pp. 434–5.
118 In *Capital*, III, p. 241, Marx vaguely anticipated one line of criticism, in asserting that the 'centralization of existing capitals in a few hands . . . would soon bring about the collapse of capitalist production *if it were not for counteracting tendencies, which have a continuous decentralizing effect alongside the centripetal one.*' (My italics.)
119 E. g. *Theories of Surplus Value*, Pt. I, pp. 385–7.
120 *Capital*, I, p. 586.
121 *Grundrisse* (trans. Nicolaus) p. 509.
122 Ibid., p. 458.
123 *Capital*, II, p. 397.
124 *Early Texts*, pp. 127–8. See S. Avineri, *The Social and Political Thought of Karl Marx* (Cambridge, 1968) ch. 2.
125 *Capital*, I p. 764.

CHAPTER 9

1 *Theories of Surplus Value*, III, p. 276.
2 *Argonauts of the Western Pacific*, p. 94.
3 *Capital*, II, pp. 16off.
4 Ibid., p. 108.
5 *Grundrisse* (trans. Nicolaus) p. 838.
6 Ibid., p. 170.
7 Loc. cit.
8 *Grundrisse* (trans. Nicolaus, slightly modified) pp. 469–70.
9 Ibid., p. 832. The phrases in quotation marks are taken from Mill, whom Marx was criticizing in this passage.
10 Ibid., pp. 239–50.
11 *Grundrisse (Anhang)* pp. 910–1.
12 *Capital*, I, p. 75.
13 *Grundrisse* (trans. Nicolaus) p. 96.
14 Marx recognised the unity of subject-matter in these various passages by throwing them together in a projected concluding section to the first volume of his *Planentwurf* of 1859 (see *Grundrisse (Anhang)* p. 974) and later developed them as part of *Capital*, I, chapter 24.
15 *Theories of Surplus Value*, Pt. III, p. 56.
16 As maintained, for example, by H. Kelsen, in *General Theory of Law and State* (New York, 1961) pp. 175ff.
17 We can also see that, to the extent that certain subsets of possessory relations are *in fact* regularly defined, as they occur, in legal terms, by legally qualified agents – as with some types of contract – that a legal description of them as voluntary attempts to conform to an ideal standard could also be an adequate sociological description of that aspect of their meaning, as social acts.
18 p. 330 above.
19 *Selected Works*, p. 321.
20 *Grundrisse* (trans. Nicolaus) p. 96.
21 Ibid., p. 45.

22 *Capital*, III, p. 857.
23 *The German Ideology*, p. 32–3.
24 *Grundrisse* (trans. Nicolaus) p. 99.
25 Ibid., p. 97.
26 See ibid., p. 463, where Marx appears to suggest that this ideological principle plays a role in the development of working-class consciousness of its product as its collective property.
27 *Theories of Surplus Value*, Pt. III, p. 485.
28 See ibid., pp. 494–5, for a good example of Marx's method of treating this phenomenon.
29 Ibid., p. 84.
30 *The Class Structure of the Advanced Societies*, Ch. 6.
31 *Theories of Surplus Value*, Pt. III, pp. 514–15.
32 Ibid., pp. 491, 476 (my italics added.)
33 The political and ideological superstructures are themselves also subsystems of the social formation, but have been omitted, as such, from the diagram, which shows only the structural inputs by which their processes are determined by the economic subsystem, through unproductive social consumption.
34 *Grundrisse* (trans. Nicolaus) p. 712.
35 'Cultivation when it 'progresses in a primitive way and is not *consciously controlled* . . . leaves deserts behind it . . . Here again another unconscious socialist tendency!' Marx to Engels, 25 Mar 1868, *Selected Correspondence*, p. 237.

Works Cited in the Text

WORKS BY MARX AND ENGELS

K. Marx *Early Texts*, trans. and ed. D. McLellan (Oxford, 1972).
  Economic and Philosophical Manuscripts, trans. M. Milligan, ed. D. J. Struik
    (London, 1973).
  Grundrisse der Kritik der politischen Ökonomie (Berlin, 1953).
  Grundrisse, Foundations of the Critique of Political Economy (Rough Draft),
    trans. and ed. M. Nicolaus (London, 1973).
  Pre-capitalist Economic Formations, trans. J. Cohen, ed. E. J. Hobsbawm
    (London, 1964).
  Marx's Grundrisse, ed. and trans. D. McLellan (London, 1971).
  Theories of Surplus Value, Pt. I, trans. E. Burns. (Moscow, n.d.).
  Theories of Surplus Value, Pt. II (Moscow, 1968).
  Theories of Surplus Value, Pt. III (London, 1972).
  Capital, vol. I, trans. S. Moore and E. Aveling (London, 1970).
  Capital, vol. I, trans. E. and C. Paul (London, 1930).
  Capital, vol. II (Moscow, 1957).
  Capital, vol. III (Moscow, 1959).
  Ethnological Notebooks, ed. L. Krader (Assen, 1972).
  'Randglossen zu A. Wagners "Lehrbuch der politischen Okonomie"',
    in Marx- Engels, *Werke*, vol. xix, pp. 355−83.

K. Marx and
F. Engels   *Werke* (Berlin, 1959).
  Selected Works, one volume (London, 1970).
  The Holy Family, trans. R. Dixon (Moscow, 1956).
  The German Ideology, trans. R. Pascal *et al.* (London, 1965).
  Selected Correspondence 1846 − 1895 (London, 1936).
F. Engels *The Condition of the Working Class in England*, trans. and ed. W. O.
    Henderson and W. H. Chaloner (Oxford, 1958).

OTHER WORKS

Adler, M. *Soziologie des Marxismus* (Vienna and Cologne, 1964).
Althusser, L. *Lenin and Philosophy*, trans. B. Brewster (London, 1971).
Althusser, L. and Balibar, E. *Reading Capital*, trans. B. Brewster (London, 1972).
Austin, J. L. *How to Do Things with Words* (Oxford. 1962).
Avineri, S. *The Social and Political Thought of Karl Marx* (Cambridge, 1968).
Barnard, C. *The Functions of the Executive* (Cambridge, Mass., 1962).
Barry, B. M. *Political Argument* (London, 1965).

Blau, P. M. *Exchange and Power in Social Life* (New York & London, 1967).
Blauner, R. *Alienation and Freedom* (London, 1964).
Bloch, M. *Feudal Society*, 2 vols (London, 1965).
Bovill, E. W. *The Golden Trade of the Moors* (Oxford, 1970).
Bukharin, N. *Historical Materialism, a System of Sociology* (London, 1926).
Campbell, J. K. *Honour, Family and Patronage* (Oxford, 1964).
Cartwright, D., & Zander, A. *Group Dynamics* (London 1960).
Coser, L. A. *The Functions of Social Conflict* (London 1956).
Dahrendorf, R. *Class and Class Conflict in Industrial Society* (London, 1959).
Dahrendorf, R. *Essays in the Theory of Society* (London, 1968).
Davis, K. *Human Society* (New York, 1948).
du Boulay, J. *Portrait of a Greek Mountain Village* (Oxford, 1974).
Durkheim, E. *The Division of Labour in Society*, trans. G. Simpson. (Glencoe, 1933).
Durkheim, E. *Professional Ethics and Civic Morals*, trans. C. Brookfield (London, 1957).
Durkheim, E. 'Two Laws of Penal Evolution', trans. T. A. Jones & A. T. Scull, *Economy and Society*, ii, 3 (1973) pp. 285–308.
Ekeh, P. *Social Exchange Theory* (London, 1974).
Elias, N. and Scotson, J. L. *The Established and the Outsiders* (London, 1965).
Emerson, R. M. 'Power-Dependence Relations', *American Sociological Review*, vol. 27 (1962) pp. 31–41.
Evans-Pritchard, E. E. *The Nuer* (Oxford, 1940).
Feilbogen, S. 'Die Solidaritätsphilosophie in Frankreich', in *Festschrift für W. Jerusalem* (Vienna, 1915).
Feuerbach, L. *The Essence of Christianity*, trans. M. Evans (London, 1881).
Feuerbach, L. *Sämtliche Werke*, ed. W. Bolin and F. Jodl.
Firth, R. *Themes in Economic Anthropology* (London, 1967).
Fortes, M. and Evan-Pritchard, E. E. *African Political Systems* (London, 1940).
Frankenberg, R. *Communities in Britain* (London, 1966).
Freud, S. *Civilization and its Discontents*, trans. J. Rivière (New York, 1958).
Freud, S. *Group Psychology and the Analysis of the Ego*, trans. J. Strachey (London, 1945).
Giddens, A. *The Class Structure of the Advanced Societies* (London, 1973).
Glotz, G. *La Solidarité de la famille dans le droit criminel en Grèce* (Paris, 1904).
Gluckman, M. *Custom and Conflict in Africa* (Oxford, 1956).
Godelier, M. 'Structure and Contradiction in *Capital*', in R. Blackburn (ed.), *Ideology and Social Science* (London, 1972).
Goffman, E. *Asylums* (London, 1968).
Goody, J. *Technology, Tradition and the State in Africa* (London, 1971).
Goody, J. 'Inheritance, Prosperity and Marriage in Africa and Eurasia', *Sociology*, vol. 3, no. 1 (1969) pp. 55–76.
Gough, J. W. *The Social Contract* (Oxford, 1957).
Gouldner, A. W. *For Sociology* (London, 1975).
Harding, A. *A Social History of English Law* (London, 1966).
Hare, A. P. *Handbook of Small Group Research* (New York, 1962).
Harris, H. S. *Hegel's Development. Towards the Sunlight, 1770–1801* (Oxford, 1972).
Hayward, J. E. S. 'Solidarity', *International Review of Social History*, iv (1959) pp. 261–84.
Hegel, G. W. F. *The Phenomenology of Mind*, trans. J. Baillie (London, 1949).

Hegel, G. W. F. *The Philosophy of History*, trans. J. Sibree (New York, 1956).
Hindess, B. and Hirst, P. Q. *Precapitalist Modes of Production* (London and Boston, 1975).
History of Religions, 8th. International Congress. 'La Regalità Sacra' (Leyden, 1959).
Homans, G. *The Human Group* (London, 1951).
Kamenka, E. and Neale, R. S. (eds.) *Feudalism, Capitalism and Beyond* (London, 1975).
Kelsen, H. *General Theory of Law and State* (New York, 1961).
La Bruyère, J. de. *The Characters of Jean de la Bruyère*, trans. H. van Laun (London, 1929).
Laing, R. D. *Self and Others* (London, 1969).
Lévi-Strauss, C. *Structural Anthropology*, trans. C. Jacobson and B. G. Schoepf (London, 1968).
Lévi-Strauss, C. *The Elementary Structures of Kinship*, trans. R. Needham *et al.* (London, 1969).
Lévi-Strauss, C. *Totemism*, trans. R. Needam (London, 1962).
Lukes, S. M. 'Alienation and Anomie', in P. Laslett and G. Runciman (eds), *Philosophy, Politics and Society*, 3rd series (Oxford, 1967).
Lukes, S. M. *Emile Durkheim, His Life and Work* (London, 1973).
Macpherson, C. B. *The Political Theory of Possessive Individualism* (Oxford, 1962).
Macpherson, C. B. *Democratic Theory* (Oxford, 1973).
Maine, H. *Ancient Law* (London, 1901).
Malinowski, B. *Argonauts of the Western Pacific* (New York, 1961).
Mandel, E. *Marxist Economic Theory*, trans. B. Pearce (London, 1968).
Maquet, J. *The Premise of Inequality in Ruanda* (London, 1961).
March, J. G., and Simon, H. A. *Organizations* (New York, 1958).
Martins, H. 'Time and Theory in Sociology' in Rex, J. (ed.), *Approaches to Sociology* (London and Boston, 1974).
Mauss, M. *The Gift*, trans. I. Cunnison (London, 1954).
McLellan, D. *The Young Hegelians and Karl Marx* (London, 1969).
Merton, R. K. 'Insiders and Outsiders', in *Varieties of Political Expression in Sociology* (Chicago & London, 1972).
Merton R. K. and Lazarsfeld, P. F. 'Friendship as Social Process', in M. Berger, T. Abel, C. H. Page, *Freedom and Control in Modern Society* (New York, 1954).
Mészáros, I. *Marx's Theory of Alienation* (London, 1972).
Moreno, J. L. *Who Shall Survive?* (New York, 1953).
Moreno, J. L., *et al.* *The Sociometry Reader* (Glencoe, 1960).
Morris, I. *The World of the Shining Prince* (London, 1964).
Nadel, F. *The Theory of Social Structure* (London, 1957).
Newcomb, T. *Social Psychology* (New York, 1950).
Ollman. B. *Alienation, Marx's Conception of Man in Capitalist Society* (Cambridge, 1971).
Park, R. E. 'Human Migration and the Marginal Man', *American Journal of Sociology*, vol. 33 (1928) pp. 881–94.
Parkin, F. (ed.) *The Social Analysis of Class Structure* (London, 1974).
Plamenatz, J. P. *Karl Marx's Philosophy of Man* (Oxford, 1975).
Postan, M. M. *The Mediaeval Economy and Society* (London, 1975).
Proudhon, P. J. *Oeuvres Complètes* (Paris, 1873).

Pufendorf, S. von *De Officio Hominis et Civis juxta Legem Naturalem*, trans. F. G. Moore (New York, 1927).

Radcliffe-Brown, A. R. *Structure and Function in Primitive Society* (New York and London, 1965).

Rawls, J. *Theory of Justice* (Oxford, 1975).

Riesman, D. *The Lonely Crowd*, abr. ed. (New Haven, 1961).

Rousseau, J. J. *The Social Contract and Discourses*, trans. G. D. H. Cole (London, 1913).

Sartre, J. B. *Critique de la Raison dialectique* (Paris, 1960).

Schacht, R. *Alienation* (London, 1971).

Searle, J. R. *Speech Acts* (Cambridge, 1969).

Seeman, M. 'On the Meaning of Alienation', *American Sociological Review*, vol. 24, No. 6 (1959) pp. 783–91.

Selznick, P. *The Organizational Weapon* (New York, 1952).

Simmel, G. *The Sociology of Georg Simmel*, trans. and ed. K. H. Wolff (Glencoe, 1964).

Simmel, G. *Conflict and the Web of Group Affiliations*, trans. R. Bendix and K. H. Wolff (Glencoe, 1964).

Terray, E. *Marxism and Primitive Societies*, trans. M. Klopper (New York and London, 1972).

Titmuss, R. M. *The Gift Relationship* (London, 1970).

Tolstoy, L. *What Then Must We Do?* trans. A. Maude (London, 1935).

Vinogradoff, P. *Villeinage in England* (Oxford, 1892; repr. 1968).

Weber, M. *From Max Weber*, ed. H. H. Gerth and C. W. Mills (London, 1948).

Weber, M. *The Theory of Social and Economic Organization*, trans. and ed. T. Parsons (New York, 1947).

Weber, M. *General Economic History*, trans. F. H. Knight (New York, 1961).

Westergaard, J. and Resler, H. *Class in a Capitalist Society* (London, 1975).

White, L. *Mediaeval Technology and Social Change* (Oxford, 1962).

Williams, E. *Capitalism and Slavery* (London, 1964).

Wittgenstein, L. *Philosophical Investigations*, trans. G. E. M. Anscome (Oxford, 1953).

Index

Adler, Max, 350
alienation: meaning, in Hegel and Marx, xi–xiii; in religion, 3–7; in social contract theory, 8–11; in Enlightenment thought, 11–15; in Rousseau, 15–19; and self-alienation, in Hegel, ch. 2, *passim*; and self-alienation, in Feuerbach and early Marx, ch. 3 *passim*; sociological concepts of, ch. 7 *passim*; of use, 260*f*, other theories of, 344
Althusser, Louis, 255, 344, 348, 361
altruism, 138–44
anomie, 28, 140
appropriation, xii, 159, 325–6; Weber on, 163–4; sociological concepts of, ch.7 *passim*; 'real appropriation', 188–90; and exploitation, 241*f*; of use, 260*f*; of title, 262; of surplus product, 278–99; 'law of appropriation', 282–7
Aristotle, 121–2, 140
attraction and repulsion, 354; in Hegel, 23–4; in sociometry, 114–19, causes of interpersonal, 119–37
authority, 153

Bacon, Francis, 36
Balibar, Etienne, 189, 357
barter, 99, 230
Bauer, Bruno, 48
beneficence, norm of, 232–5
Blau, Peter 211, 231–2, 358–60
Bloch, Marc, 263*f*, 362
bureaucratic succession, 204–5, 358

capitalism, *see* production, mode of
Cherbuliez, Antoine-Elysée, 282–8, 309
circulation of commodities, 284; and estrangement, 92–7; and private property, 173; and transmissive practices, 199*f*; and bride prestation; 215, cf. with *kula*, 216–19; and exchange, 226–8; and possessory relations, 319–20
class, Marx's model of, 153–4; monopoly of means of production, 245–72; ruling class, 269–71, 298; and exploitation,

308–13; and consumption, 310*f*, 334
coercion, 221–5; and exchange, 225–8
community, tribal, 98–100, 175–85
complementarity, 140–4
conquest, 100–1, 205–7, 221*f*
consumption: of surplus product, 299–308; and class, 310*f*; and distribution, 333*f*
contract: theory of social, 8–14, 230, 344; and exchange, 229–30, 255
contradiction, 57–8, 129, 338; in tribal community, 181, 261*f*
Cooley, Charles, 353
corvée labour, 244 *f*, 258–63, 276, 279, 286, 291, 293
Coser, Lewis, 109, 137, 351, 352
culture, 11–20, 34*f*

Dahrendorf, Ralf, 109, 150, 155, 351
deviance, 145–6
devolution, *see* inheritance
dialectic, 56–8, 112, 123, 124–5, 357
Diderot, Denis, 39
difference, *see* similarity and difference
division of labour, 63, 296
distribution, 185–8, 206–7; of surplus product, 299–308; and possessory relations, 325–38
Durkheim, Emile, 87, 90, 155, 355; on sacred, 4; and Marx, 65; on solidarity, 105–10, 121–3, 127–9, 140–4, 350; and Moreno, 113, 117–19; on segments and organs, 137; on altruism and egoism, 138–44; on morality, 147; on punishment, 148–9; on property, 162–4, 171–2

ecological system, 340*f*
egoism, 138–44
Engels, Friedrich, 54, 93, 119, 177, 206, 349
essentialism, 48–58, 64*f*, 91
estrangement: meaning, in Hegel and Marx, xiii–xvi; in religion, 3–7; in social contract theory, 8–11; in Enlightenment thought, 11–15; in Rousseau, 15–19; and self-estrangement, in Hegel, ch. 2 *passim*; and self-estrangement, in Feuerbach and

Mead, George Herbert, 133, 355
Merton, Robert, 115, 140, 352–4
migration, 101–4
Mill, James, 92*f*, 143, 164
Mill, John Stuart, 112, 241, 327, 361
Mills, C. Wright, 206
mobility, social: of intellectuals, 12–16
Montesquieu, Charles de, 9, 12
Moreno, Jacob, 121, 351; and socio-emotional matrix, 110–19; and socio-dynamic effect, 150
Mosca, Gaetano, 153, 206, 349
Murray, Gilbert, 101–2

Nadel, Siegfried, 116, 351
Newcomb, Theodore, 122, 353
Nietzsche, Friedrich, 132, 151

opposition, *see* similarity and difference, *and* contradiction
organisation as a productive force, 292*f*
ownership, 168–72; communal, 178*f*; labile and sessile 319*f*; and distribution, 325–38

Park, Robert, 101–2, 349
Parsons, Talcott, 107, 109, 137, 155, 163
Pascal, Blaise, 61
patrimonialism, 181, 244*f*; status of labour under, 258–63; and labour supply, 275–6; and *corvée* labour, 293; and distribution of surplus product, 300, 304, 306
Polanyi, Karl, 198–200, 357
polis, 26–7, 101–2
political economy, 67–71, 160
political theory, estrangement and alienation in, 8–11
possession, 164–7, 168, 259
possessory relations, ch. 6 *passim*; in tribal society, 175–85; and exploitation, 314; static and dynamic, 316–325; sessile and labile, 319; and distribution relations, 324–38
Postan, M. M., 278
potlatch, 211–13
prestige, 150–1
production, production relations; positive and negative models, 175*f*; control of, 278–99; and management, 295–9; and distribution, 325–38; mode of, 338; Asiatic mode of, 179–81, 245, 258–63, 275–6, 293, 307*f*, 356; ancient mode of production, 182–4, 245, 250–1, 256–8, 275; feudal mode of, 245–9, 263–72, 276–9, 300–2, 306–8, 363; capitalist mode of, 87–91, ch. 8 *passim*

productive forces, 290*f*
property, property relations, 355; in Hegel's 'soulless community', 28; in *Paris MSS*, 70–1; sociological concept of, ch. 6 *passim*; cf. with possession and ownership, 171–4; private property, 172–4, 182–4; communal property, 179*f*; and transmissive practices, 194; capitalist property, 247; sessile and labile, 319*f*; and distribution, 325–38
Proudhon, Pierre, 159*f*, 363
Pufendorf, Samuel von, 10, 344
punishment, 148–9, 355

Radcliffe-Brown, A.R., 109, 212–13, 355
reciprocity, norm of, 232–5
reference group theory, 353
reification, 65*f*, 294–5, 314–15, 325, 336
religion: estrangement and alienation in, 3–7, 12–3; Protestantism, 4, 8–9, 107, 307; Christianity and the Enlightenment, 14–15, 36–7; Hegel's 'unhappy consciousness', 30*f*, 43, 73; Feuerbach on, 47–52; Marx on, 73–4; and altruism, almsgiving, etc., 139, 212, 234–5
restitution, 224–5
retentitive practices, 317*f*
Ricardo, David, 64
Riesman, David, 136, 354
Rousseau, Jean-Jacques, 3, 24, 132, 344; and social contract, 8–9, 11, 12; and Hegel, 11, 24, 36, 39–43; and Enlightenment thought, 15–19, 34; and Marx, 11, 63

Saint-Simon, Claude Henri de, 94
salience, 121, 124, 131, 165
Sartre, Jean-Paul, 18, 61, 132
scepticism, 29–30, 35
Scheler, Max, 151
Schumpeter, Joseph, 206
Schutz, Alfred, 196
Searle, John, 357
self-alienation, self-estrangement, *see* alienation, estrangement
serfdom, 187, 286; and exploitation, 244*f*, 263–72, 276–8, 290–1, 293
Sherif, M., 125
Simmel, Georg, 132, 142, 190, 211, 231, 344, 351, 353; on the stranger, 101; on city life, 107–8; and formal sociology, 109–10; and sociometry, 112, 118; on similarity, 123–5; on personality, 135; on altruism and egoism, 138
similarity and difference, 121*f*
Sismondi, Jean Charles de, 282, 327